M000274632

Handbook of Improving
Performance in the Workplace

Volume Three

Measurement and Evaluation

ABOUT ISPI

The International Society for Performance Improvement (ISPI) is dedicated to improving individual, organizational, and societal performance. Founded in 1962, ISPI is the leading international association dedicated to improving productivity and performance in the workplace. ISPI reaches out to more than 20,000 performance improvement professionals in over 40 countries through publications and educational programs.

ISPI's mission is to develop and recognize the proficiency of our members and advocate the use of Human Performance Technology. This systematic approach to improving productivity and competence uses a set of methods and procedures and a strategy for solving problems for realizing opportunities related to the performance of people. It is a systematic combination of performance analysis, cause analysis, intervention design and development, implementation, and evaluation that can be applied to individuals, small groups, and large organizations.

Website: www.ispi.org
Mail: International Society for Performance Improvement
1400 Spring Street, Suite 400
Silver Spring, Maryland 20910 USA
Phone: 1.301.587.8570
Fax: 1.301.587.8573
E-mail: info@ispi.org

International Society for Performance Improvement

WHERE KNOWLEDGE
BECOMES KNOW-HOW

About Pfeiffer

Pfeiffer serves the professional development and hands-on resource needs of training and human resource practitioners and gives them products to do their jobs better. We deliver proven ideas and solutions from experts in HR development and HR management, and we offer effective and customizable tools to improve workplace performance. From novice to seasoned professional, Pfeiffer is the source you can trust to make yourself and your organization more successful.

Essential Knowledge Pfeiffer produces insightful, practical, and comprehensive materials on topics that matter the most to training and HR professionals. Our Essential Knowledge resources translate the expertise of seasoned professionals into practical, how-to guidance on critical workplace issues and problems. These resources are supported by case studies, worksheets, and job aids and are frequently supplemented with CD-ROMs, websites, and other means of making the content easier to read, understand, and use.

Essential Tools Pfeiffer's Essential Tools resources save time and expense by offering proven, ready-to-use materials—including exercises, activities, games, instruments, and assessments—for use during a training or team-learning event. These resources are frequently offered in looseleaf or CD-ROM format to facilitate copying and customization of the material.

Pfeiffer also recognizes the remarkable power of new technologies in expanding the reach and effectiveness of training. While e-hype has often created whizbang solutions in search of a problem, we are dedicated to bringing convenience and enhancements to proven training solutions. All our e-tools comply with rigorous functionality standards. The most appropriate technology wrapped around essential content yields the perfect solution for today's on-the-go trainers and human resource professionals.

Essential resources for training and HR professionals

www.pfeiffer.com

Handbook of Improving Performance in the Workplace

Volume Three

Measurement and Evaluation

Edited by
James L. Moseley and Joan C. Dessinger

Co-Published by the International Society for
Performance Improvement

International Society for
Performance Improvement
WHERE KNOWLEDGE
BECOMES KNOW-HOW

Pfeiffer
A Wiley Imprint
www.pfeiffer.com

Published by Pfeiffer
An Imprint of Wiley
989 Market Street, San Francisco, CA 94103-1741 www.pfeiffer.com

For additional copies/bulk purchases of this book in the U.S. please contact 800-274-4434.

Pfeiffer books and products are available through most bookstores. To contact Pfeiffer directly call our Customer Care Department within the U.S. at 800-274-4434, outside the U.S. at 317-572-3985, fax 317-572-4002, or visit www.pfeiffer.com.

Pfeiffer also publishes its books in a variety of electronic formats. Some content that appears in print may not be available in electronic books.

Library of Congress Cataloging-in-Publication Data
Handbook of improving performance in the workplace.
    p. cm.
''Co-Published by the International Society for Performance Improvement.''
Includes bibliographical references and index.
ISBN 978-0-470-19068-5 (v. 1 : cloth)—ISBN 978-0-470-19069-2 (v. 2 : cloth)—ISBN 978-0-470-19067-8 (v. 3 : cloth)
    1. Performance technology.   2. Employees—Training of. I.   International Society for Performance Improvement.
HF5549.5.P37H364 2010
658.3'14–dc22
                                                                                                2009026946

Acquiring Editor: Matthew Davis

Marketing Manager: Brian Grimm

Production Editor: Michael Kay

Editor: Rebecca Taff

Indexer: Sylvia Coates

Editorial Assistant: Lindsay Morton

Manufacturing Supervisor: Becky Morgan

Printed in the United States of America
Printing   10 9 8 7 6 5 4 3 2 1

This handbook is dedicated to the many students with whom I have had the pleasure to interact over the years in teaching product and program evaluation theory and practice and to those among them who have taken the material and applied their skills and strategies in evaluation and measurement to multiple workplace settings. I salute all of you on your courage to make a difference and to influence change.
—JLM

This handbook is dedicated to all the HPT, HR, IT, and other practitioners who are already doing evaluation and measurement—and to those who are open to adding evaluation and measurement to their repertoire of knowledge and skills.
—JCD

CONTENTS

LIST OF CASE STUDIES, EXHIBITS, FIGURES, PERFORMANCE SUPPORT TOOLS, AND TABLES

INTRODUCTION TO VOLUME THREE

APPRECIATING WHAT THIS HANDBOOK HAS TO OFFER

Purpose

The purpose of our Volume Three handbook is simple: it updates the field of measurement and evaluation in the workplace with new perspectives and emerging ideas that capture and blend both theory and practice. It also transforms workplace measurement and evaluation from a selected set of activities and functions about programs to evidence-based results that add value and affect an organization's bottom line. It provides the workplace practitioner with opportunities to read, think, and reflect upon issues of importance in measurement and evaluation. It may even cause the reader to be challenged and take action in learning more about this interesting discipline.

Scope

The scope of this handbook is widespread, ranging from traditional, cherished, and sometimes sacred views of workplace measurement and evaluation to more maverick thinking and application. The handbook consists of four sections: Perspectives, Pillars, Mosaics, and Frontiers in Measurement and Evaluation. The five chapters in each section are carefully selected and orchestrated to reflect the authors' thinking about and experiences with the world of workplace measurement and evaluation. We ask the readers to make a quantum leap whenever necessary in adapting the practical dimensions of the chapters and to spearhead their ability to influence change.

Goal and Objectives

The goal of this handbook is to offer new insight into the theoretical and practical worlds of workplace measurement and evaluation. The handbook will assist workplace learning and performance (WLP) practitioners to accomplish the following objectives:

1. Align workplace measurement and evaluation with business goals and objectives of the organization;

2. Conduct evaluations with an ethical and humane perspective in mind;

3. Become familiar with tools, techniques, and tips about the measurement and evaluation process and be able to integrate them into professional practice;

4. Appreciate the changing nature of evaluation and the evolving trends in the field; and

5. Challenge themselves to reflect upon the authors' thoughts and how they are or are not congruent with their own.

Audience

We group the audience for this book into five categories:

1. **Work units and organizations.** As the context for evaluation expands to units and organizations as diverse as government, private, for-profit, not-for-profit organizations, foundations, faith-based and community-based organizations, and so forth, new emphases are placed on evidence-based results in workplace measurement and evaluation. The focus now is on producing credible facts and noteworthy outcomes. This handbook addresses these needs.

2. **Individuals using measurement and evaluation data.** The definition of value in measurement and evaluation has shifted from a series of activities performed to focus, design, gather, analyze, interpret data, and report information to results that make an individual's work credible and viable. This handbook has relevance to all workplace learning and performance (WLP) specialists who want or need to demonstrate that their work in this area really matters and that their work really makes a substantial and sustainable difference.

3. **Academics and students in learning environments.** The handbook is a compendium of current thinking about measurement and evaluation. It is particularly well-suited for advanced undergraduate and graduate courses

in program evaluation in performance settings. It can be used as a stand-alone resource and reference.

4. **Professionals in the field.** Since the volume captures new thinking and future challenges about measurement and evaluation, it is very useful for consultants and others who make their living in measurement and evaluation arenas. Its focus is on perspectives, tips, and strategies that shape and challenge current discourse and dialogue in the field.

5. **Researchers, librarians, and other knowledge management personnel.** Every discipline and field of study utilizes evaluation principles and evaluation data to guide their research and planning efforts. The handbook provides initial guidance for researchers, librarians, and others to share in seeking and answering queries regarding measurement and evaluation in the workplace.

OVERVIEW OF VOLUME 3 CHAPTERS

The editors of this handbook asked the authors to provide bulleted items that represent the thoughts and essence of their chapters. These pivotal ideas are captured below to give the readers an initial glimpse of what they will discover in each chapter.

Chapter One: "Measurement, Evaluation, and Research: Feedback for Decision Making"

- Clarification of terminology
- Why measurement counts
- Units of measurement
- Measurement and the performance chain
- Behavior influences in measurement
- Standard data display for decision making

Chapter Two: "Measurement and Evaluation in the Workplace"

- Distinctions between measurement and evaluation
- Types of measurements and evaluations
- Methods and types of assessments at individual, team, and organization levels
- IBSTPI evaluator domains, competencies, and performance statements

Chapter Three: "Unleashing the Positive Power of Measurement in the Workplace"

- Importance of measurement
- Dysfunctions of measurement
- How individuals experience measurement
- Keys to transforming performance measurement

Chapter Four: "Relating Training to Business Performance: The Case for a Business Evaluation Strategy"

- Training and development as a microcosm of a broader strategy for driving talent management
- Proactive alignment of evaluation linked to business results
- Viewing Joseph from multiple perspectives
- Sharing lessons learned

Chapter Five: "Success Case Methodology in Measurement and Evaluation"

- Realities of training with impact on measurement and evaluation
- Success case method as a strategic perspective
- Practical guidelines for implementing a new mindset to view evaluation

Chapter Six: "Needs Assessment: A Lighthouse Beacon"

- Our definition of needs assessment
- Models of needs assessments
- Approaches to organizational needs assessments
- Using *Evaluation Standards* and *Guiding Principles for Evaluators* to frame a needs assessment

Chapter Seven: "The Impact Evaluation Process"

- Aligning every component of evaluation with objectives and expectations that the organization values
- The interrelationships of programs, activities, and internal results
- Desired results and benefits outweighing costs and unintended consequences
- Stakeholder expectations and the need to align efforts

Chapter Eight: "Full-Scope Evaluation: Do You 'Really Oughta Wanna'?"

- About full-scope evaluation—when, why, what
- Getting started—the importance of being focused, intentional, and purposeful
- The Full-Scope Evaluation Planning Inventory—a diagnostic tool that assesses organizational readiness for evaluation

- How to use the Inventory—distribution and analysis
- Validity and reliability of the *Inventory*

Chapter Nine: "How to Use Kirkpatrick's Taxonomy Effectively in the Workplace"

- Straightforward taxonomy that codifies professional evaluation practices
- Levels from an "evidentiary chain"
- Practical ways to make Kirkpatrick-style evaluation workable in most organizations
- Applying a systems approach to understanding and using the four levels

Chapter Ten: "Ethical Considerations in Performance Measurement"

- Areas in which ethical considerations guide professional behavior
- Performance measurement system functions
- Professional integrity and professional measurement
- Case study applications and reflection

Chapter Eleven: "Performance-Based Evaluation: Tools, Techniques, and Tips"

- Rules for evaluating needs and solutions based on facts or evidence
- Measures and metrics produce evidence-based results
- Adding value in measurement and evaluation
- Leveraging measurement activities

Chapter Twelve: "Test Strategies: Verifying Capability to Perform"

- Aligning testing strategies within business goals and constraints
- Performance testing versus knowledge testing
- Designing and developing performance tests

Chapter Thirteen: "The Business of Program Evaluation: ROI"

- Focus on a business approach
- Types of data and measurement focus
- ROI process model
- Implementing and sustaining ROI
- Benefits of this approach

Chapter Fourteen: "Integrated Evaluation: Improving Performance Improvement"

- Emphasis on fully integrated, ongoing, formative, summative, and confirmative evaluation

- Role that process, product, and impact evaluation play in performance improvement life cycle
- Providing objective answers to evaluation questions

Chapter Fifteen: "Using Evaluation Results to Improve Human Performance Technology Projects"

- Focuses on supports for evaluation and change
- Attends to critical factors for using, correcting, and adjusting evaluation results
- Makes the case for continuous evaluation and for establishing baseline data
- Evaluates every impact on interventions and makes appropriate changes

Chapter Sixteen: "Understanding Context: Evaluation and Measurement in Not-for-Profit Sectors"

- Shift in evaluation in not-for-profit sectors to outcomes measurement, impact evaluation, and sustainability
- Focus on organizational collaboration in not-for-profits
- Stakeholder analysis and employment of logic models
- Customization of evaluation designs and data collection

Chapter Seventeen: "Using New Technology to Create a User-Friendly Evaluation Process"

- Availability of technology-based evaluation tools
- Using technology to evaluate performance interventions
- Rationale for using technology-based tools in evaluation practice
- Future emphasis in applying emerging technology to evaluation
- Ethical and confidentiality issues related to using new technology for evaluation

Chapter Eighteen: "New Kids on the Block: Evaluation in Practice"

- Telling your workplace story using measurement and evaluation
- Profile of five measurement and evaluation plans
- Application of plans to measurement and evaluation in the workplace
- Criteria + plans = Workplace Alignment Guide

Chapter Nineteen: "Expanding Scope of Evaluation in Today's Organizations"

- Expanding content of evaluation in all types of organizations
- Outcomes-based approaches and systems approaches to evaluation

- Growing use of evaluation results for decision-making and shared learning
- Global competency, ethical standards, use of meta evaluation to guide practice

Chapter Twenty: "The Changing Role of Evaluators and Evaluation"

- What characterizes a profession?
- Evaluation as a profession
- Books, journals, and professional organizations
- Competencies, standards, and certification

BENEFITS OF USING THIS HANDBOOK

Because this handbook enjoys a diverse and wide audience, it similarly has benefits. The main benefit is that the handbook can be applied to any measurement and evaluation workplace or endeavor where results are demanded and where value is required. It is also beneficial in adding new perspectives about the topic to current research and development efforts. Because of its practical emphasis, and the nature of handbooks and their intended uses, it encourages dialogue among practitioners who are charged with evaluation in the workplace, and it charges them to influence change.

HOW TO USE THIS HANDBOOK

The handbook is designed to be used as a guide to update the field of workplace measurement and evaluation. Ideally, the serious scholar would read it from cover to cover modeling Sir Francis Bacon's treatise on reading books. More practically, however, the practitioner would read the general preface and the section introductions to get a flavor of the mixed threads that form the measurement and evaluation coat of many colors. He or she would proceed to read those chapters or entire sections that have specific relevance to individual workplace evaluation issues. Any individual interested in measurement and evaluation could flip through chapter figures and tables as added points of interest and personal value. The perspectives, pillars, mosaics, and frontiers provide a wealth of information to help the readers question their beliefs, guide their thinking, and reflect upon their capability and passion to make a difference in workplace measurement and evaluation.

ACKNOWLEDGEMENTS

The editors wish to acknowledge the following contributions:

All the authors who took time out of their busy lives to share their knowledge, experience, and enthusiasm with us . . . and with you.

Judy Billington for her moral support.

Michael Burton and Ann Chow for their computer expertise.

Scott Pitts for his clear thinking and his ability to wordsmith.

Sacip Toker for his research skills and words of encouragement.

Joyce A. Wilkins for her technical and editorial skills.

Matthew C. Davis, senior editor, for insight and direction.

Rebecca Taff and Lindsay Morton for editorial expertise.

Michael Kay, production editor, for changing schedules and often "walking on water" to accommodate our needs.

April Davis, Executive Director of ISPI, for support and encouragement.

Handbook of Improving Performance in the Workplace

Volume Three

Measurement and Evaluation

PART ONE

PERSPECTIVES IN MEASUREMENT AND EVALUATION

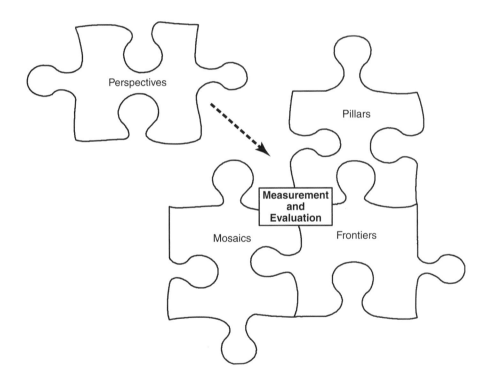

We live in a world of information. Whether reading a volume of selected texts penned with the authors' personal flavors, hearing a movie critic's reaction to the latest Hollywood blockbuster, writing a letter to friends about a recent memorable vacation, or engaging in conversations with colleagues on current affairs, we find ourselves immersed in the sensory sorting of information that ultimately leads to the formation of our perspectives. This first part of the book, "Perspectives in Measurement and Evaluation," is devoted to authors who wish to convey ideas, create impressions, and form mental images with the intent of leading the reader to develop new perspectives on each of the topics presented for consideration. Some perspectives will represent new infusions into traditional ways of considering measurement and evaluation. Whether the inclusions here are new or old, cathartic or traditional, you are invited to read, think, and react; you are invited to examine your own perspectives as well as the perspectives presented by the authors.

Chapter One: Measurement, Evaluation, and Research: Feedback for Decision Making. Binder's chapter presents a different approach to the discussion of measurement and evaluation, overlapping at points with some of the more conventional discussions, but also stepping outside the mainstream measurement and evaluation thinking to highlight several key ideas.

Chapter Two: Measurement and Evaluation in the Workplace. Bosteder and Russ-Eft's chapter is applications-based. It focuses on organizational level assessments, including financial and performance measures, audits, culture and climate surveys, and needs assessments. It considers team- or group-level assessments as well as assessments of conflict and communication style. It looks at individual assessments, including personality and skill assessments of leaders and supervisors, as well as employee satisfaction measures. It also examines customer loyalty measures.

Chapter Three: Unleashing the Positive Power of Measurement in the Workplace. Spitzer looks at measurement as the fundamental management system in any organization that triggers everything else that happens. The measurement system in most organizations is often left to chance, becomes dysfunctional, and causes counterproductive behaviors. Nothing works well when the measurement system is broken and, unfortunately, most organizational measurement systems are in various stages of brokenness.

Chapter Four: Relating Training to Business Performance: The Case for a Business Evaluation Strategy. The Tarnacki and Banchoff chapter is an adventurous case study about a young man's progress in understanding how the essence of training and evaluation truly connect to business performance. A proactive alignment of the evaluation tactic, strategically linked to business results, whether quantitative or qualitative, is essential to avoid being a reactive servant to administrative waste.

Chapter Five: Success Case Methodology in Measurement and Evaluation. Apking and Mooney posit that our professions are top-heavy in formulas, equations, and techniques for evaluation. We do not need more magic formulas or more easy-to-use techniques. The key is to unlock the mystery and to develop a fresh perspective and a new strategy that looks at *why* we do evaluation and *how* we approach it.

Measurement, Evaluation, and Research

Feedback for Decision Making

Carl Binder

In his elegant little book devoted, not to measurement and evaluation, but to the essence of sustainable performance improvement, Esque (2001, p. 18) states that:

"In its simplest form, managing work consists of three components:

- Setting goals;
- Letting work happen and comparing work completed against goals; and
- Deciding whether to change how the goals are being pursued."

In other words, there are three conditions that must be in place to say that performance is being managed: (1) clear, measurable goals; (2) measurement feedback provided to the performers in order to make decisions; and (3) the ability to control resources and conditions if the measurement feedback indicates need for a change.

In the field of human performance technology (HPT), this understanding of performance management provides a rationale for measurement and evaluation. We clearly identify the changes in performance we seek to produce. We measure and monitor the performance over time to determine whether our goals are being achieved, and at what rate. And we decide, based on the feedback provided by measurement, whether (and sometimes how) to change conditions when our goals are *not* being met.

This logic applies at two levels in our field. First, when we as performance improvement professionals are called in to help address a performance challenge, we must ensure that the three conditions described by Esque (2001) are in place. In fact, unlike many of our colleagues in the performance improvement field who conduct cause analyses at the front end of projects to determine what interventions to propose, Esque follows a simpler path: He asks whether the three conditions are in place. Then, because they usually are *not*, he helps clients to establish clear, measurable goals; continuous data-based feedback loops to the performers; and processes for making decisions to change when goals are not being achieved. Once these conditions are in place, he coaches performers and their management through a continuous, data-based performance improvement process.

At a second level, whether we choose to take such a "lean" approach to human performance improvement or follow a more traditional sequence starting with front-end analysis, the three conditions that Esque describes *should apply to our own performance as change agents*, as well as to the performance that we seek to improve. For us to be effective as performance improvement professionals, we need the feedback provided by measurement to determine whether to continue an intervention as planned—or to change. This is a simple cybernetic model of self-correction, inherent in both data-based performance improvement and in the fields of natural science and engineering upon which it has, at least in the past, been modeled. In the same way, this self-correcting approach is the raison d'etre for *evaluation*, the reason for its very existence, as described in this chapter.

A DIVERGENT PERSPECTIVE

This chapter takes a somewhat different approach to the discussion of performance measurement and evaluation, overlapping at points with some of the more conventional discussions provided in this volume, but also stepping outside of mainstream measurement and evaluation to highlight several key ideas. It covers much of the same ground as Binder's (2001) article on "a few important ideas," as well as elements of Binder's (2002–2004) online column on measurement and evaluation entitled: "Measurement Counts!"

While the field of HPT originally emerged from the natural science of behavior (Binder, 1995), with its focus on standard units of measurement and replicable descriptions of procedures similar to accepted practice in the physical sciences, HPT has come to encompass a wider array of technical and conceptual inputs, many from the so-called "softer" fields of education and the social sciences. These other fields have introduced methods and approaches to measurement and evaluation that do not always align with generally accepted criteria in the natural sciences or engineering (Johnston & Pennypacker, 1993), especially with regard to the selection of measurement units and procedures. The principles and concepts presented in the current chapter reflect the author's background and perspective and are as much as possible grounded in the philosophy and practice of natural science. One of the advantages of sticking closely to principles of natural science is that, in many respects, we can demystify measurement and evaluation and make it more accessible to front-line performance improvement practitioners. While this might seem, at the outset, counter-intuitive, continue reading to discover whether or not you think it is a fair statement. In many respects, natural science approaches to measurement and evaluation are simpler in concept, and less encumbered by statistical models and theoretical baggage, than are many approaches derived from the social sciences.

TERMINOLOGY

We use many terms in the field of performance measurement and evaluation, some of which have been defined in detail and with great technical sophistication elsewhere in this volume. For purposes of this chapter, here is a short list of concepts, defined with the intention of eliminating confusion, and appealing as much as possible to plain English explanations.

Measurement

Measurement is the process by which we identify the dimension, quantity, or capacity [of a thing] (*American Heritage Dictionary*, 2006). In the field of performance improvement, this term refers to the identification of *what* to count (business results, work output, and/or behavior); selection of relevant quantitative units of measurement (such as simple counts, kilograms, meters, liters, or other measures); and collection of data expressed in those units. For example, we might identify *a successful business proposal* as a countable work output and include criteria that define a "successful" proposal. We can then count successful proposals over successive time intervals prior to intervention to determine "baseline" levels of productivity. We might additionally count *unsuccessful* proposals and use the "success ratio" of successful to unsuccessful ones as a secondary measure. Once we have decided on an intervention to improve business proposal productivity and quality, we can continue to count during successive time intervals to monitor whether or not the quantity of proposals and/or the ratio of successful to unsuccessful proposals is improving. This is not very different from keeping score in a sporting event, after first defining what constitutes a score, an error, a foul, and so on.

Evaluation

Evaluation is a process by which we evaluate or ascertain the value or worth of [a thing]. (*American Heritage Dictionary*, 2006). In performance improvement, we use measurement, plus some sort of evaluation design, to determine the impact and worth of an intervention. If, for example, measurement shows that the proportion of successful proposals as well as the total number of proposals completed per month accelerate after an intervention, and if we also measure the dollar value of successful proposals (and perhaps the average unit cost for submitting proposals), then we can determine (that is, *evaluate*) the worth of the intervention by calculating the increased number and proportion of successful proposals and the dollar value of the increase. This process would yield what is often referred to as an estimate of return on investment (ROI) if we were to compare measures before the intervention with measures following the intervention.

Performance Analysis

Analysis is another term used frequently in the literature of performance improvement and performance evaluation. The *American Heritage Dictionary* (2006) defines *analysis* as "the separation of . . . a whole into its constituent parts for individual study." In our field, the term analysis can mean many different things, depending on what is being analyzed. In this chapter, we will first discuss *performance analysis*, which breaks down human performance into its elements as a way of describing the performance we wish to improve and developing ideas about how we might improve it. Performance analysis forms a foundation for measurement strategies and tactics described later in this chapter.

Functional Analysis

A second type of analysis, called *functional analysis*, may be unfamiliar to some HPT practitioners, but derives from a basic principle of the natural science of behavior (Binder, 1995; Johnston & Pennypacker, 1993; Skinner, 1953). Functional analysis (or functional definition) uses measurement to determine what impact, or *function*, a variable (or behavior influence) has in relationship to performance, for example, the impact of providing job aids on the frequency of correctly diagnosing equipment failure. In the literature of behavior science, a "reward" arranged to follow a specific behavior can only be called (or said to function as) a *reinforcer* if data show that it results in an increase in the behavior it follows (Skinner, 1953). Similarly, in HPT our interventions can only be considered effective if we can demonstrate through measurement and evaluation their impact on performance. In other words, functional analysis is the *actual demonstration of function or effect*, using measurement and evaluation design, rather than the assumption, perhaps based on prior research or experience, that a particular intervention "works."

While it might seem academic to introduce the term *functional analysis* in this context, there is an important reason for doing so. As managers or performance improvement specialists, we often try to create or apply *recipes*—standard procedures or interventions that, based on previous research or application, are "known" to be effective. If there is a short list of important takeaways from this chapter, it should include the recognition that *there are no sure-fire recipes*. We can never know in advance from scholarly research, or from prior real-world successes, whether or not a particular program, initiative, method, or intervention will work in the next case to which we apply it. We don't know whether a teaching program that worked with one group will be successful with all those in the next group. We don't know whether a feedback system that works in one setting will work in another, and so on. Individual and group differences, cultural variations, and many other factors often conspire to make ineffective, or to mask the effects of, procedures and programs that have previously proven successful. That is the most important reason for measurement and evaluation in HPT practice. We must continue to monitor and adjust our interventions, based on measurement feedback.

The best way that we can use prior experience and the findings of scholarly research is to formulate "good next bets" about what is likely to work in a given situation. We select programs and interventions based on scholarly research, prior experience in our own organizations, or best practice reports from others. But, as Esque's (2001) approach to performance improvement makes clear, we need to use the feedback provided by measurement to be sure what we are doing is effective here and now or to make decisions to change when the results are not as hoped. Functional analysis, according to which a program or variable can only be said to be effective when it is measurably shown to be so, is a core scientific principle that applies equally well to real-world performance improvement practice.

Research

A final term, *research*, deserves some discussion here, if only because there is frequent reference in the field of performance improvement to "research-based methods." A simple definition of research is "systematic investigation to establish facts" (Wordnet, 2006). As performance improvement specialists, we should make every effort to apply what is known from systematic and scholarly research to design our "best bet" interventions, based on the known "facts" about different types of programs and procedures. This is how as practitioners we can take advantage of formal research findings.

Hypothesis-Testing Research. Often scholarly research uses an hypothesis-testing approach in which conditions are arranged to test whether a particular program, variable, or intervention has a specific, hypothesized effect. It is often possible to isolate and test the impact of elements that one might typically combine to form a single, complex intervention in the field. Basic scholarly research often uses statistical models, comparing *average* effects of different interventions, or evaluating the relative effects of variations of an intervention across groups or individuals. This approach is often neither practical nor particularly useful in applied settings, since our goal in most field applications is to improve the performance of *all* individuals or groups whose performance we are attempting to improve, not merely to demonstrate the relative effectiveness of different types of interventions under specific conditions. Nonetheless, scholarly hypothesis-testing research can still be helpful when we are attempting to assemble programs or interventions composed of multiple elements or variables. It can provide guidelines for what we might try in our "best bet" interventions and enable us to improve the likelihood that our initial designs will be effective.

Inductive Reasoning Research. Another type of research, more closely resembling and useful for practical application, is what would traditionally be called *inductive research*: the accumulation of multiple cases (individuals, groups, or others) in which changing a particular variable produces the desired results, to the point at which we feel confidently able to generalize from many successful "replications" to new but similar situations. When researchers (or practitioners) describe performance and its conditions clearly enough so that others can reliably repeat their procedures, and when they use standard units of measurement with clearly defined evaluation designs (Johnston & Pennypacker, 1993), it is possible to become more and more confident over time about what works in particular situations and about variations that might be most likely to succeed under different conditions. The idea is that we "induce" general rules or guidelines by accumulating multiple cases that resemble each other in critical features.

With this inductive approach in mind, practitioners should make every effort to carefully define performance and conditions and to use standard, repeatable measurement and evaluation procedures so that it becomes possible to generalize the results of one project or case to another and to accumulate cases over time to build confidence about the likely impact of specific types of programs or variables. Again, we can use such information to select "best bet" interventions or designs, and then make changes going forward as measured results provide feedback. Whether conscious or otherwise, this is what we all do as practitioners when we continue to refine our ability to predict what will work in different situations or with different types of performance. And as a field, to the extent we carefully describe performance, our procedures, and our measurement methods, we will be able to accumulate growing bodies of useful, prescriptive research. We'll have better and better ideas about "best bet" procedures and interventions to try.

A NATURAL SCIENCE FOUNDATION

Historical Roots

In this chapter and elsewhere (Binder, 1995), I have repeatedly referred to the "natural science" of behavior. By this, I mean the new science created by B.F. Skinner (Bjork, 1993) and his colleagues, in which the fundamental unit of measurement was rate of response (count/time), and the methodology used in the laboratory focused on the analysis, prediction, and control of behavior in the "individual organism" (Skinner, 1938). This science led to breathtaking discoveries and developments that included intermittent schedules of reinforcement, behavior shaping through reinforcing successive approximations to desired behavior, stimulus fading, programmed instruction, performance management, and the methods of behavior therapy. The International Association for Behavior Analysis is the growing and vital home for both basic researchers and field application of this science, and founders of the International Society for Performance Improvement (ISPI)—originally the National Society for Programmed Instruction—included many professionals who were applied behavior scientists in that tradition.

The reason for mentioning this aspect of our performance improvement lineage is to highlight the value of:

- Research and practice that employ standard and universal ("idemnotic") units of measurement rather than self-referencing ("vaganotic") indicators such as percentage correct or rating scale scores whose meanings can vary within or across applications (Johnston & Pennypacker, 1993),

- A focus on analysis and evaluation methods that reveal impact on individual performance rather than averaging across groups (Binder, 1995), and

- Measurement as a continuous feedback loop, in contrast to one-time "validation" of methods (or recipes) and subsequent application without ongoing measurement feedback (Binder, 2001).

These are among the essential elements of HPT at its best, directly inherited from the science of behavior.

Role of Measurement

While earlier sections of this chapter have at points addressed the purpose or role of measurement in performance improvement, let us be very clear about the three typical purposes or types of measurement that we generally find in the development or management of human behavior.

- *Validation.* As suggested above, measurement often occurs in the context of research studies or best practices initiatives in which data collection and analysis serve the role of "validating" a particular program, type of intervention, or variable's effect. While such work can, indeed, provide good input for designing "best bet" performance interventions, validation studies simply *cannot* guarantee that any particular program or type of intervention will apply in new situations, or even in very similar situations with what might seem to the casual observer to be "slight" variations in conditions or performers. For effective day-to-day management or performance improvement, we need to evaluate each time we intervene.

- *Accountability.* Much of the data collected in organizations and schools is intended to "hold people accountable"—whether the performers themselves, managers, or performance improvement specialists. Often such data are collected and stored in spreadsheets, databases, learning management systems, or other "containers" so that people can later retrieve the data "in case" they are needed. However, such data are not often collected or organized and stored in ways that can support frequent decisions about whether, when, or how to change conditions to improve performance. By the time we obtain test scores in most courses, it's too late to change procedures. By the time we look at spreadsheet summaries of "results" weeks or months after an initial intervention, it can be too late to change that intervention in a cost-effective way. While not all data collected for accountability are so difficult to use for other purposes, they do not often support the sort of agile decision-making and course correction that Esque's (2001) approach suggests.

- *Decision making.* Following the notion that measurement can and should provide information for a feedback loop, intended to support mid-course corrections and continuous improvements, the primary purpose of measurement and evaluation in performance improvement ought to be decision making. If this is true, then we should try to collect data frequently enough and display and use it in ways that allow us to adjust conditions and resources to optimize the pace, quantity, and ultimate impact of any performance change that occurs as a result of our programs or interventions. This is the same rationale as emerged from Skinner's (1938) science of behavior in which researchers continuously adjusted experimental conditions for individuals to maximize the pace and degree of behavior change in the desired direction.

In performance improvement we likewise want to be able to use measurement and evaluation to continue changing our programs and interventions until we "get it right."

Units of Measurement

Mention of *standard units of measurement* earlier in this chapter, and in previous publications (Binder, 2001), deserves expansion. In the natural sciences, for scientists to be able to compare results from one experiment to another or to contribute to a coherent accumulation of scientific knowledge, there is an insistence on using standard, universal, and objective measurement dimensions and units. In fact, one could argue that many of the most important advances in science over the centuries have arisen from development of new, standardized measurement units and tools.

In the same way, if the field of performance improvement is to achieve the status of a true technology in the way that various fields of engineering have produced certifiable technologies, we must use standard dimensions and units of measurement. What this means (Johnston & Pennypacker, 1993) is that the measurement units and dimensions that we use to validate and make decisions about performance improvement programs and variables must mean the same from one situation to the next, from one individual to the next. Otherwise we can make nothing but very weak statements about the impact of our efforts.

Some measurement dimensions or units vary in their meaning from situation to situation. Good examples include percentage correct (Binder, 2004a) and average scores from Likert rating scales (Binder, 2003).

Percentage Correct. The trouble with percentage correct is that we cannot uniquely describe actual performance from the score. We don't know *how many opportunities* the performer was given to respond, *how many responses* were correct, or *how much time* it took to respond. Two people can achieve exactly the same percent correct scores on the same test, but with very different levels of performance, because percent correct ignores the time dimension. The same percent correct score can indicate quite different levels of performance from one situation to another, which is why accuracy-only tests, for example, are often very poor predictors of on-the-job performance. An additional, and often-confusing, aspect of percentages is that an increase by a given percentage (for example, adding 20 percent to 100, resulting in 120) is not equivalent to a decrease of the same value in percentage (for example, subtracting 20 percent from 120, resulting in 96).

Rating Scales. The results of evaluation using rating scales can also vary in meaning from one situation to another. First, the numbers on the scale are themselves relative, not absolute quantities. They simply indicate more than (>) or less than (<) lower or higher levels on the scale, respectively. In fact, the *numbers* on rating scales are actually *categories*, not quantities that can be added, multiplied, or otherwise manipulated with meaningful numerical results (Binder, 2003). Consequently, when they are combined into quantities and then averaged (for example, a score of 3.2 out of 5), the average numbers have no relationship to objective performance. It would be far more useful to use rating scales, if necessary, by counting and reporting the *numbers* of people who assign each rating value, as in "thirty-two out of seventy people said service was excellent or good, while fifteen said it was average, and twenty-three said it was below average or poor." These numbers at least describe results in standard units—the actual counts of people. We can *directly* compare these counts, and their proportions, with other results quantified in the same way.

The general point here is that if we use standard measures (count, time, weight, volume, distance, and so forth), we will be able to evaluate results based on quantities that are standard across settings and applications—and that are therefore more likely to help us communicate and reliably contribute to accumulating knowledge of what works. As you will see in a following section, if we can describe business results, work outputs, and/or behavior using standard measurement dimensions, then we will be able to conduct measurement and evaluation in an objective, meaningful, and repeatable way, comparable to measurement used in natural science.

Key Concept: Calibration

Another concept from natural science that might be helpful for those attempting to measure performance and evaluate the impact of efforts to change it in the "real world" is *calibration*. Wikipedia defines calibration as "the process of establishing the relationship between a measuring device and the units of measure." In general, calibration is the stage in any measurement process whereby we check to be sure that the tool we are using accurately measures what we want it to measure. This concept can be applied at various levels in measurement and evaluation of performance improvement.

Validity of Analysis Unit. First, are we measuring what we intend to measure? Sometimes we're not certain whether we've chosen the right unit of analysis. For example, should we count lines of code written, or some other output, in order to measure the productivity of programmers? In other words, if we find ways of increasing lines of code, will we be contributing to the productivity of the programming team? (The generally accepted answer to that question is, "No." We need to identify some other unit to judge and count, since code efficiency is an important aspect of programming productivity not reflected when we count lines of code.)

Reliability of Data. Once we've chosen something to measure, are we reliably measuring it? For example, when measuring the behavior of people in a customer call center by observing and counting, we need to ascertain whether two or more observers are counting the same instances of behavior. We compare data collected by two observers and calculate inter-observer reliability (Daniels & Daniels, 2004, p. 143), the degree to which two people are observing and counting the same behavior. This method calibrates the reliability of our instruments, in this case human observers with checklists and pencils. It's important to note, however, that two observers could be equally inaccurate but still agree in their measurement results. This would be a case of inaccurate but reliable (consistent) measurement.

Sensitivity of Procedures. Another aspect of calibration is related to the *sensitivity* of our measurement procedures. In the case of a microscope or a telescope, one might be able to observe more valuable or useful levels of detail at one magnification versus another. In some cases, the higher degree of magnification may actually be "too sensitive" for the purpose to which it is applied. We need to determine which level yields what type of information and which might be more useful for the purpose intended.

Similarly, if we are measuring human performance, the interval over which we count or the *counting period* (per hour, per day, per week, and so on) and the "chunk size" of what we are counting (for example, individual parts, sub-assemblies, or entire units) might make a difference as to what decisions we can make and how useful they might be. Among other things, the counting period determines how often we can make data-based decisions, since we need several data points in a row to determine the average level and the trend of the data. Similarly, when setting criteria for which work outputs are acceptable and which are not, it's important to determine which criteria will be more indicative of overall quality.

Refining the Measurement Plan. These are often decisions that, in the beginning, can be made only on the basis of pilot or trial runs or observations and analysis of collected data, both numerically and graphically, for the purpose of calibrating one's measurement procedures and tools. While calibration has been an important element of the quality management literature, it has not always been part of performance improvement practice. In general, it is important to recognize that metrics and measurement methods that you choose might need to be adjusted and refined during the early phases of any initiative or program evaluation process in order to be sure you are reliably measuring what you think you are measuring and that the data you collect are useful and help to inform good decisions, cost-effectively and practically. It might not always be clear in the beginning what to measure either. For this reason, it is often helpful to measure and graph results in more ways than you will after an initial calibration period, to determine what measures and presentations of the data turn out to be most indicative of what you are attempting to measure and most helpful for making decisions. These initial attempts and revisions of your measurement approach might require a number of adjustments, and it is good to plan for some time at the beginning of any project or effort for reviewing initial data, summarizing and graphing the data in various ways, and possibly adding to or changing what and how you measure performance.

MEASUREMENT AND THE PERFORMANCE CHAIN

As discussed earlier, performance analysis is an essential prerequisite for performance improvement. We analyze performance by identifying the elements of what we call the *performance chain* (Binder, 2005). The performance chain shown in Figure 1.1 depicts how behavior produces organizational results and the behavior influences that make desired behavior likely to occur.

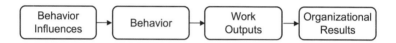

Figure 1.1 The Performance Chain.
© 2008 Binder Rhea Associates.

We typically begin this analysis by identifying the individual or team *work outputs* that contribute to desired *organizational results* and then specifying the *behavior* required to produce those work outputs. The process of performance improvement is when we identify and attempt to design or manage the combination of *behavior influences* needed to establish, support, or accelerate desired behavior that will produce the work outputs that contribute to organizational results. These four elements comprise the performance chain. This is a simple model that multiplies many times in the context of real-world organizations and complex work processes. Many team and cross-functional processes are comprised of dozens or perhaps hundreds of these chains, linked end-to-end (where the output of one chain is the input to the next) or running in parallel. At whatever the organizational level, or however complex the performance we are seeking to improve, the elements of the performance chain give us two important types of linkage:

- *Behavior influences and behavior link to outputs and business results.* Work outputs describe "what the organization needs from its people" and provide the important linkage between the activity (behavior) of people and the results they need to achieve for their organizations. Once we understand what outputs are needed, we can discover or plan for behavior to produce them and then assemble the behavior influences (Binder, 1998) needed to establish, support, or accelerate that behavior. If our analysis of the linkage is accurate, we should be able to improve behavior to improve work outputs and thereby improve organizational results.

- *Units of analysis link to measurement.* The performance chain provides a convenient way to think about what we can measure. In the elements of behavior, work outputs, and organizational results, it points to units for analyzing performance that can be measured using the appropriate dimensions or units of measurement.

Organizational Results

Business executives and owners generally have ways of quantifying the organizational results they seek to achieve. Business experts and consultants sometimes help organizations determine what measures to use and at what level. For example, Kaplan and Norton's (1996, 2004) *balanced scorecard* methodology recommends cascading sets of measures from the top of the organization down through functions and departments to help define goals and monitor progress in strategic and tactical planning and execution. Others within our own field of HPT, most notably Rummler (Rummler & Brache, 1990; Rummler, 2004), have suggested systematic methods for assigning indicators and measures, most notably those that allow evaluation of cross-functional processes.

While not all measures of organizational results are equally sensitive, useful, or expressed in standard units, performance improvement professionals—depending on their roles and positions in the organization—are often given these metrics by organizational management as targets for improvement. Our jobs are often framed as doing something with the human resources of the organization to achieve or accelerate progress toward specified business results.

Work Outputs

Work outputs are (or should be) the focus of our measurement and improvement efforts. We are often asked to improve productivity in a department, to increase the efficiency and productivity of processes that incorporate many milestones or "sub-outputs" along the way, or to enable a new performance designed to produce certain outputs (for example, problems solved for users, signed contracts delivered by sales people). Because one of the most powerful contributions of HPT as a field has been the understanding that outputs (or *accomplishments*), not behavior, should be the focus of our efforts and starting points for our analyses (Binder, 2005; Gilbert, 1978, 2007), our challenge is to help define and measure valuable work outputs that contribute to organizational results and then work to improve their quality or quantity, timeliness, and so on.

Defining Criteria. When we measure outputs, we usually need to define criteria for *good ones*—which might specify qualitative dimensions or successful outcomes that define them as acceptable. *Successful* sales presentations, for example, are those that lead to the next desired step in the sales process such as a customer request for a proposal. *Acceptable* responses to customer queries might be qualified as those that are timely, accurate, and result in the customer's saying that her problem has been solved. *Good* executive decisions of a particular kind might be those that are backed up by financial data, are sufficiently specific to be executable, and are linked to key performance indicators for the business. For any manufactured work output, quality and customer-acceptance criteria might apply, and so on.

Gilbert (1978, 2007) used the term *requirements* to describe what we are calling criteria, and categorized them into three sets of *quality*, *quantity*, and *cost*. To translate requirements more easily into measurement, Binder (2001) described "countable units corresponding to Gilbert's requirements" (p. 22) such as count of accurate and inaccurate items, count of timely or untimely outputs, or count of outputs meeting cost criteria.

Counting Output. The point is that once we have assigned criteria for judging a *good* output, we can count that output. While simple counting is not always the best way to measure work outputs, it is in many cases the simplest and most straightforward. We can monitor to see whether the counts per counting period of "good" ones go up and "bad" ones go down. In some cases (such as with resolved customer problems), we might want the total count per time interval to increase while the count of customers who say they are pleased by the service remains stable or increases. In some cases we are focused on units of volume or weight or we want timely delivery of process outputs that meet quality and cost criteria.

Behavior

Behavior is perhaps the most difficult and often the most expensive element of the performance chain to measure. We don't always need to measure behavior. If our intervention produces desired outputs at an acceptable level or accelerates outputs as planned, then we need not measure behavior. On the other hand, sometimes for diagnostic reasons or because we need to be sure that outputs are being delivered in the *right* way, we must measure behavior, if possible.

Automatic Measurement. Sometimes behavior can be measured automatically, which makes the measurement process both easier and less expensive. More and more automated systems exist for potentially capturing behavior measures, perhaps the most ubiquitous being the measurement of user and customer behavior on the Internet. Online systems can now count mouse-clicks, page visits, and other behavior of users in ways that allow web designers and business people to monitor the impact of changes in systems, content, or navigation on websites. By automating the measurement of computer usage, we are actually turning behavior (key-presses or mouse-clicks) into simple outputs (switch closures) that we can count. But that's something of a technicality. Similarly, in security systems and other electronic environments that monitor door-openings, cardkey swipes, and other user activities, measurement is straightforward. Most sophisticated assembly lines have mechanisms that automatically turn behavior into countable mechanical or electronic events.

Observing Behavior. In many cases, especially those involving face-to-face interactions between humans, behavior is much harder to capture for measurement and evaluation. In those environments, such tools as behavioral checklists for observing or self-monitoring become necessary. Specialists in behavior management (Daniels & Daniels, 2004) have devised many procedures for judging and counting desired and inappropriate behavior. While some measures of behavior conform to criteria for standard and universal measurement units (those that always mean the same thing and can be compared across situations), others, particularly those involving rating scales or percentage calculations, fall short of natural science standards. In general, we encourage practitioners to identify criteria that distinguish between acceptable and unacceptable instances of behavior or among different classes of behavior, so that observers or self-observers can learn to reliably count instances and sum them over appropriate periods of time (per minute, per hour, per day, per week). Often we use behavioral checklists to tally behavior of different types. For some applications, carrying small notebooks for collecting tallies or using such devices as golf wrist-counters can make data capture easier.

Self-Monitoring. A type of behavior measure that generally escapes discussion among managers and performance improvement professionals is *self-monitoring* (Binder, 2004b). We can use self-monitoring to count behavior (or outputs) produced by the person counting his or her own performance. While one might doubt the reliability of one's counting one's own thoughts, feelings, or actions, research has demonstrated remarkable orderliness in self-monitoring, particularly if there is no incentive for the performer to "fake" the data. Sometimes on-the-job criterion-referenced learning programs or self-monitored fluency training (Binder & Sweeney, 2002) turn measurement procedures over to the learner, with dramatic results: by becoming responsive to their own measured performance, participants take enthusiastic control of their own learning processes, much like athletes monitor their own improvements in performance through continuous measurement and feedback.

Self-monitoring is often most powerful when managers or others, interested in improving their own behavior, count specific actions or activities throughout the day. The author, for example, has occasionally counted his own use of positive and negative feedback delivered to staff as a means of monitoring efforts to use a more positive management style. When compared with other means of measuring the behavior of managers, supervisors, or others as they behave in relation to other people, behavior self-monitoring can be an attractive option.

BEHAVIOR INFLUENCES: THE INDEPENDENT VARIABLES

As the diagram of the performance chain in Figure 1.2 depicts, the factors that affect or influence behavior to produce work outputs and results are called *behavior influences*. These are the many different conditions in the performer's environment and techniques, tools, or methods that we can arrange to influence behavior. The list of such variables can be extremely long, especially if we take the relatively transient fads or "flavors of the month" in HRD or management development into account. How, in the end, we can make sense of these many different variables has been the focus of countless articles and models of performance improvement over the decades (Wilmoth, Prigmore, & Bray, 2002). This author uses the Six Boxes® Model (Binder 1998, 2005), a plain English framework that evolved from Gilbert's (1978) behavior engineering model (BEM).

Expectations and Feedback (1)	Tools and Resources (2)	Consequences and Incentives (3)
Skills and Knowledge (4)	Selection and Assignment *(Capacity)* (5)	Motives and Preferences *(Attitude)* (6)

Figure 1.2 The Six Boxes® Model.

© 2008 Binder Rhea Associates

To our knowledge, the Six Boxes Model is a *comprehensive* framework that encompasses every variable that can have an influence on behavior. Using this model, we describe all the elements in a performance improvement program or initiative, and categorize them into the six cells of the model. This is a convenient, powerful yet simple way to understand what a scientist would call the *independent variables* that we as managers or performance improvement specialists configure to provide the most cost-effective impact on performance that we can arrange.

While a thorough description of the Six Boxes Approach (www.SixBoxes .com) is beyond the scope of this chapter, suffice it to say that we use it to better understand the programs we design and to better predict what changes we can make in the factors influencing performance that are likely to produce the desired outcome. When we evaluate programs or interventions, we are in effect evaluating the impact of performance systems comprised of variables that can be described and organized according to the logic of the Six Boxes Model. With experience or based on research, the model can often help us to determine ''best bet'' changes in performance programs (such as clearer expectations, better tools, rewards for doing the right thing, and so forth) likely to accelerate progress toward the desired outcome.

STANDARD DATA DISPLAY FOR DECISION MAKING

It should not shock any reader to know that anyone can ''lie'' with charts and graphs. Most professionals involved in measurement and evaluation of performance interventions summarize and present their data in graphic form. Some even use graphic displays to analyze and support *ongoing* decision-making about performance improvement. Some authors (Jones, 2000) have turned the phenomenon of distorting facts using graphic display into good humor; others have emphasized the positive potential of graphic display for highlighting important information or conclusions (Tufte, 2001). Those of us involved with making decisions about performance improvement interventions will benefit from keeping a few key distinctions in mind.

Stretch-to-Fill Graphs Versus Standard Graphic Display

For those accustomed to using PowerPoint or other software capable of creating graphs, the *stretch-to-fill* or *fill-the-frame* phenomenon is familiar. In fact, some even use it to advantage as a tool for persuasion about the size of effects and so forth. When we specify the ranges of the data we wish to graph and the type of graph we wish to use, the software generally selects the highest and lowest values on the scales to frame the data to fill the screen or a piece of paper. From one point of view, this is an effort to maximize visual attractiveness and best use of graphic *real estate*. However, because every graph created in this way consists of customized scales and distances between values, the proportions, angles, and distances equaling a given unit of measurement generally differ from one graph to the next. This means that the viewer must look carefully at the actual numbers on the graph to truly understand rates of change (trends), sizes of effects, ratios between sets of numbers, and so on. Visual comparisons between graphs become impossible or deceptive, since the scales and proportions differ. While a standardized picture of data might, indeed, be worth a thousand words or more, idiosyncratic stretch-to-fill graphs can actually *inhibit* accurate communication of quantitative results.

In contrast, using standardized graphic displays offers the same power of comparison as does a standard twelve-inch ruler or any other tool designed to provide visual representation of quantities. By "standardized" we mean graphs in which the distance between numbers on scales for one graph is the same as for another with which we are likely to compare it. In the most general case, we might hope that an entire literature of, say, feedback effects, might use the same graphic displays. While this is perhaps unrealistic, the point is that standard graphic communication can significantly improve communication of quantitative results, comparison between cases, and so forth. One can directly compare effects, trends, proportions, and other dimensions of the data without having to look so carefully at each "customized" scale.

Lindsley (1999) illustrated this point with numerous examples of his standard celeration chart (Figure 1.3), a powerful visual tool for understanding and presenting ongoing measures of behavior, outputs, or organizational results. In

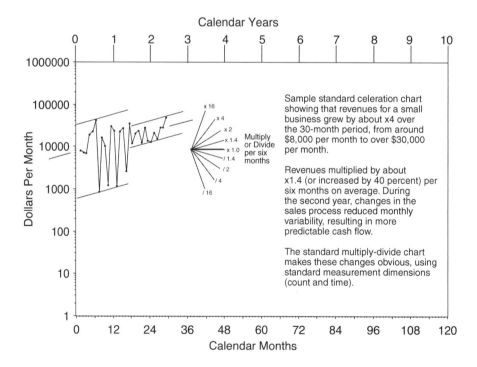

Figure 1.3 Standard Celeration Chart.

his standard charting technology, Lindsley took advantage of the human ability to quickly scan and visually compare objects for similarities and differences. Without visual standards for the display of data, we place ourselves and others at a significant disadvantage and at risk of unintentionally misrepresenting or misunderstanding the results of our performance improvement efforts.

Uninterrupted Calendar Time Versus Sessions Scales

How often have you seen graphs on which the scale across the bottom was something like *sessions* or *observations*? Quick review of many journals and other publications displaying measures of human behavior or outputs over time reveals that they often ignore standard *calendar* time, substituting instead events displayed sequentially on the time scale, regardless of the varying time intervals between points. This means that if sessions or observations, for example, are sometimes scheduled daily and sometimes only every few days, we cannot tell from the display of the data because every data point simply appears on the next line in the sequence, not taking real-time distances between measures into account. In fact, the potential effects of missed days or sessions cannot be determined from such graphs, a phenomenon that can cause us to significantly misunderstand or even be oblivious to important time-related effects on performance.

If, instead, we use standard displays of calendar or clock time so that, when there is a day on which an event did not occur, we *skip* that line on the graph and go to the next (Binder, 2001), then we can see the impact of our interventions spread over a true representation of time. If a week of vacation intervenes, we can see any effect it might have had on performance after the week. If there were more than one session on a given day, we might see data displayed with two points on that day-line. In any case, we can see the effects in "real time" of our interventions, spaced as they are in actual time on our data display.

Equal-Interval Versus Multiply-Divide Graphic Scale

Many people recognize that certain quantities such as population tend to grow in multiples. For example, population of a given area, or of a given type of organism, is likely to multiply by a given factor (x2, x3, for example) for each successive period of time, rather than adding a fixed amount. This is why we have the "population explosion"—growth that is much more rapid than a fixed amount per unit time. Rather, it tends to be a fixed multiplication.

Lindsley and his colleagues (Lindsley, 1996; Pennypacker, Gutierrez, & Lindsley, 2003), based on research showing that human behavior also grows in multiples (or proportionally, a given percentage trend) rather than in additive increments, have perfected a graphic display (Figure 1.3) that takes advantage of this finding. They created the *standard celeration chart* over the course of more than forty years of research and development. The term "celeration" was coined to reflect a standard measure of change, either AC-celeration or DE-celeration, quantified as a multiplicative or dividing trend per standard unit of time (per week, per month, per six months, and so on). A professional society, the Standard Celeration Society (www.celeration.org), exists for people who use this standardized graphic display in education, training, management, macro-economic studies, and other fields.

While description of this chart might sound very esoteric, and perhaps only useful for the mathematically inclined, its design actually allows users as diverse as elementary school children and performance improvement special-ists, performance coaches, and managers to make quick data-based decisions about trends and levels of measured performance. It is not necessary to know very much about the underpinnings of the chart to use it effectively.

What makes the standard chart helpful, with its multiplicative scale of counts up the left and its calendar time base across the bottom, is that any given angle on the chart represents the same rate of change, no matter what the level. And any given distance between two points on the chart reflects the same *ratio* (or multiplicative factor) between those two numbers, no matter what the levels. This means that one can learn to "read" the charts directly, without looking carefully at the numbers themselves, and rapidly understand the levels, bounce, or variability and trends in any data displayed on the chart. Such a graphic standard supports rapid display or sharing of data and rapid decisions. Its key features, with multiple examples, are presented in Binder's (2001) paper, available for downloading online.

SUMMARY AND CONCLUSION

While this chapter is by no means a complete discussion of performance measurement and evaluation, its intention has been to present the topic from a somewhat different perspective than usual, to introduce some new ideas, and to refer readers to additional resources for further study.

Key summary points to consider as you dig more deeply include the following:

- The most practical and directly useful purpose of performance mea-surement is to *make decisions* about whether or not efforts to improve performance are having the desired impact and whether or not to make changes before too much time has elapsed.

- Measurement provides *feedback* to performers, managers, and perform-ance improvement specialists so that they can adjust their behavior and their efforts to improve.

- Being careful to describe our procedures and methods clearly and thoroughly enough *so that others can replicate them* will advance both

HPT practice and its scientific foundations in the most reliable and sustainable way.

- The *performance chain*, linking organizational results to work outputs to behavior and its influences, provides a good reference for what we might choose to measure (behavior, work outputs, and/or organizational results).

- Using standard measurement units rather than quantities with no reliable real-world reference (such as averaged rating scales or percentage correct) allows us to bring rigor and objectivity equivalent to that of natural science to our measurement and evaluation of performance.

- How we display our data using standard graphic presentations is as important as the data themselves. We should be careful and self-critical as we attempt to truly understand results from the graphs and charts we use to analyze and display them. The standard celeration chart is a powerful tool for graphic display of performance data.

Following these guidelines will enable practitioners and researchers alike to contribute to a strong foundation in practical performance measurement and evaluation and to the accumulated knowledge base of our field.

References

The American Heritage dictionary of the English language (4th ed.). (2006). New York: Houghton Mifflin.

Binder, C. (1995). Promoting HPT innovations: A return to our natural science roots. *Performance Improvement Quarterly, 8*(2), 95–113.

Binder C. (1998). The six boxes: A descendent of Gilbert's behavior engineering model. *Performance Improvement, 37*(6), 48–52.

Binder, C. (2001). Measurement: A few important ideas. *Performance Improvement, 40*(3), 20–28. Available online at www.binder-riha.com/measurement_ideas.pdf.

Binder, C. (2002, March/2004, November). Measurement counts! www.performance xpress.org.

Binder, C. (2003, March). Using surveys and questionnaires. In *Measurement counts!* Online monthly column at www.performancexpress.org/0303/mainframe0303. html#title5.

Binder, C. (2004a, September). The dangers of percent: An example. In *Measurement counts!* Online monthly column at www.performancexpress.org/0409/mainframe 0409.html#titlemeasure.

Binder, C. (2004b, January). Counting one's own behavior and accomplishments. In *Measurement counts!* Online monthly column at www.performancexpress.org/0401/ mainframe0401.html#titlemeasure.

Binder, C. (2005). *What's so new about the six boxes?* A white paper available at www .SixBoxes.com/resources.html.Bainbridge Island, WA: Binder Riha Associates.

Binder, C., & Sweeney, L. (2002, February). Building fluent performance in a customer call center. *Performance Improvement*, *41*(2), 29–37.

Bjork, D. W. (1993). *B. F. Skinner: A life*. New York: HarperCollins.

Daniels, A. C., & Daniels, J. E. (2004). *Performance management: Changing behavior that drives organizational effectiveness* (4th rev. ed.). Atlanta, GA: Performance Management Publications.

Esque, T. J. (2001). *Making an impact: Building a top-performing organization from the bottom up*. Atlanta, GA: CEP Press.

Gilbert, T. F. (1978). *Human competence: Engineering worthy performance*. New York: McGraw-Hill.

Gilbert, T. F. (2007). *Human competence: Engineering worthy performance*. San Francisco: Pfeiffer.

Johnston, J. M., & Pennypacker, H. S. (1993). *Strategies and tactics of behavioral research* (2nd ed.). Mahwah, NJ: Lawrence Erlbaum Associates.

Jones, G. E. (2000). *How to lie with charts*. Bloomington, IN: Indiana University Press.

Kaplan, R. S., & Norton, D. P. (1996). *The balanced scorecard*. Boston: Harvard Business School Press.

Kaplan, R. S., & Norton, D. P. (2004). *Strategy maps: Converting intangible assets into tangible outcomes*. Boston: Harvard Business School Press.

Lindsley, O. R. (1996). Performance is easy to monitor and hard to measure. In R. A. Kaufman, S. Thiagarajan, & P. MacGillis (Eds.), *The guidebook for performance improvement: Working with individuals and organizations* (pp. 519–559). San Francisco: Pfeiffer.

Lindsley, O. R. (1999). From training evaluation to performance tracking. In H. Stolovitch & E. Keeps (Eds.). *The handbook of human performance technology* (2nd ed.). (pp. 210–236). San Francisco: Pfeiffer.

Pennypacker, H. S., Gutierrez, A., Jr., & Lindsley, O. R. (2003). *Handbook of the standard celeration chart*. Concord, MA: Cambridge Center for Behavioral Studies.

Rummler, G. A. (2004). *Serious performance consulting*. Silver Spring, MD: International Society for Performance Improvement.

Rummler, G. A., & Brache, A. P. (1990). *Improving performance: How to manage the white space on the organization chart*. San Francisco: Jossey-Bass.

Skinner, B. F. (1938). *The behavior of organisms: An experimental analysis*. New York: Appleton-Century-Crofts.

Skinner, B. F. (1953). *Science and human behavior*. New York: Macmillan.

Tufte, E. R. (2001). *The visual display of quantitative information* (2nd ed.). Cheshire, CT: Graphics Press.

Wilmoth, F. S., Prigmore, C., & Bray, M. (2002). HPT models: An overview of the major models in the field. *Performance Improvement*, *41*(8), 16–25.

Wordnet 3.0 (2006). Princeton University.

CHAPTER TWO

Measurement and Evaluation in the Workplace

Lori G. Bosteder
Darlene Russ-Eft

It was time—a new human being was about to come into the world. The family paced anxiously in the waiting room, watching for signs that their newest member had joined them. All eyes glanced anxiously and often toward the door that would open with the good news. Hours had passed; surely it would be soon. . . .

Eight months before, the mother of this new child discovered that she was pregnant. All her attention became focused on one thing: keeping this growing human being healthy. She immediately made an appointment with an obstetrician. The physician measured things like weight, height, and the size of her belly. Her physician asked questions about her diet and stress levels; he explored her emotional state and interpersonal relationships; and he drew blood to test numerous aspects needed for a healthy pregnancy. The nurse conducted a simple needs assessment to evaluate what learning needs she had. Did the mother need a nutrition class or prenatal training? Now they had the data, not only for that moment in time, but the baseline to compare as things changed. What would follow were many appointments filled with a well-designed process of measurement and evaluation.

Now what if the physician just sent the mother home saying, "Let me know when you go into labor." We would all be shocked. How will the physician know whether the baby is developing properly? How will the physician know whether the mother is staying healthy emotionally and physically? How can they prevent problems and educate and reinforce good habits? They cannot, and any physician who did this would likely be accused of malpractice.

Physicians have developed a process of measurement and evaluation based on benchmarks from millions of pregnancies. They measure the key indicators of health and growth over time to make sure everything progresses well and normally. They evaluate these measures at regular intervals that make sense to their desired outcome: healthy mother and child. These measurements are not just quantitative (blood, size, and weight), but qualitative (stress levels, support, and environment), because this is a human system and *all* key indicators are watched. And when that child comes into the world, he or she will have already benefited greatly from a well-designed and conducted process of measurement and evaluation.

An organization is a human system as well: it grows and changes; it can be healthy or sick. Measurement and evaluation at its best helps those that desire a healthy organization to notice when problems are brewing so interventions can take place, to educate as needed, and to reinforce good habits. So many companies fail to view their organizations as living systems, seeing them instead as money-producing "machines" (Wheatley, 2006). Nearly all organizations measure financial indicators, but many fail to measure the human side of the company. Often overlooked are human requirements of relationship, support, control, clarity, and meaning. Even more often overlooked is the need to measure over a period of time, to look for the signs of growing health or intruding dysfunction. Organizations that treat measurement and evaluation as a one-time event are like the physician in our story, sending the mother home until labor has begun. Those that do not measure over time will miss important information needed to understand the health of their growing, living systems.

Developing a well-thought-out measurement and evaluation process is more important to organizations today than ever. The rapidly changing environment in which we live can quickly make our past experience less valuable, even locking us into old perceptions that are no longer valid. Organizations that survive and thrive in change are willing to look for what is different and challenge their assumptions of what works. For many small businesses and organizations, gut feel from experience and a few internal conversations are often the only criteria they use for performance decision. Our world has changed. Paul Gaffney, COO for Staples, believes measurement is a crucial component of business performance. "You can improve performance without measurement, for example, by gut feel, by experience, by recognizing patterns and so on, but you cannot do so reliably or in a repeatable way (and eventually you run out of tricks)" (Hammer, 2007, p. 24).

Using a wide range of tested key indicators is also crucial. Companies using only financial metrics can miss trends that will eventually affect the bottom line, both positively and negatively. Like the obstetrician in our story, many companies are discovering that numbers alone are not enough. Human beings and their living systems stay healthy in different ways than balance sheets. Laurie Bassi, former vice president of research for ASTD, a former economics professor and current founder of an organizational survey firm, argues that human capital has to be measured and valued in this global economy.

> Globalization has left only one true path to profitability for firms operating in high-wage, developed nations: to base their competitive strategy on exceptional human capital management. Any benefits that, historically, have been associated with superior technology and access to capital (both financial and physical) are now too fleeting to provide sustainable advantage. As these former sources of advantage become less relevant, managing human capital by instinct and intuition becomes not only inadequate but reckless. (Bassi & McMurrer, 2007, p. 9)

Measurement and evaluation of human capital then becomes an important process for organizations to integrate into all aspects of its organizational culture. Measures such as revenue, expenses, and quality control must be joined by measures of human performance, innovation, development, and customer satisfaction. Organizations that measure the right things, the right way, embed metrics in processes over time, and create a culture that values what is learned by using it have a better chance of making good decisions in this world of constant change (Hammer, 2007).

WHAT ARE MEASUREMENT AND EVALUATION?

Organizations have always measured financial indicators. Expenses, revenues, and inventory are traditional well-known measures used to track how the organization is doing. The balance sheet and profit-and-loss documents are routinely reviewed monthly. Human performance and development, customer satisfaction and loyalty, organizational climate and innovation, all affect profitability as well and are being added to the review process (Ittner & Larcker, 2003). Measurement of these less-tangible areas can help managers make smarter strategic decisions. Managers can get a sense of the health of their businesses long before the financial reality is felt and intervene. Employees can better see where their efforts are most needed, and investors can gain a clearer sense of potential growth.

Measurement

Measurement simply refers to what information is gathered and analyzed in an organization. This includes the financial measures, such as income and expenses. Measurement can also focus on human issues, such as customer satisfaction or employee satisfaction.

Is customer satisfaction dropping? While sales may not yet be affected, that information would warn managers that reduced sales are not far behind, giving them time to identify or correct the problem. If it is a customer service issue, training can take place or changes may have to be made in how issues are resolved. If it is a product issue, then appropriate actions can and should be taken in production or design. Are innovations in the pipeline that could propel the company to new heights? Are new teams forming and performing at higher levels with potential improvements coming? These types of questions cannot be answered with accounting and financial measures alone.

Evaluation

Evaluation is the analysis of the data an organization has measured in order to determine the "merit, worth, or value" of a program, a process, or a product (Scriven, 1991, p. 139). "Evaluation, therefore, collects data, which is turned into information that, when used becomes knowledge at the individual level" (Russ-Eft & Preskill, 2001, p. 7). By evaluating key performance indicators (KPI) and assessing strengths, weaknesses, opportunities, and threats on an ongoing basis, organizations can adapt much more readily and accurately than by using their "gut" alone.

TYPES OF MEASUREMENTS AND EVALUATIONS

A quick search on Google shows there are literally thousands of already developed measuring and evaluation tools available for organizations. Frequently, organizations also develop their own sets of measures. Choosing what methods to use for collecting information can be daunting, but in the beginning it is helpful to focus on the key questions rather than on the method. What are the key indicators of health for our type of organization? What are the key drivers of performance? What do we know? What do others know? What benchmarks have already been discovered for our type of company? Some research and thought here can prevent gathering of useless data. Imagine if our physician measures the height of the mother every month and not her belly. This is a common problem when organizations use pre-created tools without their own research.

Then ask questions like: What will we do with the information? What form will we need it in to be useful? Our physician needs to keep track of the data he collects from each patient to be able to track trends and watch for problems. The physician needs to be able to communicate these data to the patient in a way that is meaningful to her. In a similar way, the organization must consider what to do with the information and in what form it will be most useful.

Consider our mother: she knows what is at stake, and she has a strong investment in keeping her appointments and letting her physician gather information. Data collection is much easier when everyone knows what is at stake, believes it will be used, and cares about the outcome. The purpose for measuring and evaluating an organization needs to be clear. What problems are we trying to solve? Where do we need improvements? What questions need to be answered? What decisions are likely to come from the information we discover? What is at stake? Why should anyone care?

When we have answered these questions, it is time to ask how to best gather the information we need. The context often determines which tools will make the most sense. Matching context with the right methodologies goes a long in helping the process go smoothly and obtain the desired outcomes. If you need rich relational data, face-to-face interviews and direct observation become very important. If you need information from a large group of people who all have access to the Internet, then online surveys may be ideal. Consider the environment, culture, number of people involved, data needed, and how you will use it as you read the next section.

Organization- and Program-Level Assessments

We will now review just a few of the many methods and/or tools used in the workplace. Table 2.1 presents further detail on the measures that will be mentioned. We will start with the big picture or organization level and continue the review with teams, individuals, and finally customer measurements and evaluations. Later chapters in this book explore some of these measurements and evaluations in greater depth.

Table 2.1 Examples of Methods and Types of Organization Assessments

Organization- and Program-Level Assessments

Examples of Methods	*Examples of Types*
Financial and Performance Assessments	Return on Investment (ROI); Benefits/Cost Ratio (BCR); Human Capital Management Survey (HCM); Organizational Dashboard; Balanced Scorecard
Audits	Alignment Audit; Program Audit; Conformability Audit; Quality Audits; Environmental Audits; Safety Audits
Culture and Climate Surveys	Denison Organizational Culture Survey; Six Seconds Organizational Climate
Needs Assessment	Training, Process, Communication

Team- or Group-Level Assessments

Examples of Methods	*Examples of Types*
Financial and Performance Assessments	Team Effectiveness Profile; Dashboards and Scorecards; ROI

(Continued)

Table 2.1 (*Continued*)

Team- or Group-Level Assessments

Examples of Methods	Examples of Types
Needs Assessment	Training Needs: Power and Possibilities Team Training Assessment; Performance Needs
Conflict and Communication	TalentSmart Team Emotional Intelligence Assessment; Team Dimensions 2.0 Profile-DiSC; Team Communication Inventory; Strength Deployment Inventory

Individual-Level Assessments

Examples of Methods	Examples of Types
Leadership Development	Leadership Personality Assessments: Dimensions of Leadership Profile-DiSC; Management Profile-DiSC; Emotional Intelligence Assessments: Goleman EQ; Bar-on EI; and TalentSmart EQ–ME; Hogan Personality Assessment; DiSC Profile; Myers-Briggs; Conflict and Communication: Strength Deployment Inventory
360-Degree Feedback	360 Leadership: Denison Leadership Development Survey; Clark-Wilson 360; Emotional Intelligence: Goleman EQ 360, Talent Smart EQ 360
Employee Satisfaction	Satisfaction, Engagement, Loyalty

Customer-Level Assessments

Examples of Methods	Examples of Types
Customer Satisfaction	Customer Satisfaction Surveys; Customer Motivation and Experience Surveys; Customer Service Survey; Net Satisfied (NS)
Customer Loyalty	Net Promoter Score (NPS); Net Delighter (ND); Net Committed (NC)

Note: Methods and examples are not intended to be exhaustive, but give practitioners some general ideas.

Financial and Performance Measurements. All organizations, whether not-for-profit or for-profit, need to gather data on the financial performance and health of the organization. Typically, such measures include income or revenue, expenses or costs, and profits or retained earnings. All organizations try to operate with expenses at a level that does not exceed the income or revenue.

But, as has been previously mentioned, the financial picture does not represent all aspects of the organization. A number of performance measurement tools exist; four that we will look at here are *return on investment, organizational dashboards, balanced scorecards,* and the *human capital management survey.*

Return on investment. Revenue and expenses have been standard measurements since humans first began to trade and barter. As the industrial age took hold, the "bottom line" was the focus. Did the company make more money than it spent? In organizational and people development, managers still want to know: "Are the activities we are conducting increasing our bottom line?" "Is it worth it financially?" Return on investment (ROI) is a key measurement to any business. Learning and development professionals need to know how to connect and track their efforts to the "bottom line" of the organization.

ROI is usually measured in one of two ways, benefit/cost ratio (BCR) and the ROI formula. The BCR formula, a long-used measure, compares the annual economic benefits to the cost of the program being measured (Phillips & Phillips, 2007). The measure currently favored by many is the ROI formula. This formula is related to the BCR, but measures the program effectiveness on a par with other types of business investments. Whenever human development professionals can speak the same language as management and CFOs, it helps to increase value and understanding. Using the ROI formula can assist in that effort as long as it is used with other types of measures. When undertaking these assessments, some use of discounted cash-flow methods may be appropriate (Brigham & Houston, 2006, 2008). It should also be recognized that requests for measures of ROI may actually be a request for data needed for decision making. It always behooves the measurement or evaluation specialist to undertake some focusing efforts as described by Russ-Eft and Preskill (2005) so that the needed information is gathered.

Organizational dashboard. The organizational dashboard and the balanced scorecard are often blurred, especially in software designed for their use. Lawson, Stratton, and Hatch (2007) explain the distinctions and why it is important to understand them. While these two tools often have similar elements, dashboards tend to track key performance indicators (KPI) and scoreboards tend to track strategic data. Dashboards provide personalized visual images, such as dials and graphs with little or no explanatory text "showing important trends, changes, and exceptions" (Lawson, Stratton, & Hatch, 2007, p. 34). Dashboards may be updated hourly, daily, or weekly. They contain historic information or look at what *has* happened and focus on comparing results to other results. Finally, they focus more on input and output measures (Lawson, Stratton, & Hatch, 2007). The purpose of a dashboard is to provide real-time information to improve efficiency, manage resources, and empower decision makers.

Balanced scorecard. Balanced scorecards, on the other hand, track strategic information and point to the future. The data in a scorecard are updated less often than the data in a dashboard, perhaps quarterly or annually. Developed in 1992, the balanced scorecard brought the concept of scorecards from the sports world into the business world (Kaplan & Norton, 2007). Scorecards allow coaches, players, and fans to keep track of their teams' performance, and individual stats track the performance of each player. It is easy to see at a glance the team's current performance, look for trends, and analyze strengths and weaknesses. Kaplan and Norton proposed a business scorecard that could provide a similar at-a-glance overview and organized it into four key categories of process, operational, financial, and growth (Phillips & Phillips, 2007).

The balanced scorecard ideally helps organizations connect "long-term strategy with its short-term actions" (Kaplan & Norton, 2007, p. 2). While the dashboard tracks historic information and is updated frequently, the score-card is typically "more focused measuring progress toward achieving strategic goals" (Lawson, Stratton, & Hatch, 2007, p. 35).

Human capital management survey. A survey tool designed to measure the human side of organizational performance is the human capital management survey (HCM), which uses the knowledge gleaned from empirical research that revealed a core set of human performance drivers. It measures the five major categories identified as most important: leadership practices, employee engage-ment, knowledge accessibility, workforce optimization, and organizational learning capacity (Bassi & McMurrer, 2007). Each of the five categories is subdivided into key components of that driver and measured in a rigorously designed survey. The survey is scored on a 1 to 5 rating that signifies the level of maturity existing in the organization, with 1 indicating low maturity and 5 indicating high maturity. Organizations can use this survey over time to watch for trends and progress.

Bassi and McMurrer (2007) have found that the most important practices can vary between organizations and can even change over time within a single organization. The benefit of this particular tool is that it starts with some well-researched key human drivers and encourages a process of linking these drivers to organizational outcomes. By starting with good drivers and linking them to actual outcomes, organizations can continue to improve and adapt this tool to their unique situations. They can significantly drive organizational performance by highlighting where developmental efforts need to be concentrated (Bassi & McMurrer, 2007).

Audits. The word "audit" may bring to mind the IRS examining financial records while people frantically pace in the hall. For this reason, the idea of audits can strike fear in hearts, but audits can be very valuable when used for improvements or adjustments. Organizational audits done in the right spirit can be a tremendous learning tool. Audits can determine the trustworthiness of studies and reduce bias error (Reichheld, 2008; Russ-Eft & Preskill, 2001) and help determine whether there is alignment within an organization's strategies, processes, materials, and external opportunities (Crotts & Ford, 2008).

It has been emphasized in research over the years that the more aligned organizations are, the more successfully they are likely to perform. Research investigating the issue of alignment or congruence has, not surprisingly, found it important. One study on organizational mission and financial performance found that the degree of alignment an organization created between its internal structure, policies, procedures, and mission increased positive employee behavior and was directly connected to financial performance (Crotts & Ford, 2008).

An alignment audit can assist organizations in identifying where they are and are not aligned and make meaningful adjustments to improve performance. Crotts and Ford (2008) identified forty-two alignment factors that they divide into three categories: strategic, staffing, and system.

Other types of audits include safety, quality, process, materials, and program audits. All these types of audits look for things like alignment with goals, consistency, reliability, and accuracy. Audits can help managers make better strategic decisions and adjustments for their companies.

Culture and Climate Surveys. Culture and climate surveys are frequently used organization assessment tools. They identify strengths and weaknesses of the workplace culture. They can shed light on the often-hidden but powerful rules that are controlling behavior, moods, and motivation. Organizational culture and climate are often confused and are often merged in the literature. A study by Dennison (1996) pointed out the confusion. For the purpose of this review, we will use the following definition of culture: a "collective, mutually shaping patterns of norms, values, practices, beliefs, and assumptions that guide the behavior of individuals and groups . . . and provide a frame of reference . . . to interpret meaning of events" (Kuh & Whitt, 1988, p. 13, as cited in Reichard & Shumate, 2005, p. 429).

If culture is the "enduring quality, climate may well be described as the current manifestation of that culture" (Reichard & Shumate, 2005, p. 429). Whether climate and culture are considered the same or different, climate or culture surveys can be very important tools. They measure areas such as communication, collaboration, ability to influence, work design, and customer focus (Reichard & Shumate, 2005).

Similar to our doctor's tools and processes, these types of surveys can help spot trends when taken over periods of time and aid in the design of interventions when they are needed. That was exactly how a climate survey was used in a community college campus study in North Carolina (Reichard & Shumate, 2005). The new incoming president was familiar with climate surveys and wanted to use one both to set a baseline and to look for areas to strengthen. Programs and changes were developed from the data of the first survey and then the college was resurveyed two years later. Improvement was noted and further work determined to be required. Two years later the climate was assessed again. Great progress was made and the organization has made assessing and improving its climate a part of its culture. Climate surveys can also be used to assess openness to change and help create better outcomes when changing processes or programs (Phillips & Phillips, 2007).

Needs Assessments. Needs assessments are often overlooked in the evaluation process; yet, they may be one of the most important evaluations an organization can conduct. Needs assessments can go a long way to ensuring that interventions are appropriate and aligned with both the organizational goals and the external environment. Needs assessments analyze the gap between what "is" and what "needs to be" (Gupta, Sleezer, & Russ-Eft, 2007). They help organizations develop a clear focus on the problem and needed outcome. According to Phillips and Phillips (2007), the number one cause of program failure is undefined needs, with the second most common cause of failure misalignment with organization needs and environmental realities.

Needs assessments are often not pursued for a number of reasons:

1. The need seems to point to the solution.
2. The solution looks obvious.
3. There are too many opinions about the cause.
4. Needs assessment takes too much time.
5. Needs assessment often seems confusing.

These misperceptions need to be addressed to help the organization value the process and willingly participate (Phillips & Phillips, 2007). Remember why a very busy woman preparing for the birth of her child takes time and money to visit the physician every month and why she attends classes in diet, prenatal care, birthing, and baby care. She sees the value and knows what is at stake. Helping the organization see the value of needs assessment is important to the process.

Team- or Group-Level Assessments

Teams have become a very important way to get work done in organizations. Among the many benefits are shared challenges, shared focus, multiple ideas and perspectives, improved problem solving, encouragement and support, and reduction of stress (Beyerlein, Freedman, McGee, & Moran, 2002). These benefits can lead to greater innovation, enjoyment of work with reduced stress, and greater work productivity. Like all human groups, however, teams can be challenging as well; conflicts, communication issues, and different working styles can reduce or eliminate the benefits. Assessments can help teams identify issues and gaps so that appropriate interventions can be created and delivered.

Team-level assessments can be undertaken that are similar to those described in the section on organization- and program-level measurements and evaluation. Thus, a team can be measured using financial measures, as is typically done with sales teams, or performance assessments can be done at the team level. Training needs assessments are often undertaken with specific teams. Finally, it may be important to assess the conflict and communication styles that exist within a team.

Individual-Level Assessments

In the following sections we will discuss the respondents for various individual-level assessments: leaders and supervisors and employees. These assessments can form the basis for both the organizational and the team-assessments described above.

Leaders and Supervisors. A variety of assessments have been used with leaders and supervisors, as shown in Table 2.1. Among them are leadership development and 360-degree assessments. As part of many supervisory training programs, trainees are asked to complete leadership development assessments, which might be used to measure the person's leadership skills or style, communication style, conflict management style, emotional intelligence, or some other facet. Many of these assessments tap into one or more of the "big five" personality factors (Barrick & Mount, 1991; Digman, 1997).

In some cases, the assessments are undertaken prior to an intervention and then again following it. This can form the basis for an evaluation of a training intervention. Taylor, Russ-Eft, and Chan (2005) undertook a meta-analysis of numerous published and unpublished studies that examined pre-training and post-training assessments.

While self-assessments may be useful, organizations are increasingly, recognizing the value of having the perspectives of other people. A 360-degree assessment is taken to see the leader or supervisor from the point of view of supervisors, colleagues, and subordinates too. A major advantage of 360-degree assessments is having various perspectives. A major disadvantage is the significant differences among the rating groups. (See Taylor, Russ-Eft, & Chan, 2005, and Taylor, Russ-Eft, & Taylor, in press, for more details.)

Employees. Assessment and measurement of employees, other than for topics such as productivity, safety, or as part of a 360-degree assessment, tend to focus on issues related to employee satisfaction. The popular literature suggests that employee satisfaction is linked to improved productivity and quality and increased customer loyalty and satisfaction (for example, Allen & Wilburn, 2002; Byham, 1998; Cook, 2008; Heskett, Sasser, & Schlesinger, 1997).

Beyond the popular management literature, however, some scholarly literature supports the link between employee satisfaction and organizational results. Judge, Thoresen, Bono, and Patton (2001) showed a positive relationship between job satisfaction and individual performance. Furthermore, Harter, Schmidt, and Hayes (2002) and Harter, Schmidt, and Keyes (2002) reported on the results of a meta-analysis using 198,514 employees in 7,939 business units. Employee engagement and satisfaction at the business-unit level showed significant correlations with an index that included turnover, customer loyalty, and financial performance. Such findings suggest that organizations should consider spending more time and more effort examining employee satisfaction and the ways in which to improve employee satisfaction.

Customer-Level Assessment

Even if organizations do not undertake assessments of teams or individuals, most are concerned about customer satisfaction, since satisfied customers translate into repeat business and higher revenues (Morgan & Rego, 2006; Russ & Zahorik, 1991). Like many organizations, Marriott conducts market research with its customers on a regular basis. Guests, focus groups, and corporate meeting planners are queried often concerning their satisfaction with Marriott's product and service (Brown, 1998). Marriott knows that communicating with their customers is essential for retaining current customers and attracting new ones. Feedback cards, surveys, phone and face-to-face interviews, and focus groups are commonly used methods. Various customer metrics are regularly tracked in dashboards and scorecards.

Typically, academic researchers suggest using customer satisfaction and repurchase intentions as key metrics in customer assessments, while consultants often recommend loyalty metrics (Morgan & Rego, 2006). Loyalty metrics, such as the net promoter score (NPS), have become popular over the last few years. Probably the best known, yet controversial, the NPS was introduced by Fred Reichheld in a *Harvard Business Review* article in 2003 (Keiningham, Aksoy, Cooil, Andreassen, & Williams, 2006). The NPS is attractive in its simplicity as it uses a key question to measure loyalty: "How likely is it that you would recommend this company to a friend or colleague?" (Levey, 2004, p. 35).

The NPS has been billed as the single best predictor of organizational profitability. A number of studies dispute that claim, however, so caution should be used in choosing your metrics (Keiningham, Aksoy, Cooil, Andreassen, & Williams, 2006, Morgan & Rego, 2006; Romaniuk & Hartnett, 2008). Morgan and Rego examined the value of customer satisfaction and loyalty metrics in large businesses, finding that several metrics stood out as useful, but the NPS was not one of them. Instead they found that average customer satisfaction index (ACSI), top two box satisfaction score, proportion of customers complaining, and repurchase intent were much more important. They suggest that companies use all four of these measures on a balanced scorecard for monitoring, goal setting, and planning (Morgan & Rego, 2006). They also point out that their study was done only with large companies and that it does not take into account the different conditions of smaller companies and all types of products and services.

Clearly, it is important to do the homework necessary to choose customer metrics that work well in the organization you are measuring. Keep in mind the measurement and evaluation lessons from obstetricians as you put together your plan and use well-tested metrics appropriate to your goals, organization, and product or service.

FUTURE TRENDS

As can be seen from this and other chapters in this book, there is a continuing expansion in the *types* of measurements and evaluations being undertaken by organizations and in the *number and kinds of organizations* undertaking measurements and evaluations. Bamberger, Rugh, and Mabry (2006) referred to the field as being "responsive and flexible," unimpeded by economic, geographic, social, or cultural barriers.

Measurement and evaluation within organizations is taking place worldwide. Indeed, the International Board of Standards for Training, Performance, and Instruction (www.ibstpi.org) recognized the importance of evaluation and measurement. Thus, IBSTPI commissioned a study to determine the competencies needed by evaluators working within organizational settings. This followed the systematic approach described by Richey (2002) involving a literature review, review of academic and training programs and courses, and listings of competencies from professional associations. The competency drafting phase included reviews by evaluation experts and practitioners from North America, Australasia, and Europe. The validation process involved an online survey (in English, French, and Spanish) of evaluators located throughout the world. Although cultural differences existed across respondents, they all confirmed the evaluator competencies. The IBSTPI Evaluator Domains and Competencies can be found in Exhibit 2.1 Further details on these competencies, including specific performance statements, can be found in Russ-Eft, Bober, de la Teja, Foxon, and Koszalka (2008).

The 2006 Evaluator Competencies include fourteen competencies clustered in four general domains and supported by eighty-four performance statements. These competencies are required by internal staff or external consultants conducting evaluations in organizational settings, such as for-profit and not-for-profit organizations, military, and government agencies evaluating their

Exhibit 2.1 The 2006 IBSTPI Evaluator Domains, Competencies, and Performance Statements*

Professional Foundations

Communicate effectively in written, oral, and visual form.

Establish and maintain professional credibility.

Demonstrate effective interpersonal skills.

Observe ethical and legal standards.

Demonstrate awareness of the politics of evaluation.

Planning and Designing the Evaluation

Develop an effective evaluation plan.

Develop a management plan for the evaluation.

Devise data collection strategies to support the evaluation questions and design.

Pilot-test the data collection instruments and procedures.

Implementing the Evaluation Plan

Collect data.

Analyze and interpret data.

Disseminate and follow up the findings and recommendations.

Managing the Evaluation

Monitor the management plan.

Work effectively with personnel and stakeholders.

---

*The 2006 Evaluator Competencies and Performance Statements are copyrighted by the International Board of Standards for Training, Performance and Instruction. Permission must be obtained from IBSTPI prior to any use, reproduction, storage, or transmission in any form. All rights reserved. A copyright request form can be obtained at www.ibstpi.org. Reprinted here with permission.

own internal programs. The competencies required by such individuals are different from those required by evaluators examining the effectiveness of large-scale state-wide or national programs, often funded by government departments or agencies. Competencies for such large-scale evaluations are provided by professional evaluation associations, such as the American Evaluation Association and the Canadian Evaluation Society, and are covered in numerous textbooks on program evaluation.

They reflect the core competencies of evaluators in these organizational settings—the skills, knowledge, and attitudes that a competent evaluator must demonstrate to successfully complete an evaluation assignment within an organization.

One factor enabling such expansion of measurement and evaluation is the increased use of technology. Certainly, organizations throughout the world are relying on computers to gather and analyze data for measurement and evaluation purposes. Online web-based surveys facilitate such data collection in diverse locations throughout the world, as was done in gathering the data for these competencies. Furthermore, digital audio- and video-recorders enable easy oral and visual capture of events for later analysis and interpretation.

Finally, the expansion in the types of measurement and evaluation as well as the expansion in the organizations undertaking such efforts has been accompanied by an increased concern about the use of the findings. Measurement and evaluation projects cost enormous time, money, and effort. If such projects are simply undertaken, but the findings are not used for decision making and direction, then all of that time, money, and effort has been wasted. In today's (or tomorrow's) economies, organizations cannot afford such waste. Patton (1978) introduced the notion of utilization-focused evaluation, and he continues to promote these ideas, which primarily involve engagement of stakeholders in order to increase their awareness and use of the measurement and evaluation findings.

Indeed, such stakeholder engagement helps to weave these future trends together. Just like skilled obstetricians, competent measurement and evaluation specialists recognize that involved and engaged stakeholders help to ensure that their efforts are responsive and flexible. Furthermore, stakeholders can aid in overcoming economic, geographic, social, or cultural barriers through technology. Finally, involved and engaged stakeholders can put findings to use in their own work as well as in the work of the organization.

References

Allen, D. R., & Wilburn, M. (2002). *Linking customer and employee satisfaction to the bottom line.* Milwaukee, WI: ASQ Quality Press.

Bamberger, M. J., Rugh, J., & Mabry, L. (2006). *Real world evaluation: Working under budget, time, data, and political constraints.* Thousand Oaks, CA: Sage.

Barrick, M. R., & Mount M. K. (1991). The big five personality dimensions and job performance: A meta-analysis. *Personnel Psychology, 44,* 1–26.

Bassi, L., & McMurrer, D. (2007, March). Maximizing your return on people. *Harvard Business Review.* Retrieved July 22, 2008, from http://harvardbusinessonline.hbsp.harvard.edu/hbsp/hbr/articles.

Beyerlein M. B., Freedman, S., McGee, C., & Moran, L. (2002). *Beyond teams: Building the collaborative organization.* San Francisco: Pfeiffer.

Brigham, E. F., & Houston, J. F. (2006). *Fundamentals of financial management: Business school edition* (11th ed.). Mason, OH: South-Western College.

Brigham, E. F., & Houston, J. F. (2008). *Fundamentals of financial management: Concise edition* (6th ed.). Mason, OH: South-Western College.

Brown, C. (1998, June). Measuring what your customers think. [Electronic version]. *Black Enterprise. 28*(11), 45.

Byham, W. C. (1998). *Zapp!: The lightning of empowerment: How to improve productivity, quality, and employee satisfaction.* New York: Ballantine.

Cook, S. (2008). *The essential guide to employee engagement: Better business performance through staff satisfaction.* London: Kogan Page.

Crotts, J. C., & Ford, R. C. (2008, June). Achieving service excellence by design: The organizational alignment audit. [Electronic version]. *Business Communication Quarterly*, pp. 233–240.

Denison, D. (1996). What is the difference between organizational culture and organizational climate? A native's point of view on a decade of paradigm wars. *Academy of Management Review, 21*(3), 619–654.

Digman, J. M. (1997). Higher-order factors of the big five. *Journal of Personality and Social Psychology, 73,* 1246–1256.

Gupta, K., Sleezer, C., & Russ-Eft, D. (2007). *A practical guide to needs assessment* (2nd ed.). San Francisco: Pfeiffer.

Gurau, C., & Ranchhod, A. (2002). How to calculate the value of a customer. Measuring customer satisfaction: A platform for calculating, predicting and increasing customer profitability. [Electronic version]. *Journal of Targeting, Measurement and Analysis for Marketing, 10*(3), 203–219.

Hammer, M. (2007, Spring). The seven deadly sins of performance measurement and how to avoid them. [Electronic version]. *MIT Sloan Management Review*, pp. 19–28.

Heskett, J. L., Sasser, W. E., Jr., & Schlesinger, L. A. (1997). *The service profit chain: How leading companies link profit and growth to loyalty, satisfaction, and value.* New York: The Free Press.

Harter, J. K., Schmidt, F. L., & Hayes, T. L. (2002). Business unit-level relationship between employee satisfaction, employee engagement, and business outcomes: A meta-analysis. *Journal of Applied Psychology, 87,* 268–279.

Harter, J. K., Schmidt, F. L., & Keyes, C. L. M. (2002). Well-being in the workplace and its relationship to business outcomes: A review of the Gallup studies. In C. L. Keyes & J. Haidt (Eds.), *Flourishing: The positive person and the good life* (pp. 205–224). Washington, DC: American Psychological Association.

Ittner, C. D., & Larcker, D. F. (2003, November). Coming up short on non-financial performance measurement. *Harvard Business Review.* Retrieved July 22, 2008, from http://harvardbusinessonline.hbsp.harvard.edu/hbsp/hbr/articles.

Judge, T. A., Thoresen, C. J., Bono, J. E., & Patton, G. K. (2001). The job satisfaction-job performance relationship: A qualitative and quantitative review. *Psychological Bulletin, 127,* 376–407.

Kaplan, R. S., & Norton, D. P. (2007, July/August). Using the balanced scorecard as a strategic management system. *Harvard Business Review, Managing for the Long Term.* Retrieved July 22, 2008, from http://harvardbusinessonline.hbsp.harvard.edu/hbsp/hbr/articles/.

Keiningham, T. L., Aksoy, L., Cooil, B., Andreassen, T. W., & Williams, L. (2008). A holistic examination of Net Promoter. [Electronic version]. *Database Marketing & Customer Strategy Management*, *15*(2), 79–90.

Kuh, G. D., & Whitt, E. H. (1988). *The invisible tapestry: Culture in American colleges and universities* (ASHE-ERIC Higher Education Report no. 1). Washington, DC: Association for the Study of Higher Education.

Lawson, R., Stratton, W., & Hatch, T. (2007, December/January). Scorecards and dashboards—partners in performance. [Electronic version]. *CMA Management*, *80*(8), 33–37.

Levey, R. N. (2004, February). Reichheld reconsiders. [Electronic version]. *Direct*, *16*(2), 35–36.

Maddox, K. (2008, January 14). Marketers pursuing new customer-focused metrics. [Electronic version]. *B to B*, *93*(1), 31–33.

Morgan, N., & Rego, L. (2006, September/October). The value of different customer satisfaction and loyalty metrics in predicting business performance. [Electronic version]. *Marketing Science*, *25*(5), 426–438.

Patton, M. Q. (1978). *Utilization-focused evaluation*. St Paul, MN: Minnesota Center for Social Research, University of Minnesota.

Patton, M. Q. (2008). *Utilization-focused evaluation* (4th ed.). Thousand Oaks, CA: Sage.

Phillips, P. P., & Phillips, J. J. (2007). *The value of learning: How organizations capture value and ROI*. San Francisco: Pfeiffer.

Reichheld, F. F. (2008). *The rules of measurement: Principals for building an effective customer feedback system*. Boston, MA: Harvard Business Press.

Reichard, D., & Shumate, D. (2005). Using campus climate surveys to foster participatory governance. [Electronic version]. *Community College Journal of Research and Practice*, *29*, 427–443.

Richey, R. C. (2002). The IBSTPI competency standards: Development, definition, and use. In M. A. Fitzgerald, M. Orey, & R. M. Branch (Eds.), *Educational media and technology yearbook* (Vol. 27) (pp. 111–119). Englewood, CO: Greenwood.

Romaniuk, J., & Hartnett, N. (2008, July 18). WOM brand detractors misunderstood. [Electronic version]. *B&T Magazine*, *58*, 16.

Russ, R. T., & Zahorik, A. J. (1991). The value of customer satisfaction. Working Paper, Nashville, TN: Vanderbilt University.

Russ-Eft, D. F., Bober, M. J., de la Teja, I., Foxon, M. J., & Koszalka, T. A. (2008). *Evaluator competencies: Standards for the practice of evaluation in organizations*. San Francisco: Jossey-Bass.

Russ-Eft, D., & Preskill, H. (2001). *Evaluation in organizations: A systematic approach to enhancing learning, performance, and change*. Cambridge, MA: Perseus.

Russ-Eft, D., & Preskill, H. (2005). In search of the holy grail: ROI evaluation in HRD. *Advances in Developing Human Resources*, *7*, 71–85.

Scriven, M. (1991). *Evaluation thesaurus* (4th ed.). Thousand Oaks, CA: Sage.

Taylor, P., Russ-Eft, D., & Chan, D. (2005). The effectiveness of behavior modeling training across settings and features of study design. *Journal of Applied Psychology, 90,* 692–709.

Taylor, P., Russ-Eft, D., Taylor, H. (In press). Gilding the outcome by tarnishing the past: Inflationary biases in retrospective pretests. *American Journal of Evaluation.*

Taylor, P., Russ-Eft, D., Taylor, H. (In press). The transfer of management training from alternative perspectives. *Journal of Applied Psychology.*

Wheatley, M. (2006). *Leadership and the new science: Discovering order in a chaotic world* (3rd ed.) San Francisco: Berrett-Koehler.

CHAPTER THREE

Unleashing the Positive
Power of Measurement
in the Workplace

Dean R. Spitzer

Effective management is based on a foundation of effective measurement, and almost everything else is based on that. Organizations are conglomerations of many systems. Measurement is actually the most fundamental system of all. The measurement system—for good or ill—triggers virtually everything that happens in an organization, both strategic and tactical. This is because all the other organizational systems are ultimately based on what the measurement system is telling the other systems to do. No organization can be any better than its measurement system. If the measurement system works well, management will tend to manage the right things—and the desired results will occur.

THE IMPORTANCE OF MEASUREMENT

So why is measurement so important? Here are some of the most compelling reasons:

- It cuts through the B.S. and gets right to the point. People can (and often do) advance their points of view with incredible vagueness until they are challenged "to measure it." Suddenly, clarity emerges.
- It makes performance visible. Even if you can't see performance directly, you can see it indirectly using measurement. This is the concept of "operational definitions" that is such a critical part of effective measuring.

- It tells you what you need to manage in order to get the results you want. Using "measurement maps," you will be able to identify, understand, and discuss the high-leverage relationships that drive results, and apply them to your benefit—and to the benefit of your organization.

- Measurement makes accountability possible. It's difficult to hold yourself—or anyone else—accountable for something that is not being measured because there's no way to determine that whatever it is that you're supposed to do has actually been accomplished. Measurement tells you whether you (and your employees) are doing the right things at the right times—the essence of accountability.

- Measurement lets people know if they are off-track so that they can do something to correct their performance. Without measurement, feedback is often too vague and too late—and feedback that is too vague and too late is useless.

- Measurement tells employees what is important. If you don't measure it, people won't pay attention to it. As one colleague said: "Measure it, or forget it."

- Measurement makes things happen; it is the antidote to inertia. We have all experienced, for example, how milestones in a project plan get people moving energetically toward a goal, while open-ended timeframes inevitably lead to complacency and low energy. Give people measurable goals—and help them measure their progress—and they will make progress.

- Measurement results in consequences (rewards and punishment) that further reinforce the inherent power of measurement. Any effective system of rewards and recognition, and any system of performance appraisal, must be based on a solid foundation of measurement.

Above all, measurement helps you to understand what is really happening in your organization and to take action based on that understanding. Measurement enables you to make comparisons, study trends, and identify important correlations and causal relationships that will help establish a roadmap for success. And this is just a sampling of what performance measurement—when well used—can contribute to organizational effectiveness.

The good news is that organizations are finally discovering the importance of measurement. The bad news is that most organizations are still using it very poorly.

THE DYSFUNCTIONS OF MEASUREMENT

Unfortunately, when used poorly, not only does performance measurement not live up to its positive promise, but it can be a very negative force in organizations. In *The Agenda*, Michael Hammer (2001, p. 105) puts the problem this way: "A company's measurement systems typically deliver a blizzard of nearly meaningless data that quantifies practically everything in sight, no matter how unimportant; that is devoid of any particular rhyme or reason; that is so voluminous as to be unusable; that is delivered so late as to be virtually useless; and that then languishes in printouts and briefing books, without being put to any significant purpose. . . . In short, measurement is a mess."

What is commonly referred to as "measurement dysfunction" occurs when the measurement process itself contributes to behavior contrary to what is in the best interests of the organization as a whole. When measurement dysfunctions occur, specific numbers might improve, but the performance that is really important will worsen. While some of the most egregious examples of measurement dysfunction in the history of business were at companies like Enron, WorldCom, and Tyco, its more mundane manifestations are being played out virtually every day in almost every organization around the globe.

Most organizations are full of examples of negative, self-serving measurement: measurement used for self-aggrandizement, self-promotion, and self-protection; measurement used to justify pet projects or to maintain the status quo; and measurement used to prove, rather than improve. Although the more routine cases of dysfunctional measurement might not appear to be very serious individually, the collective consequences of small doses of measurement dysfunction can be profound.

Probably the biggest problem with measurement is not the flaws in the system, but with the consequences, both positive and negative, that so often follow flawed measurement. There are two major types of measures, based on how they are used: *informational measurement*, measurement that is used for informational purposes, and *motivational measurement*, measurement that is used for rewards and punishment.

Most of the functionality of measurement, as described in the previous section, is related to the enormous value of measurement as a source of information—information for organizational members to use to improve management and the work that is done. However, when measures are tightly linked with rewards or the threat of punishment, the informational value of the measurement becomes subordinated to its use for inducing people to exert more effort. This is where the major problems begin.

Most organizations have very strong contingencies that tell employees, either explicitly or implicitly, "If you do this (behavior) or achieve this (result), you will get this (reward, punishment)." Because, in most organizations, behavior and results can't be directly observed, these performance expectations are operationalized by how they are measured. The performance measures become the way to achieve rewards and to avoid punishment. No matter how many other things might be measured, what is rewarded or punished becomes the focal point.

Striving for rewards is one of the most important aspects of life and work. But when rewards are at the end of the line, measurement becomes a means to that end. Furthermore, the greater the rewards that are offered, the less focus there is on the information that measurement can provide. When the focus is on the carrot, it's difficult to see anything else! And human beings are very adept at doing whatever it takes to get a reward. Because measurement is so powerful, especially when coupled with contingent rewards, measurement dysfunctions are quite prevalent and widespread. Furthermore, when people are being rewarded by the existing measurement system, they will resist any changes that will reduce their rewards.

While linking rewards and measurement does not automatically lead to dysfunction, it very significantly increases the probability of it happening.

HOW PEOPLE EXPERIENCE MEASUREMENT

People tend to refer to those things they perceive as negative and threatening as the enemy. When I ask participants in my workshops about their personal measurement experiences, the negative ones far outnumber—and, more importantly, outweigh—the positive ones. Even more distressing is that, even when I probe deeply, most people can't even think of *any* positive experiences!

Almost everybody has, at one time or another, experienced *negative measurement* used to expose negative things—errors, defects, accidents, cost over-runs, out of stock items, exceptions of all kinds—and to trigger negative emotions—like fear, threat, fault-finding, blame, and punishment. They also know how dangerous measurement can be in the hands of those who don't use it well or benevolently. Although negative measurement can get results, it is mostly short-term compliance, and it leaves a bad taste in people's mouths.

For most employees, measurement is viewed, at best, as a "necessary evil." At worst, it is seen as a menacing force that is greeted with about the same enthusiasm as a root canal! When most people think of performance measurement at work, they tend to think of being watched, being timed, and being appraised. This is why Eliyahu Goldratt (1990, p. 144) says that "the issue of measurement is probably the most sensitive issue in an organization."

The environment of measurement tends to have a major influence on how measurement is perceived by employees and, therefore, how they respond *emotionally* to it. Since measurement is such an emotionally laden subject, the environment in which it is being conducted is particularly important. Even if people aren't directly involved in measurement, almost everyone *feels* strongly about it. And yet, very few people *talk* about it—which, as we will see, is one of the primary problems with the way performance measurement is implemented in most organizations.

Measurement is powerful, and—for better or for worse—*what is measured tends to be managed.* Most employees also seem to intuitively understand that measurement provides data upon which many important decisions are made—most prominently personnel decisions. Although seldom explicitly acknowledged as such, measurement is important to people because they know that their success, their rewards, their budgets, their punishments, and a host of other things ultimately are, directly or indirectly, based on it.

Many of these negative attitudes about measurement at work are due to its association (and confusion) with evaluation. Few people, including corporate executives, know the difference between *measurement* and *evaluation*—and there *is* a very significant difference! The word "evaluation" is really composed of three component parts: "e," "value," and "ation." The central element of the concept of evaluation is *value.* When you evaluate, you *place a value* on whatever you are evaluating. Most people don't mind measuring, or even being measured; they just don't like *being measured upon.* And that's what most evaluation is—having a value placed by an external agent on us and our performance. The outcome of an evaluation is a *judgment.* Evaluation is essentially about making value judgments. People don't like being judged—especially when they are suspicious about the fairness of the evaluation process and the motives of those who are doing the judging. As long as measurement is closely associated with judgment, there will be fear. And as long as there is fear, measurement will be viewed as a negative force—rather than a positive one. And, as long as the "measurement experience" is negative, there is little hope that performance measurement will realize its potential as a powerful and transformational force in organizations.

In my book *Transforming Performance Measurement* (Spitzer, 2007), I talk about four keys to transforming performance measurement and making it a more positive force in organizations. These four keys are summarized in Table 3.1.

In the rest of this chapter, I will discuss those four keys.

CONTEXT

The first key to transforming performance measurement is *context.* Much of what we have already discussed relates to what I call the "context of measurement." Context is everything that surrounds a task, including the social and psychological climate in which it is embedded. This includes such factors as the perceived value of measurement, communication around measurement, education around measurement, measurement leadership, and the history of how measurement has been used in the organization. To a large extent, the context of measurement tends to reflect how measurement is perceived by employees and,

Table 3.1 Keys to Transforming Performance Measurement

Four Keys	Definition	Importance
Context	Context is everything that surrounds a task, including the social and psychological climate in which it is embedded.	The context of measurement tends to reflect how measurement is perceived by employees and therefore how well it will be used.
Focus	Focus is what gets measured in an organization, the measures themselves.	Selecting the right measures can create leverage and focus the organization on what is most important.
Integration	Integration is how the measures are related to each other, the relationships among the measures.	Measurement frameworks make sure that measures relate to each other and are not just isolated metrics.
Interactivity	Interactivity is the social interaction process around measurement data.	Interactivity is the key to transforming measurement data and information into knowledge and wisdom.

therefore, how they respond *emotionally* to it. Interestingly, even if it is accomplished with great technical skill, it can still carry a negative implication. How people respond to measurement is largely a function of how it is used—that is, what is *done* with the data that are collected makes a huge difference in how measurement is perceived. For example, as we have seen, it is experienced much differently if it is used to inspect, control, report, or manipulate—compared with when it is used to provide feedback, to learn, and to improve.

The importance of the context of measurement in an organization cannot be over-stated. It can make the difference between people being energized by measurement or people just minimally complying with it, and even using measurement for their own personal benefit (that is, gaming or cheating). No matter how sophisticated the technical aspects of your performance measurement system, how managers and employees experience it on a day-to-day basis will be due more to the "context of measurement" than anything else.

So what can be done to improve the context of measurement? Here are a few important points: Be aware of the sensitivity of measurement. Be vigilant for dysfunctions. Use it for learning and improvement, so that employees can see the positive side. Avoid using measurement for judgment and, above all, don't confuse measurement with evaluation. Discuss measurement openly and honestly. Educate employees about measurement and help them use it well. Make measurement less tightly connected with judgment and rewards. And make sure that evaluations are much more data-based.

FOCUS

The second key to transformational performance measurement is *focus*. The right measures will provide laser focus and clarity to management, while the wrong measures, or too many measures, will likely cause lack of focus.

What gets measured gets managed, and what gets managed gets done. Selecting the right measures can create enormous leverage for any organization. And, of course, the things that are measured command management attention. Because of the validity of *"You get what you measure,"* it is vital to select the right measures. If the right things are measured, the right things will happen. Unfortunately, most organizations' measurement systems lack focus, and most of what organizations measure is routine—the hundreds or thousands of measures that permeate every nook and cranny of organizations. This dilutes performance measurement—like trying to boil the ocean! When everything is important, then nothing is really important. This focus on the wrong things, or the lack of focus, tends to do little more than perpetuate the status quo. However, in today's competitive marketplace, organizations need to have very clear focus. Not only do companies need to do the routine things well, better and better, they must also find new measures that are high-leverage so that they can achieve competitive advantage. This can be done by focusing on a critical few *transformational measures*—measures that will make a real differ-ence to competitive advantage and that will differentiate the organization from the others with which they compete—measures that will make a real difference to the organization's competitive advantage.

While most organizations realize that measurement is essential for manag-ing, they don't realize how important the selection of their measures is. Unfortunately, organizations and organizational entities fritter away much of the power of measurement by not differentiating between the *critical few* measures that will have the greatest impact from the hundreds, or thousands, of other measures—the *trivial many*—that permeate every area of their organi-zations. Knowing what to focus on is crucial to success. Organizations must measure the right things, even if it means coming up with *new* measures.

Probably the most frequent question I am asked by clients and prospective clients is: "What should we be measuring?" This question drives me crazy, because too many executives and other managers think it is sufficient just to track generic or standard "metrics." These are what I call "routine measures," and they are satisfactory for maintaining the status quo, but not for taking the organization to the next level. Many organizations are paralyzed by billions of bits and bytes of fragmented raw data that clog their information systems—like the supermarket chain that was collecting 340 million different data points per week, but using only 2 percent of it!

An organization's routine measures are not differentiators. How can any organization differentiate itself from the competition while measuring exactly the same things as the competition? It is also important to realize that when we choose to measure a particular object of interest or dimension of performance, we are—at least by default—choosing to ignore other things. Just look at your own organization's measurement system and you will probably find a vast array of measures that keep your business running—but few, if any, that will help get your organization to the next level.

Focused measurement is not just about "getting things done; it's about being effective, and getting the *right things* done. In order to thrive—not just survive—and move to a higher level of performance, organizations need to focus their measurement on one, or a critical few, measures that matter most. The key to what I call "transformational measures" is finding the most crucial few measures that provide the organization with the greatest insight into competitive advantage.

Two great examples of transformational measures are (1) the "turnaround time" measure used at Southwest Airlines, which enabled people (from pilots, to flight attendants, to maintenance workers, to refuelers, to cleaning crews, and everyone else) to see something that was formerly invisible, the time from arrival at the gate to departure from the gate, so that it could be managed to create value and achieve competitive advantage and (2) the "cash conversion cycle time" at Dell Computer, the time from the outlay of cash for parts to the receipt of payment for completed computers, which was able to help the company conquer its cash flow problems and also provide the mechanism to make its innovative business model work in practice, not just in theory. Everybody knows that if aircraft turnaround time increases, Southwest will lose the key to its competitive advantage—and everybody knows what they have to do to keep that number low.

Most transformational measures start off as what I call "emergent measures"—measures that *emerge* through increased understanding of the major drivers of business success. They rarely come from a textbook, off a menu, or are provided by a vendor. Many of the emergent measures will be measures of difficult-to-measure intangibles, because transforming organizations are realizing that many of their key value drivers are intangible. But don't let anyone tell you that something isn't measurable. *Everything* is measurable in some way that is superior to not measuring it at all.

The next great challenge in organizations is to measure and manage intangible assets. While most of the tangible components of businesses are already being accounted for (albeit in rather traditional ways and with rather predictable effects), in today's world, the most important drivers of value in today's organizations are mostly intangible. As Herb Kelleher (1998, p. 223), former CEO of Southwest Airlines, put it: "It's the intangibles that are the hardest things for competitors to imitate. You can get an airplane. You can get ticket-counter space, you can get baggage conveyors. But it is our *esprit de corps*—the culture, the spirit—that is truly our most valuable competitive asset." That's the problem: Most of what is valuable is intangible, but most of what is measured is tangible!

According to James Brian Quinn (2002, p. 342), "With rare exceptions, the economic and producing power of a modern corporation lies more in its intellectual and service capabilities than in its hard assets." And Michael Malone (2000) insists that the biggest financial question of our time is how to value the intangible assets that account for *as much as 90 percent* of the market value of today's companies. Did you ever think that one of those unmeasured and unmanaged assets might be the key to your organization's next competitive advantage?

True transformational change will not happen until organizations begin to think much more creatively about the value of the assets, how to connect them with strategy, and how to link them to competitive advantage. One of the reasons it is so important to begin to think differently about intangibles such as intellectual capital is that the way you measure them will determine how you treat them. For example, your organization probably has already begun to manage people differently, because it is at least beginning to view them as assets worthy of investment rather than just as costs to be expensed.

The key to transformational measures is to change *perspective.* In many organizational areas, dramatic shifts in vision have taken place because of relatively minor changes in perspective, such as from "product-line profit" to "customer profit," or from "on-time delivery" to "perfect orders." In addition, few realize that one of the key success factors for supply chain management is the ability to measure trust throughout the system, and a key measure is "supply chain trust." Transformational measures measure many of the same things, but from a *different* perspective.

The biggest problem of performance measurement is that the world is different, but the measurement of performance is pretty much the same. If you were to compare the workplace of today with the workplace of fifty years ago, the difference is dramatic. But if you were to compare how most performance is measured, it looks like a throwback to yesteryear. Just think how little progress has been made in performance appraisal! And those who "mind the gates" are not particularly encouraging of those who want to change the measures—much less the "metric system"—because, after all, these gatekeepers have benefited enormously, and continue to benefit, from the legacy systems.

That is why most organizational measurement systems are dominated by antiquated, obsolete, and outdated measures. Many existing measures seriously constrain performance and prevent breakthrough performance improvements (especially in services and knowledge work), but most workplace environments still discourage trying anything new. Take for example the following typical scenario: A company sends out a team with instructions to "improve" a specific project. More often than not, the team comes back with a set of *incremental* improvement recommendations that only end up further entrenching the status quo, while declaring victory because the project came in on time and under budget! Trying to innovate without the freedom, and the mandate, to explore unconventional approaches and to take risks ultimately leads to more of the same old measures and, of course, the same old managing.

To improve the focus of measurement in your organization, make sure that you don't measure too much. Focus on what is most important. Don't just measure the financial things, the lagging indicators, and what is easiest to measure. Don't just measure what has always been measured. Focus on at least some of the things that are most important to drive future success. Adopt some innovative, emergent measures to measure those things that are difficult to measure—but vitally important to organizational success.

Selecting the right measures can create enormous performance improvement leverage. But, even great isolated measures aren't enough.

INTEGRATION

The third key to transformational performance measurement is *integration*. Integration can be defined as "the state of combination, or the process of combining into completeness and harmony; the combining and coordinating of separate parts or elements into a unified whole." Integration is the effort that must take place in order to achieve alignment of the parts. Integration is about getting things into alignment and then keeping them aligned. Much of what passes for management today, by necessity, involves trying to get the isolated pieces of work done—turning the *dis-integration* of our organizations into something that is reasonably integrated. But it is an uphill struggle. Because measurement is so crucial to management, measurement must be used in an integrative way.

As powerful as individual measures are—even transformational ones—they can be poorly used if they are not integrated into a larger "measurement framework" that shows how each measure is related to other important measures and how the constructs (which the measures represent) combine to create value for the organization.

Focusing on isolated measures has tended to build functional "silos" that focus on their own self-serving measures and disregard the measures of other functions. Most companies are composed of pieces vying for scarce resources—operating more like competitors than cooperators—acting individually, without regard to systemic interdependencies. Managers at one financial services company were tracking 142 different departmental performance measures that were totally uncoordinated. No two managers could agree on which measures were most strategically important. People were simply following the traditional, if flawed, logic, which was: "If every function meets its goals . . . if every function hits its budget . . . if every project is completed on time and on budget . . . then the organization will win." However, it should be clear that such thinking no longer works, if it ever did. Organizations should be focused on the performance of the whole, not on the independent performance of the parts.

In order to make strategy more readily executable through the use of performance measurement, Robert Kaplan and David Norton (1996) developed the concept of a "balanced scorecard," an organizational scorecard that would facilitate the integration of functional scorecards and enable better organization-wide strategy execution. The balanced scorecard is not just a four-quadrant template for categorizing existing measures—although that might be beneficial if the right measures are already in place. But a balanced scorecard will not make the wrong measures right.

A key to the integration of measurement is developing measurement frameworks, which visually depict the interdependencies between measures. In any interdependent system, you can't change one measure without affecting the others. With an overall framework that shows the relationships among measures, it is easier to make the proper tradeoff decisions, so more optimal decisions can be made.

Another key point is that the cause-and-effect logic between measures (especially between drivers and outcomes) must be understood. The payoff of doing this well is that organizations will be much better able to predict with greater confidence what should be done to *create optimal value* for the organization and its stakeholders—and that's what outstanding management is all about!

So what can be done to increase the integration of measurement? The key as far as integration is concerned is that measures must be aligned with strategy, and then must be integrated across the entire organization (even the extended enterprise). In addition, measurement frameworks will spotlight the potential of "cross-functional measures"—measures that can help to integrate functions and lead to higher levels of collaboration. Develop measurement frameworks to help you "see" the actual and hypothesized cause-and-effect relationships among measures, such as a strategy map. Make sure that everyone has a scorecard (a set of measures for their individual work), a clear line-of-sight between his or her own scorecard and the measures of the larger organizational scorecards (team, function, business unit, and so forth), and knows how his or her own measures relate to each next set of measures.

INTERACTIVITY

The fourth key to transformational performance measurement is *interactivity*. It is my contention that performance measurement isn't primarily about calculations, or data collection, or analysis—it is about the ongoing interactions that should occur throughout what I call the "measurement socialization process." In order for the full power of performance measurement to be realized, there must be considerable interaction at each phase of the process, leading to new insights about what to measure and how to measure it.

Transformational performance measurement is not a static, technical process of identifying standard measures and collecting and analyzing data on them. It is much more of a *social process*. If it is to be done well, the processes of selecting and creating key measures based on the organization's business model and strategy, relating measures to each other and developing measurement frameworks, interpreting analyzed data, negotiating commitments to action around the data, understanding tradeoffs, making decisions, and utilizing the feedback loops that are necessary at every phase will all be highly social and interactive.

One of the reasons why it is so important to establish a positive context for measurement is that the context will either encourage or discourage interactivity around measurement. If people in an organization view measurement as just routine "numerical transactions," they will be missing the most important parts of measurement—which are the "social interactions"—the communication, insight, and learning that should occur throughout the measurement process.

Performance measurement should include highly interactive and iterative (ongoing) discussions. When people carry out authentic *dialogues* about measurement, the benefits can be enormous. That's why I believe that performance measurement is, above all else, a *social process*.

Dialogue as interactivity should incorporate learning, understanding, defining, listening, modeling, hypothesizing, balancing, linking, integrating, and so forth. It is an important part of the total transformation of the measurement package. Transformational and emergent measures, especially, require the synergy and support that interactivity around measurement provides. One of the great qualities of interactivity is that it means that everybody doesn't have to be good at everything—or, for that matter, anything.

One of the major challenges of transformational measurement is to create an environment in which performance measurement data can be efficiently and effectively converted into useful information: this information can be transformed into knowledge, and this knowledge can be the basis for real wisdom. This kind of environment is very rare, because most of the time measurement is not dealt with interactively or iteratively. Data are generated and go into databases, somewhere. There is little or no interaction about the data or the information produced from the data. Without interaction, if any data-to-wisdom conversion does occur, it will be more haphazard than systematic—and it will not occur consistently. To make matters worse, in most organizations today, very few employees understand the meaning of most performance measures that are used in their organizations.

There is rarely any meaningful discussion or education on performance measures. Most organizations are performing a lot of measuring, but not learning much from their measurements. One of the reasons why measurement is still not widely accepted in organizations is that, to most people, measurement remains "just numbers," and few people understand the "the big picture" of measurement. As a result, the easy-to-measure things tend to be measured, and there is little interest in using the real power of performance measurement. Most people don't know how the *power* of measurement can be used anyway, so they don't really know what they are missing.

Most communication about measurement, when it happens, occurs within a particular function (such as within sales, within marketing, or within manufacturing). The failure to appropriately socialize measurement across the organizational enterprise continues to reinforce the silo mentality, to lead people to adopt local and suboptimal measures that work against what is best for the organization as a whole, and to cause them to react in the wrong ways to the wrong signals.

Value is only realized from performance measurement when it is turned into information, information into knowledge, and knowledge into wisdom. This data-to-knowledge-to-wisdom conversion process reflects one of the great positives of transformational measurement. Although it is possible for individuals to do this alone, the most effective way to create knowledge and wisdom from measurement is through frequent and high-quality interactions between people with complementary knowledge. Ask anyone (including yourself): "How much do you learn from data versus from interacting with other people who have a like-minded mission?" I have asked this question to hundreds of leaders in all sectors of the economy and in government, and the resounding answer is unequivocally "from our interactions with others." It is ultimately the *social things* that will help convert measurement from information into knowledge and wisdom and, in the process, positively transform the context of measurement.

The key to increasing interactivity around measurement is *performance conversations*: "Let's look at the measures and see how we're doing." "Let's look at the factors that are affecting our performance." "What do these data tell us about (customer satisfaction, profitability, quality, and so forth)?" "We are starting to see some improvement in this area. Let's discuss why we are improving here, and not here." "Do you need to come up with a new measure of . . . ?" Collegial functional and cross-functional performance conversations about measurement will become a fundamental part of new knowledge work in organizations.

Encourage communication and open discussion of measurement. Institute regular "dialogue" meetings within teams and between functions to discuss existing measurements, develop actions plans, review measurement frameworks, and consider transformational measurement issues. When there is more interactivity around measurement, there is much more self-management. Managers no longer have to be "supervisors" and micro-manage, because performance is highly visible to everyone. And when employees are more involved and engaged in measurement, they feel stronger ownership and increasingly realize that it is a key to their own, and to the organization's, success.

SUMMARY AND CONCLUSIONS

In this chapter I have discussed the four keys to transforming performance measurement from a technical, peripheral, and largely negative force in organizations to one that is social, central, and largely positive.

I have found that some organizations excel at one or two of the keys, but I have never found a single organization that was able to achieve superior results in all areas—and it is essential that all four keys work in tandem with one another. For example, without the right *focus*, the other keys will be meaningless—because if you don't measure the right things, you won't be able to manage the right things, and you won't get the right results—no matter how well you might measure them technically. On the other hand, even with the right focus, without a positive *context*, people won't be motivated to measure the right things, will tend to focus on what will bring them the largest personal rewards, and will tend to have an adversarial posture toward whatever it is that is measured. When measurement has the wrong focus *and* a negative context, a multitude of things can go wrong.

Without the right *integration*, measures will stand alone, functional silos will be perpetuated, individuals and functions will not be properly aligned, and there will be a natural tendency to maximize individual measures, often at the expense of other parts of the organization or the organization as a whole. In fact, the individual measures may actually work against each other, and even cancel each other out.

Without frequent *interaction* relative to measurement, none of the other keys can really work. Without frequent and effective interactivity, you will have a technical engine without a social engine, which is like having a Ferrari, but not being able to drive it. In addition, you might develop a scorecard or a measurement framework, but who is going to maintain it and keep it up-to-date? Without adequate interactivity, it is impossible to sustain any gains from the other three keys.

When all four keys are working together synergistically in an organization's measurement system, amazing things can, and will, happen. Together, the four keys to powerful performance measurement will work together to enable the awesome power of measurement to make a real difference—a *transformational* difference—in your organization!

The best approach for reducing measurement dysfunction is not to try to correct every system defect, but to begin by changing the factors in the context of measurement in your organization so that the motive for people to manipulate the measurement system will be reduced. If you put too much emphasis on the technical and ignore the social, the problems will just keep coming back.

If employees perceive that measurement is in place to help them to become more successful (rather than to monitor and judge them) and to empower them (rather than manipulate them), then measurement will become a powerfully positive force in the organization. Everything will feel better in a positive context, and everything will feel worse in a negative one.

Despite enormous advances in the technical areas of performance measurement (especially in scorecards, dashboards, analytics, and technology support) and some progress on the human side (for example, with lean and six sigma), the "content of measurement" has not changed very much—and neither has the experience of the average employee. For the most part, performance measurement continues to make people feel helpless, rather than empowered.

You will know things are *really improving* when people in your organization stop asking, "What do I do when I see a yellow or red light?" or "How do we keep the numbers up?" and start saying instead, "Oops, we're veering in this direction and it's adversely affecting this initiative. It's time to *talk* about a course correction!"

Positive, powerful performance measurement is not something that can be created once and for all—it is not a class you can take—it must be a continuous improvement process.

Today, most measurement still focuses on the past and the present, and it does not serve effectively as a guide for the future. This is because traditional measurement can do nothing except collect data on what has *already* happened. The "also-rans" in business can manage, for a while at least, by tracking retrospective accounting data. But the winners in business must see beyond the obvious and be able to *manage the future*. However, while some measures have more transformational potential than others, it isn't the measures alone that create the transformation. Transformational measurement is about changing organizations so that transformational measurement can become part of the DNA of the organization. Even so-called "change management" programs will ultimately fail unless the measurement *system* changes, because, as I said earlier in this chapter: the measurement system ultimately "tells" all the other management systems what is important and what to do.

References

Goldratt, E. (1990). *The haystack syndrome.* Barrington, MA: North River Press.

Hammer, M. (2001). *The agenda.* New York: Crown Business.

Kaplan, R. S., & Norton, D. P. (1996). *The balanced scorecard.* Cambridge, MA: Harvard Business School Press.

Kelleher, H. (1998). *Nuts! Southwest Airlines' crazy recipe for business and personal success.* New York: Broadway Books.

Malone, M. (2000, April 3). Digital age values. *Forbes ASAP.*

Quinn, J. B. (2002). *Intelligent enterprise.* New York: The Free Press.

Spitzer, D. R. (2007). *Transforming performance measurement: Rethinking the way we measure and drive organizational success.* New York: AMACOM.

CHAPTER FOUR

Relating Training to Business Performance

The Case for a Business Evaluation Strategy

William J. Tarnacki II
Eileen R. Banchoff

For many years organizations have been professing that the key to a truly sustainable competitive advantage is an engaged and talented workforce. "Managers are fond of the maxim 'Employees are our most important asset.' Yet beneath the rhetoric, too many executives still regard—and manage—employees as costs. That's dangerous because, for many companies, people are the only source of long-term competitive advantage" (Bassi & McMurrer, 2007, p. 115). This professed realization has pushed organizations to establish training programs (and even corporate universities) that provide opportunities for employees to develop skills and competencies related to their existing (or sometimes future) roles in the organization.

These training programs have evolved tremendously over time, becoming much more sophisticated and oriented toward creating a well-rounded workforce. Unfortunately, these training and development (T + D) efforts have not kept pace with the changing demands of business. In fact, T + D departments have evolved to be separate entities from the operations of the business, basically managing a repository of training options versus partnering with business and operational leaders to customize solutions based on evolving business needs. Recent attempts to broaden T + D efforts to encompass performance improvement (PI) are a much needed, long overdue, uphill climb. Unfortunately again, today's business leaders are looking to their human resources (HR), PI, and T + D colleagues to operate at a much higher level

59

and to develop a new language around the expectations and the demands of the business.

If our field of practice is changing (albeit slowly), it stands to reason that the traditional evaluation methods (see Table 4.1) we use to measure transfer from our training programs (skills and knowledge) are also too narrow to measure business results. These evaluation methods are being taught and even trained in the context of another narrow model—the ADDIE instructional design model (analyze, design, develop, implement, and evaluate). Evaluation strategies and tools, based on T + D and ADDIE, limit our ability to understand the overall business model and associated metrics in order to offer robust, impactful, meaningful evaluation results that help manage the business.

Table 4.1 Traditional Evaluation Types

Types of Evaluation	Which Evaluates . . .
Formative	appropriateness of all components of an instructional solution through each stage of the instructional systems design (ISD) process
Summative	learning and reaction from an instructional solution during final development and implementation, including all stakeholders, media, environment, and organization as components of that instructional solution
Confirmative	effectiveness of an instructional solution after implementation through analysis of changes in behavior, achievement, and results
Meta	evaluation methods applied to the ISD process
Level 1	participant reaction to an instructional intervention
Level 2	participant learning as a result of the instruction
Level 3	changes in participant behavior on the job due to the instruction
Level 4	results to the business as a result of the instruction
Level 5/ROI	financial value of the instruction, in terms of positive cash flow from the investment minus the cost of the program implementation

To help build the case for a more business-focused evaluation strategy, this chapter will trace the real-life professional journey of Joseph Williams (fictional name) as he matures from a young, academically prepared ADDIE advocate to a sophisticated human resources strategist and business partner. Mapping Joseph's experiential journey demonstrates how his perspectives changed to align his training results with business results without completely revamping the long-trusted tools and methods he learned in graduate school.

STUDY OF PERSEPCTIVES

The Academic Perspective

It was May 1997 and Joseph Williams had just graduated with a master's degree in instructional technology from a very reputable urban university. Basking in the glory of his new degree, Joseph was excited about applying all the wonderful concepts and practices he had just spent two plus years learning. He left the graduation ceremonies eager to employ ADDIE and its corresponding evaluation techniques to become the hero he knew some organizations were desperately waiting for.

While completing his coursework in the evenings, Joseph spent his days as a foreman and quality specialist on the shop floor of a small manufacturing organization. In this academic preparation period, he worked diligently to incorporate several new skills and techniques into his day-to-day manufacturing activities. But he soon ran into the brick wall of lack of interest and engagement and found that this organization was just too small and had too few resources to "hear his voice." In order to begin applying his new wealth of knowledge and expertise, he decided he had to move on to a bigger and more strategic enterprise.

The Novice Perspective

Soon after graduation (in 1997), Joseph jumped at an opportunity to work in the training and development department of a large automotive company's finance division. From his first day in the new white-collar environment, Joseph was sure he could make a difference by analyzing, designing, and delivering training programs that would have an immediate, positive impact on this global finance business.

Alas, it did not take long for Joseph to realize that the full application of the instructional design model was not part of the expectations of his new job. Instead, management directed him to use his ISD background to oversee projects that addressed needs they had identified during an analysis performed five years earlier! He also soon discovered that his deliverables were predetermined (seminar courses in a standard format) and that the implementers (the project trainers) would have minimal involvement in the design, development, and evaluation processes. Joseph held the title of "Instructional Designer," but he soon acquiesced to being just a project manager.

The "siloed" nature of the firm's T + D structure was perplexing to Joseph, but there were several other issues that also seemed even more counter-intuitive to this fledging ISDer.

- First, Joseph could not understand why design and development activities were focused on "old" information, especially when the organization was in the process of a major restructuring. For some time now, many department customers were indicating that much of the proposed content was out-of-date due to recent technological and organizational improvements.

- Second, he did not know why T + D operated as its own function, was not integrated with the operational areas of the business, and was only minimally assimilated with the broader human resources function.

- Third, Joseph struggled with the reality that there were stand-alone needs analysis, design, development, and delivery functions, but evaluation was not its own entity. And worse yet, evaluation was not conducted with any depth besides basic Levels 1 and 2 or summative evaluation (even formative evaluation was minimally applied).

Table 4.2 illustrates Joseph's foundational perspectives—how different types of evaluation were taught and aligned during Joseph's (and most professionals') graduate preparation.

Table 4.2 Application of Traditional Evaluation Types

Type of Evaluation	ISD Model Stages				
	A[nalyze]	D[esign]	D[evelop]	I[mplement]	E[valuate]
	Formative ————————————————→				
		Level 1 ———————————————————→			
			Summative ——————————→		
			Level 2 ——————————————→		
				Level 3 ————→	
					Confirmative
					Level 4
					Level 5

A Second Academic Perspective

Joseph knew the business had problems, but his formal ISD preparation was not robust enough to help him fix them, so in 1998 he set off to get a master's in business administration (MBA). He hoped this additional degree would give him a better understanding of how a business operates and how he could better apply his instructional systems design background to those operations. As he progressed through the finance-focused graduate program, things became much clearer in terms of how identified *gaps* have a negative effect on *organizational results.* At the turn of the century, the concept of human performance technology (HPT) was emerging in his ISD world, providing a new perspective on how to address performance gaps with instructional and non-instructional interventions. But, again, even with HPT and a deeper understanding of overall business concepts and functions, Joseph was still struggling. He was discovering that much of what happened was not a result of "pulling" business priorities to create a true linkage to results, but rather a "pushing" of functional priorities based on limited, higher-level evaluation data and a desire to justify turfs and budgets. Was this how all businesses operated? Was HR and, more specifically, T + D, simply a budgeted function of the business or could it be a strategic, value-generating consulting partner? To find out, Joseph decided to move up in his career.

The Generalist Perspective

While continuing to build his business acumen through the MBA program, Joseph ventured into an HR generalist role in 2000 with the same large automotive manufacturer, serving both the finance arm and the parent manufacturing organization. At last, Joseph was positioned to get more exposure to the operational workings of the business, and he was able to work closely *with* the business leaders to deploy solutions to address problems to close performance gaps. What a difference from his previous position in which he was a specialist working *for* the T + D function and evaluation strategy and execution were performed in a vacuum.

Joseph was getting used to being a human resources generalist, but he still knew he was not truly operating at the strategic level and really utilizing all the skills and knowledge he had learned through his new MBA and previous ISD programs. As a result, Joseph changed jobs once again in 2003 and accepted a role with a large, global, diversified industrial organization. From his first day on this new job, he felt he was really part of the leadership team and a key decision-maker and influencer in the organization (at least in the plant location in which he led the human resources function). Consequently, he learned a new way of looking at evaluation. Joseph began to understand that evaluation, as he learned it (see Table 4.2), was a very narrow application of the term, especially in relating training or general HPT interventions to business performance.

The Experienced Perspective

Joseph spent more than two years as a plant human resources manager with one diversified industrial organization and then an additional two plus years with another as a division human resources manager. Both experiences proved invaluable. Joseph learned that evaluation started with an established baseline. In other words, having a solid evaluation strategy was contingent on (1) knowing what was important to the business, (2) knowing how the business measured what was important, and (3) knowing how the organization or function was performing against specified metrics.

Once he began aligning current performance to strategic business goals and metrics, Joseph knew he could develop a solid evaluation strategy that would measure the success of the targeted interventions. At long last . . . this was something Joseph did not gain exposure to in his previous assignment as an instructional designer. His previous training and experience in evaluation was narrowly focused on being able to demonstrate that learning occurred, rather than focusing on the more meaningful metric of how the learners' enhanced job performance affected the business overall. He also was able to recognize that he had been treating training as an intervention focused solely on accomplishing specific department metrics instead of concentrating on something that was devised in partnership with the internal business customer (process owner). He concluded that this was in large part due to the segregated nature of the T + D department from the actual operations of the business.

Joseph soon learned that metrics started at the top of the house and cascaded down through the organization so that each facility and function could be aligned according to what was important. This type of top-down alignment ensured that evaluation was focused on the quantitative and qualitative priorities, as expressed in the organizations' business models. Evaluation became more than just focused on one particular aspect of a cycle (for example, formative evaluation as focused on certain portions of the ISD model). It was really ensuring that any evaluation eventually tied back to the overall business metrics no matter what the focus of measurement was. As a member of the operational leadership teams for the two large diversified industrials, Joseph learned a better way to integrate his business and instructional technology educational experiences (2003 through 2007).

Joseph found, however, that the evolution of business toward talent management, employee engagement, and business consultation by the human resources function was much broader than where many HR, T&D, and PI professionals were focused. He also observed that evaluation became an overused tool, overcomplicating the nature of business because everything became a target for evaluation, even if there really was not a valid business reason or linkage to business results. Evaluation was performed for evaluation's sake instead of determining the true value derived from performing an evaluation by relating interventions such as training, recognition, succession, and recruiting to overall business performance. This prompted him to consider a new opportunity that would allow him to take everything he had learned, good and bad, and demonstrate the type of human resources focus and alignment that would close all the gaps in the evolution of the function he had observed.

The Business Perspective

Joseph's frustrations with continuing to perform wasted activities and employ non-value-added measurement systems drove him to accept a new position as director of human resources and organization development at a much smaller, private organization (in 2008). Having spent most of his career in manufacturing, Joseph was excited about getting into a different type of organization—the information publishing and services industry. He was thrilled with the proposition of owning the development of the human performance improvement and development strategy for the organization, aptly called the "talent management" strategy. This was finally his chance to take all the great practices (perspectives) he had been exposed to and "lean out" those things that he considered waste, to produce what was bound to be considered an industry benchmark talent management system—at least in his mind!

Immediately after accepting the new position, he realized that the organization (a business that was growing very quickly) had nothing in place to build on. The non-existent program aspects did not pose a serious issue for him. But he did find the non-existent systems infrastructure—so critical in linking all aspects of a talent management and an employee engagement strategy together—to be particularly stressful.

Business Model. Beginning with this context, Joseph knew the business and its respective leaders were not looking for a narrowly focused T + D program, or a time-consuming HPT gap assessment, to determine immediate, critical solutions. They were looking for a full-scope talent management program that aligned to the business's philosophy, values, vision, and mission, as well as to their long-term organizational strategy. And they expected this to be built very quickly, with minimal resources and a focus on achieving their high-level business metrics. Joseph knew that training and development was a component of this, as well as some gap assessment and closure, but he also knew that they were small components in the grander scheme of things. He, therefore, set out to understand the business, which started with a grasp of the organization's business model, as seen in Figure 4.1.

This metrics-based, three-tiered way of thinking was critical to help Joseph understand exactly how corporate leadership defined the culture and essence of the company, how they envisioned the future of the organization, and how they measured success. Joseph knew that this was the basis for each functional strategy (including his HR operations) and the related evaluation strategy of all interventions or solutions that his group would have to deliver. Once Joseph established a foundational understanding of the business, he embarked on getting to know each function and location.

Figure 4.1 Business Model.

HR Strategic Model. Through his extensive U.S. travels, Joseph came to understand that some specific training programs were important to the firm's overall talent management program. But T + D was still a microcosm of the employee engagement strategy the organization needed in order to continue to prosper and meet its long-term objectives. His vision of a truly strategic HR partnership with the business began to take shape and he was able to see how the three pieces fit together in his mental HR strategic model (see Figure 4.2) to culminate in a high-performance culture and organization.

- *Engagement and satisfaction* would have to address the environment in which people work and interact and needed to include communication,

Figure 4.2 Strategic HR Model.

culture and change management, reward and recognition, and community, team, and employee relations (see Figure 4.3).

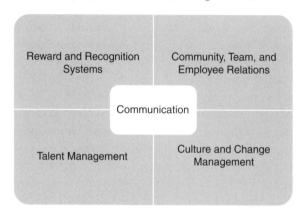

Figure 4.3 Employee Engagement Model.

- *Talent management* is integrated strategies to increase workforce productivity through having the *right* people (capacity and attitude) with the *right* skills and knowledge to meet current and future business needs. The integrated cycle had to be a continuous flow of finding talent inside and outside the organization and continuously cultivating that talent, and it needed to include assessment, identification, development, acquisition, and alignment (see Figure 4.4).

- *Functional excellence* would then become the focus on data-driven continuous improvement across the enterprise and needed to include lean/six sigma, business consulting, coaching, and competency modeling.

Figure 4.4 Talent Management Model.

The Strategic HR Model (Figure 4.2) allowed Joseph to demonstrate to the organization that managing talent effectively was at the core of ensuring an engaged workforce. Following this strategy would allow each function to perform at its very best to drive improved business performance. Together these models helped Joseph visualize and enforce with the organization that training and development are important but are minute in the context of how the organization benefits from its human capital.

Joseph reflected on how he used to "push" training programs based on the internal demands of the department versus the ever-changing needs of the business. He cringed to think how many businesses used to (and still do) create giant repositories of training to try to cover any potential employee need, rather than only producing what was actually critical to achieve true success. He finally found himself in a position to change these outdated practices and satisfy the organization's hunger for customized solutions. If, by starting with the business's overall reason for existing, he could work with individuals and managers on solutions that always linked back to those reasons. Joseph came to understand that evaluation was not just about figuring out whether people were learning, or were happy, or whether an intervention produced a return on investment (justifying financial investments versus showing whether solutions were working and serving as a means for continuous evolution and improvement). He now knew that he had to first determine what aspects of the model needed to be measured and then focus on how each piece of the puzzle was contributing to a pre-defined desired outcome, all starting with the organization's business model.

Strategic Business Model. The following systematic breakdown is how Joseph approached evaluation as a tool for his new human resources business strategy (see Figure 4.5):

1. Start with a comprehensive understanding of the overall business model.
2. Align the employee engagement program to the business model.
3. Assess the major components of the employee engagement program to establish a baseline to measure against (performance to metrics and cultural gaps).
4. Build a plan for talent management that capitalizes on the employee engagement program and linkages to the business model.
5. Assess the culture and environment to establish a baseline to measure against (performance to metrics and talent gaps).
6. Develop the gap closure strategy utilizing basic PI principles and practices.

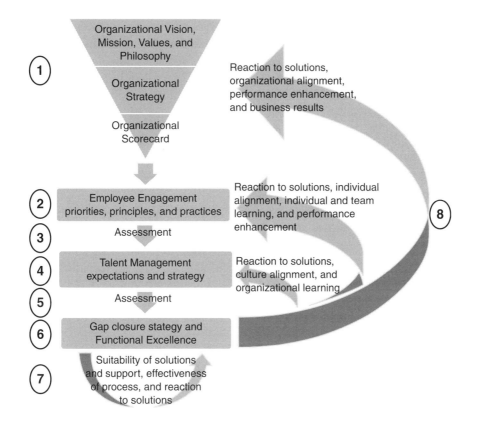

Figure 4.5 Evaluation Strategy Model.

7. Identify the evaluation needs and measurement tools based on business-defined desired outcomes.

8. Evaluate (and improve):

   • External sources of support and solutions for appropriateness

   • Processes for internally designed and developed solutions

   • Employee and manager attitudes toward solutions, culture, organizational strategy, and level of engagement

   • Knowledge transfer related to personnel development solutions

   • Job performance and individual and team capability and capacity

   • Effects of solutions on functional and organizational performance

   • Perpetual alignment of solutions to achieving the business model value proposition

By thinking business first, Joseph's process for designing, developing, and deploying solutions would never grow stale, and he would always be keeping pace with the ever-changing demands of the organization, the culture, the leadership, and each individual employee. He also came to find that he did not need to go off and design a new set of tools and processes, but that everything he had learned through his MBA and ISD programs were directly applicable. The tools and techniques just needed to be applied in a different, more holistic way, shown in Figure 4.5.

Finally! Joseph Williams ended up where he wanted to be when his graduate studies began in the mid-1990s—employing ADDIE and its corresponding evaluation techniques to become the hero he knew his new organization was desperately waiting for.

CONCLUSION

Lessons Learned

The purpose of tracing the evolution of Joseph's evaluation perspectives was to stress that the traditional ways of applying training, development, and evaluation principles no longer allow us to be the true business partners companies are seeking. Most businesses today operate very lean in terms of their human resources. The pace of corporate markets is so fast that conducting lengthy needs analyses and developing a huge array of training programs is not only impossible, but it is wasteful. Even though organizations are looking for *more, better, faster*, practitioners still have not taken the necessary steps to move toward being business experts and cultivators of functional excellence. We are still using evaluation as a tool for justification instead of valuation. While it is still true that training and development is a critical component to organizational success (for a little while longer, we hope), it must be employed as part of a broader strategy around talent management and employee engagement. Evaluation strategies, therefore, should not just be about different "levels" of *reactive measurement*; they must focus on *proactive alignment* of solutions to top-line business priorities. Practitioners first need to know these priorities and then design their evaluation systems to help create appropriate solutions and interventions.

In the study of evaluation perspectives, one can see that organizational vernacular moved away from organizational development (OD) and T + D toward human capital strategy and talent management. Although training is a component of an organization's talent management program, it cannot be the primary focus for long-term success. It must be integrated effectively with other activities to drive business results, and it must be robust enough to change as the organization's needs and directions change. The fact is, HR, T + D, and PI professionals need to transition away from being tactical specialists and move toward being strategic generalists.

There were several examples in the study of perspectives wherein the organizations and the functional leadership lost sight of their value propositions. First, in the automotive financing organization, Joseph experienced a situation in which the department was not organized as cross-functional teams, which negatively affected the speed of development, the ability to adjust effectively just in time, and the quality of alignment of design and delivery. This was in large part due to the department organizing itself to the instructional systems design model (ADDIE), which created distinct lines of demarcation where they should not have been and inhibited effective communication across groups, creating defensiveness and waste. The result was an evaluation strategy that was specific to the training itself, which helped the department learn what worked and what did not, but it was only used for future functional and departmental reference and was not linked to organizational strategy and results. This was all a result of the lack of business connectivity and integration with the operations. If this exists in an organization, the HR function's ability to move up the trend chart will be greatly diminished.

In the diversified industrial organization Joseph was a part of, training and development was viewed to be much more a component of talent management and employee engagement strategies. The issue with those organizations was the non-custom nature of their training, resulting in formal corporate universities with large repositories of training programs that simply existed for people to go out and complete as they saw fit. Training professionals were again removed from the day-to-day operations of the business and were not able to serve truly in the business consultant role. Their jobs were to maintain and, in some cases, deliver the courses made available through the universities. As a result, evaluation was again disassociated from the high-level business priorities and metrics and focused mostly on updating courses, delivery media, and support systems. Through the study of perspectives, one can see that these strategies are not representative of truly aligning training and development to a broader strategy for ensuring customized, real-time solutions to problems. Such alignment is not possible if the talent management and T + D strategies do not provide for continuous focus on business success through collective functional excellence and the flexibility to evolve to meet the changing demands of the markets the business serves. Practitioners have to assess where they are today to be able to utilize effectively evaluation as a tool for business partnership rather than program justification.

Bridging the Gap

In order to bridge a gap of any sort, one needs to understand where the gap exists and where it came from. This holds true for bridging the gap between where the majority of organizations are in terms of demonstrating the value of their training and development programs consistently and accurately, and where they need to be to align with those organizations that are already doing this well. It all starts with understanding the business goals and what is important to the business. Individual groups cannot effectively develop their own functional or process strategies without first knowing the overall business strategy. Not doing this creates chaos in the organization because everyone's efforts must be aligned to a common focus and target. Therefore, it is imperative for human resources, training and development, and performance improvement professionals to think of themselves as business associates first and HR practitioners second.

To truly understand the business goals and priorities, we must become immersed in the business. Every organization has a set of values, whether explicit or implicit, that guides the culture of the organization and the actions of its people. Those overarching values ultimately drive the strategy for the organization and the specific objectives and metrics by which the organization measures its success. From that, functional groups are expected to align themselves (with viable metrics) to these business objectives to ensure the whole enterprise is marching in the same direction. For the training and development function, this means understanding the business priorities to be able to perform an accurate gap assessment of skills and competencies required to achieve those priorities. It also means providing the right amount and type of training to match how the organization views development of people. If there is no understanding of the business objectives and values, then practitioners are simply putting out the types of things that are wanted but not needed or are simply invalid and non-value-added. Once human resources, and more specifically training and development functions, align to the broader business and devise a set of actions and expectations for them, then generating an aligned evaluation strategy follows naturally.

Designing a Business-Perspective Evaluation Strategy

Evaluation is not just a random activity that is done whenever time permits or when a request for data is submitted. If that were the case, then establishing the linkage between training and corporate results and effectiveness would be by chance and not systematic or consistent in any way. Remember the approach Joseph is using with his current employer: he starts at the corporate level first, works his way down into the details, and then links each type of evaluation back to the overarching business objective or priority. Following this process shows that designing the evaluation strategy truly starts with knowing the metrics, then establishing the measurements, then determining the process to implement those measurements, and then putting that on a timeline that aligns to every stage where evaluation serves a beneficial purpose.

Luckily, this does not mean that practitioners have to go out and learn a completely new set of tools or means for supporting their organizations. On the contrary, all our existing tools and methods are still directly applicable when designing an evaluation strategy. The change comes in no longer thinking about evaluation as a means to measure a particular solution *after* it already has been implemented. It now means using evaluation as a mechanism to help define and refine solutions and to ensure continuous alignment and improvement of solutions to keep pace with changing organization demands and needs. The key is linkage. If either the anticipated value of performing an evaluation or the availability of an appropriate measurement tool is missing or difficult to identify, then that does not negate a full evaluation strategy; it just negates evaluation of that particular solution or process.

Another important factor to composing a business-perspective evaluation strategy is linking the data back to a higher-level business metric. In the context of Level 5 of Phillips' ROI model (Phillips, 1997), every step in the process has a defined value to the organization. For example, just because a Level 1 evaluation entails gauging the reaction people have to training does not mean that it cannot be translated into a value to the organization. Satisfaction is a key component of employee retention. If employee retention is important to an organization and is understood explicitly as a core value, showing a strong positive reaction to a particular intervention or solution can quickly be correlated to employee satisfaction numbers. These results can then be translated into ongoing development and customization of solutions to drive improvement to that metric. Retention solutions also can be tied to cost-savings data through the reduced or avoided expense of recruiting and training new employees. However, performing this type of evaluation in an organization that employs a ''churn model,'' wherein turnover is expected and planned for, then evaluating satisfaction of any sort would be ill-advised and strategically misaligned. Notice that this Level 1 example is not just about training; it is about applying that concept in the broader sense of employee engagement and satisfaction and how that relates to the organization's core values, which then can be tied to financials.

Another factor important to building an effective evaluation strategy is identifying the right type of evaluation to perform based on the desired results. Practitioners must understand the desired result and the types of measurement tools at their disposal before developing the overall evaluation strategy. After all, a strategy is only as good as it is achievable. If the tools cannot yield the type of data required or the results cannot be achieved, then the strategy will not be effective. This brings this discussion to the final point about an evaluation strategy. It should focus on both *what to evaluate* to demonstrate value to the organization as well as *what not to evaluate* to avoid waste to the organization. Talent management programs vary based on both the needs of the business and the requirements of the business. Training, for example, often is completed to fill a tactical gap but not a strategic one. Although an organization may be required or feel obligated to complete some form of training and there is potential cost avoidance in terms of fines or assessments, this type of training does not really provide any substantive value in the way of improved organizational performance and, therefore, should be identified as an area in which the bare minimum will suffice in the evaluation strategy.

Joseph's evaluation strategy model (Figure 4.5) provides a picture of the eight steps for developing and deploying an evaluation strategy to ensuring business performance. This model is not all about evaluating training; it is about evaluating opportunities for solutions to solve talent issues, drive employee engagement, and create functional excellence across the organization, all of which will eventually translate into successful achievement of business results.

Devising an evaluation strategy is critical as organizations continue to push to understand how talent management strategies, including training and development activities, are enhancing business performance. Investment up-front in honing an appropriate, achievable evaluation strategy is important to being able to demonstrate value, not just justification, to the organization. A business-perspective evaluation strategy provides insight into the ongoing effectiveness of solutions and interventions in meeting organizational needs, which in turn allows for greater robustness in the process to ensure real-time changes as an organization evolves to keep pace with external pressures and market conditions.

References

Bassi, L., & McMurrer, D. (2007, March). Maximizing your return on people. *Harvard Business Review*, pp. 115–123.

Phillips, J. J. (1997). *Handbook of training evaluation and measurement methods.* Woburn, MA: Butterworth-Heinemann.

Suggested Readings

Alvarez, K., Salas, E., & Garofano, C. M. (2004, December). An integrated model of training evaluation and effectiveness. *Human Resource Development Review*, *3*(4), 385–417.

Blanchard, K., Robinson, D., & Robinson, J. (2002). *Zap the gaps! Target higher performance and achieve it!* New York: HarperCollins.

Dessinger, J. C., & Moseley, J. L. (2004). *Confirmative evaluation: Practical strategies for valuing continuous improvement.* San Francisco: Pfeiffer.

Dobrovolny, J. L., & Fuentes, S. C. G. (2008, April). Quantitative versus qualitative evaluation: A tool to decide which to use. *Performance Improvement*, *47*(4), 7–14.

Grossman, R. J. (2000, January). Measuring up. *HR Magazine*, *45*(1), 28–35.

Hale, J. A. (2002). *Performance-based evaluation: Tools and techniques to measure the impact of training.* San Francisco: Pfeiffer.

Jackson, T. (1989). *Evaluation: Relating training to business performance.* San Diego, CA: University Associates/London: Kogan Page.

Kirkpatrick, D. L., & Kirkpatrick, J. D. (2007). *Implementing the four levels: A practical guide for effective evaluation of training programs.* San Francisco: Berrett-Koehler.

Phillips, J. J., & Stone, R. D. (2002). *How to measure training results: A practical guide to tracking the six key indicators.* New York: McGraw-Hill.

Phillips, J. J. & Zuniga, L. (2008). *Costs and ROI: Evaluating at the ultimate level.* San Francisco: Pfeiffer.

CHAPTER FIVE

Success Case Methodology in Measurement and Evaluation

Anne M. Apking
Tim Mooney

Fifty years ago, Donald Kirkpatrick, one of the pioneers in the learning and performance improvement fields, developed his taxonomy, the four levels of training evaluation. His seminal work has played a vital role in structuring how our profession thinks about evaluation and in giving us a common language for how to talk about this important topic. Human resource development (HRD) professionals around the world have benefited from his valuable contribution, which identified the following four levels of evaluation:

Level 1: Did the participants like the training or intervention?

Level 2: Did the participants learn the new skills or knowledge?

Level 3: Did the participants apply the skill or knowledge back on the job?

Level 4: Did this intervention have a positive impact on the results of the organization?

Yet, when we recently went to the Internet and typed "training evaluation process" into the search engine, more than six million entries surfaced on the subject. They included recommended processes, reports, tips, books, articles, and websites. This multitude of resources was provided by universities, vendors, hospitals, state agencies, various military branches, and the federal government. We believe this extraordinarily large number of entries on this topic strongly suggests two things:

1. The concept of training evaluation is a hot topic that many HRD organizations are interested in, and

2. Our profession is still searching for *the* approach or formula that will make evaluation practical and the results meaningful.

So why does this search for the evaluation "Holy Grail" continue fifty years after Kirkpatrick first developed his taxonomy and approach? And why do we struggle as a profession to crack the code?

We suspect that many of you reading this chapter are hoping to find this magic formula for evaluation—one that is easy to use, yields compelling Level 3 and 4 results, and will solve the evaluation mystery. It is our belief that our profession does not need a slicker formula for evaluation or a new technique for performing ROI evaluation. Nor do we need more technology to make our current efforts faster and easier. Our profession is awash in formulas, equations, and techniques for evaluation. Therefore, the solution does not lie in inventing yet another formula or technique. The key to unlocking the mystery is developing a fresh perspective around the evaluation of training and performance improvement interventions—developing a whole new strategy that looks at *why* we do evaluation and *how* we approach it.

THE REALITIES OF TRAINING

After having conducted numerous evaluation studies during our careers, reviewing the evaluation studies conducted by prestigious organizations around the world, and talking with HRD professionals about the challenges associated with their evaluation efforts, we have seen two factors consistently emerge:

1. All training interventions will yield predictable results, and

2. Training interventions alone never produce business impact.

These factors are the realities operating whenever training is done. In order to perform a meaningful evaluation, we need to use a methodology that acknowledges these two realities and leverages them.

Throughout this chapter we will frequently refer to "training," "learning," or "training evaluation." To clarify our terminology, we will use these terms in the broad sense to refer to any performance improvement intervention in which there is a training component. Our intent is not to ignore or marginalize the importance of other HPT components. In reality, solutions are almost never all training or all non-training. Virtually every intervention aimed at driving performance or business results will have a training component to build employees' skills and knowledge, just as every training solution will need to be augmented with performance support tools, such as revised incentives, job aids, more explicit supervisory direction, and so forth. Our intent behind shining the bright light on the training component is to make sure that this large and visible expenditure is truly paying off and that the organization is getting full value from its investment, because frequently, organizations do not.

All Training Interventions Will Yield Predictable Results

The first reality is that all training will yield predictable results. No matter whether the training is an executive development program, customer service skills training, technical skills training, or a coaching program, there will be a predictable outcome:

1. Some participants will learn valuable information from the training and utilize it back on the job in ways that will produce concrete results for their organizations.

2. Some participants will not learn anything new or will not apply it back on the job at all.

3. And most participants will learn some new things, try to use the newly acquired knowledge or skills but for some reason (for example, lack of opportunity, lack of reinforcement and coaching, time pressures, lack of initial success) will largely give up and go back to their old ways.

The exact percentage of people in each category will vary depending on the nature of the training, the level being trained, and the organization. For example, participants in technical training typically use their new knowledge or skill back at a higher rate than participants in soft-skills training. But regardless of the specific numbers in any intervention, this pattern will emerge.

Traditional Method of Evaluating Usage and Results. Because of these two realities, relying on traditional statistical methods such as the mean (or average) can be misleading when it comes to capturing or evaluating the impact of training. Let us explain. (We promise this will not digress into an esoteric discussion of mind-numbing statistics.)

The problem with the average is that it tries to describe the entire distribution with a single number. By definition, that number is always going to be "average." There will be many cases that were much better, and there will be many cases that were much worse than the average. And they all get "smooshed" together into a number that is "average." So why is a single number a problem? As we described earlier, there are actually three categories of participants who will leave training programs, not one. To use a single number to characterize these three groups, which are very different and produced different levels of results, is misleading and not particularly useful.

Consider this simple example. If Microsoft founder Bill Gates were in a room with one thousand homeless and destitute people, the *average* net worth of those individuals would be about $40 million. In reality, that average does not begin to describe what the real situation is and to report that, on average, the people in the room are doing well economically would be an egregious misrepresentation, or possibly a dishonest deception.

In the same way, it can be misleading or dishonest to report an *average* impact of training, because those few participants who use their training to accomplish some extraordinary results may mask the fact that the larger proportion of participants received no value at all. Or vice versa: the large proportion of participants who failed to employ the concepts from the training can overshadow the important value that a few people were able to produce for the organization when they actually used the training. The average will always overstate the value of the training for people who did nothing with it, and it will always understate the good the training did for those who actually used it. In short, it obfuscates what really happened and what we as HPT professionals need to do about it. This leads to the second reality of training. It surrounds the issue of why training works or does not work to produce business impact.

Training Alone Never Produces Business Impact

Our profession largely operates with a mythical view that states: "If we are doing the training well, the business results should be good." This is depicted in Figure 5.1.

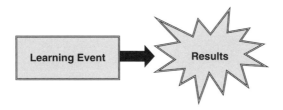

Figure 5.1 Mythical View of Training.

Unfortunately, this is not what happens in the real world. Anyone who has been in the HRD business for very long has probably experienced a situation similar to this: two people attend the same training program, taught by the same instructor, using the same materials, demonstrating comparable skills on an end-of-course assessment, even eating the same doughnuts on breaks. Yet, one of them takes what she learned and consistently applies it on the job in a way that helps improve her performance and produces a great benefit for the organization. At the same time, the second person hardly uses the new skills/ knowledge at all and has nothing to show for his efforts. How can the same training program produce such radically different levels of results? How would you judge the effectiveness of this training program?

This example dramatizes the fact that there is almost always something operating outside of the training experience that can have a significant impact on whether the trainees will even use the new skills/knowledge and what results they will achieve by doing so. Therefore, the second reality, simply stated, is that the training program alone never accounts for the success or failure of the training to produce results. There is always something else happening before or after the training that has just as much impact (or more) on whether the training is used to produce results for the individual and organization. This is depicted in Figure 5.2.

Figure 5.2 The Reality of Training.

The size of the "learning event" square is relatively small compared to the "before" and "after" rectangles to signify that the training itself is typically a smaller player in the results outcome. Other performance factors usually have a greater influence in determining the level of results. Sometimes those factors are deliberate and desirable, such as job aids, new work processes, or manager coaching; frequently, they are accidental and undesirable, such as peer pressure to stick with the old approach, lack of confidence in using the new skills, or no support or time to try out the new techniques.

Restating the Two Realities

To restate the two realities:

Reality Number 1: Training yields predictable results. Typical statistical measures used in evaluation studies can be very misleading.

Reality Number 2: Training alone never accounts for the success or failure of the training to produce results. Therefore, attempting to parcel out the results produced by the intervention is impossible and terribly counter-productive.

To be useful, an evaluation strategy must acknowledge that these two realities are operating and then leverage them. By leverage, we mean capture and report the kind of data that helps the organization maximize the impact of training and any other performance improvement interventions in the future. An evaluation that is simply "a look in the rear-view mirror" and reports statistics on what happened in the past has limited value to the organization. Moreover, it can be perceived as self-serving or defensive. "Look at the wonderful results the L&D organization produced" or "We are producing meaningful results; please approve our budgets." The message that runs through this chapter is quite simple: The goal of evaluation is *not to prove* the value of training or performance intervention. The goal of evaluation is to *improve* the value of training. Its primary purpose should be to help the organization produce more business impact from its training and performance improvement investments. This goal cannot be accomplished by creating a new and slicker formula for calculating ROI, but requires a strategy and method that will help L&D departments collect the kind of data and communicate the kind of information that will begin to change the paradigm for how their organizations view and implement training and performance improvement interventions. In other words, greater results will not be achieved by using better counting tactics, but only by taking a more strategic approach toward evaluation.

SUCCESS CASE EVALUATION METHOD

The Success Case Evaluation Method, developed by Dr. Robert Brinkerhoff, has provided this strategic perspective and has enabled HRD professionals to begin this change effort in their organizations. This strategic approach answers four basic questions:

1. To what extent did the training or performance intervention help produce valuable and concrete results for the organization?
2. When the intervention worked and produced these valuable results, why did it work?
3. When the intervention did not work, why not?
4. What should be done differently to maximize the impact of this training (or any future performance intervention) so the organization is getting the best return from its investment?

Success Case Method Case Study

Below is an actual case of one of the member companies in our user group that used the success case method (SCM) to proactively improve training, rather than just document the success of a training intervention. This organization was implementing a large and strategically critical business initiative to help employ new marketing concepts and tools in their business plans and pricing decisions. Training was an important part of this initiative for building the capabilities of the managers with these new pricing and marketing approaches. A training director discovered from the evaluation study that just one of the several dozen trainees had used the training to directly increase operating income by an impressive $1.87 million. In this case, it would have been very easy (although this training leader did not succumb to the temptation) to calculate an average impact estimate that would have made it look as if the typical participant had produced close to $100,000 of value from the training, well above and beyond what it had cost. And indeed, had this training function employed one of the typical ROI methodologies, this is exactly what they would have discovered and reported.

Instead, this training leader happily reported and shared in the recognition for the wonderful success that the training had helped one participant produce. But he also dutifully reported the darker side of the picture—that there was a large proportion of the trainees who came nowhere near this sort of outcome— and that, in fact, many trainees made no use of the training at all. This took courage to tell the whole story, but it also drew attention to the factors that needed to be better managed in order to help more trainees use their training in similarly positive ways.

By bringing critical attention to the low-level usage of the training and the marketing tools and the projected business consequences that would ensue if the strategic shift could not be made, our user group member was able to stimulate some key executive decisions in some of the business's divisions. These decisions would drive more accountability for employing the new marketing skills and more effective manager involvement. The bold actions of this training leader spawned a new attention to the many performance factors that drive impact and enabled the entire organization to accelerate strategic execution more deeply through the organization.

The SCM enables HPT professionals to dig beneath the results headline and investigate the real truth. Why were these great outcomes achieved? Who did what to cause them to happen? What would it take to get more such outcomes in future interventions? What prevented other people from obtaining similar great results? Only when the L&D organization begins reporting the complete story about training and business outcomes in ways that senior managers and line managers can understand and act on will they be able to effectively change the way that training and other performance interventions are perceived and ensure that they lead to business results.

The Success Case Evaluation Method: Five Simple Steps

The primary intent of the SCM is to discover and shine a light on instances in which training and other performance tools have been leveraged by employees in the workplace in remarkable and impactful ways. Conversely, the SCM also allows us to investigate instances of non-success and to better understand why these employees were unable to use what they had learned to make a significant difference in the organization.

The SCM is an elegantly simple approach that can be used to evaluate a multitude of organizational improvement initiatives, with training being just one. SCM employs an initial survey process to identify instances of success, as well as instances of non-success. The successful instances are then investigated through in-depth interviews to determine the magnitude of the impact these employees achieved when they applied their new skills and capabilities on the job. In addition, employees who were unable to successfully leverage the training are also interviewed to determine the likely causes for their lack of success. It is through this collection of "stories," both positive and negative, that we can gain keen insight into how the organization can get maximum impact from learning interventions.

Specifically, the SCM consists of five essential steps:

Step 1: Focus and plan the evaluation study.

Step 2: Craft an "impact model."

Step 3: Design and implement a survey.

Step 4: Interview and document both success and non-success cases.

Step 5: Communicate findings, conclusions, and recommendations.

The remainder of this chapter will look more closely at the process for conducting a success case evaluation study.

Step 1: Focus and Plan the Evaluation Study. It does not take a college degree in accounting to conclude that any dollar invested in the evaluation of learning is a dollar that will *not* be leveraged in the design, development, or deployment of learning. In other words, any effort to evaluate training diverts valuable resources from the training function's most essential products and services to the organization. In times of dwindling training budgets and downsized training staffs, evaluation efforts must be thoughtfully and strategically expended.

The focal point of this first step is to clearly articulate the business question that needs to be answered. What information would help business leaders accelerate the key results or better execute a business strategy? What information would help the organization understand how the training can support these business goals? Success case evaluation studies that place these questions "front and center" are the studies that yield the greatest value for the organization. In our experience of conducting SCM evaluation studies, we have often found the following types of training initiatives to be good candidates for this type of evaluation:

1. *A performance intervention that is an integral part of a critical business initiative such as a new product launch or a culture change effort.* The organization cannot afford these initiatives to falter. An SCM study can

help the organization assess lead indicators of success or barriers that need to be changed before it is too late and the business initiative fails to deliver the expected results.

2. *A training initiative that is a new offering.* Typically, business leaders want to be reassured that a large investment in the launch of a new training solution is going to return the favor. A new training initiative will benefit from an SCM study, especially if it was launched under tight timeframes. An SCM study can readily identify areas of an implementation that are not working as well as they should and can provide specific recommendations for modification or even redesign. In addition, an SCM study conducted following the pilot of a new initiative will provide invaluable data regarding its initial impact and help to determine whether a broader roll-out is advisable.

3. *An existing training solution that is under scrutiny by senior-level management.* Often, in good economic times, organizations perennially offer development opportunities for employees, without much thought to the relative value they add. But in times of severe "belt tightening," these training solutions are usually the first to be considered for an SCM study, in order to truly understand their worth, especially if the initiative is expansive, expensive, and visible.

4. *Any "soft-skills" learning resource.* When looking for opportunities to increase impact and business results, business leaders frequently question the value of learning solutions that teach skills that can be generally applied in many settings, such as communication skills, customer service skills, and leadership, management, and supervisory skills. An SCM evaluation study can clearly pinpoint the ways in which employees are able to leverage these broad skill sets in ways that have a positive impact on business goals.

Regardless of the initiative selected for the SCM study, it is imperative that a relevant and important business question lies at the heart of any evaluation study.

Step 2: Craft an "Impact Model." In this world of technology-enabled gadgets, where would we be without our onboard navigation systems, our GPS devices, or even mapquest.com? Well, frankly, we'd be lost, which is exactly where we would be without an impact model during an SCM study.

The impact model is the GPS device for the evaluation study. It is a simple illustration of the successful outcome of the training initiative we are evaluating. In other words, the impact model creates the "line of sight" that connects the following:

1. The skills, knowledge, and capabilities learned through our training solution;

2. The performance improvement we expect from employees back on the job in specific and important situations as a result of acquiring the skill, knowledge, and capabilities;

3. The results we expect given this new and improved performance; and

4. The business goals that will be directly impacted.

This visual depiction provides us with a snapshot of success that will drive the entire evaluation study. The model will help us to craft our survey in Step 3, to formulate the interview questions in Step 4, and to derive our findings, conclusions, and recommendations during Step 5. Table 5.1 illustrates an example of an impact model for a call center supervisor. Note that the statements within columns do not necessarily correspond with one another. An impact map works more like a funnel. For example, in this case the third column lists applications that obtain the results and help to achieve the business goals in the fourth column.

Table 5.1 Impact Model for Coaching Skills Training for Call Center Supervisors

Key Skills and Knowledge	Critical Applications	Key Job Results	Business Goals
Learn a questioning technique for effective diagnosing of development level. Understand how to assess team strengths and performance gaps. Understand how to adapt leadership style to effectively coach a CSR representative. Develop ability to help teams set goals and achieve goals. Learn techniques to reduce defensiveness in coaching situations.	Help integrate new representatives into CSR teams. Use behavior observation and targeted questions to determine skill level of representatives. Coach representatives by explaining the call metrics and their relationship to the model and impact on corporate goals. Coach by mapping day-to-day tasks and corporate goals. Ask questions like: "Why is this task important?"	75 percent of CSR representatives score 90 percent or better on the universal QA form. Attrition reduced to 30 percent.	Increase customer renewal rates by 10 percent. Maintain or improve J.D. Power rating of 92.

Step 3: Design and Implement a Survey. It is during this step of the process that our efforts with the SCM study move from being strategic to being tactical. At this point, we have selected the performance intervention we will evaluate and have an impact model documenting what success should look like in terms of behavior and results. We now need to craft a survey that will be administered to the target audience of that initiative, so that we can identify employees who successfully applied their learning in significant and meaningful ways. In addition, we also want to uncover employees who were unable to get positive results, as their stories yield valuable insights as well.

Many questions typically arise with regard to the design and implementation of this survey. The questions we are asked most frequently include:

1. *What questions should be asked on the survey?* If your only goal for the survey is to identify the most successful and least successful training participants, it is possible that the survey consists of a single question: "To what extent have you been able to leverage [the name of the performance intervention] to have a significant positive impact on [some organizational goal]?" If, however, you want to solicit additional input from the survey, such as demographic information or the degree of managerial support, you will include additional questions to collect this data. In general, it is recommended that the survey be brief, not to exceed five to eight multiple-choice questions in total, and follow accepted best practices of survey construction.

2. *To whom should the survey be sent?* While there is an extensive amount of research available on sampling theory, such as Babbie's (1990) book, *Survey Research Methods*, here are a few helpful guidelines. First, survey your entire target audience if it is fewer than one hundred participants. We anticipate, and usually experience, a 50 to 70 percent response rate, which will yield about fifty to seventy completed surveys in this case. If your target audience exceeds one hundred, then use a sample size that will result in at least fifty completed surveys assuming a 50 percent response rate.

3. *Is the survey anonymous?* No, this initial survey cannot be anonymous, as we need to be able to follow up with those survey respondents whom we believe have a success story, or a non-success story, to tell. Even though we do not provide anonymity, we steadfastly guarantee every respondent's confidentiality throughout the process.

4. *How much time should elapse between participants' attendance at the training and the receipt of the survey?* This question is best answered with another question: "How long after exposure to the training is it reasonable to expect that participants would have the opportunity to

apply what they learned and see the results from their efforts come to fruition?'' As you might imagine, the answer could range from immediately following training to one month, six months, or even longer. It is also possible to consider including participants attending earlier implementations of the learning. In any case, a good rule of thumb is to limit the survey to participants who completed training within nine to twelve months and to release the survey at the optimal point in time you would expect to see results.

5. *How should the survey be administered?* Given the technology at our fingertips today, paper-and-pencil surveys are all but extinct. If your organization uses an online surveying tool, by all means leverage it. If you do not have access to an online tool, simply construct the survey as a Microsoft Excel or Word document. You may send it via email attachment or supply a link to its location, along with instructions for its completion and submission.

6. *How are the ''success'' and ''non-success'' candidates accurately identified?* The answer to this question relates directly to the design of the survey questions. It is critical that the survey include one or a combination of key questions that specifically hone in on whether the participant leveraged the training in a way that had a significant, positive impact on the organization. The impact model you crafted in Step 2 will be very instrumental in wording these questions. The questions should provide multiple choices, and the wording should be rigorous and exclusive so that you can definitively separate true successes from the rest of the audience.

Granted, these are short-and-simple answers to some very intricate and research-oriented questions. For a more in-depth response to these and other questions regarding the SCM survey process, refer to Brinkerhoff (2003 and 2006). In both of these publications, the author provides significant detail for each step of the process, as well as numerous case study examples.

Step 4: Interview and Document Both Success and Non-Success Cases. Now that trainees have completed the surveys as a result of Step 3, our next action is to analyze the responses to select those participants whom we will interview. Our experience in conducting SCM studies indicates that the survey results are likely to fall into a traditional ''bell-shaped'' curve. Most of the survey respondents will fall in the middle of the curve, indicating that they have applied the training, but with little or no results. Interviewing these respondents will not shed much light on the relative strengths or weaknesses of the intervention. Instead, it will be in the ''tails'' of the bell-shaped curve that you will find those with the greatest success and lack of success, and therefore, those who should be interviewed. The following are all possibilities for selecting your interview candidates:

1. Randomly select from the top few candidates reporting the greatest success;

2. Randomly select from the top few candidates reporting the greatest success, as well as the bottom few candidates reporting no success;

3. Choose the top and bottom candidates across different job positions and/or business units; or

4. Choose the top candidates based on differing types of success reported.

To identify these candidates, cue in on the one or two questions that were imbedded in your survey that will help you separate the success cases from the rest of the audience. In general, you will look for those participants who responded to these items with the highest and lowest choices. For example, consider this question:

"To what extent have you been able to leverage the customer service tools taught in the 'Customer Service Excellence' course to have a significant positive impact on customer loyalty and retention?"

a. I have applied these tools with significant and positive results.

b. I have applied these tools but with little results.

c. I have not applied these tools, but plan to.

d. I have no plans for applying these tools.

Clearly, success case candidates will respond to this question with choice "a," while non-success case candidates will respond with choice "d." Interviewing participants who selected either "b" or "c" to this question will not provide much insight into the overall impact of the training intervention.

In preparation for the interviews, you will craft interview protocols for both success and non-success interviews, especially if interviews are being conducted by more than one interviewer. Having a standard interview guide will help ensure reliability across interviewers. Interviews can be conducted either face-to-face or via the telephone. Interviews conducted with successful participants typically run approximately forty-five minutes, so set this expectation when scheduling the interview.

In general, your success case interview will focus on gathering responses to the following broad categories of questions:

1. What did you use from the training that worked, and how did you use it?

2. What results did you achieve?

3. What is the value of these results to the organization?

4. Were there any aspects in the environment that helped you achieve these results?

5. Do you have any suggestions for improving the training?

At the conclusion of the interview, you should have a clear understanding of this interviewee's "success story," so much so that you could re-tell this story completely and accurately to senior management. A comprehensive "write-up" of a success case would likely include:

1. *The impact "at a glance":* In a few sentences, summarize the success that this participant experienced.

2. *The impact story:* Document the participant's complete success story in two or three paragraphs.

3. *Immediate outcomes:* Describe the results that occurred due to the participant's enhanced performance.

4. *Organizational impact:* Record the impact that this participant had on any organizational goals. However, do not force the participant to arbitrarily calculate a quantifiable measure of the impact if it cannot be readily deduced from the story. Again, refer to the impact model created in Step 2 to assist in this connection between performance and results.

5. *What helped/what did not:* Document any factors that this participant identified that helped him or her put the training to use (for example, support from his or her manager, other systems or tools, unique motivation or opportunity), as well as aspects of the training that could be improved.

Interviews with non-success case candidates are typically shorter in duration, usually running fifteen to thirty minutes. The focus of these interviews is to determine why the participants were unable to apply what they learned from a training initiative and to gather suggestions for its improvement. It is *essential* that these interviews not take on a blaming or condescending tone. Rather, the interviewer should portray empathy and seek the assistance from these non-success case participants to help identify any barriers to success so that the initiative can be improved for future participants. Documentation of these interviews also tends to be shorter than documentation for success cases. Note, however, that these interviews will still yield specific and valuable suggestions for improving the training, improving the environment into which the training is being dropped, improving external factors that undermine the performance intervention, and creating more organizational alignment and follow-up.

Step 5: Communicate Findings, Conclusions, and Recommendations. Once the interviews have been conducted, the collective wisdom from all of the stories must be compiled into a few meaningful conclusions and actionable recommendations. Most often, the conclusions within SCM study reports answer the following questions:

1. What positive actions and results is this training initiative producing?

2. What elements of the initiative are working well? What components could be improved?

3. What aspects of the work environment support the successful application of the skills, knowledge, and capabilities acquired through this training?

4. How widespread is the scope of the success of this initiative?

5. What is the return-on-investment benefit from this initiative?

6. What is the potential for additional value for this initiative?

Depending on the scope and complexity of the SCM study, the resulting report will range from simple and straightforward to quite lengthy and detailed. The typical "table of contents" for an SCM study report includes the following:

1. *Executive Summary:* This one- to-two-page section provides an overview of the purpose, methods, findings, conclusions, and recommendations of the evaluation study. This section should allow readers to view a comprehensive snapshot of the study.

2. *Methods:* This section should outline a detailed description of how the study was conducted, including the surveying and interviewing methods used. The Methods section is generally two to three pages in length.

3. *Impact Profiles:* The impact profiles make up the bulk of the SCM study report. These profiles consist of the most significant, dramatic, and colorful success stories uncovered during the interviews. Each impact profile is usually one to two pages.

4. *Summary and Conclusions:* While some of the impact profiles may speak for themselves, the researchers should offer specific conclusion statements that reflect the collective impact of the success cases investigated, as well as actionable recommendations for future implementation of the training initiative.

Piquing Interest in the Success Case Study Results

When the typical training evaluation study has been completed and the results are in, does anyone care? Surprisingly, this is a challenge that many evaluators face. While often those in the training and development function are highly interested in the findings of a training evaluation study, just as often they find that senior leadership and line management do not view the results relevant to their day-to-day concerns of growing market share, increasing profits, or launching new products.

If Step 1 of the SCM was completed well and the evaluation was strategically focused on business issues, then the answer to the question, "Does anyone care?" should be a resounding "Yes!" In fact, you should find the key stakeholders for the initiative camping outside your office door, awaiting the results. Well, that may be a bit of an exaggeration. However, senior managers who expect a performance intervention to have a significant impact on a key business goal will be keenly interested in your findings.

Remember, the primary reason for conducting any evaluation study is to answer an important business question. Therefore, the SCM gives you a vehicle for having a discussion with the primary stakeholders about this business issue. This issue and the ensuing conversation should have been jointly identified with the business leader prior to the evaluation study—perhaps even as the learning initiative was being planned and designed.

One of our customers, a leading sports equipment and apparel manufacturer, used the SCM to help the business identify ways to leverage training investments to improve the business partnerships with its largest and most important distributors (for example, national retail sporting goods stores) to grow revenues.

By using the SCM, this client found that national account managers who utilized the new account management process and tools they learned during training were able to significantly increase their sales with their key customers. Specifically, account mangers who used the training realized a 22 percent increase in sales (year over year), whereas account managers who did not apply the training saw only a 7 percent increase (year over year). Although all account managers experienced revenue increases over the previous year, the high impact group achieved a significantly greater (3X) rate of increase.

But the director of talent management didn't simply bask in the success of the training results. Instead, his team dug deeper and discovered that the account managers who leveraged the services, data, and expertise of the business planning function, in addition to using their newly acquired skills, achieved the greatest revenue gains. By digging into the "why" behind the headline with SCM, they were able to help accelerate future revenue growth. Armed with this information, the sales organization systematically forged tighter working relationships and processes with the business planning function to more effectively serve and grow the national accounts.

The Success Case Evaluation Method: Getting Started

In this chapter we have proposed a new way to think about evaluation and have provided examples of how trend-setting performance improvement leaders have successfully adopted this approach to help their organizations improve the business impact of their training. Although we have described the specific steps involved in this approach, we caution the reader that the Success Case Evaluation Method is not a new formula for analyzing training results. Instead, it is a new mindset for how to view evaluation as well as the tactics for how to do evaluation. Listed below are some guidelines for implementing this breakthrough approach, based on our experiences and the experiences of customers from our users group.

Think strategically, not tactically. Before investing valuable time and resources on an evaluation study, be clear on your intentions. Clarify the specific *business* questions, as opposed to *training* questions, the study is trying to answer and how you will use the information to benefit the organization once it is obtained.

View learning as a process, not an event. Avoid the trap of thinking of training as an event and focusing your data gathering and analysis efforts on only the training intervention. Training alone never produces the business impact; there are always factors outside of the training program that will influence whether the new skills will be applied in ways that produce business impact. Therefore, an evaluation study must effectively measure the whole learning-to-performance process and all the factors (intentional and unintentional) that influence the usage of the new skills.

Examine the good, the bad, and the ugly. To provide the organization with meaningful insights into the effectiveness of an intervention and how to improve the intervention going forward, we as HRD professionals must examine and report on when the training did *not* work, as well as when it did work. Avoid the temptation of glossing over the negatives and only reporting the positive outcomes. Often the most useful information for the organization comes from understanding when and why the training was ineffective.

Look forward, not backward. Avoid the trap of performing evaluation studies that are simply a look in the rear-view mirror, reporting on what happened in the past. The information you gather should provide useful insights for specific actions that can be taken by the organization to get even greater business impact from future training implementations.

Share credit, don't seek it. This is a corollary to the reality that training alone never produces business impact. The most productive evaluation studies—those that are perceived as credible and are acted upon—share the credit with all the stakeholders, including senior leadership, line management, trainees, and HRD. Avoid the fool's journey of trying to isolate the impact of the training program on results; it will seem naïve and self-serving to other stakeholders.

Provide the "why"; don't just publish headlines. A good evaluation study must help the organization improve future efforts. Reporting a result (for example, an average increase of 15 percent in sales) may make the HRD organization look good, but it will not help the organization move forward. Always be prepared and have an answer for the logical question a senior manager might ask: "How do we grow that 15 percent improvement to a 20 to 25 percent or even greater gain?"

Remember, the goal of training evaluation is to improve the value of training, not simply prove its value. The Success Case Evaluation Method is a practical tool for accomplishing both of these goals.

References

Babbie, E. (1990). *Survey research methods*. Belmont, CA: Wadsworth.

Brinkerhoff, R. O., & Apking, A. M. (2001). *High impact learning: Strategies for leveraging business results from training*. Cambridge, MA: Perseus Publishing.

Brinkerhoff, R. O. (2003). *The success case method*. San Francisco: Berrett-Koehler.

Brinkerhoff, R. O. (2006). *Telling training's story*. San Francisco: Berrett-Koehler.

Kirkpatrick, D. L., & Kirkpatrick, J. (2006). *Evaluating training programs: The four levels* (3rd ed.). San Francisco: Berrett-Koehler.

Mooney, T., & Brinkerhoff, R. O. (2008). *Courageous training: Bold actions for business results*. San Francisco: Berrett-Koehler.

PART TWO

PILLARS IN
MEASUREMENT
AND EVALUATION

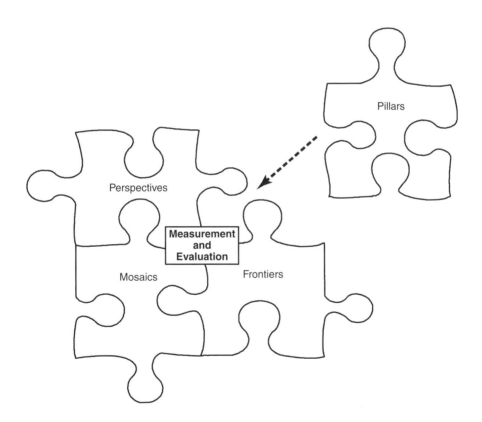

Whether wandering the well-worn paths through the remnants of ancient civilizations and visually experiencing the glory that was Greece and the grandeur that was Rome or walking through Chicago's infamous Loop district, the rambler would come face-to-face with the realization that a society's strength can be exemplified by what that society builds. As impressive as they may be, these edifices would lose their significance if they lacked the vital support of a sold foundation provided by the pillars, because the pillars form the integral element that constitutes the structure's strength. This second part of the book, "Pillars in Measurement and Evaluation," looks at strengths and supports provided by each topic as the authors examine consistency and landmark perspectives, methodologies, procedures, and practices in the field. In providing these topics, these pillars of the field, we encourage you to draw on your own experiences and perspectives in considering the strength of your ideas about measurement and evaluation. Here is what the authors will offer you.

Chapter Six: Needs Assessment: A Lighthouse Beacon. Sleezer and Russ-Eft describe major needs assessment models and approaches. They look at evaluation standards and principles that are especially important when planning, implementing, or evaluating a needs assessment, and they show how the standards and principles are applicable in workplace learning.

Chapter Seven: The Impact Evaluation Process. According to Guerra-López, each and every component of the evaluation must be aligned with those objectives and expectations that the organization values and the decisions that will have to be made with the evaluation findings. In an organizational context, all programs, activities, and internal results are interrelated and inevitably impact organizational performance, whether positively or negatively.

Chapter Eight: Full-Scope Evaluation: Do You "Really Oughta Wanna"? Dessinger and Moseley challenge organizations and workplace learning and performance (WLP) practitioners to take a full-scope approach to evaluation—an approach that encompasses formative, summative, confirmative, and meta evaluation. However, they also urge practitioners to first explore whether an organization *oughta* evaluate a performance improvement intervention, and whether it has the resources and desire or *wanna* to support evaluation. The chapter contains an inventory that is useful for diagnosing organizational readiness for evaluation.

Chapter Nine: How to Use Kirkpatrick's Taxonomy Effectively in the Workplace. Pearlstein discusses a rationale for the continued effectiveness of Kirkpatrick's taxonomy because it codifies professional evaluation practices and makes them easily applicable in a wide variety of organizations. The author covers wide-ranging tips, including applying a systems approach, treating "Level 0" seriously, addressing participants' direct experience, measuring performance, and using simple experimental designs that are workable within an organization's environment.

Chapter Ten: Ethical Considerations in Performance Measurement. Solomon's chapter focuses on ethical considerations that guide the behavior of professionals in our field. He focuses on four specific areas and challenges us to discuss and reflect upon three case studies that involve varying levels of compromise.

CHAPTER SIX

Needs Assessment

*A Lighthouse Beacon**

Catherine M. Sleezer
Darlene Russ-Eft

Those who captain ships at sea rely on a lighthouse beacon to mark a safe path to the journey's end. The bright, flashing light mounted on a tall tower that is visible over the horizon also reveals underwater areas that are too risky, too shallow, or too dangerous for safe passage. The lighthouse beacon for human learning, training, and performance improvement initiatives—whether labeled as *needs analysis, needs assessment*, or some other term—is a type of evaluation that lights the path for completing an initiative and reveals places that are too risky, dangerous, or shallow for safe passage. Such analysis takes more time and planning than simply moving forward to implement solutions; it does, however, avoid costly mistakes and greatly increases the likelihood of an initiative's success.

Indeed, evaluation expertise applied at the beginning of a project to assess needs (predictive analysis) may provide a higher return on investment than the evaluation expertise that is applied after a project is completed (summative evaluation) (Bahlis, 2008; Sleezer, 1990). Such analysis can link learning and performance improvement expertise to an organization's strategic needs, its mission and goals, and the perceived issues. For a useful visual of this linkage, see the Pershing Performance Analysis Model (Haig & Addison, 2008).

---

* *Authors' Note:* The information in this chapter on the definition of needs assessment and the four needs assessment approaches is from the *Practical Guide to Needs Assessment* (2nd ed.) by K. Gupta, C. Sleezer, and D. Russ-Eft.

In this chapter, we set the stage by first defining the term *needs assessment* and describing some needs assessment models and approaches. Then we discuss evaluation standards and principles that are especially important when planning, implementing, or evaluating a needs assessment, and we show how the standards and principles can be applied.

WHAT IS NEEDS ASSESSMENT?

Needs assessment is a diagnostic process for determining the important learning and performance needs in the situation and how to best address them. A "need" is the gap between the current condition and the desired condition. The indicators that a needs assessment should be implemented include dissatisfaction and growing concerns with a current learning, training, or performance situation; a sense that there are gaps in accomplishments, processes, or capacity; and the willingness to expend resources to improve the situation. Sometimes, a needs assessment targets a subset of gaps (for example, critical incident analysis, audience analysis, technology analysis, situational analysis, media analysis, and cost analysis).

Needs assessments are implemented in situations that are dynamic, where some information is unknown and where key players may disagree about the information that is known. Moreover, a needs assessment either supports or challenges the current power structure. In such situations, sound evaluation practices keep a needs assessment grounded and assure the integrity of the process and results.

Implementing a needs assessment involves data collection and analysis and collaboration and negotiation with key stakeholders. The data collection and analysis focus on behaviors, processes, systems, and culture that produced the current conditions and those that are required to create the future situation and the gaps between the two sets of conditions. Collaborating with the key stakeholders to implement the needs assessment assures that their relevant insights are shared, their incompatible beliefs are uncovered, and that areas that are too risky, dangerous, or shallow are identified and become common knowledge. The negotiations by the analyst and the key stakeholders during the needs assessment process about the meaning of various events and stakeholder comments clarify ambiguities and help build support for successfully implementing the solutions.

Thus, the results of a needs assessment are influenced by the characteristics of the organization, the stakeholders, and the analyst (Sleezer, 1990). The needs assessment results are also influenced by the needs assessment model that guides the process.

MODELS FOR NEEDS ASSESSMENT

Needs assessments are implemented in complex systems and organizations; thus, a change in one part of the system can affect other levels and parts. For example, a needs assessment within an organization can produce results that contribute to the larger shared society (Kaufman, 2005). Three kinds of needs commonly found in organizational settings include:

- *Learning needs:* These are gaps in knowledge and skill between the current and desired conditions. Most needs assessment experts agree that individuals have learning needs. In addition, growing bodies of literature describe team and organizational learning needs.

- *Individual performance needs:* These are gaps between current and desired conditions relative to a person's accomplishments, behaviors, or capacity for performance.

- *Strategic or operational business needs:* These are gaps between current and desired conditions for an organizational unit or for an entire organization. Closing these gaps is critical for the long-term success of the organization or one of its units.

Needs may also be determined for various groups (such as specific teams, departments, organizational units) or for groups with specific foci (such as sales performance or management).

Learning and performance needs may be only vaguely understood when they initially surface. As Harless (1970) observed, when confronted with problems, organizations tend to look for solutions even before the problem is fully defined. Harless, a leader in needs assessment, focused on accomplishment, and he coined the term "front-end analysis," which he defined as "all the smart things a manager does before addressing a solution to a human performance problem" (p. v). Front-end analysis is used to determine the root causes of performance problems. The title of Harless' book, *An Ounce of Analysis Is Worth a Pound of Objectives*, communicates well his view on the relationship between needs assessments and instructional objectives.

Gilbert (1978) proposed the behavior engineering model (BEM), which has become a classic model for measuring performance. The BEM describes the relationships among behaviors, accomplishments, and performance. Behaviors are what people do, accomplishments are their outputs, and individual performance includes both behaviors and accomplishments.

Mager and Pipe (1984) differentiated between performance problems that result from a skill deficiency and those that result from other causes, such as lack of motivation or obstacles to performing. There is little point to providing individuals with knowledge and skills if the lack of performance is caused by low motivation or obstacles to performing (such as lack of resources).

Kaufman (1992, 2005) introduced the organization elements model (OEM). In this model, needs assessment and strategic planning are used to link and define an organization's desired external and internal results. Elements in the OEM include the following:

- *Inputs:* The resources an organization uses
- *Processes:* The internal ways, means, methods, activities, and procedures an organization uses to achieve desired results
- *Products:* The results produced within an organization
- *Outputs:* The end results delivered outside an organization
- *Outcomes:* The effects or payoffs for clients and society

Rummler and Brache (1995) revolutionized the practice of needs assessment in organizations. Instead of referring to a traditional organizational chart with its departmental silos, they described an organization as a system with such components as inputs, a processing system, outputs, markets, and shareholders. They also showed the importance of the interrelationships among departments. Needs assessment practitioners who understand the systems view of organizations can move beyond focusing on activities that occur within departmental silos to focusing on activities that occur across departments.

Rummler and Brache also described the importance of diagnosing performance needs that occur at three levels: the organization, the processes, and the individual jobs and performers. Because the three levels are interdependent and critical to the whole system's optimal performance, a failure at any one level can affect the ability of the organization to perform optimally. Today most needs assessment practitioners view organizations as systems comprised of subsystems.

Today, we find that the literature describes many types of analysis (such as systems task analysis, knowledge task analysis, environmental analysis, cause analysis, extant data analysis) and many approaches to needs assessment (for example, Altschuld & Witkin, 2000; Rossett, 2009; Swanson, 2007; Van Tiem, Moseley, & Dessinger, 2004). While it is beyond the scope of this chapter and the patience of most of our readers to cover all the approaches to needs assessment, the next section describes four commonly used approaches.

FOUR APPROACHES TO ORGANIZATIONAL NEEDS ASSESSMENT

This section describes the following approaches to organizational needs assessment:

1. Knowledge and skills assessment
2. Job and task analysis
3. Competency assessment
4. Strategic needs assessment

Examples of when to use each approach and the phases and steps required for each type of needs assessment are described in the following sections. Note that these approaches can be used separately or in combination. Figure 6.1 shows the time and labor required for the each of four approaches that are described in this chapter. Additional details on each of these approaches, along with data collection instruments and other tools, can be found in Gupta, Sleezer, and Russ-Eft (2006).

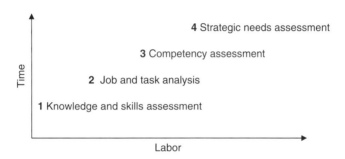

Figure 6.1 Comparison of Time and Labor Requirements for the Four Needs Assessment Approaches.

Adapted from *A Practical Guide to Needs Assessment* (2nd ed.) by Gupta, Sleezer, and Russ-Eft.

Knowledge and Skills Assessment

As a training manager for a manufacturing firm, you may be asked to provide an employee safety curriculum; as an HR manager for a government agency you may be considering training the agency's employees on newly adopted policies; or as the adult educator for an international consortium, you may be considering updating the orientation program for new employees. A knowledge and skills assessment provides just the right beacon of light for systematically examining the developmental needs of a group and for determining if training is an appropriate solution. The purposes of a knowledge and skill assessment are

1. To identify the knowledge and skills that people must possess in order to perform effectively on the job and
2. To prescribe appropriate interventions that can close the knowledge and skill gaps.

A knowledge and skills assessment has five phases:

Phase 1. Gather preliminary data provides a holistic perspective and establishes specific goals for the needs assessment. Completing this phase requires gathering background data by reviewing the available documents and talking with key individuals. During this phase, the analyst may discover that key stakeholders have different goals or that training is not an appropriate solution. Such a discovery suggests that the analyst may need to modify the direction of the assessment.

Phase 2. Plan involves developing a work plan to ensure that the needs assessment stays on target. The plan details the types of data that must be collected, the sources of data, the tools that will be used to collect data, and the approaches that will be used to analyze the data.

Phase 3. Performance training requirements analysis involves developing or adapting tools for collecting the data (for example, an interview form or a survey instrument). Data are also collected during this phase. The *Practical Guide to Needs Assessment* (2nd ed.) contains a tool book with various data collection instruments and other needs assessment documents that can be adapted for specific situations. The book also contains tips on how to collect and analyze data.

Phase 4. Analyze the data involves using the process that was specified in the plan to evaluate the data collected in the previous phase.

Phase 5. Prepare and present a report involves creating a formal report that details the needs assessment process and results. The report may be written and/or oral.

Job and Task Analysis

As an HR practitioner you may be asked to prepare job profiles or job descriptions; as a technical trainer, you may be asked to develop training for highly specialized or highly technical jobs; or as a chief learning officer, you may be involved in redesigning jobs and tasks for a work group. A job and task analysis provides just the right beacon of light for assessing needs based on detailed knowledge about the scope, responsibilities, and tasks for a particular job or job function. A job and task analysis has three phases:

Phase 1. Prepare involves collecting information individually from high performers about the details of the job. The steps of this phase include identifying the high performers, preparing the job analysis questionnaire, and preparing materials (for example, summarizing the individual responses on a flip chart).

Phase 2. Conduct job task analysis work session involves participants collaborating to identify the key responsibilities and job tasks required for effective on-the-job performance. They also identify training and non-training requirements for each job task. The participants use the materials gathered in Phase 1 of the needs assessment as a resource in this phase.

Phase 3. Develop and present job training and non-training recommendations involves first reviewing and organizing the information from the work session. Then, approval must be obtained from supervisors, HR, and others as needed for the job responsibilities, the tasks, and the training and non-training recommendations.

Competency-Based Needs Assessment

As an OD manager, you may be asked to develop career paths for various job functions; as an HRD specialist, you may be charged with conducting management development; or as an HR manager you may be required to create a system that relies on competencies for recruiting, hiring, developing, and promoting people within certain jobs. A competency-based assessment provides the right beacon of light for identifying the knowledge, skills, attitudes, or behaviors for jobs or for job functions that enable a person to perform effectively to the standards expected (that is, the competencies). One way to identify competencies relies on critical incidents and behavioral event interviewing. This approach has five phases:

Phase 1. Develop a project plan involves determining how the competency model will be used (for example, for recruiting or for development), specifying the scope and objectives for the project, selecting the people who will participate in the project, and creating a work plan.

Phase 2. Conduct behavioral interviews involves gathering and analyzing the data required to build a competency model. Data for this phase are usually gathered through surveys, behavioral interviews, or focus groups. The behavioral information collected in this phase can specify the main responsibilities for the job, the skills and abilities needed to be successful on the job and to accomplish each responsibility, the specific examples of when someone experienced success, and the specific examples of when someone experienced failure.

Phase 3. Construct competency model involves creating a competency model that specifies the competencies that are required at various levels of a job and precisely defining each competency and all the dimensions of the model. For example, the levels of jobs in the professorate could include lecturer, assistant professor, associate professor, and professor; the levels of jobs within a research function in an organization could include research assistant, research associate, research scientist, senior research scientist, and managing research scientist; the levels within a marketing function could include marketing assistant, marketing specialist, marketing supervisor, marketing manager, marketing director, and marketing vice president.

Phase 4. Assess gaps involves using the competency model to identify gaps in competencies for people who perform the job functions. This phase also involves analyzing the results. For example, a survey can be implemented that allows people to self-rate themselves on each competency. Or competencies could be assessed by supervisors or trained assessors. The analysis of data compares the competencies for various groups (for example, the top performers compared with the average performers).

Phase 5. Implement the model involves using the model as specified in the plan that was developed during Phase 1 of the needs assessment. For example, a competency model created for recruitment could focus on selecting individuals who have all the competencies for a job, while a competency model created for development could focus on employees who hold the job and lack critical competencies.

Strategic Needs Assessment

As a performance improvement specialist, you may be asked which needs in a situation are the strategic needs; or as an OD consultant, you may be asked to identify the strategic needs for a work group in a newly acquired part of the company. A strategic needs assessment, which relies on a thorough under-standing of organizational strategy, identifies the performance gaps between the current situation and the strategic goals.

A strategic needs assessment provides the right beacon of light when performance improvement needs are linked to an organization's business strategy. It also provides the right beacon when processes that do not add value to an organization must be identified or when the organization is taking on long-term performance improvement or culture change initiatives. This approach has five phases:

Phase 1. Gather preliminary information about the situation to develop a better understanding of the performance need. The senior executives in a business unit can usually provide this information.

Phase 2. Examine external environment involves first identifying and isolat-ing the external factors that affect a performance need and then determining their implications. Once isolated, this information is analyzed.

Phase 3. Examine internal environment involves answering two questions:

1. What is the organization's competitive strategy given its external environment?

2. Which business processes are affected by the performance problem or performance need?

Answering these questions involves validating the business strategy, doc-umenting current performance, and identifying causes of performance gaps.

Phase 4. Chart future events involves documenting the desired processes and performance. Also, structural, reward, and other system improvements may be developed to support the new processes and performance.

Phase 5. Develop performance improvement plans involves converting the information from the previous phase into a performance improvement plan that includes all the projects that will be undertaken to improve performance in the organization. Implementing this phase involves assessing the readiness for change and selecting the interventions.

ASSESSING LEARNING AND PERFORMANCE NEEDS FOR INDIVIDUALS

In this section, we describe three approaches for assessing an individual's learning and performance needs. In the first approach, individuals assess their situation and determine what they need based on their unique conditions, characteristics, interests, and goals. An individual's selection of a community college course or a college degree often reflects this approach. As another example, individuals often gain unique on-the-job experiences by taking actions based on their own interests as well as on their perceptions about their own knowledge and skill needs.

In the second approach, an individual's needs are determined by a source other than the individual. For example, supervisors often determine developmental needs for each of their direct reports. Also, the many instruments that assess an individual's developmental needs based on their responses to a set of questions also reflect this approach.

In the third approach, data are collected from the individual and from external sources and data are analyzed by the individual and one or more external sources. An example of this approach is a 360-degree assessment that relies on data from the individual, the supervisor, the direct reports, and the boss. Often the data are displayed using a computer-generated program. The individual and a performance improvement professional can analyze the data together and jointly agree on the high-priority needs and how they will be addressed.

Each approach has both advantages and disadvantages. An individual can provide unique observations about his or her interests and commitments for a learning or performance improvement project. However, individuals often have faulty information and assumptions about themselves, about the larger environment in which they are learning or performing, and about how they compare to others. The supervisors and others may provide needed insights from the perspective of the larger organization. At the same time, they may overlook the individual's perspectives and desires. Certainly, using data from the individual and external sources helps to link individual learning and performance needs with organizational needs. Gathering such data may be expensive in both time and cost. Therefore, regardless of which approach is chosen, care must be taken to assure that the identified needs truly reflect both the individual and the organization or larger environment.

NEEDS ASSESSMENT AS EVALUATION

A word that has nearly the same meaning as *assess* is *evaluate*. Dictionary definitions for the term *evaluate* that were found on www.dictionary.com include:

1. To determine or set the value or amount of; appraise: *to evaluate property*.

2. To judge or determine the significance, worth, or quality of; assess: *to evaluate the results of an experiment*.

3. *Mathematics*: to ascertain the numerical value of (a function, relation, etc.). (www.Dictionary.com, 2007)

Implementing a needs assessment involves determining or setting the value of various needs. The gaps between the current situation and the desired situation (that is, the needs) must be appraised because individuals and organizations have more needs than resources to address them. Moreover, the dissatisfaction with the current situation that initiates a needs assessment contains insufficient information about what is causing the needs, what must be done to address the needs, or how to best implement the solutions. The information that is gathered during the needs assessment and the options that are identified for moving to the desired condition must be judged by the decision-makers and by the others who have a stake in the situation. These judgments determine the significance, worth, or quality of the needs.

Applying evaluation principles and standards assures that the needs assessment processes and results are undertaken in a professional manner. The Joint Committee on Program Evaluation Standards developed thirty *Program Evaluation Standards* in 1981 and revised them in 1994. The standards focus on the following four areas of evaluation:

- Utility standards are intended to ensure that an evaluation will serve the information needs of the intended users.

- Feasibility standards are intended to ensure that an evaluation will be realistic, prudent, diplomatic, and frugal.

- Propriety standards are intended to ensure that an evaluation will be conducted legally, ethically, and with due regard for the welfare of those involved in the evaluation, as well as for those affected by its results.

- Accuracy standards are intended to ensure that an evaluation will reveal and convey technically adequate information about the features that determine the worth or merit of the program being evaluated.

Details on the thirty standards can be found at www/eval.org/Evaluation-Documents/progeval.html.

In 1995, the American Evaluation Association developed *Guiding Principles for Evaluators*. These principles, which were ratified by the membership in 2004, offer direction in the following areas:

1. Systematic inquiry (evaluators conduct systematic, data-based inquiries).
2. Competence (evaluators provide competent performance to stakeholders).
3. Integrity and honesty (evaluators display honesty and integrity in their own behavior and attempt to ensure the honesty and integrity of the entire evaluation process).
4. Respect for people (evaluators respect the security, dignity, and self-worth of respondents, program participants, clients, and other evaluation stakeholders).
5. Responsibilities for the general and public welfare (evaluators articulate and take into account the diversity of general and public interests and values that may be related to the evaluation).

Additional details on these principles can be found at http://eval.org/Publications/GuidingPrinciples.asp.

The *Evaluation Standards* and the *Guiding Principles for Evaluators* communicate the values and behaviors found in professional evaluation. Therefore, they provide frames that are useful when planning, implementing, or evaluating a needs assessment. For practice, review the following needs assessment and identify the unprofessional values and behaviors.

Needs Assessment Example

The goal of the needs assessment was to determine the training in a school district that would be required for updating teacher expertise. The client for the needs assessment was the school superintendent, who phoned his friend, Robert, and asked him to analyze the teachers' knowledge and skill needs in the school district. Although Robert had years of experience in developing training programs for an international manufacturing firm and no prior needs assessment experience, he quickly agreed to take on the project, saying that it would be fun to try something new. Robert submitted a proposal that offered few details about the needs assessment process, but did specify the payment amount of $100 per hour for collecting and analyzing data and for reporting results. When his friend approved it, Robert began assessing needs.

To collect data, Robert used a simple process. He looked at the file of courses he had developed over the years and picked out his favorites. Then he surveyed the 283 teachers in the school district to determine which of these topics they most wanted. The survey also contained a space that teachers could use to identify other training that they wanted (see Performance Support Tool 6.1). The survey was distributed to the teachers on the first day of the school term with instructions to submit the completed survey by the end of the week. When several teachers asked for additional time to complete the survey, Robert explained that he was an extremely busy professional trying to identify *their* training needs and that as professionals they would submit the survey on time.

PERFORMANCE SUPPORT TOOL 6.1 PST TRAINING SURVEY.

[Note the lack of descriptors for the scale.]

Help identify training that will be offered next year by rating your preference for the following training courses. Note that the survey must be submitted next week.

	4	3	2	1
Continuous process improvement				
Technical writing				
Performance appraisal				
Leading a team				
Interpersonal skills				

Suggest other training that you would like in the space below.

Fifty-five surveys were returned. However, while transporting the surveys from the car to his house, Robert dropped a few surveys, which the rain and wind blew into the mud. Because the wet, muddy surveys were impossible to read, Robert ignored them. He included an estimate of the number of dropped surveys when reporting the total number of returned surveys, but ignored the dropped surveys when estimating the ratings for each training course listed on the survey. Instead Robert analyzed the remaining surveys by first examining all the ratings for each training course. For example, he counted the number of people who rated technical writing as a 2 and divided that total by 2, the number of people who rated technical writing as a 3 and divided that total by 3, and so forth. The returned surveys contained many suggestions for other training courses, which Robert analyzed by picking out a few favorite suggestions.

The final written report for the needs assessment, which was provided only to the superintendent, gave the ratings for the five courses on the survey and listed the suggestions for other training. The report also included the participants' guide from Robert's interpersonal skills course because that course had received the highest rating on the survey. To aid in decision making, Robert also included the cost for delivering his interpersonal skills course to all teachers in the school district. Robert padded the bill a little and then submitted it.

Review the Needs Assessment

How well does the sample needs assessment reflect evaluation values and behaviors? As an aid in reflection, consider the needs assessment's utility, feasibility, propriety, and accuracy. Also consider the *Guiding Principles for Evaluators* (systematic inquiry, competence, integrity and honesty, respect for people, and responsibilities for the general and public welfare).

In truth, the example contains many violations of the evaluation standards and principles. Below are just some illustrations.

Utility

- Individuals who are affected by a needs assessment (the teachers, students, school counselors, and other school staff) should have been identified so that their needs could be addressed. After all, the teachers' lack of knowledge and skills could have profound effects on each of these groups.
- The analyst's lack of experience and competence in needs assessment and his unethical behaviors will affect how the results are viewed and accepted.

Feasibility

- A needs assessment should be practical and keep disruption to a minimum. Requiring the teachers to complete a survey during the stressful first week of a school term does *not* keep disruption to a minimum.
- A needs assessment should be cost-effective, which is inconsistent with padding the budget.

Propriety

- The contract for the needs assessment should have specified in writing what was to be done, by whom, and when.
- The needs assessment findings, including the limitations to the findings, should have been made available to those affected by the needs assessment.

Accuracy

- The dropped surveys, the number of non-respondents, and the unique way of analyzing the data resulted in data that were insufficient to appropriately determine the merit or worth of needs.

Systematic Inquiry

- Data were collected at one time using only one data collection method. Moreover, the survey was technically unsound. The survey does not include descriptors for the ratings (that is, 1 most important; 2 important . . .) so it is impossible to accurately interpret the results.

Competence

- Robert failed to decline the project even though it clearly fell outside his area of experience and competence.

Integrity/Honesty

- Robert failed to display integrity and honesty in his own behavior. He also failed to ensure the honesty and integrity of the needs assessment process and to honestly report its limitations.

- Robert's offer to provide training courses that he developed (for a fee) to address the needs that he identified created a conflict of interest.

Respect for People

- Robert's response to the teachers who requested an extension did not indicate respect for their dignity and self-worth.

Responsibilities for General and Public Welfare

- The needs assessment process neglected to take into account the diverse public and general interests and values in the situation.

These illustrations are not the only areas of infringements of the *Evaluation Standards* and the *Guiding Principles for Evaluators* evident in the example, but they are sufficient to show the importance of these evaluation resources. In real life, formal needs assessments seldom violate so many standards and principles; however, it is common for analysts (especially those who lack training in evaluation, training, and performance improvement) to unknowingly violate some standards or guiding principles. Collaborating with the stakeholders during the needs assessment process and thoroughly documenting the needs assessment process and the results provides the transparency that allows various stakeholders to carefully examine the needs assessment path and to trust it as a safe guide for future actions.

Learning and performance improvement professionals should also use the *Evaluation Standards* and the *Guiding Principles for Evaluators* as a frame when participating in informal needs assessments that are an unspoken and natural part of communication. Consider the following example: While on the way to lunch with a friend, he asks to pick your brain about what training to provide a group of employees who report to him. Before responding with answers, it would be wise to determine what approach was used to assess the needs and to frame the request using the *Evaluation Standards* and the *Guiding Principles for Evaluators*.

SUMMARY

Needs assessments are lighthouse beacons that evaluate the gaps between a current learning or performance condition and the desired condition. Using the *Evaluation Standards* and the *Guiding Principles for Evaluators* to frame a needs assessment assures the trustworthiness of both the needs assessment process and the results. A needs assessment that ignores these resources can easily run a learning or performance improvement initiative aground. Surely, our clients, stakeholders, and the profession deserve better.

References

Altschuld, J. W., & Witkin, B. R. (2000). *From needs assessment to action: Transforming needs into solution strategies*. Thousand Oaks, CA: Sage.

American Evaluation Association. (2004). *Guiding principles for evaluators*. Retrieved July 25, 2006, from www.eval.org/Publications/guidingPrinciples.asp.

Bahlis, J. (2008). Blueprint for planning learning. *T&D, 62*(3), 64–67.

Dictionary.com (n.d.). Los Angeles: Lexico. Retrieved on December 17, 2007, from http://dictionary.reference.com/

Gilbert, T. J. (1978). *Human competence: Engineering worthy performance*. New York: McGraw-Hill.

Gupta, K., Sleezer, C., & Russ-Eft, D. (2006). *A practical guide to needs assessment* (2nd ed.). San Francisco: Pfeiffer.

Haig, C., & Addison, R. (2008). *Trendspotters: Pershing performance analysis improvement process*. Retrieved May 5, 2008, from www.performanceexpress.org.

Harless, J. (1970). *An ounce of analysis (is worth a pound of objectives)*. Newman, GA: Harless Performance Guild.

Joint Committee on Standards for Educational Evaluation. (1994). *The program evaluation standards: How to assess evaluations of educational programs*. Thousand Oaks, CA: Sage.

Kaufman, R. A. (1992). *Strategic planning plus: An organizational guide*. Thousand Oaks, CA: Sage.

Kaufman, R. A. (2005). Defining and delivering measurable value: A mega thinking and planning primer. *Performance Improvement Quarterly, 18*(3), 6–16.

Mager, R. F., & Pipe, P. (1984). *Analyzing performance problems: Or, you really oughta wanna* (2nd ed.). Belmont, CA: Pitman Management and Training.

Rossett, A. (2009). *First things fast* (2nd ed.). San Francisco: Pfeiffer.

Rummler, G. A., & Brache, A. P. (1995). *Improving performance: How to manage the white space in the organization chart*. San Francisco: Jossey-Bass.

Sleezer, C. M. (1990). *The development and validation of the Performance Analysis for Training Model* (Project No. 35). St. Paul, MN: University of Minnesota, Training and Development Research Center.

Swanson, R. A. (2007). *Analysis for improving performance: Tools for diagnosing organizations and documenting workplace expertise* (2nd ed.). San Francisco: Berrett-Koehler.

VanTiem, D. M., Moseley, J. L., & Dessinger, J. C. (2004). *Fundamentals of performance technology: A guide to improving people, process, and performance* (2nd ed.). (pp. 22–25). Silver Spring, MD: International Society for Performance Improvement.

CHAPTER SEVEN

The Impact Evaluation Process

Ingrid J. Guerra-López

In our daily lives, people encounter decision points on an almost continuous basis: What actions should they take? Should they do something now or later? Should they do it themselves or have someone else do it? In this point, life is no different in an organizational setting; people are continuously faced with decisions about what programs to sustain, which to change, and which to abandon, to name but a few organizational dilemmas. How do organizational members go about making sound decisions? They make decisions with the use of relevant, reliable, and valid data, gathered through a sound evaluation process that is aligned with desired, long-term outcomes.

BACKGROUND OF THE IMPACT EVALUATION PROCESS

The impact evaluation process (Guerra-López, 2007) is the product of research, applied work, and teaching. One key underlying idea of this process is that everything is aligned to some greater purpose (whether people are conscious of it or not, and whether they are aligning it well or not), and evaluation is no different. The evaluand—"thing" being evaluated—is always considered a means to an end, with the end manifesting itself in three levels of result:

1. *Strategic.* Long-term organizational impact or benefit your organization delivers to its clients and society (for example, improvements to clients' quality of life).

2. *Tactical.* Shorter-term organizational results from which the organization benefits (for example, profits, revenues, and other measures).

3. *Operational.* The internal building-block deliverables that, when well aligned and coordinated, allow the organization to reach its tactical and strategic results.

While the contributions of an evaluand are more readily observed at the operational level, any evaluand must ultimately get us closer to long-term, strategic results, as well as to the more immediately expected organizational level results. The evaluand would have to positively contribute toward specific results at each of these levels, as measured by relevant performance indicators and other measures.

The performance indicators must be appropriate measures of desired performance, rather than typical or standard measures that, while perhaps related to the result to be measured, do not say anything about the impact of the evaluand and the value of that impact. One classic example is using the number of participants as an indicator of the success of a program. The fact that there were many or few participants says nothing about the quality of the participation, or the impact of participating in such a program on human and organizational performance, or even the desirability of improving that particular performance in the first place. Measuring impact on the three levels mentioned above ensures that all relevant perspectives are considered.

Scriven's consumer-oriented evaluation approach is consistent with this view. Scriven (1991) argues that, rather than accepting a developer's goals as given, the evaluation must judge whether the achievement of the goals would contribute to the welfare of clients and consumers. Regardless of the products and outputs, Scriven argues that the evaluator must also identity outcomes and determine their value as they relate to the consumer's needs.

Needs should have, of course, been identified through a needs assessment process, which in turn gives us the inputs or raw material for a causal analysis. It is through a sound needs assessment and causal analysis that performance improvement professionals are able to identify the causes for those needs, and in turn, solution requirements, solution alternatives, and finally a selected solution. This "solution" later becomes the evaluand during an evaluation process. If the front-end work was done, and it was done well, then there should be a high probability that the evaluand will in fact add positive and measurable value to the organization and its customers through its various levels of results.

If the evaluand was the best alternative for closing the gap, then one evaluation hypothesis is that the evaluand should have helped eliminate or reduce such gaps in results/performance. The basic evaluation question would then be: "Did Solution X contribute to the reduction or elimination of Performance Gap Y?"

Consistently, Scriven also calls for identifying and ranking the alternative programs or solutions that are available based on the relative costs and effects and in consideration of the needs identified through a needs assessment based on societal value added (1991).

Additionally, the impact evaluation process is also influenced by decision-oriented theory, and Patton's (1997) utilization-focused evaluation, an approach to evaluation concerned with designing evaluations that inform decision making. From an impact evaluation perspective, every evaluation starts with a practical purpose: to help stakeholders make sound decisions. Thus, the entire evaluation process must begin with the identification of what decisions have to be made and what data and subsequent information will help us make them.

BUILDING A CASE FOR IMPACT

When evaluators set out to evaluate programs, initiatives, or any solution, the usual focus of the evaluation is the nature of the program and the results of the program in terms of the predetermined expectations. For example, did the participants like the new training program? Did the participants master the new training program content? Are they applying the content in their jobs? What is usually taken for granted or assumed is the desirability of mastering that particular content. Usually, the program is reported as effective depending on the:

- Resources consumed (for example, within time and budget);
- Participation level (for example, attendance; completion);
- Perceived satisfaction (for example, participant reactions or reactions of those using the intervention; reactions of others such as the recipient of any change caused);
- Usage (for example, self-reports about "if" and "how" they are using the intervention or actual usage statistics); and
- Other indicators that tell us little about the program contributions toward the organizational objectives.

This common evaluation focus centers around the means (for example, the new leadership development program) rather than the organizational ends organizational members wish to accomplish (for example, increased sales, increased revenues, growing market share, enhanced quality of life of our customers). This is not all that different from the way organizations are usually led. If our planning and implementation are focused on means, likewise our evaluation questions will probably stop at this level. If you look at the bulleted items above, one could certainly claim to have relevant data about effectiveness in reaching the predetermined objectives: people liked the program, they mastered the content, and it was done within the time and budget allotted.

However, if evaluation is going to be worth the trouble, evaluators and other stakeholders must look further. The approach proposed here requires that the evaluation also focus on whether these indicators link to valued organizational ends, and in turn, the external needs of our clients and consumers. In an organizational context, all programs, activities, and internal results are inter-related and inevitably impact organizational performance—whether positively or negatively. If not purposely linked, this very fact in itself could be negatively impacting the organization, by virtue of this activity's consumption of re-sources, with no known, or expected, return to our bottom lines (financial or social).

For this reason, the evaluation process must be linked to a rigorous needs assessment (rigorous does not imply lengthy and unfocused). Needs assessment is essentially the process of identifying gaps in results and placing them in, priority order based on the costs to meet the needs versus the costs to ignore the needs (Kaufman, 2006). It is data from this process that should inform what programs, activities, and other solutions will help us accomplish our organiza-tional vision and mission.

THE SEVEN STEPS OF IMPACT EVALUATION

The notion that "evaluation's most important purpose is not to prove, but to improve" is an idea originally put forward by Egon Guba when serving on the Phi Delta Kappa National Study Committee on Evaluation circa 1971 (Stufflebeam & Shinkfield, 2007). This should be the foundation for all evalua-tion efforts to come. Each and every component of the evaluation must be aligned with those objectives and expectations that the organization values and with the decisions that will have to be made as a result of the evaluation findings. These decisions are essentially concerned with how to measurably improve performance at all levels of the organization: internal deliverables, organizational gains, and public impact.

While there are approaches to evaluation that do not focus on predetermined results or objectives, the approach taken by using the impact evaluation process is based on the premise of performance improvement. The underlying assump-tion is that organizations, whether fully articulated or not, expect specific results and contributions from programs and other solutions. However, this does not prevent the evaluator or performance improvement professional from employ-ing means to help them identify unanticipated results and consequences. The worth or merit of programs and solutions is then determined by whether or not they delivered desired results; whether these results are worth having in the first place; and whether the benefits of these results outweigh their costs and unintended consequences.

While evaluation, at its core, is straightforward, the situations in which it is applied can be complex and at times make evaluation daunting. The impact evaluation process is primarily directed at individuals who want a clear map that guides them through the process and helps them keep a pragmatic and responsive focus. The idea is that, with a well-articulated plan, the actual evaluation process will be a lot simpler and more straightforward.

The impact evaluation process consists of seven steps that, while conveying sequence, can and should be considered reiteratively. The basic steps and approach are illustrated in Figure 7.1, and each of the seven phases is described in more detail below.

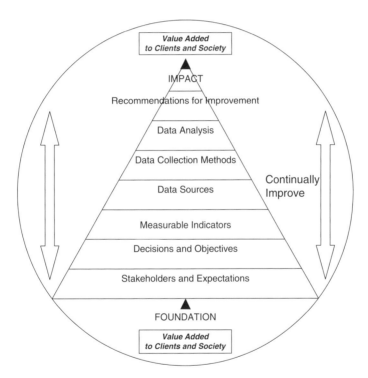

Figure 7.1 The Impact Evaluation Process.

© Ingrid J. Guerra-López, 2007

1. Identify Stakeholders and Expectations

The evaluator must identify the key stakeholders involved. The stakeholder groups include those who will be making decisions, either throughout the evaluation process or directly as a result of the evaluation findings. Those with the authority to make critical decisions are often the ones who finance the evaluation project, but if it is someone different or a different group, they too should be included. Also important are those who will be affected by the evaluation—either in the process or potentially as a result of the findings. Including this group will make the implementation of the evaluation plan a lot easier, particularly during the data collection stage. The driving question for identifying stakeholders is "Who is/could be either impacted by the evaluation or could potentially impact the evaluation in a meaningful way?" While not every single stakeholder must be a direct member of the evaluation project team, it is wise to have each group represented.

Now, with a diverse group of stakeholder representation, you will also have a diverse group of expectations. These expectations are the basis for your contract, whether verbal or written and should explicitly articulate what is expected of you (as well as of the stakeholders!). If you feel they are unreasonable, this is the time to discuss, educate, discuss again, educate again, and come to a consensus . . . not after you have completed what in your own mind you think is a successful evaluation. *If you do not have the specific stakeholder expectations clearly defined from the start, it is nearly impossible to align your efforts to such expectations without sheer luck . . . and if you do not align your efforts with stakeholder expectations from the start, it is very unlikely that you will ever meet those expectations.*

2. Determine Key Decisions and Objectives

Asking the stakeholders to articulate what decisions will be made as a result of your findings is a primary step. The discussion about the decisions that must be made should also be about the objectives that must be reached. All organizations have objectives—both external and internal—and everything within the organization must contribute toward those objectives (Guerra, 2005). The relative worth of any intervention or solution is primarily contingent on whether it is helping or hindering the achievement of organizational objectives.

While some stakeholders may not provide you with the specific objectives they expect, they will give you "clues" about the relevant effects they are expecting, even if these are about means rather than results. Your task here (and actually, throughout the process) is to be the *educator* and *facilitator* and to approach the conversation from the standpoint of . . . *and if the organization were to accomplish that, what would the result be?* And to continue that line of inquiry until key results have been identified.

With these decisions and objectives clarified, the overarching questions that will drive the evaluation process and purpose of the evaluation should also become clear, articulated, and agreed on.

3. Derive Measurable Indicators

Sound decisions are made on the basis of relevant, reliable, and valid data related to desired results and the related questions that must be answered (Guerra, 2003). Therefore, the heart of your evaluation plan will be to gather the data required to answer the questions that guide the inquiry. People often end up making judgments based on wrong or incomplete data, particularly when they try to force connections between inappropriate data (just because it happens to be available) and the decisions that must be made. (Kaufman, Guerra, & Platt, 2006).

The data you will seek to collect are essentially about key performance indicators. Indicators are observable phenomena that are linked to something that is not directly observed and can provide information that will answer an evaluation question. Results are not always neatly and directly observed. When measuring results, there are a number of indicators, or to borrow Gilbert's (1978) term, "performance requirements," that could be relevant. For instance, profit is a result that has various metrics, which collectively indicate its level (for example, money collected; money paid out; assets, and others). Indicators for customer service include referrals, repeat business, customer retention, length of accounts, and satisfaction survey scores.

4. Identify Data Sources

With a list of specific indicators for which to collect data, you must first determine where you can find those data. The data drive the appropriate source. You can likely find the data that you are looking for right in your own organization. Existing records about past and current performance may already be available, but collected by different parties in your organization and for different reasons. Some excellent sources include strategic plans, annual reports, project plans, consulting studies, and performance reports, to name a few.

Telecommunications and other technologies can often be used to link to reports, documents, databases, experts, and other sources like never before possible (the Internet is a great vehicle for efficiently linking up to these!). A number of companies, government agencies, and research institutions, nationally and internationally, publish a series of official studies and reports that could prove to be valuable sources of data.

5. Select Data Collection Methods

The right data collection methods and tools are a function of the data you are seeking. Likewise, the data you collect is a function of the methods you select. When evaluators limit the data they collect by employing an overly narrow set of observation methods because they don't know how to use others, their data set will not be complete and, in turn, their findings will not be valid. If you are after hard data such as sales figures, don't use a survey to get people's opinions of what these sales figures are. Rather, review relevant sales reports. Conversely, if it is people's attitudes you want, there are a number of ways to ask them (interviews, focus groups, and surveys are some appropriate possibilities). There is extensive literature about these and other data collection methods. Be sure to make your selection based on their pros and cons, specifically with regard to important criteria such as appropriateness of the instrument for the required data, time, characteristics of sample, comprehensiveness of tool, previous experience with tools that are being considered, and feasibility among others (Guerra, 2003).

Again, the "secret ingredient" for successfully collecting valid and reliable data is *alignment* of data type, data source, data collection tools, and data analysis procedures.

6. Select Data Analysis Tools

While the data analysis is often thought to be mere "number crunching" it is more than that. The analysis of data as part of an evaluation effort is the organization of information to discover patterns and fortify arguments used to support conclusions or evaluative claims that result from your evaluation study. In a nutshell, what is happening is a mere summarizing of large volumes of data into a manageable and meaningful format that can quickly communicate its meaning. In fact, one might say that the analysis of the data begins even before its collection by virtue of analyzing the characteristics of the required data, as it is done before the methods for data collection are selected.

If you have quantitative data, various statistical operations can help you organize your data as you sort through your findings. Qualitative data is also subject to analytical routines. Qualitative observations can be ordered by source and by impact, or sorted according to general themes and specific findings. Checking the frequency of qualitative observations will begin to merge qualitative into quantitative data.

7. Communicate Results and Recommend Improvements

The importance of effective communication cannot be overstated. A rigorous evaluation does not speak for itself. Communicating with key stakeholders throughout the evaluation process keeps them aware of what you are doing and why, which in turn increases the amount of trust they place in you and your efforts. In addition, it allows them the opportunity to participate and provide you with valuable feedback. By the time the final report and debriefing come along, these products will not be seen as something imposed on them, but rather as something that they help create. With this type of buy-in, resistance to the findings will likely be lower.

Things to consider in the communication include medium, format, language, and timing, among others.

CONTINUAL IMPROVEMENT

No useful and responsive evaluation model or guide would be complete without addressing continual improvement. Continual improvement depends on knowing where the organization is headed and continually monitoring the course to get it from where it is to where it should be. This is accomplished by asking the right questions, collecting useful data on an ongoing basis, and then applying that data to make sound decisions about required changes and/or which current initiatives to sustain. The goal of a continual improvement culture, thus, is to support the ongoing journey toward reaching the organizational vision through the use of performance feedback.

Continual improvement is much talked about but is actually done but rarely in practice. A likely reason is that there is much confusion about exactly what continual improvement is. There are two major components to continual improvement: *monitor* and *adjust*. Monitoring is about measurement and tracking. Organizational members measure what matters and track its progress. Adjusting is about change. Organizational members use the feedback obtained from the monitoring stage to promote and facilitate desirable change. The discussion below focuses on these two central functions.

Monitoring Performance: Using Evaluation to Build Continual Improvement in Organizations: A Self-Evaluation Framework

The benefits that evaluation can provide are not something that happen once and stop after the final report. Evaluation, if conducted properly, can give us useful feedback about how much closer (or further) the organization is from our ultimate goal. In the context of continual improvement, evaluation helps us to do this by establishing an evaluation framework that allows things that matter to be consistently and reliably measured. You might say that this evaluation framework is the backbone of a performance management system. You cannot manage performance, at least not effectively, without the required performance data.

Once the evaluation framework is developed, which includes performance objectives at the various organizational levels, measurable indicators, and respective initiatives that target each of these, the data collected will almost naturally fall into meaningful categories. In this sense, it is a lot like facilitating an ongoing, self-evaluation that provides just-in-time feedback for opportune adjustments. Feedback is a central concept here and depends on effective communication systems. If developed appropriately, it will allow leaders and employees to track, manage, and sometimes forecast performance at opportune times. In this sense, it is very much like monitoring the vial signs of the organization.

Another function that the evaluation framework can fulfill is facilitating collaboration among the various departments of the organization. When the individual yet complementary contributions of the various departments are published broadly, people more readily understand their interdependent roles and see that the key to organizational (and their) success is not to compete for limited resources, but rather to collaborate so that resources can be maximized. This in turn leads to the recognition and elimination of redundant processes and/ or internal products. Again, open, accurate, and consistent information is critical.

Characteristics of the Evaluation Framework

The following is a list of characteristics meant to guide in the development of a personalized evaluation framework based on Guerra-López (2007). Every organization is different and has its own set of goals, values, strengths and weaknesses. Thus, while all evaluation frameworks should possess the following five characteristics, they will likely look and feel different.

1. *Align all key results at various organizational levels (systemic):* Recall that the value of any intervention is whether it ultimately helped the organization get closer to achieving its vision. Thus, do not track only immediate results at the intermediate level, but be sure to hypothesize and test the linkages all the way up to the vision level goals.

2. *Provide linkages between interventions or initiatives and the indicators they are to impact:* Remember that one of the en-route tasks of evaluation is to provide evidence of the effectiveness of implemented solutions. Thus, it is important to articulate for everyone the linkages among these solutions and between the solutions and the organizational indicators they are intended to impact. The clearer the linkages, the better able people will be to understand and use the data.

3. *Responsive and dynamic:* The evaluation framework is more of a template than a confining structure. While the framework might remain pretty constant, the actual indicators may change, or the result itself, as objectives are met, and new ones are derived. Recall that, while solutions might solve old problems, they may also bring with them a new set of challenges. Modifying this framework in order to keep its indicators current should not be done at the expense of the constancy of your organization's purpose. Changing your mission every year does not make you current, but rather gives you a moving target your organization will not likely reach.

4. *Accessible by all decision-makers:* While all these characteristics are critical, this one is probably one of the most difficult for leaders to grasp. The idea that the organization's report card will be open for all to see is quite scary for many. It is important to remember that the purpose of evaluating is to collect and interpret data for improving performance, not for pointing fingers and blaming. All must have ready access so that they can make timely decisions about how to improve performance— individual and organizational. These efforts, of course, should be coordinated and integrated.

5. *Feedback and communication:* You cannot talk about continual improvement without considering the feedback loop upon which it rests. The feedback loop represents the reiterative nature of tracking and adjusting. Performance data should not only be accessible by all, but should be clearly understood by all. Thus, providing consistent feedback about performance is part of bigger communication systems. Progress, milestones reached (or not reached), action plans for reaching desired goals, and so forth should be consistently and accurately communicated throughout the organization.

All this, of course, has to take place in the context of a supportive environment. An environment where using relevant, reliable, and valid data before making decisions is part of the organizational culture. This can only be accomplished by modeling this from the top of the organization on down and aligning the proper consequences with the desired accomplishments and behaviors related to continually improving.

A Note on the Nature of Inquiry of the Impact Evaluation Process

It is worth noting that, much like instructional systems and performance systems are based on systems theory concepts, the impact evaluation process is also based on a systemic approach to evaluation and performance improvement. Traditional science and research has been heavily based on studying independent variables and, in this sense, the focus of evaluation would be to study the impact of one variable throughout the system in order to understand what is going on with the system. However, as one looks around in organizations and programs across sectors, it is obvious that there are no such things as purely independent variables. In fact, all variables are interdependent, and as "systems become more and more sophisticated, the reality of interdependency becomes more and more pronounced" (Gharajedaghi, 1999).

(Continued)

(Continued)

Understanding the interdependency of factors that impact human, program, and organizational performance requires a shift from a pure analysis (taking apart that which is sought to be understood in order to explain behavior of the separated parts and extrapolate an explanation of the whole) (Gharajedaghi, 1999) to synthesis (looking at system components and their interdependencies in order to understand their impact on the whole). Performance improvement professionals and evaluators alike must look at the entire performance system and understand that any impact observed is rarely ever attributable to one solution or one cause alone. It is only responsible, ethical, and pragmatic to look for and communicate the whole story.

ADJUSTING PERFORMANCE

The monitoring framework, or performance dashboard (Eckerson, 2006), itself is a potent agent of organizational change. It helps the organization clearly define, communicate, and focus on important results. It also provides consistent and timely feedback that informs decisions about what changes are required for the benefit of the organization, its clients, and its employees. Up to this point, the concept of improving performance has been discussed in general terms. But what is actually involved in improving performance, specifically, where actual change is concerned? The discussion below attempts to answer this question.

CHANGE PROCESSES

What are the dynamics of the change process for those being mandated to change by their leaders? Everyone, including individuals, teams, and interdepartmental groups, goes through three critical change processes (Coghlan, 2000):

1. *Perception:* The meaning the change has for them; the degree to which they have control over the change; and the degree of trust individuals have in those mandating or promoting the change.

2. *Assessment of the impact of change:* Will the change be for the better; uncertain, but probably positive; uncertain; uncertain though probably negative, threatening, or destructive?

3. *Response:* The individual can deny; dodge, oppose, resist, tolerate; accept, support, or embrace the change.

What factors impact these processes? One factor that has a significant impact is the availability of information about the change and the process of communication between those mandating the change and those affected by it. Recall that, in an earlier discussion about stakeholders, it was noted that stakeholders include both those who can impact the evaluation process, as well as those who will be potentially impacted by its results. Open communication of the evaluation process, findings, and recommendations directly impacts the change process. Lack of information promotes a sense of anxiety and resistance, particularly when individuals begin to make their own stories about what is going on and what will happen in the future.

Any change initiative, whether the evaluation process itself or the recommendations that stem from it, must address these three processes. A change plan that takes into account how these changes will be perceived and evaluated by employees must be derived so that the desired responses are elicited.

While it is critical to take steps to manage the change appropriate so that it is useful, it is important to consider the other side of the coin: change creation. Change creation is essentially what is being done when the direction for that change is set. This happens during an authentic strategic planning and needs assessment process, whereby organizational leaders identify where they would like to be years from now and what they have to accomplish in the meantime in order to get there. Hopefully, it was through those processes that the solution you are now faced with evaluating was selected. Change management is, then, what you do to make sure that things go as smoothly as possible on your way to your ultimate destination. Evaluation is one of the tools that facilitates this smooth sailing by providing you with important information required for navigation.

CONCLUSION

The impact evaluation process rests on the premise that everything used and done is aligned to some greater purpose. Ethical and responsible evaluators and performance improvement professionals must look beyond the generic measures of program success (for example, Did the participants like the new training program? Did the participants master the new training program content? Are they applying the content in their jobs?). They must also look for the desirability of mastering and applying that particular content in the first place, which requires us to align the evaluand to strategic, tactical, and operational results. Establishing this chain of impact, and realistically accounting for the myriad of intervening variables along the way is the only way to truly know what is working and what is not, why, and what to do about it.

References

Coghlan, D. (2000). Perceiving, evaluating, and responding to change: An inter-level approach. In *Handbook of organizational consulting* (2nd ed., Vol. 81, p. 1045). New York: Marcel Dekker.

Eckerson, W. (2006). Deploying dashboards and scorecards. Business Objects and the Data Warehouse Institute. Retrieved April 26, 2008, from *DMReview Magazine* website: www.dmreview.com/portals/portal.cfm?topicId=230006.

Gharajedaghi, J. (1999). *Systems thinking: Managing chaos and complexity, a platform for designing business architecture*. Boston: Butterworth Heinemann.

Gilbert, T. F. (1978). *Human competence: Engineering worthy performance*. New York: McGraw-Hill.

Guerra, I. (2003). Asking and answering the right questions: Collecting relevant and useful data. *Performance Improvement*, *42*(10), 24–28.

Guerra, I. (2005). Outcome-based vocational rehabilitation: Measuring valuable results. *Performance Improvement Quarterly*, *18*(3), 65–75.

Guerra-López, I. (2007). *Evaluating impact: Evaluation and continual improvement for performance improvement practitioners*. Amherst, MA: HRD Press.

Kaufman, R. A. (2006). *Change, choices and consequences: A guide to mega thinking and planning*. Amherst, MA: HRD Press.

Kaufman, R. A., Guerra, I., & Platt, W. (2006). *Practical evaluation for educators: Finding out what works and what doesn't*. Thousand Oaks, CA: Corwin Press.

Patton, M. Q. (1997). *Utilization-focused evaluation: The new century text* (3rd ed.). Thousand Oaks, CA: Sage.

Scriven, M. (1967). The methodology of evaluation. In R. W. Tyler, R. M. Gagné, & M. Scriven (Eds.), *Perspectives of curriculum evaluation* (Vol. 1, pp. 39–83). Chicago: Rand-McNally.

Scriven, M. (1991). *Evaluation thesaurus* (4th ed.). Thousand Oaks, CA: Sage.

Stufflebeam, D. L., & Shinkfield, A. J. (2007). *Evaluation theory, models, and applications*. Hoboken, NJ: John Wiley & Sons.

Suggested Reading

Drucker, P. (1995). *Managing in a time of great change*. New York: Harper Business.

Fitzgerald, L., Johnston, R., Brignall, S., Silvestro, R., & Voss, C. (1991), *Performance measurement in service businesses*. London: CIMA Publishing.

Guerra, I., Bernardez, M., Jones, M., & Zidan, S. (2005). Government workers adding societal value: The Ohio Workforce Development Program. *Performance Improvement Quarterly*, *18*(3), 76–99.

Guerra-López, I. (2008). *Performance evaluation: Proven approaches for improving program and organizational performance*. San Francisco: Jossey-Bass.

Kaplan, R. S., & Norton, D. P. (1992). The balanced scorecard—measures that drive performance. *Harvard Business Review*, pp. 71–79.

Lynch, R. L., & Cross, K. F. (1991). *Measure up! How to measure corporate performance.* Oxford, UK: Blackwell.

Neely, A., Adams, C., & Kennerley, M. (2002). *The performance prism: The scorecard for measuring and managing business success.* London: FT Prentice-Hall.

Porter, M. E. (1996, November/December). What is strategy? *Harvard Business Review*, pp. 61–78.

CHAPTER EIGHT

Full-Scope Evaluation

Do You "Really Oughta, Wanna"?

Joan C. Dessinger
James L. Moseley

Among many "wish-we-had-said-that" statements, this is probably one of our favorites: "While some executives argue that a successful measurement and evaluation process is very difficult, others quietly and deliberately implement effective evaluation systems" (Phillips & Phillips, 2008, p. 12). The process we call "full-scope evaluation" is all about "quietly and deliberately" **doing** evaluation from the beginning to the end of a performance improvement intervention—because HPT practitioners "really oughta wanna" (Mager & Pipe, 1970) go beyond identifying the performance problem and finding solutions (aka interventions) to judging whether the solutions (aka interventions) really do solve the problem and add value to the organization.

"Full-scope evaluation is **not** for the faint hearted" (Dessinger & Moseley, 2006); it **is** for the believers and the doers who know they "oughta" and "really wanna." Knowing when, why, and what to evaluate is important; determining whether we should and even can evaluate is crucial to evaluation success. The success of any evaluation—full-scope or not—relies on designing, developing, and implementing an evaluation that:

- Meets the expressed needs of the organization;
- Gives the organization what it needs to judge the merit, worth, and/or value of the program or intervention; and
- Is actionable.

As the voice of the organization, the internal and external stakeholders should be involved in pre-planning an evaluation. Smith's (2008) analogy of "building bridges'' comes to mind here. While discussing the need for workplace learning and performance professionals (WLP) to "speak the language of business and contribute to business results," Smith suggests: "Bridges could be built between WLP professionals, our measurement practices, and the organizations that we serve." (p. 59).

BEGIN WITH WHAT, WHEN, AND WHY

Full-scope evaluation carries evaluation to the fourth power (E^4), offering HPT practitioners a choice of all four types of evaluation: formative, summative, confirmative, and meta. Table 8.1 shows when and why HPT practitioners oughta use some or all of the four types of evaluation and what they should focus on during each type of evaluation.

Table 8.1 The When-Why-What of Full-Scope Evaluation

Type	When	Why
Formative	☑ during Analysis ☑ during Design ☑ during Development ☐ during Implementation ☐ 3 mon. + after Implementation ☐ during/after Evaluation	Judge the "goodness" of the intervention analysis, design, and development process and products
Summative	☐ during Analysis ☐ during Design ☐ during Development ☑ during Implementation ☐ 3 mon. + after Implementation ☐ during/after Evaluation	Judge the immediate impact of the intervention on the learner and on the organization
Confirmative	☐ during Analysis ☐ during Design ☐ during Development ☐ during Implementation ☑ 3 mon. + after Implementation ☐ during/after Evaluation	Judge the long-term impact of the intervention

(Continued)

Table 8.1 (*Continued*)

Type	When	Why
Meta	☐ during Analysis ☐ during Design ☐ during Development ☐ during Implementation ☐ 3 mon. + after Implementation ☑ during/after Evaluation	Judge the validity and reliability of the formative, summative, and/or confirmative evaluation process and products

HPT practitioners use a systematic, five-phase process—Analyze, Design, Develop, Implement, Evaluate (ADDIE)—to develop instructional or non-instructional performance improvement interventions. Using this process as a framework, HPT practitioners oughta conduct *formative* evaluation up-front to judge the "goodness" of the inputs, processes, and outputs of the analysis, design, and development phases of both one-time and long-term interventions. Then, they oughta conduct *summative* evaluation during the implementation phase to judge immediate outputs such as participant reaction, behavior change, and anticipated usefulness of the intervention. If the intervention is long-term—three months or longer—HPT practitioners oughta conduct *confirmative* evaluation at established intervals over the lifecycle of the intervention to determine whether the intervention should be maintained "as is," maintained with revisions, deleted, or deleted and replaced. Finally, *meta* evaluation oughta take place concurrently with or after evaluation activities to verify the reliability and validity of the evaluation process and products.

Evaluation is vital; over-evaluation is worthless. Over-evaluation strains the available resources and damages the credibility of the HPT profession. Evaluation should be intentional and purposeful and should stay focused on that purpose from beginning to end. Knowing which type(s) of evaluation to conduct is an essential first step to take for achieving successful evaluation outcomes. The decision to use a specific type of evaluation should be based on the following:

1. What type(s) of evaluation will provide what the stakeholders need to know to make decisions about the merit, worth, or value of the intervention?

2. What type(s) of evaluation will the available resources support?

3. What type(s) of evaluation will the organization and/or organizational culture support?

Pre-planning with the stakeholder oughta answer all or most of these crucial questions and moves the WLP professional into that bridge-building mode, where talk "shifts subtly from how the WLP program aligns and attunes with the organization and what can be accomplished with the outputs and outcomes, toward how many measurement levels (aka 'types') have been, could have been, or should be applied" (Smith, 2008, p. 59).

PERFORMANCE SUPPORT TOOL 8.1 INVITATION TO PARTICIPATE IN A FULL-SCOPE EVALUATION PRE-PLANNING ACTIVITY FOR _____ [NAME OF INTERVENTION] _____

Dear _____,

The purpose of evaluation is to judge the merit, worth, and/or value of something. As a person who has a stake in the outcomes of _____ [*intervention*] _____ we would like you to help us answer the following questions:

- Do you think we *can* evaluate this program/intervention? Does the organization have the resources and will to conduct an evaluation?

  _____

- Do you think we *should* evaluate this program/intervention? Is it important to you to prove the merit, worth, or value of this program/ intervention?

  _____

- If we can and should evaluate, what do you need to know about the program/intervention to judge whether it has merit, worth, or value for you and the organization?

  _____

Please complete this inventory by _____ [*date*] _____ and return it to _____. We will analyze all the inventories, let you know the results by _____[*date*] _____, and give you our recommendations based on your input.

Thank you,

[*Sender's name/position_____*]

[*Sender's contact information_____*]

THE FULL-SCOPE EVALUATION PRE-PLANNING INVENTORY

The Full-Scope Evaluation Pre-Planning Inventory is a diagnostic tool that assesses or audits organizational readiness before planning and implementing an evaluation. The results help the HPT practitioner decide whether an organization *oughta* evaluate a performance improvement intervention and has the resources and desire or *wanna* to support evaluation. If evaluation is appropriate, the Inventory also helps the HPT practitioner select, design, and implement the most appropriate types of evaluation for the intervention based on stakeholder information needs. The Inventory can also help the HPT practitioner achieve buy-in from the organization's stakeholders.

Successful evaluation should begin with a dialogue among the stakeholders who have an interest in what happens as a result of the performance improvement intervention and the practitioners who will design and implement the evaluation. The dialogue should provide the answer to the following three questions:

1. Can the organization evaluate the training program or performance improvement intervention? Does it have the will and the resources?

2. Should the specific training program or intervention be evaluated? Do the stakeholders need to make a judgment regarding the merit, worth, or value of the program or intervention? Will evaluation provide the data they need to make a judgment?

3. If the organization can and should evaluate the intervention, how should it be evaluated? What do the stakeholders need to know about the results of the training program or intervention? What type of evaluation will meet their information needs? (Dessinger & Moseley, 2007)

Overview

The Inventory contains a series of statements that help to answer the three questions listed above: *Can* the organization evaluate? *Should* the specific program or intervention be evaluated? If yes, *how* should it be evaluated? The respondents qualify and quantify their response to each statement by selecting a response that ranges from 6 = strongly agree to 1 = not sure. The statements related to the stakeholders' information needs are randomly scattered and are identified on the practitioner's scoring copy as items related to formative, summative, confirmative, or meta evaluation.

Distribution

The Full-Scope Evaluation Pre-Planning Inventory should be distributed to *all* organizational stakeholders who will need to know the outcomes of the performance improvement intervention in order to make a judgment of merit, worth, and/ or value. Stakeholders may also include external customers of a product or service that is impacted by the intervention. In the Analysis section below, we will discuss how to classify the stakeholders and weight their responses if desired (Section C).

HPT practitioners who are involved in planning the intervention are also encouraged to complete the Inventory. They can then compare their responses as practitioners to those of the other stakeholders; for example, other stakeholders may respond from a broader organizational perspective than the HPT practitioner.

The Inventory may be delivered in hard copy via mail or fax or as an electronic file, which allows respondents to directly input their responses and email the completed Inventory back to the sender. If possible, the Inventory should be presented during a real-time or virtual meeting, which will make it possible to provide immediate feedback to the respondents.

Analysis

The simplest way to analyze Sections A and B of the Inventory is to assess the frequency of each response to each item. Once the frequency assessment is completed, the data collector or analyst can determine whether a majority of the respondents feel that the organization can and oughta evaluate the training program or performance improvement intervention.

In Section C, the data collector or analyst will follow the same process; however, this time the data are grouped according to the type of evaluation. For example, the data collector/analyst totals the number of respondents who selected "strongly agree" or "agree" for the items relating to formative evaluation. If a majority of respondents "strongly agree" or "agree" with *all* the items related to formative evaluation, then that type of evaluation is appropriate.

If the Inventory is to be most useful, the analyst should categorize the respondents in advance and take into consideration which category(ies) responded favorably or unfavorably to each item. The analyst may even consider weighing the frequency count to reflect the relative impact of the stakeholders in terms of the success of the evaluation. Table 8.2 suggests some categories and weights and Performance Support Tool 8.3 gives some samples of scoring for the Inventory.

Table 8.2 How to Categorize Stakeholders and Weight Their Responses

If the stakeholder . . .	Add this number to the response	Example: if the stakeholder responds 6 (strongly agree) to a statement the weighted score is . . .
Will provide essential political and/or economic support	+ 3	6 + 3 = 9
Will use the product or service impacted by outcomes	+ 2	6 + 2 = 8
Will help implement the program or intervention	+ 1	6 + 1 = 7
Is not directly involved but should be kept informed	+ 0	6 + 0 = 6

PERFORMANCE SUPPORT TOOL 8.2 FULL-SCOPE EVALUATION PRE-PLANNING INVENTORY

Program/Intervention _____

Respondent's Name _____

Title/Position _____

Date _____

Instructions: Please read each numbered statement in Sections A, B, and C and circle the number that best describes your response. Your immediate response is usually the most accurate:

6 = Strongly Agree

5 = Agree

4 = Agree Somewhat

3 = Strongly Disagree

2 = Disagree

1 = Not Sure

Section A. Can the organization evaluate the training program or performance improvement intervention? Does it have the will and the resources?

A-1. This organization acknowledges the value of evaluating training programs or other performance improvement interventions.
6   5   4   3   2   1

A-2. This organization has or has access to the resources (time, money, experienced personnel) required to conduct an effective and efficient evaluation.   6   5   4   3   2   1

A-3. This organization will support an evaluation of the training program/intervention by authorizing the required resources.   6   5   4   3   2   1

Add additional comments here:

_____

Section B. Should this program or intervention be evaluated? Is it important to establish that this program or intervention has merit, worth, and/or value to the organization.?

B-1. It is important to this organization to judge the merit, worth, or value of this program/intervention.   6   5   4   3   2   1

B-2. It is important to my business area to judge the merit, worth, or value of this program/intervention.   6   5   4   3   2   1

B-3. It is important to me to judge the merit, worth, or value of this program/intervention.   6   5   4   3   2   1

B-4. It is important to our industry to judge the merit, worth, or value of this program/intervention.   6   5   4   3   2   1

B-5. It is important to our customers to judge the merit, worth, or value of this program/intervention.   6   5   4   3   2   1

Add additional comments here:

Section C. If we can and should evaluate this program or intervention, what would you need to know about this program/intervention in order to judge whether it has merit, worth, or value?

C-1.   I would need to know how the participants reacted to the training program/intervention.   6   5   4   3   2   1

C-2.   I would need to know the long-term cost/benefit ratio or ROI (return on investment) of the program/intervention.   6   5   4   3   2   1

C-3.   I would need to know whether the evaluation produced information of sufficient value to justify the resources expended.   6   5   4   3   2   1

C-4.   I would need to know whether the objectives of the program/intervention are aligned with the organization's goals and objectives.   6   5   4   3   2   1

C-5.   I would need to know whether the participants were able to change their workplace behavior as a result of the program/intervention.   6   5   4   3   2   1

C-6.   I would need to know whether the participants' managers, supervisors, and/or customers are satisfied with the long-term results of the program/intervention.   6   5   4   3   2   1

C-7.   I would need to know whether the evaluation results were reliable.   6   5   4   3   2   1

C-8.   I would need to have feedback from a pilot test before I can sell the program/intervention to my boss or staff.   6   5   4   3   2   1

C-9. I would need to know whether the participants predict they will be able to change their behavior as a result of the program/intervention. 6 5 4 3 2 1

C-10. I would need to know whether the program/intervention was designed to meet the goals and objectives established in the plan. 6 5 4 3 2 1

C-11. I would need to know whether the program/intervention had an immediate impact on the knowledge and skill level of the participants. 6 5 4 3 2 1

C-12. I need to use the results of the program/intervention to make informed decisions about immediate performance improvement in my business area. 6 5 4 3 2 1

C-13. I need to know whether the evaluation maintained ethical standards. 6 5 4 3 2 1

C-14. I need data to prove that this program/intervention is effective and efficient over time. 6 5 4 3 2 1

C-15. I need data to prove that this program/intervention has a positive impact and value over time. 6 5 4 3 2 1

C-16. I need data to prove that the program/intervention supports the short-term competence of the participants. 6 5 4 3 2 1

C-17. I need data to decide whether to maintain, change, or eliminate this program/intervention. 6 5 4 3 2 1

C-18. I need to know whether the evaluation outcomes were valid. 6 5 4 3 2 1

C-19. I need to know whether the evaluation-based recommendations for future action were implemented. 6 5 4 3 2 1

C-20. I need to know whether the program/intervention plan was based on complete and accurate information from the stakeholders. 6 5 4 3 2 1

C-21. I would need to know whether the products or outputs of the program/intervention design were designed to meet the goals and objectives established in the plan. 6 5 4 3 2 1

C-22. I need to use the results of the evaluation for certification or accreditation purposes. 6 5 4 3 2 1

C-23. I need to know whether the results of the training or intervention transferred to the workplace. 6 5 4 3 2 1

C-24. I need to be able to prove that evaluation was necessary for this program or intervention.   6   5   4   3   2   1

Add any additional information you may need here:

PERFORMANCE SUPPORT TOOL 8.3 FULL-SCOPE EVALUATION PRE-PLANNING INVENTORY SCORING GUIDE

Purpose: Use the Section A and B guides to tabulate the frequency data and determine whether a majority of the respondents feel the organization can and should evaluate this training program or other performance improvement interventions. Use the Section C guide to tabulate the frequency data and help you decide what type of evaluation would be most appropriate.

INSTRUCTIONS FOR SECTIONS A AND B

1. On a blank survey form, change the Column 1 heading to "Frequency Count," indicate the number of participants (N = ___), and use the column to record the results.

2. Add a **row** after each item to record the total number of participants who strongly agreed or agreed with the item.

EXAMPLE: SECTION A TABULATION

Section-Item   Frequency Count (N = ___)

A-1. This organization acknowledges the value of evaluating training programs or other performance improvement interventions.

___ Strongly Agree

___ Agree

___ Agree Somewhat

___ Strongly Disagree

___ Disagree

___ Not Sure

A-1 Total who strongly agree or agree   ___

3. Add a summary box at the end of each section to record whether a simple majority of the respondents strongly agree or agree with the items in the section.

EXAMPLE: SECTION **A** SUMMARY

Summary of Section A

___ Total number of respondents to this section (n).

___ Number required for a simple majority (2/3n).

___ Total who strongly agree or agree with *all* the statements in this section.

___ Yes ___No   A majority of the respondents strongly agree or agree that the organization can evaluate this program or intervention and that they have the will and the resources.

INSTRUCTIONS FOR SECTION **C**

1. On a blank survey form, change the Column 2 heading to "Frequency Count," indicate the number of participants (N = ___), and use the column to record the results. Also, add the type of evaluation [___] represented by the item.

Example: Section C Tabulation

Section-Item and [Type of Evaluation] Frequency Count (N= ___)

C-1. I would need to know how the participants reacted to the training program/intervention [Summative]

___ Strongly Agree

___ Agree

___ Agree Somewhat

___ Strongly Disagree

___ Disagree

___ Not Sure

___ Total who strongly agree or agree

2. Follow the example below when developing the summary for Section C.

EXAMPLE: SECTION **C** SUMMARY

Summary of Section C—If the organization *can* and *should* evaluate this program or intervention, then what type of evaluation is most appropriate?

Formative Evaluation items C1, 4, 8, 10, 20, 21

___ Total number of respondents who responded to the formative evaluation items (n).

___ Number required for a simple majority (2/3n).

___ Total who strongly agree or agree with the formative evaluation items.

___ Yes/___ No, a majority of the respondents strongly agree or agree that they need information provided by formative evaluation.

Summative Evaluation items C5, 9, 11, 12, 16, 23

___ Total number of respondents who responded to the summative evaluation items (n).

___ Number required for a simple majority (2/3n).

___ Total who strongly agree or agree with the summative evaluation items.

___ Yes/___ No, a majority of the respondents strongly agree or agree that they need information provided by summative evaluation.

Confirmative Evaluation items C2, 6, 14, 15, 17, 19

___ Total number of respondents who responded to the confirmative evaluation items (n).

___ Number required for a simple majority (2/3n).

___ Total who strongly agree or agree with the confirmative evaluation items.

___ Yes/___ No, a majority of the respondents strongly agree or agree that they need information provided by confirmative evaluation.

Meta Evaluation items C3, 7, 13, 18, 22, 24

___ Total number of respondents who responded to the meta evaluation items (n).

___ Number required for a simple majority (2/3n).

___ Total who strongly agree or agree with the meta evaluation items.

___ Yes ___ No, a majority of the respondents strongly agree or agree that they need information provided by meta evaluation.

The input from stakeholders who *must* provide the political and economic support for the program or intervention will have greater impact on the success of the program or intervention than the input from stakeholders who just "need to know." Evaluation plans can die an untimely death if they lose their political or economic support. In addition, supporters and customers whose stated information needs are not met by the evaluation may not support future evaluations because they did not find that this evaluation was valuable.

Validity and Reliability

The Full-Scope Evaluation Pre-Planning Inventory is an informal diagnostic tool. It was piloted in a graduate program evaluation class with groups of students from all areas of business and representing all types of organizations. It has both content and face validity. *Content validity* refers to inventory items representing the content that the inventory is designed to measure. *Face validity* is the subjective appraisal of what the content of the inventory measures. The population that piloted the inventory concurred on both kinds of validity.

Reliability data for the Full-Scope Evaluation Pre-Planning Inventory are not available. Increasing the number of items and observing the stability of the responses over time will address reliability issues.

SUMMARY

The Inventory sets the stage for successful evaluation by exploring the environment in which the evaluation will take place and ensuring that the stakeholders as well as the HPT practitioners feel they oughta and wanna evaluate a particular performance improvement intervention *during* and *after* the evaluation is planned, designed, and implemented. The Inventory is primarily intended to generate dialogue and inquiry about the evaluation process as an integral part of a performance improvement intervention. It can also be used to examine the stakeholders' personal beliefs about a well-planned and carefully designed and implemented evaluation plan and as a learning tool for the many uses of evaluation in organizational settings.

References

Dessinger, J. C., & Moseley, J. L. (2006). The full scoop on full scope evaluation. In J. A. Pershing (Ed.), *The handbook of human performance technology: A guide to improving people, process, and performance* (3rd ed.; pp. 312–330). San Francisco: Pfeiffer.

Dessinger, J. C., & Moseley, J. L. (2007). Full-scope evaluation planning inventory. In E. Biech (Ed.), *The 2007 Pfeiffer annual: Training* (pp. 135–154). San Francisco: Pfeiffer.

Mager, R. F. & Pipe, P. (1970). *Analyzing performance problems or "you really oughta wanna."* Belmont. CA: Fearon.

Phillips, J. J., & Phillips, P. P. (2008, July). Distinguishing ROI myths from reality. *Performance Improvement, 47*(6), 12.

Smith, S. (2008, September). Why follow levels when you can build bridges. *Training + Development*, pp. 58–62.

Additional Reading on Full-Scope Evaluation

Dessinger, J. C., & Moseley, J. L. (2004). *Confirmative evaluation: Practical strategies for valuing continuous improvement*. San Francisco: Pfeiffer.

Guerra, I. J. (2003). Key competencies required of performance improvement professionals. *Performance Improvement Quarterly, 16*(1), 55–72.

Moseley, J. M., & Dessinger, J. C. (1998). The Dessinger-Moseley evaluation model: A comprehensive approach to training evaluation. In P. J. Dean & D. E. Ripley (Eds.), *Performance improvement interventions: Instructional design and training—Methods for organizational learning*. Alexandria, VA: International Society for Performance Improvement.

CHAPTER NINE

How to Use Kirkpatrick's Taxonomy Effectively in the Workplace

Richard B. Pearlstein

D onald L. Kirkpatrick introduced his four-level evaluation taxonomy in 1959 and 1960; since then it quickly became the most widely used evaluation model. Many evaluators encounter it frequently in for-profit, not-for-profit, and governmental organizations. Even those who believe that Kirkpatrick's taxonomy is "old school" and does not focus tightly enough on performance improvement outcomes admit that it is still prevalent in organizations. For example, Pulichino (2006), reporting on 2006 research published by the eLearning Guild, categorized results as showing that 88 percent of that organization's twenty thousand participants were at least "fairly knowledgeable about Kirkpatrick's four levels of evaluation," with 62 percent being "very or highly knowledgeable."

IS KIRKPATRICK'S TAXONOMY STILL EFFECTIVE?

Despite the taxonomy's widespread use, some claim it is no longer relevant. For example, Kathy Dye (2003, p. 11) noted, "It is generally ineffective as an overarching paradigm for today's business." She further argues that "evaluation is a complex process of organizational decision making," while models, such as Kirkpatrick's, that focus on measuring effectiveness are technical. However, the author has found that Kirkpatrick's taxonomy offers a good framework for influencing organizational decision making. For example, organizations have used results of Kirkpatrick's taxonomy-based evaluations he has conducted to cancel programs, modify programs, and initiate new programs.

Others claim that Kirkpatrick's taxonomy is often misused, and discount it on that basis. It is true that it is often misused, but discounting it for that reason is like suggesting that automobiles should be banned because they are a leading cause of accidental death. Still others point out that, because data are hard to come by, especially at Kirkpatrick Levels 3 and 4, evaluators who use the taxonomy often rely on opinion data rather than measures that are more reliable. Again, just because it is often not used well is not a valid reason to disregard Kirkpatrick's taxonomy.

Kirkpatrick's model did not introduce new technologies—evaluators had already been considering multiple levels long before he advanced the taxonomy. His taxonomy was important because it codified professional evaluation practices and made them easy for managers in a wide variety of organizations to understand. Managers easily grasp that there may be gaps between what people like, what they learn, what they actually do, and what outcomes result from what they do.

Kirkpatrick's four levels are simple, straightforward, and useful. This chapter examines them, some extensions to them, and provides tips for using the levels effectively in organizations. It also shows how Kirkpatrick's taxonomy works well with performance interventions other than training.

KIRKPATRICK'S FOUR LEVELS OF EVALUATION

Kirkpatrick noted that the four levels address increasingly important organizational questions. The higher the level at which one evaluates, the more important the findings will be for the organization.

Level 1. Reaction

Some evaluators call it "the dog food test," as the following apocryphal story illustrates. A few years ago, a team of veterinarians and nutritionists at a large agricultural school spun off a commercial enterprise to create and market a wonderful new dog food. They designed it to be highly nutritious, produce glossy coats, and reduce the amount of bolus produced by dogs. When they test-marketed it, the new dog food failed miserably. Why? The dogs didn't like it.

But Level 1 has value outside of determining whether participants liked training (customer satisfaction). Participants can give useful input on their experience. For example, they can tell you whether the training environment was distracting. In addition, tracking participant ratings can raise warning signals if reactions change markedly over time. If a given instructor consistently gets high ratings, but then ratings fall off markedly, it is worth examining what caused the drop. Another example: Participants can tell you whether course exercises are realistic in terms of their jobs.

Level 2. Learning

Can the participants do things at the end of training that they could not do prior to training? This is easy to measure by comparing scores between pre-course tests and end-of-course tests. If participants test better at the end of the training than they do at the beginning of it, learning has occurred. The higher the test gains at the end of training, the greater the learning.

Learning is NOT the same as knowledge acquisition, although it often includes it. Instead, in terms of performance interventions, learning includes most types of behavioral change. In the training world, these changes often involve skill acquisition or skill building. Examples include using new equipment and software, following new processes, making decisions in various professions in the same ways that exemplars in those professions make them, and trouble-shooting specific types of problems. The point is that Level 2 measures what people CAN do at the end of an intervention, not necessarily what they WILL do back on the job.

Level 3. Behavior

Evaluation at this level asks whether training participants actually use learned behavior on the job. For example, a course may train inspectors to examine products in a new way. End-of-course tests may show that they in fact have learned to conduct the new examinations. But this does not mean that they will behave accordingly on the job. If they do not, it is probably due to factors outside training that inhibit the new behavior from occurring on the job. For example, perhaps their supervisors encourage them to keep conducting inspections the "way it has always been done around here."

It is also possible that learning is not applied on the job due to lack of retention. This may happen if learners are trained too far in advance of when they need to apply their learning.

Level 4. Results

This level measures the degree to which new behavior used on the job leads to improved work outcomes. These outcomes will depend on context—specifically on the group(s) to whom the intervention was directed. If the intervention is organization-wide, then the outcomes will be at least at the level of the whole organization. If the intervention is for a part of the organization, then the outcomes will be at least at the level of the units in that part. But, because organizations are complex systems, it is likely that changes in a single unit of an organization will impact other units, if not the entire organization. For example, changes in a design unit may affect workflow in many other organizational units.

KIRKPATRICK'S LEVELS AND PERFORMANCE IMPROVEMENT INTERVENTIONS

Practitioners can apply Kirkpatrick's taxonomy to evaluating most types of performance improvement interventions—not just training. Kirkpatrick's levels mate well with human performance technology (HPT) models. Whether an intervention addresses learning, environmental factors, feedback, reward systems, communications and expectations, or other elements, it can be evaluated in terms of reaction, immediate impact, on-the-job impact, and benefits that result. Table 9.1 shows Kirkpatrick's taxonomy applied to a few types of HPT interventions. (Note that the questions in the cells of the table are NOT inclusive: They are illustrations of how Kirkpatrick's levels apply across interventions.)

Before offering a few examples based on Table 9.1, it is necessary to distinguish between primary interventions and follow-up interventions. In her seminal article, "Maintenance Systems: The Neglected Half of Behavior Change," Karen Brethower (1967) showed that skill acquisition is only the beginning of behavior change. Ongoing follow-up efforts are critical to ensure that people actually use new skills on the job.

Brethower's concept addressed behavior change interventions—largely training interventions. However, one can easily apply the concept to other types of performance improvement interventions. Instead of "skill acquisition," the first half of behavior change is shaping, requiring, or supporting new behavior. The second half—"maintenance"—needs no change; its focus remains on maintaining new behavior. Examples of primary and follow-up interventions are shown in Table 9.2.

The left column of Table 9.2 shows examples of the first part of Brethower's paradigm. All of these interventions would be designed to help people acquire new behaviors, shape new behaviors, recognize management requirements for new behaviors, or obtain support for their new behaviors. The right column of Table 9.2 shows matching examples for the second part of Brethower's paradigm.

Note that, while performance can be easily noted at the conclusion of training or other skill/knowledge-based interventions, changes just after initiation of other types of interventions—for example, those relating to reward or feedback systems or changes in the work environment—may not be easily measured at that time because it may take a while for those interventions to have impact. For

Table 9.1 Questions Asked by Kirkpatrick's Taxonomy for Various Types of HPT Interventions

Focus Skills/	Kirkpatrick's Levels 1	2	3	4
Knowledge	Are the learning system's characteristics acceptable to participants?	Did learning result from the course, coaching, or other training interventions?	Do participants continue to use the new learning on their jobs?	Does the learning system give benefits to the organization with positive ROI?
Environment	Is the change of environmental factors suitable to employees?	Do initial environmental changes support performance better? Are staff members aware of new environmental resources?	Does full installation of environmental changes improve performance?	Are the organizational outcomes worth the investment in environmental change?
Feedback	Is the type of feedback clear, timely, and specific to employees?	Do initial changes of feedback systems yield improved performance? Do staff members know how to use the new feedback system features?	Does full installation of new feedback systems yield improved performance?	Are the organizational outcomes worth the investment in the feedback system?
Rewards	Do employees understand and accept changes to reward systems?	Do initial changes to reward systems improve performance? Do staff members know the changes to the reward system that apply to them?	Does full installation of the new reward system improve performance?	Are the organizational outcomes worth the investment in the reward system?
Communica- tions	Are management communications of expectations clear and at intervals useful for employees?	Do initial changes in communication of expectations improve performance? Can staff members recall receiving new information on management expectations?	Does full installation of the new communication system improve performance?	Are the organizational outcomes worth the investment in the communication system?

Table 9.2 Examples of Primary and Follow-Up Interventions

Primary "Acquisition" (or Shaping, Requiring, Supporting New Behavior)	Follow-Up "Maintenance"
Participants attend training.	Supervisors encourage use of new skills.
Participants receive performance support tools (job aids).	Management sends repeated reminders that it expects job aids to be used consistently.
Participants come under a new feedback system or a new reward system. Management introduces and explains the new systems.	Management uses the new reward system fairly and the new feedback system consistently. Management provides appropriate incentives and feedback for required new behaviors.
Management modifies the work environment, introducing and explaining the changes beforehand.	Management monitors and solicits comments about the new work environment, changing elements as necessary to maintain effectiveness.
Management works with staff to initiate newsletters to improve communication. Management rolls out first issues with appropriate publicity.	Management and staff meet regularly to assess effectiveness of newsletters, adjusting content to make the newsletters more useful as needs evolve.

those types of interventions, it might be more useful to note simply whether people in various parts of the organization are aware of the changes and their characteristics. For instance, when rolling out a new reward system, it might be useful to see how many employees and managers are aware of how the new system is supposed to work. But it would be highly unlikely that the new system would bring about performance changes right after roll-out. One would expect lag time before changes would begin, depending on the reward contingencies and how long before people began receiving them.

Example of Applying the Four Levels to a Non-Training Intervention

Suppose you conducted an evaluation of a new reward system that you installed in an organization. At Level 1, you found mixed results. Supervisors reported that during meetings introducing the new rewards system, employee responses indicated that they understood the changes to the existing reward system but were skeptical that they would be implemented appropriately. On the other hand, Level 2 results were entirely positive: Productivity at six months following roll-out compared with that before roll-out, when contrasted to a group that did not come under the new reward system in that same timeframe, showed increases in productivity attributable to the new reward system. Also, you found positive results at Level 3: Productivity continued to increase as the new reward system was installed across the organization, and a follow-up survey at one year showed that employees believed that the new system rewarded productivity fairly. Finally, at Level 4, you calculated that productivity gains had a higher dollar value than the costs of installing and maintaining the new reward system. So, all-in-all, your evaluation demonstrated the effectiveness and cost benefits of the non-training performance intervention you conducted.

EXTENSIONS OF KIRKPATRICK'S TAXONOMY

Kaufman's Level 5

One indication of the continued impact of Kirkpatrick's taxonomy is the fact that it continues to stimulate others to build upon it. For example, if interventions are organization-wide, Level 4 outcomes will be at least at the level of the whole organization. But Kaufman (2006; personal communication, April 2, 2008) has argued that evaluating outcomes should also be done at what he labels the mega-level, a level that includes the society or even world of which the organization is a part. An organization that aims to make a profit by selling medicine must address not only profit-making outcomes but also societal health outcomes. In other words, in Kaufman's model, evaluation should also address benefits at a level higher than the organization doing the intervention. In fact, Kaufman finds the mega level so important that he separates it from Level 4 and calls it Level 5.

Phillips Level 5

Jack Phillips (1997) has elaborated usefully on Kirkpatrick's Level 4, defining a Level 5 in a different manner than Kaufman. Phillips posits Level 5 as return on investment (ROI). Although Kirkpatrick specifically included ROI as an important component of results (Level 4), Phillips' addition provides much greater emphasis on ROI by devoting an entire level of evaluation to it. After all, results are questionable if the cost of getting them exceeds their value.

Elaborations on Level 1

Others have explored the low end of the taxonomy. For example, Watkins, Leigh, Foshay, and Kaufman (1998) discussed Level 1 in some detail. They suggested modifying Level 1 to separate evaluation of processes from evaluation of resources, noting that doing so would encourage performance improvement practitioners and evaluators to address two separate questions (1998, p. 91):

1. "Are books, computers, reference materials, and other resources readily available and of the quality required for training and/or educational experience," and

2. "Are the training and/or educational processes efficient and acceptable."

Similarly, Pearlstein (1995) developed several Level 1 checklists that examine the process by which training interventions are developed and the training materials that result. For example, he developed checklists for the USDA Forest Service, providing easily used guidelines for selecting commercial training packages based in part on how they were developed. Exhibit 9.1 shows a

Exhibit 9.1 Truncated Checklist for Level 1 Evaluation of Self-Instructional Training Packages

Directions: Use this checklist to see whether a self-instructional package is likely to meet employees' needs. Review the self-instructional package against this checklist. Place a check mark ($\sqrt{}$) in the box to the left of each question, if the answer is "yes." If you are not sure, leave the box blank.

☐ 1. Do the package objectives, or the overall description of the package, match what employees need to learn? The overall package description may be misleading. Always read the package objectives, if they are included. They will state more specifically what the package is designed to teach. Skills listed under topic areas should give an overview of what employees need to learn. If only a small proportion of the package objectives apply to employees' learning needs, the package is not suitable.

☐ 2. Are the directions for using the package clear? That is, do the directions explain how to set up or install the package? Could employees follow them without help?

☐ 3. Is the package easy to understand? Ask a few candidates for the self-instruction to try a little of the package: Is it clear? Were they able to follow the exercises? Would most employees be able to follow them?

☐ 4. Is the package easy to use? Ask a few candidates to try a little of it. Does it seem to flow well, or did they find it tiresome and hard to follow?

☐ 5. Does the package include materials, such as quick reference cards or summary sheets, that would help on the job? Would they work in employees' job settings?

☐ 6. Are the package examples and exercises relevant to employees' jobs, or at least not distracting?

☐ 7. Does the package provide an opportunity to practice all skills specified by its objectives? The package should provide many exercises in which employees need to respond actively. Clicking a button to turn a page does NOT count as active responding.

☐ 8. Does the package provide appropriate feedback? Well-designed self-instruction will anticipate the most common mistakes and provide information addressing them. It will reward correct responses in a factual, non-fawning manner.

Scoring: If you checked six or fewer items, find a more suitable self-instructional package.

---

truncated version of a Level 1 checklist that supervisors can use to select commercial, self-instructional training packages.

Pearlstein's Level 0

Pearlstein (2008) posited an additional level below the first level of Kirkpatrick's taxonomy. Level 0 is the "hallway evaluation," in which an executive asks a trusted compatriot something like "Fred, how'd you like the training last week?" Although this level provides only anecdotal data, and often very slim anecdotal data at that, it may be the most widely used form of evaluation practiced in organizations. It has less value than Level 1 evaluation, but, unfortunately, it may have even more impact on training and other performance improvement decisions than all other levels of evaluation combined. For this reason, evaluators ignore it at their own—and their organizations'—peril.

KIRKPATRICK'S LEVELS AS LINKS IN AN "EVIDENTIARY CHAIN"

Although some regard Kirkpatrick's levels as independent, Kirkpatrick (1994) offered them as an integrated approach. Practitioners should carry this integration of levels a step further by making sure that clients understand that each step is a link in an "evidentiary chain."

Sivasailam Thiagarajan (personal communication, May 2, 2007) suggested that only Level 4 is important in the final analysis, and this author agrees. However, an evidentiary chain is necessary to show that results at Level 4 are in fact due to actions taken and results achieved at lower levels. Suppose, for example, that one measures changes in organizational outcomes and determines that they are significant in those parts of the organization that have had Intervention X compared with changes in the same outcomes in those parts of the organization that have NOT had Intervention X. Can one then say that Intervention X brought about those changes? The author submits that one cannot without first tracing the evidentiary chain backward.

For example, moving backward through the chain, what if one measures changes at Level 3 and discovers that they are not significant for either group? In other words, one finds that there is no significant change in Behavior X on the job compared to pre-intervention Behavior X in those units that received the intervention, nor in an equivalent period in those units that did NOT receive it. Since the behavior that the intervention was supposed to change did NOT change, any change in organizational outcomes at Level 4 could not have been due to the intervention.

Now, moving further backward, suppose that one finds positive results at Level 2. For example, in a training intervention, measurement showed that those who took the training could perform in the desired new way at the end of training, while those who did not have the training could not. In this case, a Level 3 finding of no measurable change would suggest that something in the workplace inhibited the new behavior. In Brethower's terms, maintenance variables were neglected.

Level 1 may not be a real part of the evidentiary chain when participation in the intervention is mandatory because participants' reactions to the intervention may not prevent behavior change from occurring. However, it must be considered a part of the chain when participation in the intervention is voluntary because, if people don't like the intervention, they are less likely to participate.

Level 2 data are always a real part of the chain. One must be able to show that new skills/knowledge exist at the end of the preliminary intervention or, for non-training interventions, that people are at least aware that they are operating with new support or under new contingencies. Similarly, without Level 2 data, Level 3 findings cannot be linked to the primary intervention.

Level 3 shows the extent to which the desired new performance is occurring on the job; without these data, organizational outcomes cannot be linked to the preliminary or follow-up interventions. Level 4 data show the extent to which an organization has benefited from the intervention(s)—these data are the end of the chain.

USING AN APPROACH BASED ON KIRKPATRICK'S TAXONOMY

Misuses of Kirkpatrick's approach are rampant, and almost anyone working in evaluation can give you numerous examples. For example, some organizations collect only Level 1 data but represent them as Level 2 or Level 3 data. In other words, they take opinions as evidence of behavior change or impact on the job.

Merely ensuring that progress is measured at all levels of Kirkpatrick's taxonomy is not sufficient for evaluation to be useful. Organizations first need to prepare the ground for evaluation. An effective way to do this is to use a systems approach to conduct evaluation.

A Systems Approach to Evaluation

The most important success factor for evaluation is to incorporate it as an integral part of a systems approach. In any type of performance improvement work, evaluation is most likely to be successful if it is conducted in conjunction with initial stages of the work, during the work, at the conclusion of an intervention's roll-out, and for some time after the intervention has stabilized. Moseley and Dessinger (2008) refer to these stages as *formative* (initial analysis and during design and development), *summative* (at the conclusion of roll-out), and *confirmative* (some time later).

In other words, evaluation is NOT done solely at the end of the analysis-design-development-implementation (ADDIE) cycle, but throughout it. Evaluation and initial assessment are based on the same data. Front-end analysis and needs assessment determine what an organization should change in order to solve problems or take advantage of opportunities, while evaluation determines ways to improve the interventions to achieve those changes and the extent to which the desired changes are actually achieved. Accordingly, organizations need to determine desired outcomes before they begin to work on an intervention.

Contracting with Management in Advance

The key to determining and supporting these outcomes is contracting with management for evaluation in advance of implementing interventions. This may be more easily said than done because managers are often leery of evaluation.

Mintzberg (1973) may have the explanation for this leeriness. He suggested that, because managers serve many different stakeholders amidst a swirl of constantly changing circumstances, they need *manipulatable* data. That is, they need data that are easily adapted to meet the often-conflicting needs of various stakeholders. They need data that they can interpret in varying ways to suit the needs of the particular stakeholders they are addressing.

Good evaluation data, however, are not easily manipulated. If evaluation research is properly designed and implemented, the resulting data will answer questions unequivocally. So, given this "problem" with evaluation data, how does one successfully contract with management in advance?

The answer is to meet with key decision-makers before engaging in a perform-ance improvement project and let them know the benefits of careful evaluation in terms of meeting their specific needs. Show them how evaluation can improve programs or identify and support eliminating ineffective ones. Although evaluation results are not easily manipulated, in the end, management chooses whether and how to implement recommendations based on evaluation data.

Once you have worked out a general agreement, establish an appropriate contract for evaluation with the organization's management. The contract should spell out the responsibilities that the evaluator and management have for the evaluation. Record the contract with a memo (or e-mail) of understanding. In it, specify the evaluator's side of the contract, which is that one will conduct a well-planned, systematic evaluation that addresses the issues that senior management finds important. Provide an attachment that briefly summarizes the evaluation plan.

Senior management's side of the contract involves supporting the effort in word and deed. The memo of understanding should describe the resources management will provide and when they will provide them; messages of support they will send to others in the organization, and when they will send them; terms of access to themselves and other key personnel; and a guarantee for anonymity of sources during data collection.

Other Initial Factors for Ensuring Evaluation Success

Enlist the support of other stakeholders by showing them how evaluation outcomes link to their needs. Their needs will vary and may include support for budget; input for improving interventions; impact on job results; and many others. Describe the value of information at each level in terms appropriate to specific stakeholders. For example, training departments may want information on the relative effectiveness of courses as measured by course test results (Level 2), while supervisors might want to know the benefit of interventions in their work units (Level 3), and general managers might be most interested in the value received for their investment in the intervention (Level 4).

TIPS FOR MEASURING EACH LEVEL OF KIRKPATRICK'S TAXONOMY

Tips for Level 0

First, don't ignore it—Level 0 doesn't go away just because it is not systematic, well-considered data. Senior managers are likely to listen to and value the opinions of a few confidants. Therefore, request and document Level 0 quotes from figures widely respected in your organization. Use these anecdotes informally in chats with members of the "C Suite," and consider using them as highlights or sidebars in evaluation reports. For example, one might write something like: "Three supervisors in the XYZ division attributed recent increases in production to the new reward system that went into effect several months ago."

When using Level 0 data, always also include Level 2 or higher data. Otherwise, one runs the risk of trivializing evaluation data. For example, one might use the attribution of the three supervisors in the example above for a section in which one presents data comparing units' production levels as a function of the installation dates of the new reward system.

Tips for Level 1

Measure only reactions that are in participants' direct experience, NOT their opinions. Ask for descriptions of their experiences, not judgments of them. Use Likert-style psychometrically sound items.

For example, one might ask: "To what extent did the instructor make sure your questions were answered" or "How easily were you able to hear the instructor?" Both of these questions are based on and describe an individual's direct experience. If the first had been worded, "How well did the instructor answer your questions," the query would be asking for a judgment rather than a descriptive reaction.

When using Likert scale items to estimate participants' future use of what was learned, ask how comfortable they would be using specific skills back on the job—an estimate of self-efficacy, NOT how well they learned something. Their answers may be more meaningful. Research (for example, Clark, 1982) shows that participants' self-ratings of their skills do not correlate well with actual proficiency.

For example, ask for opinions on something like "I would be comfortable on the job translating the following article from French to English." (Provide a typical example of the type of article to be translated on the job.) This gives a concrete way for participants to estimate their degree of learning. One would get less accurate results if one asked for their opinions on a more general item, such as "I am comfortable translating French to English."

Tips for Level 2

The most important tip for Level 2 is to test performance, which may be either a skill used under specified conditions to meet specified standards or knowledge applied under specified conditions to meet specified standards. Table 9.3 provides an example and non-example of each.

Another important tip for measuring at Level 2 is to select or develop criterion-referenced tests (CRTs) whenever possible. CRTs measure what learners need to do (or knowledge they need to apply) in order to perform satisfactorily on the job. CRTs may address an entire job, a task, or a subset of a task, depending on the objectives of the intervention for which it is used.

Table 9.3 Examples and Non-Examples of Performance Test Items

	Example	Non-Example
Knowledge-based	"Review this article and list at least three areas requiring analysis for impact on the United States."	"List four key criteria for selecting targets of analysis."
Skill-based	"Use the provided cotton swab and antiseptic solution to prepare an area on the triceps for subcutaneous injection (standard is circular swabbing motion for thirty seconds)."	"Select the correct sequence for preparing to perform a subcutaneous injection from choices a through d below."

At least one item on a criterion-referenced test is required to measure each objective addressed by the training or other intervention (Swezey & Pearlstein, 2001, p. 927). The first practical guide for criterion referenced test development and use was written by Swezey (1981), based largely on work conducted by Pearlstein & Swezey (1974). Shrock and Coscarelli (2007) offer a recent practical guide.

Base end-of-intervention performance tests on intervention objectives. For example, ask: "What does Objective **X** state that employees will do differently on the job?" Then ask: "What can I measure at the end of the intervention to see whether employees can do that Objective **X** thing to a standard on the job?" For example, if an objective stated that employees would be able to prepare a work breakdown structure to **X** standards, the test item would be something like: "Given the following information, prepare a work breakdown structure meeting **X** standards."

When possible, measure pre-intervention performance before measuring end-of-intervention performance. Comparison of pre- and post-measures provides a basis for showing that improvement resulted from intervention. However, sometimes logistics, safety considerations, or other factors prevent taking pre-measures. When measuring pre-intervention performance is not possible, screen the candidate for previous experience. In other words, avoid putting people through interventions if they already perform at a post-intervention level. In addition, if one is not able to measure pre-intervention performance levels, report that post-measures show only that participants could perform at the end of the intervention. Acknowledge that they may have been able to perform before the intervention, but point out that candidates were screened to reduce the chances that those with the necessary prerequisites or experience participated in the intervention.

Tips for Level 3

First, use existing measures of on-the-job performance whenever possible. Doing so meets two goals: (1) addressing on-the-job performance that management already considers important enough to measure and (2) minimizing the data collection effort, thereby maximizing the probability that data will be collected.

Second, use a simple quasi-experimental design—pre- and post-measures of those who have completed the intervention compared to equivalent time series measures of those who have not yet begun the intervention. Shadish, Cook, and Campbell (2002) provide an excellent text on quasi-experimental designs.

Third, keep the research design as simple as possible. Table 9.4 shows a model of a simple Level 3 quasi-experimental design.

Table 9.4 Example of Quasi-Experimental Design for Level 3 Research

When Measured		
Quasi-Experimental Condition	No Intervention Subgroup	Intervention
Subgroup Just Before Intervention	A = Performance at Time X	B = Performance at Time X
Appropriate Later Time	C = Performance at Time X + 3* months (*–same interval as used for measurement D)	D = Performance at Time X + 3** months (**–will vary by type of intervention)

Using this design, one randomly assigns employees from the same group to two subgroups, a subgroup that receives the intervention and another that does not. Then measure the performance of both subgroups just before the intervention. If the assignment is truly random, there should be no significant difference between the two subgroups' behaviors at this point.

After an interval that allows participants in the intervention to demonstrate behavior change on the job, measure on-the-job performance of both subgroups. Random assignment to groups should ensure that other factors balance out. Therefore, the difference between the two subgroups after the intervention reflects that intervention's impact on on-the-job behavior.

Use appropriate inferential statistics—such as Chi square or analysis of variance—to establish the significance of results. If the subgroup with the intervention showed significantly more improvement over the period than the similar subgroup that did not receive the intervention, one can reject the hypothesis that the intervention had no impact on performance. If one fails to find a significant difference, one fails to reject that null hypothesis.

The timing of measurement is critical and will depend on the nature of the intervention. For example, while training or job aids may produce results quickly, a change in feedback or reward systems is more likely to take longer to achieve results. Therefore, consider doing several comparisons like the one shown in Table 9.4, one at three months, for example, and another at six months.

Tips for Level 4

Tips for Level 4 are similar to tips for Level 3. First, measure what senior management regards as organizational benefits. One should already know this information because of the contract with senior management done as the initial step of evaluation. In the same vein, use senior managers' existing measures whenever possible. This time, focus on macro-level outcomes—those that affect the entire organization, and, if the organization is willing, at the mega-level.

Table 9.5 shows how to modify the quasi-experimental design used for Level 3 to work with Level 4. Instead of measuring unit-level performance before and after interventions, measure the targeted organizational outcomes.

Table 9.5 Example of Quasi-Experimental Design for Level 4 Research

Quasi-Experimental Condition

First Round of Measurement	*No Intervention Subgroup*	*Intervention Subgroup*
Just Before Intervention	Organizational Outcomes at Time X	Organizational Outcomes at Time X
Appropriate Later Time	Organizational Outcomes at Time X + 3* months (*–same interval as used for post-intervention measurement)	Organizational Outcomes at Time X + 3** months (**–will vary by type of intervention)

New Quasi-Experimental Condition

Second Round of Measurement	*Intervention Subgroup*	*No New Intervention Subgroup*
Just Before Intervention	Organizational Outcomes at Time Y	Organizational Outcomes at Time Y
After Intervention	Organizational Outcomes at Time Y + 3* months	Organizational Outcomes at Time Y + 3* months
	(*–This time, use the same after-intervention delay that you used during the first round of measurement.)	

For example, one might measure organizational productivity before and after the intervention, just as one measured subgroup performance at Level 3. However, at Level 4 there is an additional difficulty: It will NOT be possible to assign individuals randomly in work units to the intervention condition because the intervention will impact entire groups of work units in specific divisions or locations. Instead, one will need to use separate entities, whether entire divisions or separate geographical locations, in order to have at least one condition in which the intervention has impact and another in which it cannot yet have had impact.

Thus, even if the entities show significant differences in achieving organizational results, one may not be able to attribute those differences to the experimental condition alone. A second round of measurement becomes necessary, as shown in Table 9.5. During this second round, organizational entities that did not receive the intervention during the first round will receive it. If the intervention resulted in the change in organizational outcomes, then a pre- to post-intervention comparison should show a significant improvement in the same way that it did in the first round of measurement. If the difference does NOT surface, factors other than the intervention may have affected the entities in the first comparison.

Another tip for Level 4 is to include ROI as an integral part. Any organizational benefit may be accomplished at a price, but are the benefits worth the price? If one cannot show that the value of the benefits exceeds the cost of the intervention, then one would NOT want to repeat the intervention without serious modification.

Finally, when considering the cost of interventions in a cost/benefit analysis, use senior management's standard approaches to costs. For example, if senior management does not normally include certain overhead costs in determining ROI, do not include those overhead costs. Phillips (1997) has shown numerous ways to calculate both the costs and the benefits sides of the equation.

SUMMARY

Kirkpatrick's evaluation taxonomy can be used as an effective part of organizational performance improvement interventions. It lends itself to a systems approach. Systems start by specifying desired outcomes—and an organization can adjust its processes and practices until those outcomes are achieved. By providing data along an evidentiary chain, evaluation gives an organization the information it needs to align processes and practices to achieve desired outcomes.

A key to effective evaluation is keeping it simple. Overly complex systems are hard to initiate and harder to maintain. Keeping it simple means using existing data as much as possible; and using replicable, sound methodology to show links between evaluation levels and outcomes. Although inferential statistics intimidates some, their use can be described in simple terms to show that changes benefiting the organization were the result of the applied performance improvement interventions, as opposed to other factors.

Done well, evaluation meets many stakeholders' needs by showing the overall worth of a performance improvement intervention and by helping to improve ongoing interventions so that they achieve organizational benefits. Because various stakeholders see benefits in different ways, evaluation should address benefits according to their differing perspectives. When evaluation is done well, everyone wins. Those paying for performance interventions get evidence of their worth. Those developing, implementing, and supporting the performance interventions find ways to improve them. Various organizational entities benefit from the interventions. Finally, when organizations address the mega level, society itself may benefit.

References

Brethower, K. S. (1967). Maintenance systems: The neglected half of behavior change. In G. A. Rummler, J. P. Yaney, & A. W. Schrader (Eds.), *Managing the instructional programming effort*. Ann Arbor, MI: University of Michigan, Bureau of Industrial Relations.

Clark, R. E. (1982). Antagonism between achievement and enjoyment in ATI studies. *Educational Psychologist, 17*(2), 92–101.

Dye, K. (2003). Dye's two-tier framework of evaluation: A practical approach for determining the effectiveness of HRD activities. Retrieved September 14, 2007, from http://kathydye.com/IDEAS/2tier.pdf.

Kaufman, R. A. (2006). *Change, choices, and consequences: A guide to mega thinking and planning*. Amherst, MA: Human Resource Development Press.

Kirkpatrick, D. (1994). *Evaluating training programs: The four levels*. San Francisco: Berrett-Koehler.

Mintzberg, H. (1973). *The nature of managerial work*. New York: Harper & Row.

Moseley, J. L., & Dessinger, J. C. (2008, April). *The kaleidoscope of full scope evaluation: Differences that matter*. Session presented at the International Society for Performance Improvement 2008 Annual Conference, New York, New York.

Pearlstein, R. B. (2008, April). *Using Kirkpatrick's four levels of evaluation in real-world organizations*. Session presented at the International Society for Performance Improvement 2008 Annual Conference, New York, New York.

Pearlstein, R. B. (1995). *Job aids for evaluating skill acquisition methods*. Arlington, VA: Kajax Engineering, Inc. [Under contract to the USDA Forest Service.]

Pearlstein, R. B., & Swezey, R. W. (1974, November). *Criterion-referenced measurement in the Army: Development of a research-based, practical test construction manual*.

Valencia, PA: Applied Science Associates. [Under contract to the Army Research Institute.].

Phillips, J. J. (1997). *Return on investment*. Houston, TX: Gulf.

Pulichino, J. (2006). The eLearning Guild's online forums. Re-examining Kirkpatrick's four levels. December 7 & 8. Retrieved October 15, 2007, from www.elearningguild.com/olf/olfarchives/index.cfm?action = viewonly&id = 290.

Shadish, W. R., Cook, T. D., & Campbell, D. T. (2002). *Experimental and quasi-experimental designs for generalized causal inference*. Boston: Houghton Mifflin.

Shrock, S. A., & Coscarelli, W. C. (2007). *Criterion-referenced test development: Technical and legal guidelines for corporate training* (3rd ed.). San Francisco: Pfeiffer.

Swezey, R. W. (1981). *Individual performance assessment: An approach to criterion-referenced test development*. Reston, VA: Reston Publishing Company.

Swezey, R. W., & Pearlstein, R. B. (2001). *Selection, training, and development of personnel*. In G. Salvendy (Ed.), *Handbook of industrial engineering* (3rd ed.; pp. 920–947). Hoboken, NJ: John Wiley & Sons.

Watkins, R., Leigh, D., Foshay, R., & Kaufman, R. A. (1998). Kirkpatrick plus: Evaluation and continuous improvement with a community focus. *Educational Technology Research and Development*, 46(4), 90–96.

CHAPTER TEN

Ethical Considerations in Performance Measurement

David L. Solomon

Long before the Standards of Performance Technology and Code of Ethics (International Society for Performance Improvement) were published in 2002, ethical considerations for performance improvement professionals represented a growing concern in a developing field. In 1977, the Joint Certification Task Force, sponsored by the Association for Educational Communications and Technology (AECT) and the National Society for Performance and Instruction (NSPI, now the International Society for Performance Improvement), was established (The International Board of Standards for Training, Performance and Instruction). Since then, there have been various efforts to create guiding principles within the field (Dean, 1993; Guerra, 2006; Kaufman & Clark, 1999; Westgaard, 1988), including work from The International Board of Standards for Training, Performance and Instruction, which grew out of the Joint Certification Task Force. Still, these standards, ethics, and codes of conduct never really explain what to do or how to handle an ethical dilemma (the "PT Standards" and "Code of Ethics" may be found at www.ispi.org/). Kaufman (1987) asked a very important question: "Do we ask questions of ourselves and others relative to the merit, worth, and usefulness of what to do, or do we simply do that which we are asked and obliviously follow instructions?" (p. 48). The goal of this chapter is to provide a range of responses to Kaufman's question, since the answers are rarely going to be clearly defined and will likely involve varying levels of compromise.

Human performance technology (HPT) is all about people, and people vary. In addition, there are many different stakeholders involved in measuring performance, each with different responsibilities, values, goals, and a broad range of organizations to which they belong. Clearly, there are some organizations in which measurement is part of the culture and others in which measurement is the newest strategic goal. With so many variables, performance measurement is not the easiest workplace challenge, and ethical considerations add another layer of complexity. Further, ethics as an area of inquiry can be quite complicated because the topic is quite expansive.

It would be easy to devote an entire chapter to an exploration of ethics; however, the focus of this chapter is really about finding the best path to follow at the "moment of truth"—that moment when an ethical decision must be made. Before delving into ethical considerations for HPT professionals, the question remains, what are *ethics*? Generally, ethics are the principles of conduct that govern individuals and groups (Dean, 1994) and it is reasonable to assume that there are generally accepted ethical principles that can be broadly applied (Brown & Stilwell, 2005). For example, a generally accepted code of ethics would not cause harm to others, would be anchored in truth, and would strive to make society a better place. Further, a discussion about ethics should also address the notion of integrity, where one's actions become aligned with principles of conduct. Later in this chapter, a definition of integrity is offered for consideration. For those who are interested in learning more about ethical theory as it relates to HPT, there are excellent resources available (Dean, 1993; Guerra, 2006). Given the Standards of Performance Technology and Code of Ethics (International Society for Performance Improvement), along with "common ethical values that are applicable and knowable to all, regardless of gender, race, age, wealth, class, politics or religion" (Josephson Institute as cited in Brown & Stilwell, 2005, p. 23), there are four areas in which ethical considerations can guide the behavior of professionals in the field:

- Designing performance management systems (PMS);
- Collecting data;
- Analyzing performance; and
- Reporting findings.

OVERVIEW OF PERFORMANCE MANAGEMENT SYSTEMS

As members of a professional community, we have an obligation to preserve and safeguard public confidence in our field, and performance measurement can pose a number of challenges. HPT professionals are expected to focus on results and to be very clear about what will be measured or the evidence that will be used to evaluate success. Accordingly, there are design considerations that follow, and it is helpful to clarify the functions of the performance measurement system, since each function will influence design (Kerssens-van Drongelen & Fisscher, 2003). Further, from a systemic viewpoint, the various functions of performance measurement systems are interrelated, and HPT professionals are expected to understand how each of the various parts influence the work, the worker, and the workplace. A taxonomy of possible performance measurement system functions (Kerssens-van Drongelen, 1999, p. 46) has surfaced in the literature, which offers a systematic approach to the design process. See Exhibit 10.1.

Exhibit 10.1 Taxonomy of Performance Measurement System Functions

1. Provide insight into deviations from objectives and into environmental factors to support the diagnosis by manager as to whether, and if so, which steering measures to apply.
2. Support learning, which may lead to improved knowledge about the organization and its processes and about the impact of external factors and corrective measures on performance and that way facilitate better organization and steering in the future.
3. Support the process of alignment and communication of objectives.
4. Support decision making on performance-based rewards.
5. Provide insight into deviations from objectives and into environmental factors to support the diagnosis by employees as to whether, and if so, which steering measures to apply.
6. Help to justify existence, decisions, and performance.
7. Motivate people by giving them feedback about the measured performance.

Measurement Considerations

Once the HPT professional has identified desired outcomes and considered the various functions of the performance measurement system, another logical step in the process will be clarifying what will be measured. In recent years, there seems to be an obsessive focus on metrics, often in the absence of well-designed performance measurement systems. While this is not entirely bad—in the sense that the desire for data-driven decision making is honorable—it becomes problematic when the desired workplace behaviors are not included in the discussion. Performance measurement can be a tremendous challenge for organizations that do not have the experience or expertise with systematic approaches to improving productivity and competence, which also adds a layer of complexity for the HPT professional. Often, performance measurement will reside within human resources or training departments, where one of the functions of the system will be to support learning. In these situations, one should expect to have discussions about "the four levels of measurement," derived from Kirkpatrick's (1959) evaluation model. While a discussion about the relevancy of Kirkpatrick's model is well beyond the scope of this chapter, it is interesting to note that Kirkpatrick's original article introduced "four steps" for evaluating training programs. By today's standards, measuring human performance and Kirkpatrick's four steps for evaluating training programs appear incongruous; however, the model can be a useful tool for helping organizations adopt a culture of measurement. Kirkpatrick's model is widely used because it is simple and practical and offers guidelines for how to get started and how to proceed (Kirkpatrick, 1996). Sometimes, getting started is more important than (what appears to be) endless dialogue for business executives who are unfamiliar with performance measurement. And, while the four-level model may not be ideal, it offers a pragmatic compromise for introducing the concept of measurement to organizations that want to get started with "metrics" quickly.

The four-level model also suggests the importance of creating a balanced representation of performance, which is one of the most important ethical considerations involved in the design of performance management systems (Kerssens-van Drongelen & Fisscher, 2003). *The Balanced Scorecard* (Kaplan & Norton, 1996), which was popularized in the 1990s, promoted the need for focusing on the human issues related to performance in addition to financial measures. As a result, a balanced scorecard provides a comprehensive view of a business, which in turn, provides guidance in the design of performance measurement systems. The fundamental idea is that performance measures will guide and direct behavior within an organization, so it is important to measure a range of activities or results that are important to successfully achieving organizational goals.

Managing Expectations

Finally, one of the most important design considerations involved in creating a performance measurement system is managing the scope and establishing realistic expectations. Sometimes, it can take years to implement a performance measurement system and HPT professionals should be prepared for a broad range of possibilities when undertaking such an endeavor. Ethically, there is a responsibility to explain these possibilities, which will vary from one environment to the next. In organizations in which there is evidence of a functional performance measurement system, the project scope could be relatively stable compared to an environment in which performance measures are conspicuously absent. In the latter case, the potential for "scope creep" exists as the functions of the performance measurement system could shift and more stakeholders are introduced to the design process as a project evolves. Experienced HPT professionals should be able to assess an organization's readiness for performance measurement during the discovery process, while someone with less experience may not have the breadth of experience to identify various factors that may influence scope. One good approach to address these concerns is to create a phased strategy whereby a project can be grouped into a number of different activities that can be implemented over time. Regardless, there is an ethical responsibility to communicate and clarify the assumptions associated with the design process up-front so that changes in scope can be managed in a professional manner.

Typical Conflicts

While one might encounter a number of conflicts designing performance management systems, some have ethical implications for the HPT professional. Some of the more typical conflicts surround the notion that performance measures will influence behavior in organizations. Although the connection between performance measurement and behavior may appear obvious, conflicts may arise when the system is designed around objective observations of performance, while subjective opinions are used to distribute rewards—particularly financial ones. For example, a performance management system may be in place to support the performance review process—a seemingly objective process; yet discretionary bonuses are subjectively determined. This conflict between managing objective observations (performance) and subjective opinions that are linked to financial rewards can have a negative impact on morale and performance. Another common flaw in performance measurement systems deals with rewarding individual performance in a team-oriented environment. When organizations value collaborative work and the interpersonal skills needed to promote strong teams, the performance management system should be designed to formally reward these types of desired outcomes (Kerr, 1975). HPT professionals should be prepared to identify conflicts arising from an imbalance between rewards for individual and team performance. Managers can also become demotivated when they are punished for delivering bad news, so another typical conflict involves "shooting the messenger." When the function of the performance management system is to support continuous improvement efforts, blaming the person who brings bad news can have serious repercussions. All of these examples, and countless others, illustrate situations in which behaviors that should be discouraged are actually being rewarded, while desired performance is not being rewarded at all (Kerr, 1975).

In addition to conflicts arising from reward systems, HPT professionals are likely to encounter situations in which there is friction regarding time horizons, which has ethical consequences. The desire for quick results can be problematic because performance measurement takes time. Yet, in economically challenged times, there could be clients who may want to act on incomplete or unbalanced performance data. Dealing with fragments of performance data can cause serious problems because, like the proverbial "elephant's ear," the picture is incomplete. For example, sales professionals are often evaluated on sales volume; yet, product availability, poor quality, or customer service can have a serious impact on the ability to sell. With so many factors influencing performance, is it ethical to evaluate a sales professional on a single piece of performance data? Although this example is simplistic, it illustrates the need for a complete set of metrics to guide decision making.

In contrast to organizations that may be in a rush to take action, there are also organizations that have difficulty choosing which metrics are important and they become mired in "analysis paralysis." Much has been written about organizations that wish to make a transition from training to performance improvement, and there can be many hurdles along the way. For example, in larger companies in which the function of the performance measurement system is to support learning, data can be quite revealing, which can pose threats, especially in highly political environments. Further, as performance measurement systems are implemented, there is a need to manage change, which can be challenging for some managers. In these situations, it is not uncommon to find clients who are more comfortable analyzing data than making difficult decisions that impact large groups of people.

A Range of Responses

A number of hypothetical situations have been described that HPT professionals could encounter while designing performance measurement systems:

1. What should be done when a client is inadvertently rewarding undesirable behaviors?

2. How should clients be handled when they want to act on incomplete or unbalanced performance data?

3. How can the HPT professional help the client move beyond analysis paralysis?

Interestingly, the ISPI Code of Ethics provides the following example of ethical behavior: "Even in the face of client resistance, use and promote the ISPI Standards." The ISPI Standards offer clearly stated performances and examples that illustrate how to implement the standards; yet, there is little guidance for dealing with client resistance. Moreover, situations like the ones previously described require consulting skills that are not necessarily outlined in the various standards, ethics, and codes of conduct that are connected to HPT. At the same time, managing client expectations requires consulting skills, especially when ethical considerations are involved (Solomon, 1997). The

Standards for HPT professionals outline what to do and what *not* to do in clearly defined situations; however, ill-defined problems can be addressed with a range of responses based on the people involved and the situation at hand. Accordingly, "doing the right thing" is contingent upon a multitude of factors. In a field that is so focused on outcomes, success is often defined in terms of the quantitative results that are produced. Because this chapter is devoted to ethical considerations in performance measurement, there are certain qualitative outcomes that are equally important:

1. *Client relationships.* The Net Promoter Score provides feedback based on one simple question: "Would you recommend us to a friend or colleague?" (Reichheld, 2003). Promoters are seen as a valuable asset based on repeat business, long-term customer relationships, and referrals. In our efforts to generate results, we need to be focused on producing an exceptional customer experience, as well.

2. *Client education.* HPT professionals have an ethical responsibility for educating clients. Another measure of our success can be determined by the degree to which our clients have acquired new knowledge and skills through our interactions with them. We should be focused on improving client competence through the consulting relationship and progressively moving the client toward a desired state through a long-term customer relationship.

3. *Adaptability.* When working with performance measurement, compromise is often a valuable outcome. I have been honored to work with some true pioneers in the field of HPT, and each of them demonstrates an uncanny ability to sense and respond to clients in very productive ways. While our methods and procedures are often systematic, true masters are flexible and adaptable to client needs.

In evaluating the three hypothetical situations that were introduced in this chapter, it is possible to reflect on the strength of the client relationship, the degree of client education provided, and the ability to compromise as "soft" measures of success. In the paragraphs that follow, the same ideas can be used to interpret cases that breathe life into ethical considerations involving data collection, data analysis, and reporting.

ETHICAL CONSIDERATIONS, INTEGRITY, AND PERFORMANCE MEASUREMENT

The concept of integrity will guide and direct the remainder of this chapter, as integrity and ethics—principles of conduct for individuals and groups—are intimately connected. As with the word "ethics," the word "integrity" means different things to different people, so a definition is needed to promote clarity. In his book, *Integrity*, Stephen Carter (1996) offers the following definition:

> Integrity, as I will use the term, requires three steps: (1) *discerning* what is right and what is wrong; (2) *acting* on what you have discerned, even at personal cost; and (3) *saying openly* that you are acting on your understanding of right from wrong. The first criterion captures the idea of integrity as requiring a degree of moral reflectiveness. The second brings in the ideal of an integral person as steadfast, which includes the sense of keeping commitments. The third reminds us that a person of integrity is unashamed of doing the right. (p. 7)

This concept of integrity provides a framework for individuals who are involved in performance measurement, especially as ethical issues arise. Working with data—collection, analysis, and reporting—may involve challenging situations depending upon the stakeholders involved, so cases will be presented for reflection and/or discussion with peers. More importantly, there are best practices that apply more broadly to working with data than the occasional ethical dilemmas that occur throughout a person's career. Each of the following sections (Data Collection, Data Analysis, and Reporting) begins with a discussion of best practices and concludes with a case study.

Data Collection

Specifying data collection methods are an integral part of designing a PMS, and it is important during this phase of a project to ensure that realistic and attainable goals have been established for data collection. Data should provide insight into performance and should focus on the vital few metrics—as opposed to measuring everything, which is a trap for many novice evaluators. Nevertheless, educational activities promote success, and everyone who will be working with data should be oriented to the PMS function(s) and trained for their specific roles in the process. For multiple data collectors, consistency and researcher bias are important concerns that educational activities can address. Whether the goal is collecting quantitative, qualitative, or "soft" metrics (often intangible assets that may not be apparent), consistency of data collection should be a goal.

Sample size is another area in which ethical considerations arise. Often, the desire for statistical significance may impact data collection costs and it is important to evaluate whether or not statistical significance is mandatory. In his book, *The Wisdom of Crowds: Why the Many Are Smarter Than the Few and How Collective Wisdom Shapes Business, Economies, Societies, and Nations*, James Surowiecki (2004) suggests that a diverse collection of people are likely to make better decisions than subject-matter experts. While Surowiecki's thesis is controversial, the insight that applies to performance measurement is that smaller, diverse samples often yield results that are comparatively close to statistically significant samples. Working with smaller samples may contribute to improved efficiency and data collection costs, which should be considered and evaluated by all stakeholders.

Finally, as a best practice, unanticipated outcomes and non-solicited data should be embraced, and management should be briefed about the value derived from unexpected findings. It is important and healthy to communicate that performance measurement may yield some surprising discoveries, and thus evaluators need to assess the readiness of stakeholders to receive information that may be difficult to accept. This type of discussion should occur throughout the life of a project so that data collection efforts can be conducted without incident. Performance measurement reveals opportunities and stakeholders need to be prepared for a range of possibilities *prior to* data collection. In the following case, client interference with data collection poses a challenge that may be encountered, and it is helpful to think about potential approaches for mitigating these concerns.

Case 10.1. Client Interference with Data Collection.
A brand manager for a pharmaceutical company was concerned that sales representatives did not have the prerequisite knowledge and skills to support the launch of a new product. The sales force consisted of both newer and more tenured employees and the level of knowledge, skills, and abilities was highly variable. In partnership with the sales training department, the brand team relied on a training manager to work with a supplier who was selected to design the launch training program. The supplier designed a study to evaluate performance using a group of randomly selected sales representatives. When presented with this plan, the training manager insisted on selecting all of the subjects. The supplier explained the importance of collecting data from a random sample that was representative of the larger group. The training manager rejected this approach and explained that sales representatives need to be seeing customers, and it is a tremendous challenge to randomly pull subjects out of the field, even if only for a few hours. During a weekly status meeting, the supplier explained this predicament to the brand manager, who said: "He's just afraid that you're going to find out his sales training program isn't working!"

Discussion Questions
1. What opportunities exist for the supplier to build a relationship of trust with the training manager?
2. What can the supplier do to help the client acquire new knowledge and skills through interactions with them?
3. How can the supplier and training manager arrive at a compromise whereby everyone's needs can be reasonably addressed?
4. Given the definition of integrity (Carter, 1996), what options exist for the evaluator to maintain integrity throughout this phase of the project?

Data Analysis

Although data analysis typically follows data collection, the data analysis plan should be clearly outlined as the PMS is designed. Data analysis involves examining data and summarizing it so that useful information can be derived for formulating conclusions or recommendations. It is very important to contextualize the data analysis activities; therefore, it helps to establish a framework for applying these analyses. It may be useful to revisit the functions of the performance measurement system (Kerssens-van Drongelen & Fisscher, 2003) so that analyses can support the intended purposes of the PMS. The human performance technology (HPT) model (Van Tiem, Moseley, & Dessinger, 2004) can also provide a context for understanding data analysis because performance analysis and cause analysis provide guidance for working with data as well.

Once a framework has been established for data analysis, it is important to revisit the data analysis plan that was specified during the design phase of the project. At first glance, there should be alignment between the analyses (frequencies, averages, content analysis) and the function of the PMS. The methods and procedures that were documented in the design phase need to be revisited and evaluated, as adjustments may be necessary. Perhaps there were fewer subjects available or extant data that was expected was not delivered. One should expect that a data analysis plan may require revision once the data are collected and the framework for analysis has been clarified and understood. From an ethical standpoint, communicating any changes in the analysis plan to stakeholders is paramount.

With a focus on ethical considerations, a detailed explanation about how to prepare data, interpret results, and summarize findings is beyond the scope of this chapter. Nonetheless, ethical dilemmas may surface during these activities and it helps to be prepared. Common sense has not yet been introduced from an ethical perspective, and it is most fitting to discuss it here. Just as there are generally accepted ethical principles that can be broadly applied (Brown & Stilwell, 2005), common sense refers to good judgment based on what people in common would perceive in a given situation. For performance improvement professionals, common sense suggests that we do not alter data as it is being prepared for analysis and that there is rigor behind any interpretation of results. When findings are summarized, common sense tells us that we must be truthful and transparent. In fact, the Standards of Performance Technology and Code of Ethics (International Society for Performance Improvement) remind us all what common sense should look like in our profession. Nonetheless, performance improvement professionals will encounter ethical challenges to our common sense, and the following case offers a situation that is riddled with complexity.

Case 10.2. Falsifying Data.

The automotive industry spends significant money on dealership training, and one manufacturer conducts a "fall tour" that visits twenty-five cities in the United States to promote its products, which includes experiential "ride-and-drive" activities with competitive products. The client responsible for this event supervises a multi-million-dollar budget and wields a lot of power. Well-known for being politically motivated, he often "manages by fear." The agency working on the fall tour was busy collecting a variety of data from each of the cities, including information such as attendance, test scores, certification data, and exit surveys. In a number of cities, inclement weather appeared to have a drastic impact on attendance, and satisfaction scores were much lower in these markets. The client instructed the agency to falsify the attendance records and eliminate survey data from any market where there was bad weather. Barbara was the account supervisor at the agency and did not know what to do. When she tried to explain that she was uncomfortable following his instructions, he reminded her that "This isn't something worth getting fired over." Distraught, she went to her supervisor, who explained that if they reported him to a senior executive, the agency would likely lose millions of dollars in business. Barbara decided to follow instructions; and she also made sure to conduct an accurate analysis for safekeeping.

Discussion Questions

1. If part of the definition of integrity includes "*acting* on what you have discerned, even at personal cost" (Carter, 1996, p. 7), how would a performance consultant describe Barbara's response to this situation?
2. Is there any room for compromise in this case?
3. What would a performance improvement specialist do in this situation?

Reporting Findings

So, we have progressed from design to data collection and analysis to one of the final steps, where ethical considerations are of supreme importance. Reporting findings should be one of the easiest steps because the previous activities consume most of the time that is involved in the overall process. Given the concepts of ethics and common sense previously discussed, reporting findings should be relatively straightforward. In addition, the ISPI Code of Ethics also provides further guidance. The "Integrity Principle" instructs professionals in our field to "exhibit the highest level of professional objectivity in gathering, evaluating, and communicating information about the activity or process being examined, or the results achieved" (International Society for Performance Improvement). Straightforward, right?

With so many options available, perhaps the most challenging ethical consideration is determining how to report the findings in a way that is useable and "actionable" by the audience. Preparing a reader-centered report involves a deepened understanding of one's audience, beyond the specific needs that motivated the inquiry to a more generalized point of view about the way in which people communicate within an organization. Over time, performance improvement professionals may develop their own "voice" for reporting information to stakeholders, and the challenge is learning how to adapt that voice across media disciplines. There was once a time when most reports were written documents; however, Microsoft Office PowerPoint has influenced the way in which findings are reported in organizations. Not too long age, people used transparencies to support speakers in live presentations. While Power-Point is promoted as a presentation tool, the fact remains that more and more reports are prepared in PowerPoint, which has implications for writing style, the use of graphic support, and presentation skills. Performance improvement professionals should be prepared to write reports in PowerPoint that include the visual display of data. Although there are many resources available to develop these skills, Edward Tufte's work should be included in the perform-ance improvement professional's review of the literature. Tufte is a professor emeritus at Yale University, where he taught courses in statistical evidence, information design, and interface design; he has also written seven books. One of his pieces, *The Cognitive Style of PowerPoint* (Tufte, 2003), is particularly relevant to reporting findings, and it offers interesting insights for the perform-ance improvement professional.

Beyond PowerPoint, digitally enhanced methods for reporting data can be seen across company intranets with scorecards or dashboards that provide people with just-in-time metrics for managing performance. While ethics is concerned with the principles of conduct that govern individuals and groups (Dean, 1994), performance improvement professionals should be tuned in to organizational culture in order to select the most effective methods for com-municating findings. Again, these types of decisions should be made during the design phase of a project; a best practice for determining effective methods for communicating is to request and evaluate exemplary reports.

There are many faces of performance measurement in the workplace, and it helps to have a solid understanding of the functions of the PMS (see Exhibit 10.1) prior to reporting. Measurement activity may represent a specific point in time, a continuous pulse on performance, or it may be the impetus for a significant performance improvement effort. Regardless, the ethical and moral considerations involved in reporting should be very clear at this point. Un-fortunately, performance improvement professionals may encounter challeng-ing situations that test one's integrity and present an ethical dilemma. In the following case, the graphic representations of data are completely accurate but misleading, which provides a final opportunity to reflect.

This last case is a little different from the other two because the sales manager acted alone, and in the other cases the evaluators were engaged in a client relationship where an ethical dilemma surfaced. Our common sense tells us that

Case 10.3. Deceptive Graphics.

In one sales organization, a decision had to be made to reduce headcount, and there were many debates about whether or not it made sense to retain the more experienced and seasoned sales force or to develop the less-experienced sales professionals who had lower base salaries. Although the more experienced sales professionals had higher sales volume, they also had higher base salaries. A decision was made to collect performance data to guide the decision-making process. The sales manager was torn. He had developed several deep and lasting relationships with the more experienced sales force and also knew that he had a fiduciary duty to the company. He decided that he would prepare his report and present the facts. While preparing his PowerPoint presentation, he cut and pasted a bar chart comparing the performance of the experienced and novice sales professionals. The chart was a bit small for the slide, so he dragged one of the corners of the graphic to fill the page. To his surprise, the tall, thin graphics made the differences between the two groups appear extreme; and, he did not have to manipulate any data. Now, slight differences between the two groups appeared to be significant.

Discussion Questions

1. If the data reported are factual, how should the sales manager respond to the question, "How would the difference in performance between the two groups be explained?"
2. Would this situation to be an ethical dilemma if the sales manager did not realize that he was distorting the data?
3. What are the ethical responsibilities of the audience in this situation?

---

the sales manager acted inappropriately; yet, Kaufman's (1987) question is still relevant. The audience for a presentation has an ethical responsibility to challenge the sales manager instead of simply going through the motions and accepting information at face value. This is the very essence of ethical responsibility. Aristotle's concept of responsibility includes the notion that human action is either voluntary or non-voluntary and that acting in ignorance is a choice whereby a person has lost some degree of responsible self-control (Broadie, 1991). Kaufman's question is riveting because it is as trenchant and meaningful today as it was decades ago: Do we challenge ourselves and others or do we blindly follow instructions?

CONCLUSIONS

One of the goals of this chapter was to clarify that the performance improvement professional will likely encounter situations that represent a challenge to personal integrity, and the path is not always going to be clear. The Standards of Performance Technology and Code of Ethics (International Society for Performance Improvement) provide some guidance and direction, but they do not address the gray areas where situational factors and circumstances yield a range of acceptable responses. The performance improvement professional's world may not be well-defined like the Standards and Code of Ethics. Another goal of this chapter was to place greater emphasis on the "human" element and focus less on "performance technology." As a field of inquiry, HPT is *still* all about people—first and foremost. While the Standards tell us to focus on results, sometimes people need to be reminded to be human too. The "Integrity Principle" does not even come close to that!

Integrity, as defined by Carter (1996) is reminiscent of Polonius' advice to his son Laertes in *Hamlet*: "To thine own self be true." Ethics may address principles of conduct (Dean, 1994), and common sense may reflect what people deem to be good judgment; yet, the performance improvement professional still has to look in the mirror each day. That is when integrity becomes very important. Performance technology is an evidence-based field of practice and sometimes it can appear to be cold or mechanistic. When working with verifiable evidence, performance may appear to be black or white. Hopefully, this chapter will help performance improvement professionals tap into some of the underlying *human* feelings and emotions that guide practice. It is important to reflect on these feelings and to feel good about that value we provide while working ethically to strengthen the field. At all times, performance improvement professionals should remember the importance of integrity in relation to the people we serve.

References

Broadie, S. (1991). *Ethics with Aristotle*. New York: Oxford University Press.

Brown, M., & Stilwell, J (2005). The ethical foundation of performance measurement and management. *Public Management*, *87*(5), 22–25.

Carter, S. (1996). *Integrity*. New York: HarperCollins.

Dean, P. (1993). A selected review of the underpinnings of ethics for human performance technology professionals. Part one: Key ethical theories and research. *Performance Improvement Quarterly*, *6*(4), 6–32.

Dean, P. (1994). Some basics about ethics. *Performance and Instruction*, (33) *10*, 42–45.

Guerra, I. (2006). Standards and ethics in human performance technology. In J. A. Pershing (Ed.), *Handbook of human performance technology: Principles, practices, potential* (3rd ed.). San Francisco: Pfeiffer.

The International Board of Standards for Training, Performance and Instruction "Milestones." [www.ibstpi.org/AboutUs/milestones.htm]. July 2008.

International Society for Performance Improvement "PT Standards" and "Code of Ethics" [www.ispi.org/]. July 2009.

Kaplan, R. S., & Norton, D. P. (1996). *The balanced scorecard: Translating strategy into action*. Boston: Harvard Business School Press.

Kaufman, R. A. (1987). Means and ends: On ethics. *Educational Technology, 5*(27), 48–49.

Kaufman, R. A., & Clark, R. E. (1999). Re-establishing performance improvement as a legitimate area of inquiry, activity, and contribution: Rules of the road. *Performance Improvement, 38*(9), 13–18.

Kerr, S. (1975). On the folly of rewarding A, while hoping for B. *Academy of Management Journal, (18)*4, 769–783.

Kerssens-van Drongelen, I. C., & Fisscher, O. A. M. (2003). Ethical dilemmas in performance measurement. *Journal of Business Ethics, 45*(1 & 2), 51–63.

Kerssens-van Drongelen, I. C. (1999), Systematic design of R&D performance measurement systems. Unpublished doctoral dissertation. University of Twente, Enschede.

Kirkpatrick, D. L. (1959). Techniques for evaluating training programs. *Journal of American Society for Training and Development, 13*(11–12).

Kirkpatrick, D. (1996). Revisiting Kirkpatrick's four-level model. *Training and Development, 50*(1), 54–59.

Reichheld, F. F. (2003). The one number you need to grow. *Harvard Business Review, 12*(82), 46–54.

Solomon, D. L. (1997). Entering the consulting relationship: A guide for instructional technologists. *Performance Improvement, 4*(36), 24–28.

Surowiecki, J. (2004). *The wisdom of crowds: Why the many are smarter than the few and how collective wisdom shapes business, economies, societies and nations*. New York: Doubleday.

Tufte, E. R. (2003). *The cognitive style of PowerPoint*. Cheshire, CT: Graphics Press.

Van Tiem, D. M., Moseley, J. L., & Dessinger, J. C. (2004). *Fundamentals of performance technology: A guide to improving people, processes, and performance* (2nd ed). Silver Spring, MD: International Society for Performance Improvement.

Westgaard, O. (1988). *A credo for performance technologists*. Western Springs, IL: International Board of Standards for Training, Performance, and Instruction.

PART THREE

MOSAICS IN
MEASUREMENT
AND EVALUATION

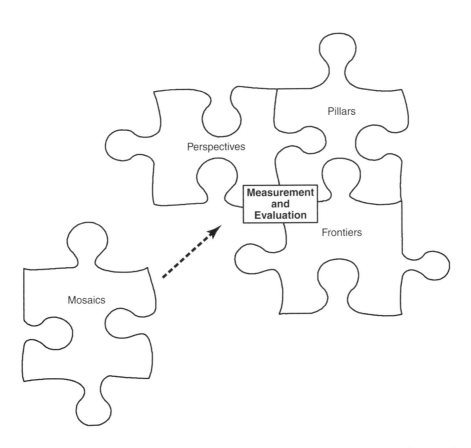

If a picture is worth a thousand words, could it just as easily spark a thousand ideas? Of all the various art forms, mosaics most clearly demonstrate to even the casual observer how it is possible to transform the known into the new simply by creating a different way of delivering the message. Mosaics remind us that our perceptions about a concept can be adjusted by how the concept is presented. This third part of the book is titled "Mosaics in Measurement and Evaluation" because each of the five chapters represents variations on a theme. They take old-fashioned attention and craftsmanship and present a new assemblage of ideas, processes, and perspectives. The strategies are diverse and, therefore, influence change by breaking with accustomed patterns and traditional methodologies. The "real life" application of measurement and evaluation differs from expert to expert, organization to organization. The mosaics presented in these chapters were selected to breathe "new life" into well-known topics while reflecting the authors' personalities and their individual work-related consulting experiences.

Chapter Eleven: Performance-Based Evaluation: Tools, Techniques, and Tips. Hale's chapter delves into tools, techniques, and tips for performance-based evaluation. Her focus is on six rules for measuring the magnitude of problems and the effect of solutions so that evaluations are more evidence-based. Evaluations based on actual observations or outcomes, rather than on hypothetical events or hearsay, are credible and improve bottom-line results.

Chapter Twelve: Test Strategies: Verifying Capability to Perform. Hybert takes the position that, beyond general impressions, the best way to verify someone's capability to perform on the job is to engage the person in testing. Why? Businesses are testing to establish a baseline entry point, to determine unneeded training, and to ensure capability at the end of training. His extensive consulting experience with Fortune 500 companies colors his mosaic patterns.

Chapter Thirteen: The Business of Program Evaluation: ROI. The Phillips' chapter presents a business approach to evaluation using ROI. Traditional evaluation success measured numbers of people involved, money spent, time to complete tasks, product waste, and so forth. Today the value definition has shifted, and value is defined by results versus activity.

Chapter Fourteen: Integrated Evaluation: Improving Performance Improvement. Hastings' mosaic is that performance improvement requires fully integrated, ongoing formative, summative, and confirmative evaluation. Her "Integrated Evaluation Structure" acknowledges that all three types of evaluations—process (formative), product (summative), and impact (confirmative)—should be integrated throughout the performance improvement life cycle and not completed separately at predetermined times.

Chapter Fifteen: Using Evaluation Results to Improve Human Performance Technology Projects. Diroff focuses on supports for evaluation and change and attends to critical factors for using, correcting, and adjusting evaluation results. She makes a strong case for continuous evaluation and for establishing the necessary baseline data. She takes the position that practitioners must evaluate every impact on interventions and make appropriate changes as necessary.

CHAPTER ELEVEN

Performance-Based Evaluation

Tools, Techniques, and Tips

Judith A. Hale

T his chapter focuses on six rules and their associated tools, techniques, and tips for measuring the magnitude of problems and the effect of solutions so that the evaluations are more evidence-based, that is, they are based on actual observations or outcomes, not hypothetical events or hearsay. Collectively, the rules, tools, techniques, and tips are meant to support the evaluation of interventions or solutions designed to improve human performance. Their use increases the chances that evaluation is based on valid information that is useful to decision-makers. Rules are prescribed guides for what to do, when, and why. The rules begin with how to get agreement on what measures and metrics to use as the basis of the evaluation. They conclude with how to present findings to clients to facilitate understanding and decisions. *Tools* are instruments used in the execution of a task. They are a means to an end. *Techniques* are suggestions about how to carry out a task or make better use of a tool usually with the intent of saving time or reducing error. *Tips* are bits of expert advice intended to make the application of a rule or the use of a tool easier. Tools, techniques, and tips are meaningless without rules; likewise, rules without tools, techniques, and tips are difficult to apply.

THE RULES

The rules for evaluating needs and solutions based on facts or evidence are

1. *Get sufficient clarity*—Have clients explain what they perceive as a need or goal in detail. The factors and observations they are using as a basis for determining there is a problem are the same factors they will use to judge improvement or success. Clarity about the details facilitates gaining consensus about the need and the evidence.

2. *Set a baseline*—Set a baseline or describe the current state of affairs sufficiently so that improvement can be measured. Clients cannot determine whether circumstances have changed unless they have something against which to compare the new situation.

3. *Leverage data already being collected*—Leverage data the client already has to measure whether change is happening and the desired level of improvement occurred. This saves time, reduces the cost of evaluating, and increases the likelihood the evidence will be accepted.

4. *Track leading indicators*—Leading indicators are the presence of interim behaviors or results that predict results if they continue. When clients track leading indicators, they are in a better position to take corrective action in time to make a difference.

5. *Analyze the data*—Examine the data for patterns, frequency, and significance so they guide future decisions. The analysis should lead to insights and better understanding of the current situation and how much change has occurred.

6. *Tell the story*—Communicate the logic behind the decision and the evidence used to measure the effectiveness of the solution. This will facilitate commitment to the solution and meaningful dialogue about the need for any next steps to further support improvement.

The rules are somewhat linear or similar to a procedure; however, it helps to have a deeper understanding of some of the more common performance improvement measures and metrics to use them efficiently.

MEASURES, METRICS, AND EVIDENCE

In the world of learning and performance, *evaluation* is the act of passing judgment on the value of a problem and its proposed solutions. *Measurement* is the act of gathering data and then using what is found out as a basis for decisions as to the worth of a problem and the value of a solution. *Measures* are the attributes that the people doing the evaluation pay attention to when making a judgment, such as customer service, timeliness, security, return on investment, and so on. *Metrics* are units of measurement such as how frequently a behavior occurs, how long before a behavior appears in seconds or hours, how many checks or levels of approval there are, and how much money is gained in hundreds or thousands of dollars. For example, if a client wants to measure customer service, the metric might be how frequently people exhibit the previously determined desired behaviors. If the measure is time, the metric may be years, days, or milliseconds, depending on the circumstances. Taken together measures and metrics are what people accept as *evidence* that there is a problem and that circumstances improved after a solution was imposed.

1. Get Sufficient Clarity

The first rule is to get sufficient clarity as to what stakeholders are using as evidence that a need exists and what information they will accept as proof that performance improved. A desired by-product of getting clarity is consensus among stakeholders as to the importance of the need and what they will accept as evidence of improvement. Clients typically dictate solutions, such as training, coaching, new software, or a change in personnel to improve performance. They may assume the basis for the request is obvious and accepted by others. However, until the information on which they are making the request is explicit, it is difficult to determine whether there is agreement or whether there is sufficient evidence to warrant action. The best time to help clients articulate the basis for their request is at the time of the request. There are tools, techniques, and tips to help clients better articulate or express what they are using as evidence a need exists or what they will take as evidence that the situation improved as a result of some intervention.

Tool 1a: Getting Clarity. A simple, but effective tool is shown in Table 11.1, Getting Clarity. It can be a spreadsheet or table that lists the problem and the evidence in different columns. Clients use it to capture what is known and what is suspected. The Issue column is where clients list the problem they are concerned about. The Evidence column is where clients note what information they are using as a basis for their conclusion that there is a problem and how pervasive it is. It helps clients connect the problem with the evidence. For example, the issue might be customer complaints, turnover of key personnel, or cost overruns. The questions then are about how clients know these are the issues. Tool 1a. Getting Clarity, as shown in Table 11.1, has examples in it. However, when using the tool put only that information in each column that is relevant to the situation.

There are at least two ways to use Tool 1a: (1) ask questions and fill it out based on what is learned or (2) prepare it ahead of time using one's best guess or past experience.

Table 11.1 Tool 1a. Getting Clarity

The Issue	The Evidence
Most issues can be classified under one of the following categories.	List source of the data on which the request is based.
1. Unhappy people (customer, employee, investor, supplier)	1. Annual morale survey; customer satisfaction surveys, angry emails
2. Poor productivity (too little work being done, too slow, using too many resources)	2. Call center productivity reports, missed production schedules
3. Poor financials (costs of sales or service too high, inadequate cash flow, margins too low)	3. Aging accounts receivables; product margins reports
4. Poor product performance (volume or quality too low, life cycle too short)	4. Error reports; customer complaints, service calls, warrantee calls
5. Inefficiencies (lack of coordination across units, underused capacity)	5. Project status reports
6. Lack of compliance (too many violations)	6. Regulatory citations; audit reports
7. Slipping image (negative reputation or public perceptions)	7. Investor confidence; frequency of recommendations by investment houses
8. Lack of safety (increasing of incidents or accidents)	8. Health insurance claims; number of incidents
9. Human resources (turnover, talent management, complaints, cost of training)	9. Exit interview data; number of complaints or grievances
10. Other	10. Other

Technique and Tip 1. Ask Questions. A simple technique is to probe, simply asking for more information about the logic behind the request. For example, if clients were told it seemed they had given the situation a lot of thought and the goal was to not waste their time or misuse their resources, they may be more willing to openly discuss the basis on which they decided there was a problem. They may be more willing to share what led them to the conclusion that an action or a solution was needed. The intent is to get clients to explain what they have seen happening that convinced them that a solution is needed and what behaviors will convince them that the situation had improved. A tip is to position the questions asked of them as a desire to save time, avoid mistakes, and use resources wisely.

Most people are willing to share their experiences and reasoning if the request is not experienced as a statement of doubt about how they made the decision but rather a genuine interest in better understanding the problem.

Technique and Tip 2. Come Prepared and Have an Organization Scheme. It is best to have measures and metrics already in mind before discussing a problem or a solution. This is easier to do when one has more experience with a client or a performance problem. The list of measures and metrics are used to facilitate a more robust conversation with clients. A technique that supports this tip is to develop an organizing scheme for measures that quickly presents a mental image or reference point about how to evaluate a need or a solution. Table 11.2, Function and Program, Measures presents one way of organizing measures. It separates measuring a function's worth from that of a solution's worth. It also suggests measures that clients may already be thinking about, but may not express.

Measures of Contribution. These measures are used to judge the degree overall that the learning and performance function adds value to the organization. Examples of contribution might be

1. *Alignment*—The degree clients see the link between what actions are being proposed and their needs being met. The metric might be the number of programs explicitly tied to major initiatives.
2. *Productivity*—The degree clients see how much was delivered and how timely the work was done. Metrics might be the number of programs produced within a year and the lapse time in days or weeks between the request and the delivery.
3. *Cost competitive*—The degree clients see the use of cost competitive resources and their being used wisely. Metrics might be the number and cost of internal and external resources used to develop solutions.

Table 11.2 Function and Program Measures

Function's Measures of Contribution	Program's Measures of Success
Alignment	Satisfaction
Productivity	Learning
Cost competitive	Transfer or behavior
Customer relations	Goal accomplishment
	Time to proficiency
	Cost of proficiency

4. *Customer relations*—The degree clients experience the learning and performance improvement function as easy to work with. Metrics might be the average rating of customers' opinion on a survey and the number of anecdotes commending the function's work.

Program Measures. These are the factors clients consider when judging the worth of specific products, programs, and services. They might include:

1. *Satisfaction*—How satisfied stakeholders are with the current state and how satisfied they are after implementing the solution. Metrics might be the average rating of opinions on a survey and the standard deviation (the amount of variance) among those opinions.

2. *Learning*—How proficient workers were before a solution was implemented compared to after it was implemented. Metrics might be pre- and post-test scores, how frequently completed work met standards, and how quickly tasks were done.

3. *Transfer or behavior change*—How many people's behavior changed after the solution was implemented and how quickly did it change. Metrics might be the frequency of discrete behaviors and how many days it took for those behaviors to show up consistently.

4. *Goal accomplishment*—To what degree did the solution deliver on the promise? The metric depends on the goal. If the goal was increased sales, the metric might be the number of proposals accepted or the number of leads that converted to sales.

5. *Time to proficiency*—How long does it take to bring people to proficiency compared to what it was after the implementation of the solution. The metric might be quantity of work performed within a given time frame, accuracy of work, or how quickly people could do the work to standard without supervision.

6. *Cost of proficiency*—What it costs in time and dollars to bring a workforce to proficiency and how much it would cost to increase the level of proficiency. The metrics might include the fee for external resources compared to the aggregate cost of using employees, such as salary, benefits, facilities, equipment, and so forth.

Measures by Level. Table 11.3 is another example of how to organize issues, that is, at the workplace, work, or worker levels. The issues listed are examples.

Each identified issue then lends itself to questions about what the evidence is to determine whether there is a problem and what can be used to measure improvement. For all three levels, the measures and metrics might be the frequency of rework, misused resources, loss of talent, and the like. What may be different are the cause and the solution. When clients are given a menu of measures and metrics, they are in a better position to pick the ones that are most

Table 11.3 Issues by Level

Workplace	Work	Worker
Lack of or inconsistent direction	Poorly designed jobs, tasks, or process	Lack of skills or knowledge
Inadequate resources, equipment, or job tools	Lack of meaningful work	Insufficient capacity
Insufficient feedback	Unclear or inefficient procedures	Lack of physical capability
Inappropriate incentives	Inadequate job or task supports (job aids)	Lack of interest
Inadequate compensation	Other	Other
Other		

relevant, accessible, and would help them make better decisions. Having an organizing schema and using tools like that shown in Table 11.1 also allow clients to add metrics meaningful to their situation. In the process it will become clear on what basis clients currently judge that there is a problem, the adequacy of the work done to address those problems, and the value of the solutions.

2. Set a Baseline

The baseline is simply the current state of affairs. Without this information there is little or no basis for determining whether circumstances improved as a result of an intervention or solution. The tool used to gain clarity (Table 11.1) can be expanded to record the baseline by simply adding another column, as shown in Table 11.4. The second column lists what is being used as evidence of a need,

Table 11.4 Tool 1b. Getting a Baseline

The Issue	The Evidence	The Current State/Baseline This is where as many of the actual metrics that exist go
Unhappy employees	Survey data	Satisfaction rating of 3.7 on 5-point scale
Loss of key talent	Turnover rate	Turnover for last twelve months
Unhappy customers	Complaints	Complaints for last years
Poor cash flow	Aging receivables	Receivables at 90, 120 days
Inadequate sales	Loss of sales	Percentage of proposals that are accepted

and the third column is where the baseline is recorded. Table 11.4 has examples of the type of information to might capture in the Getting Clarity Tool.

Technique and Tip 3. Do Not Be Afraid of Fuzzy Data; Instead Improve It. Sometimes in our desire to be precise, people too easily reject or are suspicious of information about the current state of affairs because it is old or the client has doubts about its accuracy. A technique that helps is to take the data in whatever condition they are and suggest using the solution as an opportunity to get better data. For example, when clients say "yes, but. . . . " to the suggestion to use customer satisfaction survey results as a baseline, first discuss what other data might be available. For example, in the retail industry the number of returns and aging receivables might be used to augment customer satisfaction data. In the financial services industry, the number of referrals and renewal of contracts for services could augment customer satisfaction data. Next acknowledge that the data may be incomplete, but offer that they still provide a baseline, and future measurement will produce better data. Finally, offer suggestions about how to get more accurate baseline data such as leveraging data from other sources.

3. Leverage Data Already Being Collected

One of the frequently cited excuses for not evaluating program effectiveness is the argument that evaluation costs money and takes time. What people unfortunately conclude is that they lack the money and the time to measure change efficiently or cost-effectively. The argument presumes the measurement has to start from scratch or the beginning, so to speak. However, if clients leverage the measurement that is already occurring, they can save time and avoid unnecessary expenses. Table 11.5 has examples of measurement activities commonly done. All of these measures could be leveraged to identify needs, set baselines, and measure improvement.

Table 11.5 Typical Ongoing Measurement

Annual employee morale survey usually done by human resources

Customer satisfaction survey done by marketing

Exit interviews done by human resources

Safety reports usually done by safety or quality control

Call center technical and customer support call sheets, usually done by the call centers themselves

Periodic compliance studies done by internal audit or quality assurance

Aging receivables report usually done by accounting, specifically accounts receivables

Sales logs with number of calls, who was called, usually done by sales staff or their managers

Technique and Tip 4. Assume the Data Already Exists. Most organizations collect an immense amount of data about their costs, operations, customer satisfaction, and the like. Therefore, the tip is to assume someone in the organization can already produce meaningful measures and metrics. The technique is to partner or collaborate with other departments that already capture different types of performance data. Going back to Tool 1a, the table has a column for current evidence. These are the data the organization is already getting. A question clients might be asked is, ''How do they use these data to measure change or improvement?' A challenge might be getting access to the data. A tip is to offer to help the other departments get better data or help them argue their case for greater management support.

4. Track Leading Indicators

Leading indicators are data that predict success or failure. A common mistake is to wait until a lot of time has passed to determine whether circumstances improved. Waiting also results in lost opportunities to reinforce a solution or to take corrective action. Examples of leading indicators have been added to Tool 1a. Getting Clarity in Table 11.6. Another column can be added or replace the baseline data column with one for suggested leading indicators. In most instances, the data sources for the leading indicators are the same as the baseline, but are captured and reported more frequently.

Table 11.6 Tool 1c. Expanding Clarity

The Issue	The Evidence	Leading Indicators
Unhappy employees	Survey data	Number of grievances monthly
Loss of key talent	Turnover rate	Turnover monthly or quarterly plus ongoing exit interview data
Unhappy customers	Complaints	Monthly complaints or complaints from key customers
Poor cash flow	Aging receivables	Receivables at 30, 60 days
Inadequate sales	Loss of sales	Number of monthly proposals submitted, number of customers that meet the qualification criteria.

In other instances, the information sources for the leading indicators are not the same as for the baseline, and, therefore, would have to be collected. Here are some examples:

- If the goal is for employees to get more timely feedback on their performance on the premise that this will result in fewer grievances and improved efficiencies; and the solutions include asking supervisors to do more frequent performance reviews, to redesign the performance review form, to automate the process, and to train supervisors on how to use the form, the leading indicators might be

- The number of supervisors asking for technical support to use the new system each month
- The number of reviews posted on the automated system monthly
- The number of employees reporting that they got reviews in the last thirty or sixty days

- If the goal is to improve customer retention on the premise that it will increase profits or margins and cash flow because repeat customers require less technical support and are more likely to buy more product and buy it more quickly; and the solutions are to offer technical training to customers, to certify customers who complete the training, and to have account executives call customers more frequently, then the leading indicators might be

- The number of customers requesting information about the training and certification
- The number of customers participating in the training and applying for certification
- The number of account executives calling key customers more frequently
- The average sales cycle times of customers who are signed up for training and eventually certified compared to those who do not sign up for training
- The frequency and time duration of technical support to clients who are participating in training and later certified compared to those who are not trained or certified

Technique and Tip 5. Think of Leading Indicators as Formative Evaluation or a Way to Measure Transfer. Typically, formative evaluation occurs before the launch of a product or program. It is done to confirm the usability of a solution and the accuracy of the information. However, formative evaluation can also be done after the launch to measure usability rates and the target audience's initial perceptions. In this case what is being measured is the rate of transfer; the goal is to identify early what needs to be done to increase usage and overcome resistance. Unfortunately, organizations often invest in a program, launch it, and then believe the target audience will automatically use it or adopt the new desired behaviors without further intervention. However, if the target audience does not use the program or adopt the new behaviors in a timely fashion, the odds are they will not do it later. Therefore, formative evaluation that is done after the launch can increase the odds that a program will be successful. A technique is to more purposefully do post-launch formative evaluation, or measure transfer, and to decide ahead of time what indicators to use to measure acceptance and resistance. In this case, the indicators become leading indicators or predictors.

Technique and Tip 6. Use Self-Report and Let People Know It. Self-report is the process of asking a target audience to report on its own behavior. Should someone question the validity of self-report, there is some research that shows it is valid (Norwick, Choi, & Ben-Shachar, 2002). The technique is to survey the people whose behavior is expected to change, usually the target audience of the solution. For example, if the solution was for people to use a procedure, system, or performance support tool, simply ask them how frequently they are using it. A tip is to let people know in advance that they will be asked at some time in the future about their usage. Another tip is to be sure to get permission from the target audience's supervisor to solicit their input and then be sure to tell them permission was granted so they know any future questions are legitimate. Tool 2a, as shown in Table 11.7, suggests a five-point scale for surveying a target audience and possible questions.

Table 11.7 Tool 2a. Survey for Self-Report

Possible Questions:

1. How helpful was the pre-work (training, job aid, and so forth)?
2. Think about the first time you did X (used X and so forth), how well did you do X?
3. How often since the training (program launch) have you done or used X?

Scales:

5 = Very helpful	4	3 = Somewhat helpful	2	1 = Not helpful	0 = Didn't do
5 = Very well	4	3 = Somewhat okay	2	1 = Not well	0 = Didn't do
5 = Daily	4	3 = Off and on	2	1 = Rarely	0 = Didn't do

Technique and Tip 7. Poll Vested Parties to Confirm Self-Report Data. Should clients continue to doubt the self-report data, a technique is to confirm the results by polling others who have a vested interest in the adoption of the new behaviors, such as supervisors, team leads, or customers. However, let people know in advance that they will be asked for their observations, and remind them what the behaviors are that they should be looking for. Tool 2b, as shown in Table 11.8, suggests some questions and scales for polling vested parties to corroborate self-report data.

Table 11.8 Tool 2b. Confirming Self-Report Data

Possible Questions:

1. How well did the training (or information announcement, roll-out of the new procedure, and so forth) prepare X to do the task?

2. How much assistance did he or she require immediately after the training (information, launch, roll-out)?

3. How effectively did he or she do X?

Scales:

5 = Very prepared	4	3 = Somewhat prepared	2	1 = Not prepared	0 = Didn't do
5 = Worked independently	4	3 = Required assistance on more difficult assignments	2	1 = Required a lot of guidance on easy assignments	0 = Didn't do
5 = Executed very well	4	3 = About average	2	1 = Not executed well	0 = Didn't do

5. Analyze the Data

The value of data comes from the insights they provide. However, insights require some analysis, which usually means some mathematical and statistical manipulation. Analysis also requires skill in sampling, instrument design, and quantitative and qualitative analytics.

Technique and Tip 8. Get Help from the Experts. Experts can suggest the best ways to get data, how to design data instruments so they are effective, how to sample people or work products so clients can have confidence in the conclusions, and how to analyze the data. A tip is to form a relationship with staff in the statistics department at a local university. Such faculty and graduate students have access to and experience in using data analysis software and, therefore, can save time and increase clients' confidence in the results.

Technique and Tip 9. Understand the Different Types of Data. In the world of learning and performance, data come in many forms; therefore, it is important to understand the differences when starting to interpret the data. Data are usually classified as:

- Hard data or data that can be independently verified, whether they are facts or opinions, or expressed in numbers or words.

- Soft data or data that cannot or are not independently verified, whether they are in the form of numbers or words.

- Quantitative data are numerical data (counts, percentages, weights, degrees, and so forth) and, therefore, lend themselves to some mathematical or statistical manipulation. They are used to predict outcomes or show relationships between variables. Quantitative data may be hard or soft, depending on whether or not they were independently verified. They are usually collected through the use of tests and measurement instruments such as weight scales, temperature probes, rulers, and the like.

- Qualitative data are data that reflect opinions and may be expressed in words or numbers, as in the example, "On a scale of 1 to 5 with 1 meaning strongly disagree and 5 meaning strongly agree, how much do you agree or not with the statement X?" When they are expressed as numbers, they can be mathematically manipulated, but the data are still qualitative because they are measures of opinions. Also, when opinions are expressed as words or phrases, the frequency of specific words or phrases can be counted and manipulated mathematically. Qualitative data may be hard or soft, depending on whether or not they were independently verified. Qualitative data are usually collected through the use of interviews, observations, document checks, and surveys, in-basket exercises, and the like.

Here are two examples:

- Self-report data using a five-point scale are soft (not verified), qualitative data (opinions even though the opinions have a numerical rating and can be averaged). Because a scale is used, the opinions can be mathematically manipulated. The ratings can be added and an average calculated along with percentages. Even the standard deviation of the cumulative scores can be computed. However, if data from another independent source are added, such as a survey sent to bosses, audit reports, or marketing studies, the data become hard data because now the results can be validated.

- Results from a focus group session are soft qualitative data; however, adding corroborative data from another source such as exit interviews or surveys makes the data hard qualitative data.

The tip is to use data gathering methods that get the required data and to find ways to independently validate the initial findings. For example, test data that measures how much people know about how to do a task (quantitative data), might be validated by examining data from time sheets or production reports (measures of how much they did), quality assurance (measures of how well they did it), or direct observation of their performing the task in the work setting (measures of how they did the task). Test data alone is not a valid measure of whether or not people can do a task. A technique is to go back to Tool 1 designed to help get clarity and add yet another column for how you will validate the data you gather when measuring the effectiveness of your solutions as shown in Table 11.9. Getting Clarity Expanded More.

Table 11.9 Tool 2c. Getting Clarity Expanded More

Issue	Evidence	Baseline	Leading Indicators	How Validate
Unhappy employees	Morale surveys	3.7 rating	Number of grievances monthly	Exit interviews

Technique and Tip 10. Understand What Descriptive and Inferential Statistics Do and When Each Is Used. The tip is to understand the more common statistical methods and what questions each is intended to answer or to measure. There are two types of statistics, descriptive and inferential.

Descriptive Statistics. Descriptive statistics are used to evaluate data derived from interviews, surveys, focus groups, document checks, observations, time studies, and the like. They are also used to analyze test data by calculating how many people received what score, what the average score was, and how many scored significantly higher or lower than the majority of the group. Commonly used descriptive statistics are

- *Frequency count*—Answers the question of how often a value occurred, such as how many people took a test, how many passed the test, how many scored 70 or above, how many used the sales job aid, and so forth.
- *Percentage*—Answers the question of how many compared to the whole group did each of these activities, such as what portion of the group could have taken the test, passed the test, and used the job aid.
- *Averages*—Answer the question about what is typical. There are three ways to calculate the average. One is to calculate the *mean*, or the arithmetic average. *Mode* is the most frequent value, and *median* is that point at which there are an equal number of values above it as there are below it. Collectively, the mean, mode, and median help clients determine what is typical or common. For example, averages answer questions like, "Overall how well did people do on the test? There are three ways to answer this question: (1) the mean test score was X; (2) the most frequently earned test score was Y; and (3) half of the people scored above Z and half of the group scored below Z.

- *Standard deviation*—Answers the question about what is not typical because a value is too far above or too far below the mean. Values that are one or more standard deviations above or below the mean are considered significant.

Inferential Statistics. Inferential statistics are used to determine whether there is a relationship between two variables, whether from two groups or different data from the same group. Inferential statistics help compare people's performance before the intervention and their performance afterward, match people's actual performance to what was expected of them, and answer the question of whether changing something produced a change in something else. Inferential statistics require the use of formulas and statistical tables to interpret the results. There are many different types of inferential statistical formulae. Here are three commonly used ones:

- *Correlation coefficient (Spearman Rho)*—Answers the question of whether there is a relationship between two sets of data. For example, it answers the question of whether or not success on a test influences people's tenure on the job, or the opposite question: Did people's tenure on job influence their performance on a test?
- *Chi-square goodness of fit*—Answers the question of whether or not a value is different from what was expected. For example, it answers the question of whether people's performance on a test was what bosses expected.
- *Two-tailed t tests*—Commonly used to determine whether pre- and post-tests scores are significantly different.

Working with an expert is especially helpful when deciding how to analyze data, what methods to use, and what conclusions can be safely drawn from the results.

Technique and Tip 11. Do Not Confuse Correlation with Causation. Correlation measures the relationship between two factors, such as test scores and job retention. It answers the question about the degree to which a factor is influenced by a change in another factor. The influence may be positive in that, when there is a change in one factor's value, the other factor's value changes in the same direction, that is, they both increase or decrease. For example, assume you want to know whether people with higher test scores stay in a job longer than those with lower test scores. The correlation is positive if those with higher test scores do stay in the job longer. A negative correlation means that, as the value of the first factor increases, the value of the second factor decreases, that is, they go in opposite directions. For example, people with higher test scores seem to spend less time in a job. If there is no correlation, then there is no relationship between test scores and job tenure.

Causation measures the degree to which one factor causes a change in another factor. In this case, a goal may be to determine whether higher test scores (seemingly being smarter) causes people to stay in a job longer. Causation is much more difficult to prove because the other factors that may contribute to tenure have to be ruled out or eliminated. In the case of job tenure, it is important to isolate test scores from age, proximity to work, the relationship with the boss or co-workers, salary, the presence of other employment opportunities, and so on. Because of the need to isolate the one variable being measured, tests of causation require controlling the other variables, called "controlled studies." These studies select two identical groups and do something to one group (such as train or offer incentives) and see whether something happens to the first group compared to the other. For example, to determine whether offering tuition reimbursement reduced turnover, it would be offered to one group of employees, but not to another group, and then we would see whether there was any effect on retention. However, it would be essential that the two groups be identical on other factors, such as education, job experience, and age, work with bosses with identical characteristics and management styles, and so on. Therefore, the tip is to do correlations unless there is the luxury of doing a controlled group study and sufficient time to determine whether the assumptions about how performance will be affective come true.

Technique and Tip 12. Use Tools and Guidelines Already Available. A tip is to make use of the proven tools and guidelines developed by others. For example, the book *Performance-Based Evaluation* (Hale, 2002) comes with a disk that has forty-four tools, including ones for developing surveys, designing and conducting interviews, conducting focus groups, and doing observation. It also has guidelines on how to analyze the results from interviews, surveys, focus groups, and observations. The book *The Value of Learning* (Phillips & Phillips, 2007) is full of guidelines on how to get and interpret data. This handbook and the references in this and the other chapters also provide a list of proven resources that can help save time and money. It is smart to leverage the work of others.

6. Tell the Story

It is not enough to gather and analyze data. It is important to communicate what was done, what data were used, and what changes were tracked. Communicating helps keep clients engaged and may prevent the misuse of the data or the propensity to draw the wrong conclusions. Telling the story goes beyond reporting the results or comparing the before and after states. It means presenting information in ways that help clients see relationships and implications.

Technique and Tip 14. Use Pictures or Graphics. Once data are analyzed, the numbers may be sufficient by themselves to tell the story. However, clients may not be willing to spend the time reading the detail. A technique is to develop an illustration that reflects the whole story. The illustration can take many different forms. For example, it may be a chart, graph, diagram, or another form. The goal is to communicate what was done, the agreements made, and the results achieved in one picture. One side benefit of simply telling the story is a more productive conversation about what was accomplished and what must still be done to fully appreciate the benefits of the solution. Figure 11.1 shows Tool 3. Tell the Story. Tool 3, like Tool 1, is meant to be modified or adapted to each situation. For example, it is missing a timeline, which can be easily added when illustrating a specific story.

The Story

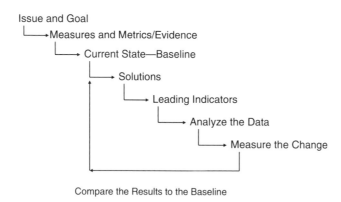

Figure 11.1 Tool 3. Tell the Story.

Example: Reducing the Cost of Sales. Assume a consultant, as part of a team, is asked to help reduce the cost of sales. The cost of sales is mostly driven by the time and related travel expenses invested by the salesperson in prospecting (repeatedly calling the prospect to negotiate a convenient time to meet and finally meeting with the prospect to get enough information to develop a proposal), then developing and delivering the proposal, conducting follow-up calls and meetings, and so on. The more time the salesperson spends on getting the contract, the more costly the sale. The costs are even higher when the time invested does not result in a sale, since this cost of time has to be spread across successful sales. Currently 40 percent of the proposals are unsuccessful as they do not result in a sale. A deeper examination of the problem showed that one factor that contributed to the failure to get the contract was that sales-persons do not appropriately qualify the prospects; instead they engage in the full sales process independent of whether the prospect is potentially a viable customer. It is also learned that that sales persons are rewarded for the number of prospects they have in their sales pipelines, not for doing a good job of screening out prospects less likely to buy.

The team recommended that the company change the way it measures and rewards the sales staff and adopt a more rigorous process for qualifying prospects. The sales staff was trained on the new qualifying process. Sales management endorsed the new qualifying process and agreed to reward sales staff on using the process. Sales management tracked and reported monthly the number of pre-qualified prospects in the pipeline compared to the number not pre-qualified and percent that resulted in sales. Finance compared and reported last year's aggregate sales call expenses with the coming year's expenses on a monthly basis. Everyone agreed the leading indicators were the frequency the new process was used and the number of qualified prospects in the pipeline. Finance also agreed to correlate the number of sales people trained in the qualifying process with sales and the cost of sales. At the end of the year, 80 percent of the leads were qualified using the new process and the number of unsuccessful proposals dropped to 12 percent and the cost of sales dropped by almost 25 percent. Figure 11.2 helps tell the story.

Example: Shorten the Time to Proficiency. Assume a team is commissioned to shorten the time it takes to bring new hires to full proficiency, meaning they can independently perform all of the tasks to standard measured in terms of accuracy, completeness, and safety. Currently new hires complete a 9-week training program; however, according to their managers it takes an additional five months of on-the-job experience before they are considered "proficient." Nine weeks plus five months were accepted as the baseline. The team recommended that electronic performance support tools be created to reinforce the

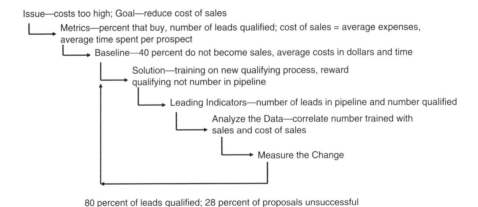

Issue—costs too high; Goal—reduce cost of sales
    Metrics—percent that buy, number of leads qualified; cost of sales = average expenses, average time spent per prospect
        Baseline—40 percent do not become sales, average costs in dollars and time
            Solution—training on new qualifying process, reward qualifying not number in pipeline
                Leading Indicators—number of leads in pipeline and number qualified
                    Analyze the Data—correlate number trained with sales and cost of sales
                        Measure the Change

80 percent of leads qualified; 28 percent of proposals unsuccessful compared to 40 percent successful; Cost of sales down 25 percent.

Figure 11.2 Reducing Cost of Sales.

training and support new hires when they are doing the more complex tasks. The team also recommended that new hires be told what criteria will be used to judge their proficiency. Information about the evidence of proficiency and the use of the performance support tools was then incorporated into the training. Once the support tools were developed, new hires reported weekly on how frequently they used them and which ones they used; this also reinforced the use of the tools. Managers were asked monthly to rate the new hires' level of proficiency. Asking managers to rate the new hires on a monthly basis also focused the managers' attention on the behaviors and results they had agreed were evidence of proficiency; this also reinforced the desired behaviors. Usage and managers' ratings were accepted as leading indicators in that the data were reported in monthly management meetings to sustain interest in the initiative and support for the tools. To determine if the new training format with the added performance support tools was effective, the time to proficiency of new hires trained in the new format was compared to that of new hires trained using the old format. The time to proficiency went from five months to six weeks. Figures 11.3 and 11.4 were used to tell the story.

Technique and Tip 15. Remember That Two Heads Are Better Than One. Consolidating information into one or two graphics helps to focus on the important metrics, the assumptions about what behaviors will more likely lead to improved results, and what clients are willing to accept as evidence of improvement. It also is more respectful of clients' time. A tip is to collaborate with clients and colleagues when deciding how to best tell the story. Another tip

Unstructured job experience

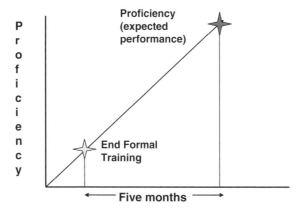

Figure 11.3 Old Time to Proficiency.

Performance Support and Feedback

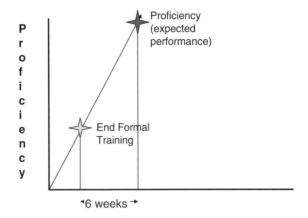

Figure 11.4 New Time to Proficiency.

is to create a draft using Tool 3, for example, and let clients modify it. The goal is to learn ways to more quickly communicate the situation, the measures and metrics, and the measurement process. A tip is to think less is more and simpler is easier. However, communicating complex relationships is not simple, which is why it helps to work with a team to come up with innovative ideas for telling the story.

When to Apply the Rules, Tools, Techniques, and Tips

Rules and tools are best used when clients are considering a significant investment of money and resources either to fix a problem or take advantage of an opportunity. They are also helpful when anticipating questions or doubts about the usefulness or wisdom of a future or past investment.

SUMMARY

This handbook contains many resources and guidelines for evaluating interventions. This chapter has focused on six rules, three tools, and fifteen tips and techniques for measuring the need for intervention and the results of intervening. Collectively, the rules, tools, techniques, and tips are intended to increase the odds that evaluation is done, is cost-effective, and is meaningful. For example, to increase the odds that evaluations:

- Add value to clients—Make sure there is clarity of purpose and agreement on the measures and metrics.

- Are done and done well—Leverage the measurement activities of other groups in the organization.

- Produce results that will be accepted as valid—Work with measurement experts and involve clients in the process of identifying metrics.

- Help interventions fully realize their potential—Track leading indictors to identify the need for further intervention early.

- Are appreciated—Learn to tell the story simply of what was done and the results that were achieved.

References

Dessinger, J. C., & Moseley, J. L. (2004). *Confirmative evaluation: Practical strategies for valuing continuous improvement*. San Francisco: Pfeiffer.

Guerra-López, I. (2008). *Performance evaluation: Proven approaches for improving program and organizational performance*. San Francisco: Jossey-Bass.

Hale, J. A. (2002). *Performance-based evaluation: Tools and techniques to measure the impact of training*. San Francisco: Pfeiffer.

Hale, J. A. (2007). *Performance consultant's fieldbook: Tools and techniques for improving organizations and people* (2nd ed.). San Francisco: Pfeiffer.

Norwick, R., Choi, Y. S., & Ben-Shachar, T. (2002). In defense of self-reports. *The Observer, 15*(3).

Phillips, P. P., & Phillips, J. J. (2007). *The value of learning: How organizations capture value and ROI and translate into support, improvement, and funds*. San Francisco: Pfeiffer.

Stolovitch, H., & Keeps, E. (2004). *Analysis and return on investment toolkit*. San Francisco: Pfeiffer.

CHAPTER TWELVE

Testing Strategies

Verifying Capability to Perform

Peter R. Hybert

W hat is the best way to assess that someone

- Knows how to do the job?
- Is ready to "go solo"?

Beyond general impressions, what is the best way to verify someone's capability to perform the job? The standard answer would be "create a test."

Presently, the business climate seems to be increasing its emphasis on testing and certification. Seemingly, more businesses are using testing in a training context—as a way to establish a baseline entry point, as a way to "test out" of unneeded training, or as a way to ensure capability at the end of training. Many professional associations and outside companies are offering certifications (for example, Microsoft, Project Management Institute, American Society for Quality, American Society for Training and Development, International Society for Performance Improvement) as a way for employees to build up credentials as evidence of their capability. In some cases, especially in regulated environments, testing is even used as a "gate" to control entry into the workplace (meaning that employees need to be qualified before they are allowed to go "solo").

Once it is decided that a test is needed, it is easy to jump directly to creating a series of multiple-choice and true-false questions. However, testing is too important for this haphazard approach. It is worth taking the time and effort to define an overall strategy for testing that fits the performance and the business situation. Many, if not most, of the key decisions are business decisions, not training decisions. How does management want to run the workplace? How much control do they need or want over who is allowed to perform what work? What regulatory requirements exist? What liability and risk are they accepting when they allow employees to perform work for which they may not be capable? How much effort (that is, infrastructure, time, attention) are they willing to spend on testing?

Another reason that test strategy is important is that testing can be challenged. All testing involves evaluating a sample of the total performance and, if someone dislikes the result, he or she may well challenge whether the test was fair or relevant. Legal challenges can be expensive and damaging to the credibility of the organization. If a business intends to test, then it will want to be on solid footing.

An important business consideration is that effort spent creating and implementing testing adds cost to the business. Technically, it also adds no value . . . at least not to the learner or the ultimate performance. It is similar to quality inspection in manufacturing. Testing is necessary to ensure an acceptable end product, but the actual act of checking for quality is verification; it only provides peace of mind. From the standpoint of cost, the fewer resources needed for inspection, the better. The best result is when no defects are found . . . which means the test was unnecessary after all. Much like insurance, it is better if it is never needed. How much to invest in testing is a business decision.

As an aside, when the performers receive feedback on their test performance, there is value. But, if the feedback is used for learning, the ''inspection'' has become more than a test—it is now a learning activity. And, because it changes the performance, it is no longer a measure of capability but a continuous improvement mechanism.

Finally, there are times when testing is just poorly done—superstitions and ungrounded assumptions are often built into the way tests are developed and administered which undermine their usefulness and accuracy.

COMMON PROBLEMS AND MISCONCEPTIONS ABOUT TESTING

There is no such thing as a completely objective test. All tests require judgment, even ''objective'' tests. Making a single defendable correct answer does not make a test objective. How was that test item selected? How was it worded? How was the test administered? All these decisions affected the question in front of the learner and all probably involved some subjective decision making. If the testing is intended to reflect capability to perform, consider how many job situations occur in which there is one right answer that the performer simply needs to choose from a list of options . . . not many.

Tests test whatever they ask the performer to do. If a test asks a participant a multiple-choice question, it tests the ability to perform "trial and error" reasoning. Good test-takers can eliminate some of the options and improve their chances of getting it right. In fact, there are books published to help college students figure out how to do just that. On the other hand, token testing is set up merely to meet a compliance requirement; everybody passes because they have to. In this kind of test, all that is tested is the employee's ability to "go through the motions because in life there are stupid rules that should just be followed"— it may be easier, but it is probably not something to encourage.

The common "cut score" of 80 percent is more a custom than a reasoned decision—at the least, there is judgment involved (Shrock & Coscarelli, 2007). In some cases, people insist on 100 percent as the passing score because they are unwilling to specifically identify the 20 percent that is not important. In other cases, there is a perceived risk about any employee who does not pass a test, even if he or she passes it later. The concern is that, if something happens in the future, those test records could be used as evidence that the company knew the employee was not capable. So to cover this eventuality, the tests are made very easy; they no longer test the boundary conditions that would clearly delineate capability from non-capability (FDA, 2008).

In short, many tests really do not measure what their authors really want to know. At best, they test only memory, test-taking skills, or the ability to do abstract reasoning. But they rarely look at the overall ability to execute a task or perform a job in a real situation. If memory, test-taking skills, or abstract reasoning skills were reliable indicators of capability, it might be an acceptable tradeoff but people can perform poorly at tests and still get the job done quite well. This is the same phenomenon as people who do poorly in school but exceptionally well in business. This is not saying anything about school or business, but simply that the criteria for success in school are not necessarily the same as for success in business. *If the goal is to verify that employees have the capability to perform, then test the ability to perform.* Knowledge testing does not do this; performance testing does.

Finally, there is the question of cost for value. Using a knowledge test for important decisions such as hiring, promotion, or pay requires a significant investment to ensure that the company is not exposed to legal risk through challenges of bias or validity. It takes a lot more effort to develop and implement a knowledge test. In many business settings, there is time and cost pressure. Large corporations are typically risk-averse. Performance testing can reduce these concerns while also providing a better picture of learner capability.

What can be done to implement effort testing? Below are four keys to a testing strategy that verifies capability to perform.

- Develop an overall testing plan that supports and is integrated with business management practices.

- Develop testing plans for strategic areas of the performance; do not test everything.

- Design a logical "library" of tests that can be used in training, on-the-job, or even in selection situations.

- Use performance testing when possible and knowledge testing only when required or when there is no other alternative.

WHAT IS A PERFORMANCE TEST?

Performance tests are exactly what they sound like—the candidate performs a task and the evaluator observes the process or evaluates the output using the same criteria used to evaluate real job performance. If employees can perform, they pass.

A knowledge test, on the other hand, asks employees questions about facts, rules, classifications, and occasionally even situations so that the employees can describe a response believed to be correct. In many cases, test-makers make these tests easier to grade by making employees select options from a list, rather than generate their answer from scratch.

These two approaches to testing are much different—see Table 12.1 below.

To take these definitions even further, let's look at the difference between a *performance* test and a *skill* test. They are really not the same thing. A skill test may consist of performing something, but it may still not be a test of the actual performance.

Table 12.1 Performance Tests vs. Knowledge Tests

Performance Tests	Knowledge Tests
Test real, usable "chunks" of work.	Test a sample of the supporting information needed to perform a real, usable chunk of work.
Incorporate "noise" factors normally present in the work environment (such as working in a respirator or on a ladder).	Assume the "noise factors" are not relevant to performance.
Can be used as a coaching or training tool as well as a test. (They don't have to be kept hidden.)	Require additional administrative overhead, for example, extra versions or effort to scramble/randomize the questions and keeping the answers secret.
Test the ability to do.	Test ancillary abilities that may not really be required for the job (such as facility with reading, writing, interpretation).

For example, consider the typing test that is often used as a requirement for data-entry jobs. The assumption is that, if applicants can manipulate a keyboard at a certain rate with only a certain amount of errors, they will be able to perform the job. This may be true. Yet, many jobs are measured by more than just the rate of data entered. Imagine someone making a hiring decision for a data-entry job. Is it better to hire the fastest typist or to hire someone who notices when something seems to be incorrect? Is someone who just types whatever is provided more desirable than someone who notices gaps or errors? The employer may be better off hiring someone who would actually look up and insert an address into a letter, instead of someone who would literally type ''put address here'' right into the document.

A typing test measures a skill, not the entire performance. A better test would be to identify some typical work products (for example, letters, reports, presentations) and give the individual a reasonable amount of time to create them and then review the complete performance. This testing would be more reflective of that person's actual capability to perform on the job.

COMMENTS ON KNOWLEDGE TESTING

Until now, the chapter has emphasized performance tests. However, there are still occasions wherein a knowledge test must be used. A knowledge test can be an effective way to confirm that learners remember information they have received, can apply rules they have learned, and even determine strategies about performance.

Where knowledge tests are used, it is important to be clear about the reason for using them, their limitations, and how the results will be used. A great deal of complexity can arise from introducing statistics and validation into the discussion and is beyond the scope of this chapter. However, a key principle to apply is ''get as close as possible to performance.''

As mentioned earlier, work situations almost never present a decision with a clear list of five options or only a binary (true or false) decision. But portions of the process may require a decision or an answer to a question. Those situations can be developed into performance-like questions—where the performer can demonstrate, if not ''know-how,'' at least ''know-what'' as in ''know what to do.''

GUIDELINES FOR TESTING—A PRACTITIONER'S VIEW

Training professionals working on designing or developing tests often have to work within a set of limitations and challenges.

- Most practitioners have to move quickly.

- In many cases there is a small audience to address, frequently under one thousand people.
- There are often multiple stakeholders. The testing strategy needs to meet the requirements of business leaders, regulators, line managers, and employees.
- Budgets are typically limited, especially for something that may only be a quality check.
- There are cultural expectations and biases against tests that must be overcome due to people's experience in school.
- Changes in the business climate drive ongoing maintenance of the content over time and, possibly, even re-testing.
- They need to avoid rewriting things that already exist, for example, taking the procedure and turning it into a test by putting checkmarks next to each step.
- Finally, they need to really test what their learners need to know and whether learners actually have the capability to perform.

Performance tests meet the requirements above and should be the weapon of choice for most testing, especially when it is being used for decisions that affect the employee's future. Knowledge tests make most sense for prerequisite concepts and informal "checks for understanding."

TEST PLANNING PROCESS

If testing is used in a larger context, whether a qualification/certification system or as part of a training strategy, it is important to design an approach that applies testing at the right places and in the right amounts to meet the business need without unnecessarily adding time and cost to the process.

The first consideration is how testing supports the overall business intent. After that, specify individual tests and how they fit into the performance sequence, learning strategy, and role requirements. The final phase is actually designing and developing the test instruments. Although there are many alternatives paths to take, a general concept structure such as the one shown in Table 12.2 can help to guide thinking and provide a basis for the communication needed to make the combined business and training decisions.

TEST PLANNING CONCEPT MODEL

The model in Figure 12.1 illustrates a way to think through the decisions needed to define a test strategy. It is a way of visually breaking down the performance to

Table 12.2 Test Planning Process

Phase	Key Considerations/Activities
Define the Test Strategy	Where are "gates" or "checkpoints" needed?
	What will happen in the case of failure?
	Will employees need to pass a test only once or will periodic re-testing be required?
	Who will perform the testing?
	Where will testing be conducted?
Define the Overall Test Library	Identify the "assignable chunks" of performance
	Define individual tests (considering what is a manageable number as well as how to comprehensively cover the performance)
	Define an organization scheme for the test inventory
Design and Develop Individual Test Instruments	Define the scope and boundaries
	Decide whether to test "process" or "output"
	Decide whether to test actual or simulated performance (or whether in the workplace or in training)
	Define the specific "micro-criteria" to be evaluated

identify the key components. This breakdown can help the test designer choose where to place the measurements, that is, where to use testing to get the best information with the least risk and effort.

At the top of Figure 12.1, at the level of "Workplace/On-the-Job," is the actual work the employee performs. It could be a call center agent answering an incoming call, in which case the output would be an order or a refund or an answer. Or it could be a manufacturing operator, in which case the steps might be the actual manufacturing process and the output could be a component or even a finished product.

The middle level shows a partial view of the supporting capabilities needed to perform the work in the level above. This model is essentially like a learning hierarchy (Gagné, 1977) but instead of showing what is required to learn, it shows the "chunks" of capability needed to perform. This model works well for visualizing the relationship but it has a weakness. Quite often, the supporting capabilities are needed to perform multiple steps. Consequently, in trying to include all the links, the diagram can become unhelpfully complicated.

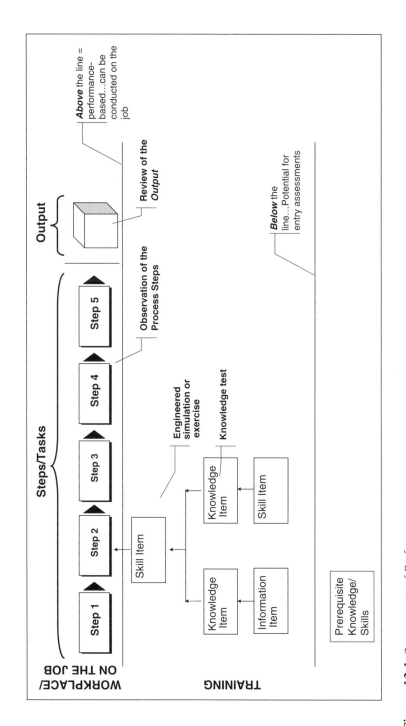

Figure 12.1 Components of Performance.

Source: Peter R. Hybert, 2007. Reproduced with permission.

The bottom level includes supporting capabilities that are outside the scope of consideration and are, as a result, "prerequisite."

The "callouts" in the figure indicate potential test points within the model. At the Workplace level, evaluate the importance of the performance. Is it necessary to actually verify that employees can execute the performance per the company standards before allowing them to do so? In other words, does this performance require a "gate" or "checkpoint"?

If it does, identify the output criteria. For example, if the output is a component design, the criteria may be that the component can be readily manufactured. Or that it meets cost targets. Or even that the design documents (drawings, specifications, and so forth) meet internal format standards.

Next, identify the process criteria. For example, for a manufacturing process, each step may require specific things to be done in a specific order. For example, does the operator wait until the tank has cooled before beginning to drain it?

Moving down to the Training level, decide whether you need any verification of the supporting capabilities. If so, it may be appropriate to define knowledge or skill tests for individual capabilities.

The supporting capabilities may be trained and tested separately; they may be grouped and trained all at once but then tested only at the step level; or they may be tested only at the output level. All those decisions depend on the amount of learning and doing involved in the work and the capability of the audience.

At the prerequisite level, decide whether to create entry assessments (for example, literacy, typing accuracy, and so forth) to confirm that learners have the necessary prerequisites to begin learning the supporting capabilities they need to perform in the workplace.

An important insight is that, from the bottom to the top of the model, all of the supporting capabilities below must be present in order to perform the blocks above. That means that if an employee can perform the steps and produce the output, it can be assumed that he or she has the underlying capabilities as well. However, testing for the underlying capabilities doesn't necessarily prove that employees will be able to perform the steps and produce the output.

A common sense way to prove this point is to consider the question: "Who would a reasonable person rather have performing an operation on her loved one? Would she rather have someone who earned good grades in medical school and has great skills in identifying the appropriate organs, suturing, or whatever, or someone who has actually performed the specific procedure in question on over one hundred patients with no undesirable outcomes?" Most people would probably choose the second physician, assuming that, by definition, anyone who can consistently and successfully perform the procedure must also have enough of the needed medical skills and smarts to do the procedure, whereas there is no evidence that the first physician, who may be very skilled and smart, can actually "put it all together" or integrate the supporting capabilities into the desired performance.

The question above also surfaces another key point—real performance deals with "noise factors" and non-standard occurrences. The physician is expected to be able to execute the procedure not only when everything is normal, but also when confronted with unexpected circumstances. What if an abnormal heart rhythm develops? What if the patient goes into shock? What if the patient has a reaction to the anesthetic? All the knowledge and skills learned in a "safe learning environment" are necessary but not sufficient. Performers who can "get it all done" in real situations constitute the desired outcome. As much as possible, learners should be trained and tested to deal with those real-world situations.

DESIGN DECISIONS FOR PERFORMANCE TESTS

When it comes to actually creating tests, there are two separate activities, design and development. Although these terms are often used interchangeably in the training business, they are really two different processes. Design is synthesizing analysis data and then defining or specifying a solution. Development is actually building that solution. Development is where the team can "divide and conquer" to build several tests in parallel, as long as there is a clear design that provides a framework within which the developers can work.

In general, it is more efficient to design all of the tests and test-related business processes before beginning development.

Assuming a need for verification tests, additional business decisions must be made regarding how the testing will be implemented. They include:

- Where will the testing be done? In the training environment, the work environment, or both?

- Who will administer the testing? In most cases in which performance tests are used, the best resource to implement the test is a master performer, that is, someone who is very capable at performing the task, rather than a trainer or supervisor who does not regularly do the work.

- Is the organization willing and ready to implement performance testing? If the use of certification is being driven primarily by political or marketing motives, there may not be support for the work analysis and processes needed to implement true performance testing in the workplace. If sponsors are more interested in just getting a test in place, rather than a true verification of capability, they would probably be satisfied with a simple one-shot written test, probably delivered via computer.

Companies that do decide to seriously implement performance testing may choose to collect and sequence a number of tests into a qualification path for key roles or sections of the organization. One advantage of these systems is that they can allow people to legitimately "test out" of training if they already have the capability, while still giving the company a way to verify that employees are, in fact, capable.

One company built a performance-test-based qualification system when several critical factors came together. They had a sponsor who had always wanted to change the compliance-oriented approach of "going through the motions" that was used historically. The company had a plant shutdown scheduled, which gave the test development team and master performers a window of time to implement the tests without impacting production. And they had a business reason—they needed to qualify the operators when they returned from shutdown on the new/changed equipment and processes. Of course, it is not necessary to wait for all the stars to align to make performance testing viable, but in this case it made it an easier decision for management.

Defining Test "Chunks"

After solving the business direction questions, the next step is beginning to design the tests. The first design problem is how to "chunk" the work into areas for which to build tests. And, once again, this is really a business question.

For example, in a manufacturing environment, a supervisor may decide she wants all operators to be qualified before allowing them to perform specific tasks. But does she want them qualified to do *everything* in the area or on subsets of the work, such as operating a specific machine? One view says to qualify them in the entire area so that supervisors know they can assign anyone in the area to any task that needs to be done. Another school of thought is to qualify employees on smaller tasks so that they can be put to work more quickly instead of waiting for them to get qualified on everything. That is a management question. A smart test designer will design the tests to be as reconfigurable as possible, though, just in case.

Once the big blocks of performance are identified, the test designer needs to decide whether each requires one or many actual tests. For example:

- Are separate tests necessary for each product or product variation?
- Can different shifts or locations use the same test?

The key here is the concept of the "assignable chunk." If a supervisor can assign someone to a task with discrete boundaries, that may be the appropriate chunk for a test. For example, quality control technicians often use test equipment in a lab to perform similar tests on a range of products. But the actual test steps and parameters may vary. This will require a decision about the number and scope of tests needed. If the performer can perform the test on one product, can he or she perform the test on any product? The answer is "it depends." The best person to make the decision is probably the master performer.

One option that can be tempting is to reduce this to simply "how to use the particular piece of equipment." This seems appealing, but it is really downgrading the test from a performance to a skill test. It is a bigger leap of faith to assume the learner will be able to put the entire performance together in the real environment.

The "assignable chunk" approach allows a test designer to break a larger performance into smaller parts that can be tested practically. If an employee might conceivably only perform a portion of some process, it becomes difficult to test the complete process in the real environment. For example, some manufacturing processes run over several days and several shifts. That means that the employee may be assigned to one set of tasks one day and another the next day. A second-shift operator may never perform certain tasks. Breaking the performance into the blocks an employee will likely be assigned to within one shift makes it easier to keep track of who is partially qualified and what parts remain to be observed.

For very long-term (multi-year) processes, a "portfolio approach" can be used. For example, engineers may contribute to a large number of product development projects. Engineers maintain a portfolio and, when they have actually performed all the pieces, even if over several different projects, they can submit the portfolio for review by an evaluator. The evaluator would critique the end-product (the portfolio), not a process, so it doesn't affect accuracy to have the evaluator checking it all at once. A downside though is that the employee will have been doing the work for quite a while without being officially qualified; this may or may not be acceptable in some situations. (This is usually managed with supervisor/mentor oversight.)

Using the "assignable chunk" approach is also a good way to figure out the library of tests needed for a specific role or area and then sequencing them for individual qualification. Perhaps the second-shift quality control technicians do not perform all the same tests as the day shift. Maybe the first part of the process is not the easiest to perform, so it may not be the first part to learn. Or maybe the Line 2 operators make a variation of the end-product that does not require some of the same tasks as needed by the Line 1 operators. Does the supervisor need to be able to shift people from one manufacturing line to the other or do people always work on the same line? The answers to these questions describe the assignable chunks that can be used to create the overall list of tests for qualification requirements for specific roles, shifts, areas, and so forth.

Product or Process?

A good way to think about the difference between testing the product and testing the process is thinking about how someone's ability would be tested to make the turkey for a family's Thanksgiving dinner. The model in Table 12.3 answers

Table 12.3 Product vs. Process Testing

A Product Test . . .	
An Everyday Example	*A Work-Related Example*
Decide whether a turkey is cooked based on a temperature reading, the color of the skin, and other means	Reviewing a printout of a computer program

A Process Test . . .	
An Everyday Example	*A Work-Related Example*
Watching someone stuffing a turkey to ensure the use of safe food-handling techniques	Observing a technician starting up a piece of equipment in the field

additional test design questions. Assuming performance is being tested, should the test measure the end-product or the process?

In general, testing the product offers many advantages, but it will not work for every situation. If evaluators only have to assess the product and not also observe the process, they can schedule the assessment at a convenient time, rather than having to be present during the performance. It also allows flexibility in how people get things done—as long as they generate the desired end-result. Of course, there are times when flexibility is exactly what the business does NOT want. In those cases, evaluators may need to observe the process.

When necessary, testing both the product and process is certainly feasible. However, additional testing generates additional effort and cost so it is important to evaluate the cost/benefit.

Real or Simulated Work?

To test performance, is it better to test the actual performance in the job environment or in a simulated setting? Testing the performance of real work has the benefit of including "noise" factors, as well as possible boundary situations. And the employee is getting work done during the testing—the downtime of being off the job to be tested is eliminated. But sometimes it is more effective to design a simulated test to ensure that specific challenges are built into the test and will always occur. There are advantages to both approaches, depending on the performance being tested, some of which are shown in Table 12.4.

Regardless of which setting is utilized, performance tests should be "open book" tests. When employees are being tested, they should be able to reference any information or tools they would normally be able to use on the job. Procedures, computer look-up's, reference guides, "cheat sheets," and other performance support tools (PSTs) should be allowed. The only document the

Table 12.4 Real Work vs. Simulation

Real Work Environment	Simulated Setting	Comments
Actual work is done while testing—don't have to take an employee "off-line" for testing.	Provides an opportunity to verify capability without the risks of the real environment.	A clear example is qualifying as an airplane pilot. Simulation allows a potential test failure without risking passenger safety (or an expensive airliner).
Will definitely transfer to the task—the test is the work.	Can be close to, but will not be exactly the same as, the work. Perhaps the equipment will be slightly different. Certainly the risk and distractions will be different.	Some tasks have pressure built into them that is very difficult to simulate. Troubleshooting a piece of equipment in a customer's facility while he or she is looking over your shoulder is more difficult than in a lab simulation.
May not test all the conditions—something to observe might not happen every time.	Can be constructed to address specific challenges.	One common concern is that troubleshooting problems or handling emergencies are difficult to address with performance testing because they don't happen every day (and it is often a bad idea to cause them, just to test someone). Simulations can address these issues.

employee should not have access to during the actual testing is the performance test itself, since it isn't actually a reference resource used on the job.

Overall Pass/Fail—"Deal Breakers"

Eventually, specific criteria must be defined, either for individual process steps or for the characteristics of the end-product. However, prior to that, the overall "deal breakers" must be decided upon and delineated. "Deal breakers" are any criteria that, if not met, result in failure on the test, regardless of the performance on individual steps. These criteria usually involve safety or legal requirements as well as general criteria for the end-product. For example, if drivers can perform all the steps to change a tire, they should still fail if they forget to secure one of the lug nuts (end-product criteria). They should also fail if they put their feet under the wheel while jacking up the car because this is a safety violation (process criteria). In most business settings, these overall criteria minimally include compliance with laws and procedures and the use of safe work practices.

TIPS FOR DEVELOPING TESTS

Once all of the tests are designed, the development process is fairly straightforward—anyone who can perform a detailed task analysis can probably develop a performance test. Just like any tool, the test has to be designed for usability in the environment by the audience.

Identify the Critical Elements (Performance "Micro-Criteria")

To create the test, one needs to understand the work at a very detailed level. One of the most effective ways to accomplish this is through in-person observation of a master performer doing the work, augmented by questions and explanations. Although a comprehensive treatment of performance analysis will not be discussed in this chapter, it is very important to the development of effective performance tests. Below are a set of key "watch-fors" and tips to be aware of when doing this.

- Find a master performer, not just an expert, but someone who does the job well.
- Have the official procedure available, if there is one.
- Actually watch the person work or talk through examples—interviews can be helpful, but it is much better to be in the environment, see how the performer organizes the workspace, uses tools and information during the process, and so forth.
- Imagine performing the work yourself.
- Ask questions until the person's answer is completely understood. Any question that the test designer would ask is probably a question that a learner would ask and quite possibly something that should be trained on and tested for. Besides, master performers are often better at doing the job than at explaining it.
- Build rapport. Especially in a manufacturing setting, employees may be concerned that anyone observing them is trying to find something wrong. In this same vein, it is essential to handle the situation delicately when

variances from the procedure are observed or when an operator explains something about how things "really get done."

- Focus on what the performer is doing: decisions he or she has to make, how he or she knows what to do next. Remember, it is a performance test, not a process audit. Quite often the human performance is not the same as the work process.

- Look for "boundary conditions" and non-standard decisions and actions. Use questions like "Why?" "What happens if X doesn't happen?" or "What determines when X is ready for Y?" to find out tacit know-how.

The goal of the analysis is simple enough—to identify the critical criteria for each step of the performance. The intent is to find out, when the performer does the task, what is important about it and what can be more or less ignored because it doesn't affect the outcome.

To capture the information during the analysis process, simply take notes. Try to capture as much as possible at the time, but try to keep up with the work in real time. Creating quick diagrams or taking digital photos can also help with recalling details later. Remember, every observation might not be captured the first time around, so some situations require multiple observation sessions.

An effective approach might use a performance checklist as the actual test instrument so that the steps and criteria are visible and so that the coach can use the test as a recording tool during the observation process. Additionally, this format can also be used as a coaching tool or practice document for the learner during training.

An Example of Performance Test Content

Using an example of a product-labeling process operator, a partial example of the performance test with detailed criteria is included in Figure 12.2. In this case, the steps from the perspective of what the *employee* would be doing and the criteria the evaluator would use to determine whether the employee met the requirements of each step are provided. In the case of an output review, this would describe the steps the *evaluator* should perform and criteria to evaluate when reviewing the output.

Identifying the detailed criteria often results in generating new know-how. Looking at each step and deciding what the key criteria are may be a level of focus that has never been done on the work. Often, procedures are developed when the process is new, but over time the focus moves to newer work processes. As a result, continuous improvement (or evolution) and best practices are not always fed back into job documents. When performance tests are developed for existing work, there are often discoveries that can be used to standardize, or even streamline, the work.

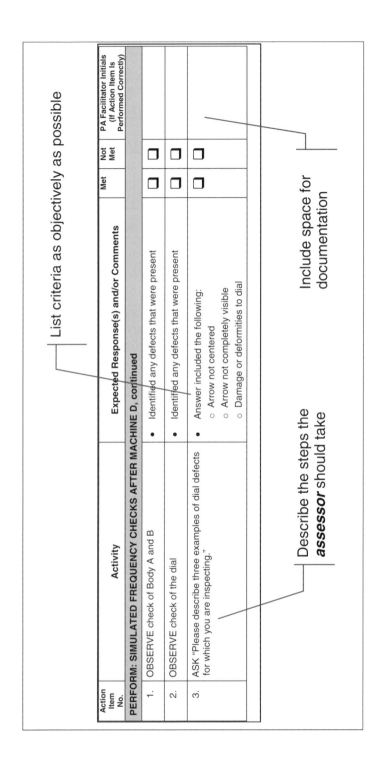

List criteria as objectively as possible

Action Item No.	Activity	Expected Response(s) and/or Comments	Met	Not Met	PA Facilitator Initials (If Action Item Is Performed Correctly)
PERFORM: SIMULATED FREQUENCY CHECKS AFTER MACHINE D, continued					
1.	OBSERVE check of Body A and B	• Identified any defects that were present	☐	☐	
2.	OBSERVE check of the dial	• Identified any defects that were present	☐	☐	
3.	ASK "Please describe three examples of dial defects for which you are inspecting."	• Answer included the following: o Arrow not centered o Arrow not completely visible o Damage or deformities to dial	☐	☐	

Describe the steps the *assessor* should take

Include space for documentation

Figure 12.2 Performance Checklist Example.

On occasion, merely watching the performance is not enough. Some situations require finding out whether an employee understands what to do in non-standard situations or situations that are unlikely to occur during the observation process. "What if there was a problem here?" "What should be done if there are three rejects in a row?" These types of questions can be inserted into the performance checklist at appropriate times to check for this know-how without having to actually observe it. When creating the test, keep the flow of the work in mind, because evaluators may not be able to interrupt employees with questions when they need to be focused on the work they are doing.

TIPS FOR DEVELOPING KNOWLEDGE TESTS

With a little work, a number of the same principles from performance testing can be applied to knowledge testing:

- Define an overall strategy for testing—where are tests really necessary and why? Figure out the business requirements for testing and be clear about whether a test is a verification step or simply an in-process check within training.

- Design the test before developing it. This sounds obvious but, in practice, test developers often just write questions. Designing it first means identifying the key capabilities to be tested and then allocating test items proportionally across those capabilities.

- Include tests of knowledge of what to do in non-standard situations to ensure that capability in "boundary situations" is verified.

- Consider making the test open book, in the sense that the employee is allowed to use reference materials and information that would normally be available on the job. This will help keep the test closer to the performance.

CONCLUSION

Ultimately, testing is a way to confirm, or verify, capability of employees to perform a task, duty, or job. Testing that is used for important human resource decisions such as hiring, promotion, compensation, or even work assignments should be fair and valid. Performance tests can be an effective way to teach, coach, and test capability if the organization can implement the processes and build the culture to support them. The benefits are significant—improved performance, reduced liability, and even more consistent work processes.

For effective performance testing, start from the top and identify the most critical work performances. The most critical tasks are those that require extensive employee capability to perform or those that, if performed poorly, may pose risk to customers, employees, or equipment.

First, decide whether a test is necessary to ensure employees are capable of performing. Then, selectively target testing where it will give the best view of capability. Base "pass or fail" on job performance criteria. Test the boundary conditions—don't make it easy. But do design the tests to reflect the real job challenges, the "noise factors," and situations that people will likely encounter.

Performance testing will yield improved clarity of what is really required on the job. The information and tools can be used in training and coaching as well as for testing. Because performance tests are almost a mirror image of analysis, they can be developed rapidly and early in an overall training process. Ultimately, performance testing will give people who can do the job a fair and valid way to demonstrate it.

References

Coscarelli, W. C., & Shrock, S. A. (1996). *Criterion-referenced test development; Technical and legal guidelines for corporate training* (2nd ed.). San Francisco: International Society for Performance Improvement/Pfeiffer.

FDA (2008, May). *Guideline on general principles*. www.fda.gov/cder/guidance/pv.htm.

Gagné, R. (1977). Analysis of objectives. In L. Briggs (Ed.), *Instructional design: Principles and applications*. Englewood Cliffs, NJ: Educational Technology Publications.

Gilbert, T. F. (1978). *Human competence: Engineering worthy performance*. New York: McGraw-Hill.

Hybert, P. (2006). *Project profile: Designing a performance measurement system*. www.prhconsulting.com.

Hybert, P., & Smith, K. (1999). *It only counts if you can do it on the job!* www.prhconsulting.com.

Lentz, R.(2008, August). *Feynman Challenger report appendix*. www.ralentz.com/old/space/feynman-report.html.

Merrill, M. D. (2002). First principles of instruction. *Educational Technology Research and Development* (pp. 43–59). Logan, UT: Utah State University Press.

Practical assessment research and evaluation. (2008, August). http://pareonline.net/.

Shrock, S. A., & Coscarelli, W. C. (2007). *Criterion-referenced test development: Technical and legal guidelines for corporate training* (3rd ed.). San Francisco: International Society for Performance Improvement/Pfeiffer.

Svenson, R., & Wallace, G. (2008). *Performance-based employee qualification/certification systems*. www.eppic.biz/services/Performance-basedEmployeeQualification-CertificationSystems2008.pdf.

CHAPTER THIRTEEN

The Business of Program Evaluation: ROI

Patti P. Phillips
Jack J. Phillips

The process for measuring return on investment (ROI) is a comprehensive, systematic methodology that includes defining the types of data, conducting an initial analysis, developing objectives, forecasting value (including ROI), using the ROI process model, and implementing and sustaining the process. This chapter presents a business approach to evaluation using ROI. We begin with a discussion of why a business approach to evaluation is needed. Then we explain why and how the ROI process can help business achieve the level of accountability demanded in today's economic climate for both public and private settings.

WHY A BUSINESS APPROACH?

"Show me the money." There is nothing new about the statement, especially in business. Organizations of all types want value for their investments, and the ultimate value is the financial return on that investment. What's new is the method that organizations use. While ROI is the ultimate report of value, organization leaders recognize that value lies in the eye of the beholder; therefore, the method used to show the money must also show the value as perceived by all stakeholders.

Measuring ROI represents the newest value statement. In the past, program or project success was measured by activity: number of people involved, money spent, hours involved, and so forth. Today the value definition has shifted: value is defined by results versus activity.

The "Show Me" Generation

Figure 13.1 illustrates the requirements of the new "show me" generation. "Show me" implies that stakeholders want to see actual data (numbers and measures). This accounted for the initial attempt to see value in programs. This evolved into "show me the money," a direct call for financial results. But this alone does not provide the needed evidence to ensure that projects add value. Often, a connection between projects and value is assumed, but that assumption soon must give way to the need to show an actual connection. Hence, "show me the *real* money" was an attempt at establishing credibility. This phase, though critical, still left stakeholders with an unanswered question: "Do the monetary benefits linked to the project outweigh the costs?" This question is the mantra for the new "show me" generation: "Show me the real money, and make me believe it." But this new generation of project sponsors also recognizes that value is more than just a single number: value is what makes the entire organization system tick—hence the need to report value based on people's various definitions.

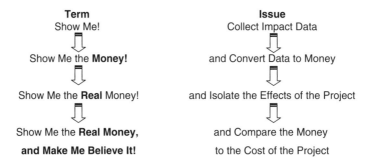

Term	Issue
Show Me!	Collect Impact Data
⇩	⇩
Show Me the **Money!**	and Convert Data to Money
⇩	⇩
Show Me the **Real** Money!	and Isolate the Effects of the Project
⇩	⇩
Show Me the **Real Money, and Make Me Believe It!**	and Compare the Money to the Cost of the Project

Figure 13.1 The "Show Me" Evolution.

2009 ROI Institute, Inc.

The New Definition of Value

The changing perspectives on value and the shifts that are occurring in organizations have all led to a new definition of value. Value is not defined as a single number. Rather, its definition is composed of a variety of data points. Value must be balanced with quantitative and qualitative data, as well as with financial and non-financial perspectives. The data sometimes reflect tactical issues, such as activity, as well as strategic issues, such as ROI. Value must be derived using different time frames and not necessarily represent a single point in time. It must reflect the value systems that are important to stakeholders. The data composing value must be collected from credible sources, using cost-effective methods; value must be action-oriented, compelling individuals to make adjustments and changes.

The Changing Definition of Program Success

In the past decade, a variety of forces have driven additional focus on measuring the impact of programs, including the financial contribution and ROI. These forces have challenged old ways of defining program success.

Program Failures. Almost every organization encounters unsuccessful programs or projects that go astray, costing far too much and failing to deliver on promises. Project disasters occur in business organizations as well as in government and non-profit organizations. The string of failures has generated increased concerns about measuring project and program success—before, during, and after implementation.

Program Costs. The costs of projects and programs continue to grow. As costs rise, the budgets for projects become targets for others who would like to have the funds for their own projects. What was once considered a mere cost of doing business is now considered an investment, and one to be wisely allocated.

Accountability Trend. A consistent and persistent trend in accountability is evident in organizations across the globe: almost every function, process, project, or initiative is judged based on higher standards than in the past. Various functions in organizations are attempting to show their worth by capturing and demonstrating the value they add to the organization. They compete for funds; therefore, they have to show value.

Process Improvement Mandate. The increased use of ROI and the need to show monetary value is due to organizational improvement processes that have dominated many organizations, particularly in North America, Europe, and Asia. These process improvement efforts, such as lean six sigma, have elevated the need to show value in two important ways. First, these processes themselves often create or enhance a measurement culture within organizations. Second, the quest to show the value of these change processes has created the need for tools to show their actual monetary impact, up to and including ROI.

Fact-Based Management. Recently there has been an important trend to move to fact-based or evidence-based management. Although many key decisions have been made using instinctive input and gut feelings, more managers are now using sophisticated and detailed processes to show value. Quality decisions must be based on more than gut feelings or the blink of an eye. With a comprehensive set of measures, including financial ROI, better organizational decisions regarding people, products, projects, and processes are possible.

Outsourcing. Support functions are often regarded as overhead, a burden on the organization, and an unnecessary expense. The approach of many managers is to outsource, automate, or eliminate the overhead. Great strides have been made in all three approaches. These days, staff support departments must show value to exist as viable support functions or administrative processes.

Executive Interest. Providing monetary contribution and ROI is receiving increased interest in the executive suite. Top managers who watch budgets continue to grow without appropriate accountability measures are frustrated, and they are responding to the situation by turning to ROI. Top executives now demand ROI calculations and monetary contributions from departments and functions where they were not previously required.

These major forces are requiring organizations to shift their measurement processes to include the financial impact and ROI. The processes necessary to meet this challenge must be systematic, logical, and credible. All are described next.

TYPES OF DATA

The richness of the ROI methodology is inherent in the types of data monitored during the implementation of a particular project. These data are categorized by levels. Figure 13.2 shows the levels of data and describes their measurement focus.

Level 0—Input

Level 0 represents the input to a project and details the numbers of people and hours, the focus, and the cost of the project. These data represent the activity around a project versus the contribution of the project. Level 0 data represent the scope of the effort, the degree of commitment, and the support for a particular program. For some, this equates to value. However, commitment as defined by expenditures is not evidence that the organization is reaping value.

Level 1—Reaction and Perceived Value

Reaction and Perceived Value (Level 1) marks the beginning of the project's value stream. Reaction data capture the degree to which the participants involved in the project, including the stakeholders, react favorably or unfavorably. The key is to capture the measures that reflect the content of the project, focusing on issues such as usefulness, relevance, importance, and appropriateness. Data at this level provide the first sign that project success may be achievable. These data also present project leaders with information they need to make adjustments to project implementation to help ensure positive results.

Level 2—Learning and Confidence

The next level is Learning and Confidence (Level 2). For every process, program, or project there is a learning component. For some—such as projects for new technology, new systems, new competencies, and new processes—this component is substantial. For others, such as a new policy or new procedure, learning may be a small part of the process but is still necessary to ensure successful execution. In either case, measurement of learning is essential to success. Measures at this level focus on skills, knowledge, capacity, competencies, confidence, and networking contacts.

Level	Measurement Focus	Typical Measures
0-Inputs and Indicators	Inputs into the project, including indicators representing the scope of the project	Types of projects Number of projects Number of people Hours of involvement Cost of projects
1-Reaction and Perceived Value	Reaction to the project, including the perceived value of the project	Relevance Importance Usefulness Appropriateness Fairness Motivational
2-Learning and Confidence	Learning how to use the project, content, materials, system, including the confidence to use what was learned	Skills Knowledge Capacity Competencies Confidences Contacts
3-Application and Implementation	Use of project content, materials, and system in the work environment, including progress with implementation	Extent of use Task completion Frequency of use Actions completed Success with use Barriers to use Enablers to use
4-Impact and Consequences	The consequences of the use of the project content, materials, and system expressed as business impact measures	Productivity Revenue Quality Time Efficiency Customer Satisfaction Employee Engagement
5-ROI	Comparison of monetary benefits from project to project costs	Benefit/Cost Ratio (BCR) ROI (%) Payback Period

Figure 13.2 Types and Levels of Data.

Level 3—Application and Implementation

Application and Implementation (Level 3) measures the extent to which the project or program is properly applied and implemented. Effective implementation is a must if bottom-line value is the goal. This is one of the most important data categories, and most implementation breakdowns occur at this level. Research has consistently shown that in almost half of all projects, participants and users are not doing what they should to make it successful. At this level, data collection involves measures, such as the extent of use of information, task completion, frequency of use of skills, success with use, and actions completed.

Data collection also requires the examination of barriers and enablers to successful application. This level provides a picture of how well the system supports the successful transfer of knowledge, skills, and attitude changes.

Level 4—Impact and Consequences

This level is important for understanding the business consequences of the project. Here, data are collected that attract the attention of the sponsor and other executives. This level shows the output, productivity, revenue, quality, time, cost, efficiencies, and level of customer satisfaction connected with the project. For some, this level reflects the ultimate reason the project exists: to show the impact within the organization on various groups and systems. Without this level of data, they assert, there is no success. Once this level of measurement is achieved, it is necessary to isolate the effects of the program on the specific measures. The link between the project and business measures is not evident.

Level 5—ROI

The ROI is calculated next. This shows the monetary benefits of the impact measures compared with the cost of the project. This value is typically stated in terms of either a benefit/cost ratio, the ROI as a percentage, or the payback period. This level of measurement requires two important steps: first, the impact data (Level 4) must be converted to monetary values; second, the cost of the project must be captured.

Accommodating Intangibles

Along with the five levels of results and the initial level of activity (Level 0), there is a sixth type of data—not a sixth level—developed through this methodology. This sixth type of data is the intangible benefits—those benefits that are purposefully not converted to money but nonetheless constitute important measures of success.

THE INITIAL ANALYSIS

Our research suggests that the number one reason for projects failing is lack of alignment with the business. The first opportunity to obtain business alignment is in the initial analysis. Several steps are taken to make sure that the project or program is absolutely necessary.

Payoff Needs

The first step in this analysis examines the potential payoff of solving a problem or taking advantage of an opportunity. Is this a problem worth solving, or is the project worthy of implementation? For some situations, the answer is obvious: yes, the project is worthy because of its critical nature, its relevance to the issue at hand, or its effectiveness in tackling a major problem affecting the organization. A serious customer service problem, for example, is one worth pursuing.

Business Needs

The next step is to ensure that the project is connected to one or more business measures. The measures that must improve, as a reflection of the overall success of the project, are defined. Sometimes the measure is obvious; at other times it is not.

Job Performance Needs

Next, the job performance needs are examined with the question, "What must change on the job to influence the business measures previously defined?" This step identifies the cause of or opportunity to resolve the business need. This step may involve a series of analytical tools to determine the cause of the problem and ensure that the project is connected with business improvement. This appears to be quite complex, but it is a simple approach. A series of questions helps: What is keeping the business measure from being where it needs to be? If it is a problem, what is its cause? If it is an opportunity, what is hindering it from moving in the right direction? This step is critical because it provides the link to the project solution.

Learning Needs

After job performance needs have been determined, the learning needs are examined by asking: "What specific skills, knowledge, or perceptions must change or improve so that job performance can change?" Every solution involves a learning component, and this step defines what the participants or users must know to make the project successful. The needed knowledge may be as simple as understanding a policy or as complicated as learning new competencies.

Preference Needs

The final step is identifying the structure of the solution. How best can the information be presented to ensure that necessary knowledge will be acquired and job performance will change to solve the business problem? This level of analysis involves issues surrounding the scope, timing, structure, method, and budget for project implementation and delivery. Collectively, these steps define the issues that lead to initiation of a project. When these preliminary steps are completed, the project can be positioned to achieve its intended results.

Developing Objectives

Positioning a program or project requires the development of clear, specific objectives that are communicated to all stakeholders. Objectives should be developed for each level of need and should define success, answering the question "How will we know the need has been met?" If the criteria of success are not communicated early and often, process participants will go through the motions, with little change resulting. Developing detailed objectives with clear measures of success will position the project to achieve its ultimate objective.

Forecasting Value

Before a project is launched, forecasting the outcomes may be important to ensure that adjustments can be made or alternative solutions can be investigated. This forecast can be simple, relying on the individuals closest to the situation, or it can be a more detailed analysis of the situation and expected outcome. Recently, forecasting has become a critical tool for project sponsors who need evidence that the project will be successful before they are willing to plunge into a funding stream for it.

USING THE ROI PROCESS MODEL

The next challenge for many project leaders is to collect a variety of data along a chain of impact that shows the project's value. Figure 13.3 displays a detailed view of the sequential steps that lead to data categorized by the five levels of results. This figure shows the ROI methodology, a step-by-step process beginning with the objectives and concluding with reporting of data. The model assumes that proper analysis is conducted to define need before the steps are taken.

Evaluation Planning

An important first step in planning is to establish or refine the objectives. Ideally, objectives are developed from the initial analysis, described earlier.

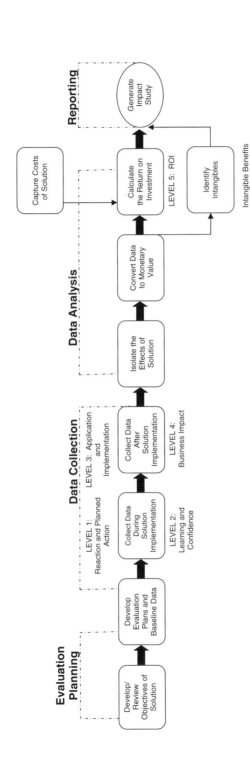

Figure 13.3 ROI Process Model.

2009 ROI Institute, Inc.

On occasion, the evaluation may stop with Level 3 objectives, excluding the impact objectives that are needed to direct higher levels of evaluation. If application and impact objectives are not available, they must be developed using input from job incumbents, analysts, project developers, subject-matter experts, facilitators, and on-the-job team leaders.

Three simple planning documents are developed next: the data collection plan, the ROI analysis plan, and the project plan. These documents should be completed during evaluation planning and before the evaluation project is implemented—ideally, before the program is designed or developed. Figure 13.4 shows a completed data collection plan for a project undertaken to reduce bus drivers' absenteeism in a major city. This document provides a place for the major elements and issues regarding data collection, described in the next section.

This planning document also captures information on key items that are necessary to develop the actual ROI calculation—all described in the data analysis section. The final plan developed for the evaluation planning phase is a project plan. A project plan consists of a description of the project and brief details, such as duration, target audience, and number of participants. It also shows the timeline of the project, from the planning of the study through the final communication of the results. This plan becomes an operational tool to keep the project on track.

Most of the decisions regarding the process are made as these planning tools are developed. The remainder of the project becomes a methodical, systematic process of implementing the plan.

Collecting Data

Data collection is central to the ROI methodology. Both hard data (representing output, quality, cost, and time) and soft data (including job satisfaction and customer satisfaction) are collected. Data are collected using a variety of methods, listed in Figure 13.5. These are commonly used methods. This figure also shows the methods which are appropriate for the different levels of data.

The important challenge in data collection is to use a method or methods appropriate for the setting and the specific program, within the time and budget constraints of the organization. Figure 13.4 shows the methods, timing, and sources for data collection in the absenteeism reduction project. Additional details on data collection can be found in other references (Phillips & Stawarski, (2008).

Figure 13.4 Data Collection Plan.

Evaluation Purpose: To measure the effectiveness of the no-fault policy and selection process in reducing absenteeism

Program: _Absenteeism Reduction_   Responsibility: _Jack Phillips_   Date: _January 15_

Level	Broad Program Objective(s)	Measures	Data Collection Method/ Instruments	Data Sources	Timing	Responsibilities
Level One: Reaction/ Planned Action	**After the project is implemented:**					
	1. MTA will experience little or no adverse reaction from current employees.	5-point scale	Feedback questionnaire	Employees	At the end of the employee meetings	Supervisors
	2. Employees will see the project as appropriate, given the excess absenteeism.	5-point scale	Feedback questionnaire	Employees	At the end of the employee meetings	Supervisors
	3. The employment staff will see the new selection step as necessary.	5-point scale	Feedback questionnaire	Employment staff	Just after launch	Evaluator
	4. Supervisors will see the project as appropriate.	5-point scale	Feedback questionnaire	Supervisors	Just after launch	Evaluator
Level Two: Learning	**During project implementation:**					
	5. Employees must be able to explain how the no-fault policy works.	Simple true/false tests. Score of 3 out of 5 is acceptable.*	Test	Employees	At the end of employee meeting	Supervisors

(Continued)

Figure 13.4 (Continued)

Evaluation Purpose: To measure the effectiveness of the no-fault policy and selection process in reducing absenteeism

Program: Absenteeism Reduction   Responsibility: Jack Phillips   Date: January 15

Level	Broad Program Objective(s)	Measures	Data Collection Method/ Instruments	Data Sources	Timing	Responsibilities
	6. Employees must be able to describe their role in the no-fault policy.	Simple true/false tests. Score of 3 out of 5 is acceptable.*	Test	Employees	At the end of employee meeting	Supervisors
	7. Employment staff will demonstrate the successful use of the selection instrument.	Simple skills practice	Observation	Employment manager	Just after launch	Evaluator
	8. Supervisors will demonstrate skills for conducting the employee meetings.	Simple skills practice	Observation	Training coordinator	Project launch meeting with supervisors	Training coordinator
Level Three: Application/ Implementation	**Within thirty days of project launch:**					
	9. The new selection instrument will be used for each selection decision, resulting in a systematic and consistent process.	Yes/no	Simple feedback and check of selection records	Company records and selection staff	30 days after program launch	Evaluator
	10. In meetings with employees, supervisors will communicate the no-fault policy, including how the policy will be applied and the rationale for it.	Yes/no	Questionnaire and check of selection records	Supervisors	Thirty days after program implementation	Evaluator

11. The no-fault policy will be consistently enforced throughout all operating units.	Yes/no	Questionnaire	Supervisors	Thirty days after program implementation	Evaluator
Level Four: Business Impact					
After one year of implementation:					
12. The driver absenteeism rate will be reduced by at least 2 percentage points.	Number of employees absent (unplanned) divided by number of employees in unit	Monitor absenteeism records	Company records	Monitor monthly and analyze one year pre- and one year post-implementation	Evaluator
13. The present level of job satisfaction will be maintained.	5-point scale	Questionnaire	Supervisors	Evaluator	Evaluator
14. Schedule delays caused by absenteeism will be reduced by 50 percent.	Percentage of delays due to absenteeism	Monitor records, bus schedule delays	Dispatch records	Evaluator	Evaluator
15. Customer satisfaction increases with fewer delays	10-point scale	Survey	Customers	Quarterly survey	Marketing-customer support
Level Five: ROI					
After one year of implementation:					
The return on investment for the project will be at least 25 percent.	N/A	N/A	N/A	N/A	N/A

*Three questions address how the policy works (employee must answer two correctly); two address employees' role (employee must answer one correctly).

Method	Level 1	2	3	4
• Surveys	√	√	√	√
• Questionnaires	√	√	√	√
• Observation	√	√	√	
• Interviews	√	√	√	
• Focus Groups	√	√	√	
• Tests/Quizzes		√		
• Demonstrations		√		
• Simulations		√		
• Action planning/improvement plans			√	√
• Performance contracting			√	√
• Performance monitoring			√	√

Figure 13.5 Data Collection Methods.

2009 ROI Institute, Inc.

Data Analysis

Data analysis involves all steps from data collection to reporting. Five distinct steps are always addressed: isolating the effects of the project, converting data to monetary values, tabulating project costs, calculating ROI, and identifying intangible benefits. Each is briefly discussed next.

Isolating the Effects of the Project. An often overlooked issue in evaluation is the process of isolating the effects of the project. In this step, specific strategies are explored that determine the amount of output performance directly related to the project. This step is essential because many factors will influence performance data. The specific strategies of this step pinpoint the amount of improvement directly related to the project, resulting in increased accuracy and credibility of ROI calculations. The following techniques have been used by organizations to tackle this important issue:

- Control groups
- Trend line analysis
- Forecasting models
- Participant estimates
- Managers' estimates
- Senior management estimates
- Experts' input
- Customer input

Collectively, these techniques provide a comprehensive set of tools to handle the important and critical issue of isolating the effects of projects. Additional information on methods of isolation are available in other references (Phillips & Aaron, 2008).

Converting Data to Monetary Values. To calculate the return on investment, Level 4 impact data are converted to monetary values and compared with project costs. This requires that a value be placed on each unit of data connected with the project. Many techniques are available to convert data to monetary values. The specific technique selected depends on the type of data and the situation. The techniques include:

- Use of output data, as standard values
- Cost of quality, usually as a standard value
- Time savings converted to participants' wage and employee benefits
- An analysis of historical costs
- Use of internal and external experts
- Search of external databases
- Use of participant estimates
- Use of manager estimates
- Soft measures mathematically linked to other measures

This step in the ROI model is important and absolutely necessary in determining the monetary benefits of a project. The process is challenging, particularly with soft data, but can be methodically accomplished using one or more of these strategies. Additional information on data conversion techniques are available in other works (Phillips & Burkett, 2008).

Tabulating Project Costs. An important part of the ROI equation is the calculation of project costs. Tabulating the costs involves monitoring or developing all the related costs of the project targeted for the ROI calculation. Among the cost components to be included are

- Initial analysis costs
- Cost to design and develop the project
- Cost of all project materials
- Costs for the project team
- Cost of the facilities for the project
- Travel, lodging, and meal costs for the participants and team members
- Participants' salaries (including employee benefits)

- Administrative and overhead costs, allocated in some convenient way
- Evaluation costs

The conservative approach is to include all these costs so that the total is fully loaded.

Calculating the Return on Investment. The return on investment is calculated using the program benefits and costs. The benefits/costs ratio (BCR) is calculated as the project benefits divided by the project costs. In formula the BCR is;

$$BCR = \frac{\text{Project benefits}}{\text{Project costs}}$$

The return on investment is based on the net benefits divided by project costs. The net benefits are calculated as the project benefits minus the project costs. In formula form, the ROI is

$$ROI(\%) = \frac{\text{Net project benefits} \times 100}{\text{Project costs}}$$

This is the same basic formula used in evaluating other investments, in which the ROI is traditionally reported as earnings divided by investment. Additional information on costs and ROI are contained in other works (Phillips & Zuniga, 2008).

Identifying Intangible Benefits

In addition to tangible, monetary benefits, intangible benefits (those not converted to money) are identified for most projects. Intangible benefits include items such as:

- Increased employee engagement
- Increased organizational commitment
- Improved teamwork
- Improved customer service
- Fewer complaints
- Reduced conflict

During data analysis, every attempt is made to convert all data to monetary values. All hard data—such as output, quality, and time—are converted to monetary values. The conversion of soft data is attempted for each data item. However, if the process used for conversion is too subjective or inaccurate and the resulting values lose credibility in the process, then the data are listed as an intangible benefit with the appropriate explanation. For some projects, intangible, nonmonetary benefits are extremely valuable and often carry as much influence as the hard data items.

Reporting

The final step in the ROI process model is reporting—a critical step that is often deficient in the degree of attention and planning required to ensure its success. The reporting step involves developing appropriate information in impact studies and other brief reports. Careful planning to match the communication method with the audience is essential to ensure that the message is understood and that appropriate actions follow.

IMPLEMENTING AND SUSTAINING THE PROCESS

Operating Standards and Philosophy

To ensure consistency and replication of the ROI process model, operating standards must be developed and applied. The results of the study must stand alone and must not vary with the individual conducting the study. The operating standards detail how each step and issue of the process will be handled. The twelve guiding principles listed below form the basis for the operating standards:

1. When conducting a higher-level evaluation, collect data at lower levels.
2. When planning a higher-level evaluation, the previous level of evaluation is not required to be comprehensive.
3. When collecting and analyzing data, use only the most credible sources.
4. When analyzing data, select the most conservative alternative for calculations.
5. Use at least one method to isolate the effects of a project.
6. If no improvement data are available for a population or from a specific source, assume that little or no improvement has occurred.
7. Adjust estimates of improvement for potential errors of estimation.
8. Avoid use of extreme data items and unsupported claims when calculating ROI.
9. Use only the first year of annual benefits in ROI analysis of short-term solutions.
10. Fully load all costs of a solution, project, or program when analyzing ROI.
11. Intangible measures are defined as measures that are purposely not converted to monetary values.
12. Communicate the results of ROI methodology to all key stakeholders.

These guiding principles serve not only to consistently address each step, but also to provide a much-needed conservative approach to the analysis. A conservative approach may lower the actual ROI calculation, but it will also build credibility with the target audience.

Process Sustainability

A variety of environmental issues and events will influence the successful implementation of the ROI methodology. These issues must be addressed early to ensure its success. Specific topics or actions include:

- A policy statement concerning results-based projects;
- Procedures and guidelines for different elements and techniques of the evaluation process;
- Formal meetings to develop staff skills with the ROI process;
- Strategies to improve management commitment to and support for the ROI process;
- Mechanisms to provide technical support for questionnaire design, data analysis, and evaluation strategy;
- Specific techniques to place more attention on results; and
- Period review to determine if the process is adding value.

The ROI process can fail or succeed based on these implementation issues. Additional information on implementation is offered in other works (Phillips & Tush, 2008).

BENEFITS OF THIS APPROACH

The ROI methodology presented in this chapter has been used consistently and routinely by thousands of organizations in the past decade. Much has been learned about the success of this methodology and what it can bring to the organizations using it. Some of the benefits of this approach are described below.

Aligning with Business

The ROI methodology ensures alignment with the business and is enforced in three steps. First, prior to project initiation, the methodology ensures that alignment is achieved up front, at the time the project is validated as the appropriate solution. Second, by requiring specific, clearly defined objectives at the impact level, the project focuses on the ultimate outcomes. In essence, this drives the business measure by its design, delivery, and implementation. Third, in the follow-up data, when the business measures may have changed or improved, a method is used to isolate the effects of the project on that data. This proves the connection to that business measure (that is, showing the amount of improvement directly connected to the project and ensuring there is business alignment).

Validating the Value Proposition

In reality, most projects are undertaken to deliver value. As described in this chapter, the definition of value may on occasion be unclear or may not be what a project's various sponsors, organizers, and stakeholders desire. However, there are often value shifts. Once the values are finally determined, the value proposition is detailed. The ROI methodology will forecast the value in advance, and if the value has been delivered, it verifies the value proposition agreed to by the appropriate parties.

Improving Processes

This is a process improvement tool by design and practice. It collects data to evaluate how things are—or are not—working. When things are not where they should be—as when projects are not proceeding as effectively as expected—data are available to indicate what must be changed to make the project more effective. When things are working well, data are available to show what else could be done to make them better. A continuous feedback cycle of results and action is critical to process improvement and inherent in the ROI methodology.

Enhancing the Image

Many functions and entire professions are criticized for an inability to deliver what is expected. For this, their public image suffers. The ROI methodology is one way to help build the respect a function or profession needs.

The ROI methodology can make a difference in any function, not just those under fire. Many human resources (HR) executives have used ROI to show the value of their projects and programs, perhaps changing the perception of a project from one based on activity to one that credibly adds value. This methodology shows a connection to the bottom line and shows the value delivered to stake-holders. It removes issues about value and a supposed lack of contribution to the organization. Consequently, this methodology is an important part of the process of changing the image within the function of the organization and building needed respect.

Improving Support

Securing support for projects is critical, particularly at the middle-manager level. Many projects enjoy the support of top-level managers who allocated the resources to make the projects viable. Unfortunately, some middle-level managers may not support certain projects because they do not see the value the projects deliver in terms the managers appreciate and understand. Having a methodology that shows how a project or program is connected to the manager's business goals and objectives can change this support level. When middle managers understand that a project is helping them meet specific performance indicators or departmental goals, they will usually support the process—or at least resist it less. In this way, the ROI methodology may actually improve manager support.

Justifying or Enhancing Budgets

Some organizations have used the ROI methodology to support proposed budgets. Since the methodology shows the monetary value expected or achieved with specific projects, the data can often be leveraged into budget requests. When a particular function is budgeted, the amount budgeted is often in direct proportion to the value that the function adds. If little or no credible data support the contribution, the budgets are often trimmed—or at least not enhanced. Bringing accountability to this level is one of the best ways to secure future funding.

Building a Partnership with Key Executives

Almost every function attempts to partner with operating executives and key managers in the organization. Unfortunately, some managers may not want to be partners. They may not want to waste time and effort on a relationship that does not help them succeed. They want to partner only with groups and individuals who can add value and help them in meaningful ways. Showing the project's results will enhance the likelihood of building these partnerships, with the results providing the initial impetus for making the partnerships work.

Earning a Seat at the Table

Many functions are attempting to earn a seat at the table, however that's defined. Typically, "earning a seat at the table" means being at the strategy- or decision-making table and in high-level discussions at the top of the organization. Department and program leaders hope to be involved in strategic decision making, particularly in areas that will affect their functions and the projects and processes in their functions. Showing the actual contribution and getting others to understand how the function adds value can help earn the coveted seat at the table. Most executives want to include those who are genuinely helping the business and will seek input that is valuable and constructive. The use of the ROI methodology may be the single most important action that can earn one a seat at the table.

FINAL THOUGHTS

The business approach to program evaluation helps organizations improve, as well as show the impact of programs, processes, and initiatives—that sometimes means ROI. But the ROI in and of itself is insufficient. Data important to all stakeholders provides a more comprehensive and balanced approach to accountability. A business approach to evaluation is not for every project. ROI evaluation is needed for expensive, strategic, important, and high-profile projects. Studies at this level are aimed at process, improvement-making adjustments to improve the project, and that is refreshing. Much to the surprise of many, the ROI methodology is user-friendly, CFO friendly, and credible. Using ROI is a minimal risk tool with many rewards.

References

Phillips, J. J., & Aaron, B. C. (2008). *Isolation of results: Defining the impact of the program*. San Francisco: Pfeiffer.

Phillips, J. J., & Burkett, H. H. (2008). *Data conversion: Calculating the monetary benefits*. San Francisco: Pfeiffer.

Phillips, J. J., & Zuniga, L. (2008). *Costs and ROI: Evaluating at the ultimate level*. San Francisco: Pfeiffer.

Phillips, P. P., & Stawarski, C. A. (2008). *Data collection: Planning for and collecting all types of data*. San Francisco: Pfeiffer.

Phillips, P. P., & Tush, W. F. (2008). *Communication and implementation: Sustaining the practice*. San Francisco: Pfeiffer.

CHAPTER FOURTEEN

Integrated Evaluation

Improving Performance
Improvement

Nancy B. Hastings

valuation models intended for use with training initiatives, such as Kirkpatrick's four levels of evaluation and Phillips' return on investment (ROI)
model, are not designed to meet the evaluation needs of the performance
improvement field. This fact is well documented in the literature. Much has
been written about the misalignment between the second of Kirkpatrick's levels,
learning, and non-training interventions (Alexander & Christoffersen, 2006;
Kaufman, Keller, & Watkins, 1995; Phillips, 1996). Some have suggested that the
easy solution to this is to continue to use the model, skipping any levels that are
misaligned with the subject of the evaluation (Ford, 2004). This adaptation by
elimination methodology is dangerous. The model is based on a causal relationship between each of the four levels; if they like it (Level 1) they are more
likely to learn (Level 2), and if they learn they are more likely to change their
behaviors (Level 3), and if they change their behaviors the training intervention
is more likely to have a positive impact on the organization (Level 4) (Ford,
2004). If Level 2 is eliminated to accommodate non-training interventions for
which learning is not a factor, the causal relationship collapses and the model
becomes significantly less capable of identifying the cause-and-effect relationships key to the evaluation. Similar limitations are evident in all models
designed specifically for training.

Evaluations of performance improvement efforts are further limited by the
terminology of the field. It is generally accepted that the term "evaluation" refers
to three separate activities: formative evaluation, summative evaluation, and

confirmative evaluation. While they are collectively referred to as evaluation, each is addressed as a separate process with a unique purpose, occurring at a predetermined point during design, development, and implementation. These terms grew out of the research related to the evaluation of training. Formative evaluation is considered a developmental process. Its purpose is to evaluate the effectiveness of a training program prior to implementation, affording the designer an opportunity to revise materials and methods prior to implementation. This definition relegates formative evaluation to the intervention selection and design phases of performance improvement. The term summative evaluation is used to refer to the post implementation evaluation of immediate changes in behavior related to the training program. Summative evaluation is the evaluation of the learning, or Level 2 of the Kirkpatrick and Phillips' ROI models (Kaufman, Keller, & Watkins, 1995; Phillips, 1996). Its purpose is to verify that short-term objectives have been met. In performance improvement, summative evaluation is aligned with the implementation process. The final of the three types of evaluation, confirmative evaluation, focuses on long-term changes in behavior and the impact of those behaviors on the organization. In training, confirmative evaluation refers to Levels 3 and 4 of the Kirkpatrick model or Levels 3, 4, and 5 of the Phillips' ROI model (Kaufman, Keller, & Watkins, 1995; Phillips, 1996). Its purpose is to make long-term decisions about the success of the program and its future. In performance improvement confirmative evaluation is aligned with the post-implementation change process (Dessinger & Moseley, 2004).

Using the terms "formative," "summative," and "confirmative" in both training and performance improvement is a highly effective way to categorize the purpose of an evaluation effort. This methodology provides the evaluator with guidance in selecting evaluation questions and identifying appropriate measures, data collection sources, and data collection methods. The limitation of the formative, summative, confirmative terminology is that it does not acknowledge the fluid nature of performance improvement and the importance of evaluating all processes at all levels throughout the life of the intervention. Improving performance improvement requires fully integrated, ongoing formative, summative, and confirmative evaluation.

Beer and Bloomer (1986) explain that the categorization of evaluations by type "does not contribute much to the planning of an evaluation" (p. 336). They note that the terminology "does not allow for differences between formative evaluations of a program that is in the pilot stage and formative evaluations of a program that has been implemented but is still amenable to change" (p. 336). They suggest that process (formative) and product (summative and confirmative) evaluations should occur concurrently. They recommend a strategy that categorizes evaluation into three levels, also based on timing, but incorporating both formative and summative components throughout. The recommended levels are "Level 1 for programs in the pilot stage, Level 2 for implemented programs and Level 3 for follow-up on the relevance and usefulness of implemented programs'' (p. 337). The limitation of the levels of evaluation strategy is that, like the Kirkpatrick levels of evaluation and Phillips' ROI evaluation model, it is best suited for training initiatives, not performance improvement.

Van Tiem, Moseley, and Dessinger (2000; 2004) addressed the role of integrated, ongoing evaluation in performance improvement by modifying the representation of evaluation in the human performance technology model. The modification included the addition of directional arrows showing the input and output relationships between evaluation and each of the performance improvement processes. Dessinger & Moseley (2006) explain that evaluation ''should take place during all HPT processes: performance and cause analysis, intervention selection and design, and implementation and change'' (p. 312). This integrated approach is evident in the Dessinger–Moseley Full-Scope Evaluation Model. The full-scope model is based on the traditional formative, summative, and confirmative evaluation structure. It also includes an additional type of evaluation, meta evaluation, focusing on the ''attributes of the evaluation process itself, such as validity, reliability, and accountability'' (p. 319). Dessinger and Moseley (2006) state that full-scope evaluation was developed to blend ''formative, summative, confirmative, and meta evaluation into a seamless, iterative flow for making judgments about the continuing merit and worth of any performance improvement intervention'' (p. 317). The Dessinger-Moseley full-scope evaluation model, unlike Kirkpatrick's four levels of evaluation, Phillips' ROI model of evaluation and other popular models, does not limit its focus to training interventions. The model is aligned with the processes associated with performance improvement: performance analysis, cause analysis, intervention selection and design, implementation and change, and evaluation. The limitation of the model is that it is based on the formative, summative, confirmative structure and fails to communicate that each type of evaluation is relevant throughout the performance improvement life cycle.

The integrated evaluation structure proposed in this chapter addresses the misalignment between training-based evaluation models and performance improvement as well as the over-reliance on the timetable prescribed by the formative, summative, and confirmative terminology.

INTEGRATED EVALUATION STRUCTURE

The integrated evaluation structure is very closely related to the full-scope evaluation model (Dessinger & Moseley, 2006). Like the full-scope evaluation model, the integrated evaluation structure acknowledges the need to bring evaluation into the process earlier, evaluating not only intervention design, implementation, and change, but also the process steps of performance analysis, cause analysis, intervention selection, and evaluation. Like the full-scope evaluation model, the integrated evaluation structure acknowledges the need to evaluate processes, products, and impact. The only significant difference between full-scope evaluation and the integrated evaluation structure is the acknowledgement that all three types of evaluations, process (formative), product (summative), and impact (confirmative) should be integrated throughout the performance improvement life cycle and not completed separately at predetermined times.

Integrated evaluation requires individual consideration of each of the five primary steps in the human performance technology (HPT) model: performance analysis, cause analysis, intervention selection and design, implementation and change, and evaluation (Van Tiem, Moseley, & Dessinger, 2000, 2004). The traditional evaluation structure suggests that the first three steps in the model, performance analysis, cause analysis, and intervention selection and design, are aligned with formative evaluation. Evaluations at this point in the performance improvement initiative would focus on the processes related to the collection and interpretation of the analysis data, the intervention selection decision-making process, and the actual design of the intervention. This narrow focus on formative evaluation ignores the fact that each of these tasks involves processes that lead to products that may have a positive or negative impact on the overall success of the performance improvement initiative. The traditional evaluation structure also suggests that the fourth and fifth steps in the model, implementation and change, and evaluation, are aligned with product-based summative evaluation and impact-based confirmative evaluation but not the process-based formative evaluation. This is again a very limited view of these important activities. Implementation and change and evaluation, like performance analysis, cause analysis, and intervention selection and design, involve processes and products that may have a positive or negative impact on the overall success of the performance improvement intervention. To fully understand the effects of our efforts at all stages in the performance improvement process, we must plan evaluations, identify standards and measurements, and collect, analyze, and report process, product, and impact data at each of the five phases represented in the HPT model. This integrated evaluation structure when based on sound principles of evaluation and measurement will lead to improved performance improvement.

PLANNING AN INTEGRATED EVALUATION

All evaluations, whether formative, summative, or confirmative, or training or performance improvement focused, require careful planning. Planning allows the evaluator an opportunity to determine what questions need to be answered, what measures are best suited for answering them, what standards the measures should be compared to, how and when to collect data, and who should receive the final report of the evaluation activities.

Evaluation is always undertaken for the purpose of answering one or more questions: Was enough data collected to make an informed decision about the current and ideal performance situation? Is the selected intervention the most efficient for the identified problem? Was the intervention design appropriate for the needs of the organization? Was the implementation schedule timed correctly? Was the intervention institutionalized? Did the intervention effectively close the gap between pre-intervention performance and desired performance? The specific questions depend on the intervention and the organization. The answers, however, are always the same. What went right? What went wrong? What can be done better the next time? Identifying evaluation questions that will provide answers to these three overarching questions provides stakeholders with the information necessary to judge the merit or worth of a program and/or to make decisions regarding program continuation, modification, or abandonment. The answers to these questions also provide performance improvement practitioners with the information necessary to improve performance improvement.

Identification of relevant evaluation questions is the first step in planning an integrated evaluation. The next step is to determine how those questions can be answered. Generally speaking, evaluation questions are answered by collecting and analyzing data. More specifically, objective answers to evaluation questions are arrived at by identifying desired performance standards, stated in terms of units and time, measuring actual performance against those standards, and identifying discrepancies between the desired performance and actual performance. Performance standards should be linked directly to the objectives of the subject of the evaluation. If the objective is to improve customer satisfaction ratings by 20 percent, then the standard is whatever customer satisfaction rating correlates to a 20 percent increase. Binder (2001) warns against using the percentage as the standard. He explains that percentages fail to acknowledge the sample size, stating that "there is a huge difference between, for example, 90 percent of ten and 90 percent of one thousand" (p. 23). Binder also reminds us that, in addition to converting the 20 percent increase in customer satisfaction ratings to a non-percentage-based unit of measure, we must also include a time factor. The time component of the standard is affected by the type of evaluation the question pertains to. A 20 percent increase in satisfaction measured shortly after implementation of the intervention will show immediate changes in behavior and provide answers for product or summative evaluation questions. The data would need to be collected across a longer period of time or at a single predetermined time in the future to determine whether the 20 percent increase in satisfaction was sustainable, a fact that would be required to answer impact or confirmative evaluation questions.

Measurement provides the data that are compared to the standards. Measurement is the heart and soul of the evaluation process. Without measurement we have no data regarding the post-intervention environment. Without data we cannot compare the post-intervention environment to expectations. Without comparisons we cannot accurately judge merit or worth or make decisions. Measurement planning is therefore essential to the overall evaluation plan. Decisions regarding what to measure are driven by the previously identified standards. If we have determined that the standard or expectation is an increase in overall customer satisfaction ratings from 3.5 to 4.2 (a 20 percent increase) on a 5-point scale, four weeks after the intervention is fully implemented, then the data to be collected are customer satisfaction ratings on the same 5-point scale used prior to the intervention, and the timing of the collection is four weeks after implementation. This example illustrates the four key components of measurement planning, what to collect (customer satisfaction ratings), when to collect it (four weeks after implementation), from whom to collect it (customers), and how (existing customer satisfaction survey).

The final step in planning an integrated evaluation is planning for the data analysis and reporting processes. How data are analyzed is dependent on the type of data. Ideally, the measurement of factors associated with predetermined, objective-based standards will provide significant quantitative data. These quantitative or numerical data can be mathematically manipulated to provide correlations as well as descriptive statistics. Qualitative data, based on attitudinal surveys or interview questions or observations is more subjective and therefore more difficult to analyze. The planning phase should include decisions regarding the thematic, semantic differential, or taxonomic analysis of these data. Data analysis planning should always be linked to three factors: the type of data, how data are reported, and to whom they are reported. Data must be presented to organizational stakeholders in terms that are easily understood and relevant to them. This is the strength of Phillips' ROI model; it presents data in financial terms (Phillips, 1996). This seems like an excellent approach, and for some measures it is. But for other measures, those Phillips refers to as "intangible," conversion to financial units is highly subjective, which in turn weakens the evaluation.

Table 14.1 presents a simple matrix that can be used to plan an evaluation based on the integrated evaluation structure. For each step on the left, identify process, product, and impact-related evaluation questions and enter those into the appropriate place on the matrix. The completed matrix can then be used to develop standards and to plan measurement, analysis, and reporting activities. The matrix also clearly illustrates that process (formative), product (summative), and impact (confirmative) evaluation efforts are relevant throughout the performance improvement process. It is important to note that the integrated evaluation plan must be developed and implemented in steps because of the interdependent nature of the HPT processes. The outputs of the performance analysis step are the inputs for the cause analysis and the outputs of the cause analysis are the inputs for the intervention selection and design. The outputs of intervention selection and design are the inputs for implementation and change.

Table 14.1 Integrated Evaluation Matrix

	Process Evaluation (Formative)	Product Evaluation (Summative)	Impact Evaluation (Confirmative)
Performance Analysis			
Cause Analysis			
Intervention			
Selection and Design			
Implementation and Change			
Evaluation			

Only the evaluation step receives inputs and provides outputs throughout the entire process.

IDENTIFYING PROCESSES, PRODUCTS, AND IMPACT

This section looks at each step in the HPT model in more detail, examining the related activities to identify processes, products, and impacts associated with the individual steps. The identification of these components drives the development of the integrated evaluation, aiding in the development of evaluation questions, standards, measures and analysis, and reporting activities.

Performance Analysis

Performance analysis is the first step in the HPT Model (Van Tiem, Moseley, & Dessinger, 2000, 2004). Performance analysis encompasses three activities: organizational analysis, environmental analysis, and gap analysis. The goal is to analyze the organization and the environment to determine the current state of workplace performance and any discrepancies between actual performance and desired or ideal performance. Organizational analysis involves collecting data regarding the mission, vision, values, goals, and strategies of the organization. The output of organizational analysis is a picture of the desired level of performance. Environmental analysis considers many factors, including the organizational environment, the work environment, the work, the worker, and the world. Factors of interest related to the organizational environment include how the stakeholders and competition influence performance (p. 33). Factors of interest related to the work environment include hiring and promotion practices, management support, and feedback, and the availability of resources and tools required for optimal performance. Factors related to the work include job design and performance support, and factors related to the worker include knowledge, skill, motivation, expectations, and abilities (p. 33). Factors related to the world refer to societal impact. The output of environmental analysis is a picture of actual performance and the factors that contribute to it. The third component of performance analysis, gap analysis, is based on the outputs of the previous components. The desired performance, identified through organizational analysis, and the actual performance, identified through environmental analysis, are compared to identify any gaps that may exist between the two. Gaps or discrepancies between actual and desired performance are performance improvement opportunities. They are also the inputs for the cause analysis step in the HPT Model.

The integrated evaluation structure categorizes the data collection and analysis activities associated with performance analysis as processes, aligned with formative evaluation. The output of each of the three steps, desired performance, actual performance, and gaps in performance, are categorized as the products of the performance analysis, aligned with summative evaluation. The impact of the performance analysis activities is the long-term effects of the products of the task group on the subsequent performance improvement steps. Did the outputs provide the information necessary to complete the cause analysis and select, design, and implement an appropriate intervention? This impact is aligned with confirmative evaluation. See Table 14.2.

Process or formative evaluation during performance analysis involves evaluation of the data collection plan, the data collection process, and the data analysis. Evaluation questions related to data collection focus on from whom data were collected, how it were collected, and when. Evaluation questions related to data analysis focus on how the data were recorded, analyzed, and reported.

Table 14.2 Application to Performance Analysis

	Process (Formative)	Product (Summative)	Impact (Confirmative)
Performance analysis	Data collection planning	Ideal performance	Cause analysis
	Data collection process	Actual performance	Intervention selection
	Data analysis	Gap	

Implementation of the integrated evaluation structure during performance analysis, as with all other phases in the HPT process, involves determining what questions should be asked, the appropriate standards, the method, timing, and frequency of measurement against standards, and the data reporting and analysis associated with the evaluation activities. Relevant measures during this phase include the timing and method of data collection, the diversity of the population from whom the data was collected, and the recording and reporting methodology.

Cause Analysis

Cause analysis is the second step in the HPT model (Van Tiem, Moseley, & Dessinger, 2000, 2004). Cause analysis is based on the outputs of the performance analysis. Performance analysis clarifies "what" the problem is. Cause analysis takes that information, digs deeper, and provides the "why." Thomas Gilbert's Behavior Engineering Model (1978) categorized the causes of performance gaps as being related to environmental factors (data, instruments, and incentives) or individual factors (knowledge, capacity, and motives). Binder (1998) used the Behavior Engineering Model as the foundation for the Six Boxes Model. The boxes in Binder's model, like those in Gilbert's, focus on identifying enablers or positive behavior influences and obstructions or negative behavior influences to identify the cause of gaps in performance. The six boxes represented in the model are expectations and feedback, tools and resources, consequences and incentives, skills and knowledge, selection and assignment (capacity), and motives and preferences (attitude).

Cause analysis, like performance analysis, is primarily a data collection and analysis process. Data are collected from all relevant sources of information and analyzed to identify all factors contributing to the identified gap in performance. The data are then further analyzed to prioritize causes. The integrated evaluation structure categorizes the data collection and analysis process associated with the cause analysis as process, aligned with formative evaluation. The output data, the prioritized list of causes of the identified performance gap, are the product of the cause analysis and the input to the next step in the HPT process, intervention selection, and design. See Table 14.3.

Table 14.3 Application to Cause Analysis

	Process (Formative)	Product (Summative)	Impact (Confirmative)
Cause Analysis	Data collection Data analysis	Prioritized list of causes	Intervention selection

Implementation of the integrated evaluation structure during cause analysis, like performance analysis, involves determining what questions should be asked, the appropriate standards, the method, timing, and frequency of measurement against standards, and the data reporting and analysis associated with the evaluation activities. Relevant measures during this phase are very similar to those related to performance analysis. They include the timing and method of data collection, the diversity of the population from whom the data was collected, and the recording and reporting methodology. Additional measures of interest unique to the cause analysis are related to how identified causes are prioritized and reported.

Intervention Selection and Design

The third step in the HPT Model is intervention selection and design (Van Tiem, Moseley, & Dessinger, 2000, 2004). The inputs for this step are the outputs, or products, from the cause analysis. During intervention selection, the performance improvement specialist is responsible for using the cause analysis data and his or her expertise to determine "which interventions are most appropriate, timely, and cost-effective" (p. 67). During intervention design, the performance improvement specialist turns his focus to the creation of the selected intervention. Depending on the performance issue and selected intervention(s) this may involve creating job aids, designing instruction, modifying the work environment, instituting new policies and procedures, and so on. Design may involve benchmarking, where interventions used by other organizations are modified and applied to the current organization, repurposing of existing materials from previous interventions within the organization, or designing a situation-specific intervention from scratch. Intervention design is a costly and time-consuming process. If design is based on inaccurate input data from the performance analysis and cause analysis or poor intervention selection, the time and money invested here may not provide the desired outcomes.

Intervention selection is primarily a process activity. It, like performance analysis and cause analysis, is based on available data and the expertise of the performance improvement specialist. The performance improvement specialist may choose to begin by determining with which intervention category the identified situation is most closely aligned. Van Tiem, Moseley, and Dessinger (2000, 2004) provide the following list of intervention types:

1. Performance Support
2. Job Analysis/Work Design
3. Personal Development
4. Human Resources Development
5. Organizational Communication

6. Organizational Design and Development

7. Financial Systems

8. Other Interventions (p. 63)

Another common method of categorizing interventions is by level of impact on the organization. This methodology recognizes the importance of selecting the least invasive of the potential interventions to minimize unintended impacts on the organization.

After one or more suitable interventions are selected and authorized by the organization, design begins. Intervention design is the point at which traditional training-based evaluation models suggest evaluation efforts should begin, with the formative evaluation of the design process. Formative evaluation is indeed relevant at this point, but again, it is not the only type of evaluation that should be associated with intervention design.

Design, like analysis, is often a time-consuming and expensive activity. If materials can be repurposed from previous internal or external interventions, the timeline and expenses can be reduced, but often this is not the case. Often the intervention involves a new and significantly invasive program or project. Design activities may involve the development of individual, team, or organizational learning events, the development of work design changes such as those related to job specifications, job rotations, job enlargement, work methods continuous improvement, quality initiatives, ergonomics or safety engineering, or the development of personal interventions such as coaching and mentoring initiatives and career development structures (Van Tiem, Moseley, & Dessinger, 2000, 2004). It may focus on human resources initiatives like motivation, compensation, and benefits or health and wellness, organizational initiatives such as globalization, team building, and ethics or financial interventions such as financial forecasting, mergers, acquisitions, and joint ventures. Clearly, the list of potential interventions is limitless and, therefore, it is very difficult to compartmentalize the intervention design process. It may involve a small number of employees in a very limited way or it may have a significant impact on the entire organization. Evaluation efforts should be aligned with the scope of the intervention. More limited, informal evaluations may be suitable for smaller interventions with limited impact on the overall organization, but global interventions warrant significant measurement-driven evaluation efforts, focused on the process, product, and impact of the intervention selection and design.

Based on the integrated evaluation structure, process evaluations during intervention selection and design should focus on the categorization and decision-making processes associated with intervention selection and the content, audience, and delivery decisions made in conjunction with the intervention design. Product evaluations during intervention selection and design should focus on the selected intervention, which is the product of the intervention selection component, and the designed intervention, which is the product of the intervention design component. Impact evaluations related to intervention selection and design should focus on time, cost, and the intervention's success at resolving the identified performance issue. See Table 14.4.

Table 14.4 Application to Intervention Selection and Design

	Process (Formative)	Product (Summative)	Impact (Confirmative)
Intervention selection and design	Intervention categorization Selection decision-making process Design activities of identifying audiences, content, and format Design validation through traditional formative evaluation	Selected intervention Designed intervention	Time Cost Resolution of identified performance issue

Implementation of the integrated evaluation structure during the intervention selection and design phase of the HPT process will likely consist of both formal and informal evaluation activities, again focused on identifying evaluation questions, standards, and the method, timing, and frequency of measurements against those standards. Specific measures will vary based on the selected intervention and the complexity of the design process, but the relevant measures will always be related to the decision-making process and the quality of the design, including the input of subject-matter experts and stakeholders.

Implementation and Change

The fourth step in the HPT Model is implementation and change. These processes are generally linked to confirmative evaluation, represented in Kirkpatrick's four levels of evaluation as Levels 3 and 4, in Phillips' ROI Model as Levels 3, 4, and 5, and in the Dessinger-Moseley Full-Scope Evaluation Model as confirmative evaluation (Dessinger & Moseley, 2006; Kaufman, Keller, & Watkins, 1995; Phillips, 1996). The integrated evaluation structure argues that this focus is limited and that implementation and change, like performance analysis, cause analysis, and intervention selection and design, includes processes, products, and impacts and should, therefore, be evaluated at multiple levels.

Moseley and Hastings (2005) identify implementation as "the process of communicating, piloting, launching, monitoring and modifying interventions"

(p. 8). They add the "intended outcome is the institutionalization of the planned intervention, resulting in long-term change within the organization" (p. 8). Implementation and change do not occur overnight. They require careful planning, purposeful communication, specific action steps, and auditing and feedback over a period of time as the intervention moves through the implementation stages of plan, do, stabilize, and institutionalize.

The integrated evaluation structure indicates that processes associated with implementation and change include introduction of the initiative, the development of a structured roll-out scheduled for larger interventions, monitoring based on observations, feedback, and other data collection methods, and the development of design or implementation plan modifications. Each of these processes is aligned with traditional formative evaluation, targeted at identifying weaknesses in the process in order to strengthen the product. The integrated evaluation structure notes that the products related to the implementation and change task group include organizational support, a structured roll-out of the intervention based on need, analyzed data from the monitoring process, and revised interventions based on the completion of identified design modifications. These products are all aligned with traditional summative evaluation, targeted at evaluating the effectiveness of the product. The impact of the implementation and change phase focuses on the resolution of the identified performance issue and the institutionalization of the intervention. Like all impact or confirmative evaluations, this portion of the evaluation must occur after a reasonable amount of time has elapsed and should be focused on very well-defined evaluation questions, standards, data collection methods, and timing targeted at measuring performance against the identified standards and thoughtful analysis and reporting. See Table 14.5.

Table 14.5 Application to Implementation and Change

	Process (Formative)	Product (Summative)	Impact (Confirmative)
Implementation and Change	Introduction of the initiative	Organizational support	Resolution of the identified performance issue
	Implementation roll-out schedule	Structured roll-out based on need	Institutionalization of the intervention
	Monitoring	Analyzed data	
	Design or implementation modifications	Revisions	

Application of the integrated evaluation structure during implementation and change should be more formal than informal. Process (formative) evaluations should involve stakeholders at all levels and should be targeted at answering evaluation questions that will lead to final modifications of the intervention, ensuring institutionalization of the change. Product (summative) evaluations should focus on the organizational acceptance of the intervention. At this point the evaluator should be concerned with behavior changes, attitudes, and barriers that may impact outcomes. Again, specific evaluation questions should be used and measurements collected from a variety of stakeholders. The impact of the implementation and change is also the final impact of the performance improvement initiative. If formal and informal process, product, and impact evaluation has taken place throughout the performance improvement life cycle, the evaluation of the implementation and change should indicate a successful resolution of the performance-related issue. It should also provide valuable input data for future performance improvement activities.

Evaluation

Evaluation is the fifth and final step in the HPT process. Evaluation is unique in that it permeates the entire HPT process, receiving inputs from and providing outputs to all of the other steps in the HPT Model (Van Tiem, Moseley, & Dessinger, 2000, 2004). Evaluation is the overarching process that ensures that each step is completed effectively and that each step receives quality inputs from the previous process. Evaluation, whether formative (process), summative (product), or confirmative (impact), involves many activities. These activities, like those that take place at other times during the performance improvement process, can be categorized as processes, products, and impacts. The integrated evaluation structure identifies the processes associated with evaluation as identifying evaluation questions and standards, the method, timing, and frequency of measurements against those standards, and data analysis plans. The product of evaluation is the knowledge provided by the analysis and interpretation of the data. The knowledge is dependent upon the timing of the evaluation. It may be related to the accuracy of the performance analysis, the prioritization of the causes of the gap in performance, the quality of the intervention design, or the effectiveness of the implementation effort. Likewise, because evaluation permeates the entire HPT process, it impacts all processes and products associated with the performance improvement effort, the organization, the stakeholders, and the performance improvement process. See Table 14.6.

Implementation of the integrated evaluation structure during the evaluation phase of the HPT process consists of evaluation of the evaluation strategies implemented throughout the performance improvement process. Specific

Table 14.6 Application to Evaluation

	Process (Formative)	Product (Summative)	Impact (Confirmative)
Evaluation	Evaluation questions	Output data related to:	Performance analysis
	Standards and measures	Performance analysis	Cause analysis
		Cause analysis	Intervention selection and design
	Timing and method of measurement	Intervention selection and design	
			Implementation and change
	Data analysis	Implementation and change	Organization
			Stakeholders
			Performance improvement specialist

measures will vary based on what is being evaluated, but the relevant measures will always be related to the decision making, data collection, and analysis processes.

CONCLUSION

It is important to acknowledge that evaluation of processes, products, and impact for all five steps in the HPT process is not always practical and that every evaluator must decide, based on budget, timing, and other organizational constraints, what is and is not possible in any given situation. The goal is to strive for fully integrated evaluation and to be cognizant of the fact that each task associated with performance improvement involves processes that lead to products that will impact the organization, the environment, and the worker. It is, therefore, essential that we not limit formative, summative, and confirmative evaluation by associating each with a single place on the performance improvement process chart or time in the performance improvement life cycle. We must allow process (formative), product (summative), and impact (confirmative) evaluation efforts to permeate the entire performance improvement process.

The integrated evaluation structure does not challenge the current evaluation methodology. It supports full-scope evaluation and the role of measurement in the evaluation process. But it does challenge the ideas that performance analysis and cause analysis are strictly process-related activities, that intervention selection and design are strictly product-related activities, and that implementation and change are strictly impact-related activities. The integrated evaluation structure challenges the performance improvement specialist to identify and evaluate these three components throughout the performance improvement process, understanding that improving evaluation will improve performance improvement.

References

Alexander, M. E., & Christoffersen, J. (2006). The total evaluation process: Shifting the mental model. *Performance Improvement*, *45*(7), 23–27.

Beer, V., & Bloomer, A. C. (1986). Levels of evaluation. *Educational Evaluation and Policy Analysis*, *8*(4), 335–345.

Binder, C. (2001). Measurement: A few important ideas. *Performance Improvement*, *40*(3), 20–28.

Binder, C. (1998). The six boxes: A descendent of Gilbert's behavior engineering model. *Performance Improvement*, *37*(6), 48–52.

Dessinger, J. C., & Moseley, J. L. (2006). The full scoop on full scope evaluation. In J. A. Pershing (Ed.), *Handbook of human performance technology* (3rd ed.) (pp. 312–329). San Francisco: Pfeiffer.

Dessinger, J. C., & Moseley, J. L. (2004). *Confirmative evaluation: Practical strategies for valuing continuous improvement*. San Francisco: Pfeiffer,

Ford, D. J. (2004). Evaluating performance improvement. *Performance Improvement*, *43*(1), 36–41.

Gilbert, T. F. (1978). *Human competence: Engineering worth performance*. New York: McGraw-Hill.

Kaufman, R. A., Keller, J. M., & Watkins, R. (1995). What works and what doesn't: Evaluation beyond Kirkpatrick. *Performance and Instruction*, *35*(2), 8–12.

Moseley, J. L., & Hastings, N. B. (2005). Implementation: The forgotten link on the intervention chain. *Performance Improvement Journal*, *44*(4), 8–14.

Phillips, J. J. (1996). Was it the training? *Training and Development*, *50*(3), 28–32.

Van Tiem, D. M., Moseley, J. L., & Dessinger, J. C. (2000). *Fundamentals of performance technology: A guide to improving people, process and performance*. Silver Spring, MD: International Society for Performance Improvement.

Van Tiem, D. M., Moseley, J. L., & Dessinger, J. C. (2004). *Fundamentals of performance technology: A guide to improving people, process and performance* (2nd ed.). Silver Spring, MD: International Society for Performance Improvement.

CHAPTER FIFTEEN

Using Evaluation Results to Improve Human Performance Technology Projects

Carol K. Diroff

The human resources department (HRD) was extremely proud of its newly acquired ability to handle human performance technology projects. Its first project was to analyze and improve performance in the company's accounting department, with the goals of reducing cost and increasing productivity. After analysis, HRD created solutions for all the productivity problems that were discovered within accounting. Those solutions required training on a new process to reduce cost, adjusting staff work schedules from two shifts to three to be available for the company's worldwide locations, and new work stations to drive more efficient productivity. After implementation of these solutions, the human resources department conducted evaluations and found that everything worked as planned and they all lived happily ever after. This is, of course, a fairly tale.

If they had actually evaluated their solutions, here's what they would have found. There was a decrease in individual performance and a minor increase in customer satisfaction because of the third shift (the international locations were extremely happy with the new twenty-four-hour operation). If they had isolated the evaluations of the three interventions, they would have discovered that increasing the number of shifts had a negative effect on all three shifts that resulted in reduced productivity overall, the new work stations produced a neutral impact, and the training didn't work because the content was confusing.

If they had adjusted the training and the shift issue a few times based on evaluation results, re-evaluation would have shown that performance did improve.

The simple conclusion that could be drawn from this story is that evaluation results that correct deficiencies in human performance technology interventions can indeed create effective, positive change. The truth is that, with multiple interventions, the complexity of evaluating those solutions increases, and an organization may re-evaluate and adjust solutions or interventions several times before achieving the desired success. The organization may also discover that other critical factors such as support for feedback and change, evaluation timing, accurate baseline data, selection of changes, implementation of changes, and relationships between solutions may enable or interfere with their ability to implement change successfully. Finally, implementing changes to existing solutions may be difficult, but certainly not impossible, to sell to the organization.

SUPPORT FOR EVALUATION AND CHANGE—THE ENABLERS

Alignment for successful implementation, evaluation, and performance improvement within any organization begins with the organization itself. It is necessary that the organization do the following:

- Support the concept that performance is defined, measurable, holistic, and that performance elements are interrelated. This support is evident in aligned vision, mission, strategic initiatives, goals and objectives, and competencies. The support is also evident in the culture and environment of the organization. Rather than prescriptive interventions, the organization supports diagnostic methods that get to the root causes of problems and preventive interventions that reduce or eliminate problems before they happen.

- Provide and support resources for forging effective change, even if it takes several tries and some failures. The organization takes ownership of both the problems and solutions and works with solutions providers to continuously improve its results. The critical word here is ''continuously.'' Smart organizations look at performance improvement as ongoing and continuous and do not wait until a critical mass of problems triggers a response.

- Have processes and tools for investigation, design, development, implementation, and evaluation of simple interventions or of cross-functional or complex interrelated solutions for performance problems. These processes and tools should also be aligned *between* solution providers, and there must be a mechanism for coordination between those providers. This simply means that, if the compensation group, training, and ergonomics experts share the responsibility for a solution set, all three organizations must coordinate their efforts. If each solution provider works independently, ability to impact performance and subsequently measure that impact is limited and may even be counterproductive. For example, if ergonomics installs new work stations that revise where parts to be assembled are located, training shouldn't ignore the impact that the work stations have on processes that they are teaching for assembling those parts.

- Attend to the critical factors for using evaluation results to correct and adjust HPT projects. This begins with careful investigation and baseline data collection and ends with appropriate, successful interventions and, in between, allows for measurement against that substantiated baseline data. It also requires that all solution providers ultimately agree on the interpretation of the data upon which changes are made.

Having defined the ideal state for nurturing changes based on evaluation of HPT projects, note that the opposite state is an organization that:

- Does not have mechanisms for cross-functional interventions.
- Cannot or will not align goals, strategies, and objectives within the organization, making it impossible to measure project success (let alone any success).
- Does not do anything with evaluation results or, indeed, does not evaluate at all.
- Has no HPT process or staff and/or has no governance within the HPT process (if there is one), preventing feedback from having an impact.
- Truncates the HPT process by preventing accurate data collection before, during, and after interventions, permits flawed interpretation of the data based on biases and political whims, and promotes the use of wrong (but perhaps politically correct) interventions.
- Waits until problems achieve a critical mass before reacting to them, causing a panic reaction instead of prevention of problems. Needless to say, this drives cost of interventions up in at least two ways: (1) cost for fixing the problems is greater and (2) the cost for lost opportunities because the problems result in lost business, no money to cover the intervention costs, and a need to reduce human resources.

If the stars align and enablers are in place, such as a nurturing environment for change, the potential for refining and revising human performance based on evaluation should be achievable.

CONTINUOUS EVALUATION: CRITICAL ASPECTS OF EVALUATION TYPES AND TIMING

The Van Tiem, Moseley, and Dessinger (2004) model in Figure 15.1 shows evaluation as a feedback to every other part of the model and, while it divides evaluation into discrete timing (formative, summative, confirmative, and meta), the arrows indicate the need and recommendation for evaluation throughout the HPT process (p. 3).

Shrock and Geis (1999) go one step further by stating that, when evaluation is used correctly in an organization, it becomes a *continual* process (p. 189). Brinkerhoff (2006) supports this practice by saying that ''HPT practitioners must continuously revisit earlier decisions and assumptions, changing plans and direction as needed'' (p. 295). The nature of the data collected, evaluated, and used to adjust interventions can and will change during continuous evaluation and feedback. Another recommendation that supports the model is to evaluate at each step in the HPT process—analysis, design, development, and implementation (Geis & Smith, as cited in Gilley & Maycunich, 2000, p. 417).

A simple definition of continuous evaluation combines traditional evaluation methods and timing with access to and use of additional sources of information and data that can affect HPT interventions. Rather than just scheduling evaluations, the HPT practitioner can use multiple sources of information, as they occur, to assess whether or not interventions are working and relevant to the organization. Both solicited and unsolicited data and information can alter the course of single and multiple interventions.

Understanding the multifaceted nature of continuous evaluation, we can identify three types of evaluation in a continuous evaluation model: *formal evaluation, informal evaluation*, and *relative evaluation*. The first, formal or discrete evaluation is evaluation done at specific times in the process to measure impact of performance interventions. This evaluation is defined in the HPT model and is done at specific times during the process, generally by the HPT organization. These evaluations usually seek information on results of interventions and their measurable impact to the performer, the performance, and the organization as a whole. Kirkpatrick and Kirkpatrick (2006) have labeled these evaluations by the types of information they collect: reaction, learning, behavior, and results (p. 21).

The second type of continuous evaluation is anecdotal evaluation. Data sources may be internal or external to the organization. Data generated from within the organization may include production statistics, numbers of calls taken or dropped in a call center, sales results, or opinion surveys of performers, product, management, and customers. Unlike traditional evaluation information, these evaluation data may, in fact, be generated *by the organization* and fed to the

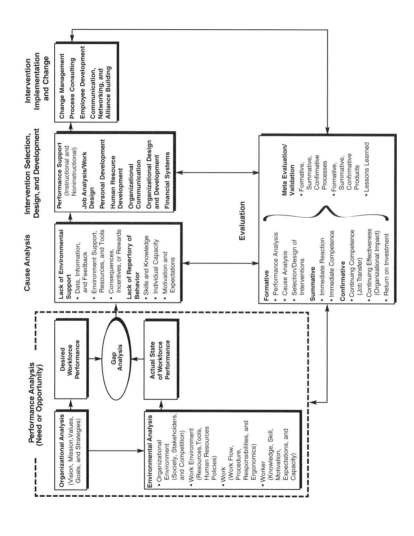

Figure 15.1 Human Performance Technology Model.

HPT practitioner instead of the reverse. Philips (1986) cites several key indicators of performance that are generated just by the HRD function: employment data, EEO data, training use tracking, employee evaluations, safety data, absenteeism, and salary and benefit administration (p. 41). While the triggers for collecting these statistics may have nothing to do with evaluating ongoing HPT projects, they may have everything to do with the successful evaluation and outcomes of those projects.

External anecdotal data may influence HPT solutions. For example, companies that report changes in market conditions to their employees may very well be supplying information to their HPT practitioner that can alter existing interventions. Organizations that track market share may be able to draw a direct line from these interventions to their performance and to their market share result.

Note that, as with formal evaluation, anecdotal evaluation data do not always trigger change. The organization will need to weigh every potential alteration to methods and interventions against the gains that change would produce and decide whether or not change is necessary or warranted.

The third element of continuous evaluation is relative evaluation, which measures performance between and among multiple interventions. While it provides traditional measurements, it can also measure the impact of changes that are external to the interventions, such as a change in senior management or changes that are outside of the organization. Relative evaluation can either be formal, done at specific times, or anecdotal. Table 15.1 describes each of these facets of evaluation, some possible methods to use in doing them, and the timing for each.

The literature covers formal evaluation thoroughly, and the same methods used to apply corrective actions resulting from these types of evaluations will work regardless of the sources of information. What does change is the notion that evaluation data are collected at specific times and corrections to interventions are done at those times, if warranted. Because anecdotal data may appear at any time, the HPT practitioner will have to decide, at the times when significant data appear, whether or not to make changes. When several interventions are involved, that decision becomes more complex.

RELATIVE EVALUATIONS OF INTERRELATED SOLUTIONS

Relative evaluations covering multiple interventions requires considerable thought and skill. Anderson (2003) recommends some important tactics. The first is to choose to measure only what is important by isolating the critical factors impacting change. If an organization reacts to every change, the cost and time involved could be overwhelming. The second tactic Anderson

Table 15.1 Evaluation Timing

Evaluation Element	Possible Methods/ Measurements	Timing
Formal Evaluation		
• Traditional evaluation assessing the success of each intervention • Proactive solicitation of feedback by the HPT practitioner • May be included routinely with the intervention or planned for based on intervention timing	• Formative • Meta evaluation • Summative • Confirmative • Methods and tools are specific to the type of evaluation data required and to the timing	Specified timing for both evaluation and feedback • Pre-implementation of solutions (needs assessment, pilot) • Implementation (reaction) • Post-implementation (evaluation of methods, results, impact) • Validation (after interventions and evaluation instruments have been used for a specified period of time) • Adjustments to the intervention may occur after evaluation data collection and analysis
Anecdotal or Continuous Evaluation		
• Data are collected as they occur • Indications are that data will affect the performance interventions in some way • Data are significant only as they relate to the interventions and may result in changes to baseline data	• Interim performance reviews • Normal business data collection, such as sales figures, quality data • Anecdotal information from meetings, focus groups, existing surveys • External information, such as stock market changes, competitive changes	• Timing is not fixed but based on when information is available • Data may be available more frequently than when using formal evaluation methods • Timing for feedback and adjustments to the interventions will depend on the data criticality and ability and desire of the organization to react

Relative Evaluation

• Assesses the impact that multiple interventions have within each intervention and between all related interventions • May result from both formal and informal evaluation • Relies on ability to collect data specific to each intervention and align data between multiple interventions • Will be most significant for adjusting interventions that have the same general goal • May also be required when non-intervention changes occur	• May be qualitative or quantitative data • Correlation is a factor • Isolation is a factor • It may be collected through traditional methods, such as focus groups, tests, surveys, and observations, or may be anecdotal • Will need to assess significance to all interventions to verify effects	• Timing may be informal to enable critical, quick adjustments to multiple interventions • Timing may be formal to enable consistent time-bound data collection • Timing for feedback and adjustments to the interventions will depend on the data criticality and ability and desire of the organization to react

recommends is to attend to other influences on performance both inside and outside the organization The third tactic is to build a case for change based on the isolation of causes and effects and, finally, to create valid, credible evaluations (p. 77). The complexity of interrelationships will arise again when implementing interrelated revised solutions.

Why are interrelated solutions hard to evaluate? In statistical terms, there is a need to isolate and evaluate within each intervention as well as a need to examine the interactions between interventions. There is also a valid concern that any intervention may cause a halo effect that makes other interventions appear successful. In the example that started this chapter, a change in work stations could be responsible for making the accounting staff more productive, or the training could have produced the increased productivity, or both.

Another factor that impacts evaluations is that solutions exist within environments or contexts that are outside the organization's control. Factors such as the economy, political environment, competition, and laws are elements that the

HPT practitioner must consider. It is especially critical when changing interventions to revisit these environmental influences to test for changes that impact possible corrections to interventions. This examination should occur as part of the decision-making process which results from evaluation. This is required in all continuous evaluation processes.

IMPORTANCE OF BASELINE DATA

One more major component that needs to be addressed is baseline information collected during needs assessment. Having accurate baseline data directly impacts the evaluation of performance. It is only possible to measure changes in performance when there is an indication of what the original performance was (worst, average, exemplar) prior to implementing interventions. If the baseline remains static, you can evaluate performance against the data. If, however, the baseline appears skewed, evaluation may require that you update the baseline. For example, if the baseline number of accounts payable transactions processed per hour by an exemplar performer was seven and the evaluation results after intervention reveal that the worst performer can still only do two, the intervention may not be working or the baseline may have been flawed. Therefore, in implementing changes to HPT projects, the evaluation data may become the new baseline data. If the original interventions were flawed, inaccurate baseline data might be the reason. In any case, with baseline comparisons pre-and post-intervention can be made.

If an HPT project is done correctly within an environment that nurtures performance improvement, the measurement of the HPT project will have a better potential for success. If evaluation is successful and the organization draws valid conclusions from the data, making change based on evaluation feedback is the next logical step. This is the point at which the HPT practitioner can evaluate the need for changes to existing interventions and decide what to do.

SELECTION OF CHANGES

After evaluation is done, selection of changes is the next logical step. Remember that change based on evaluation is a "second" change. During the determination of original solutions, the HPT practitioner justified the need for the original changes. Feeding back evaluation results to the organization that result in alterations to interventions is *additional* change. Justification for an additional round of changes may require even more rigorous substantiation than for the original recommendations.

Criteria for selecting appropriate changes are complex, especially with the potential need to justify them. The HPT practitioner will have to consider the following questions:

- Is there enough information to determine the critical changes that would have the most *impact* on the organization? To find out, the HPT practitioner may have to

  - Estimate the cost and resource utilization the change requires and compare that to the original estimates from the first intervention.

  - Estimate the resulting gain/loss and the business impact, again compared to the first intervention.

  - Isolate the effects of each of the interventions to concentrate on those that have the greatest potential for impact.

  - Rebalance the combinations of existing interventions to do more or less with each, according to evaluation results.

  - Justify doing nothing based on real or perceived benefit to staying the course.

- Will the organization welcome additional changes? To prepare an answer for that question, it will be necessary to define why a second (or more) round of changes is going to work any better than the first interventions did. Therefore, the HPT practitioner may want to gauge and plan for the potential reactions and resistance from the organization. The HPT practitioner may also have to accept that needed changes are, because of organizational factors, difficult or impossible to implement. Internal political factors may prevent the achievement of optimal results, and foster politically correct results.

- Is there enough information to accurately pinpoint *what* the critical changes should be? If evaluation results indicate that one or more of the selected interventions failed, revisiting the initial investigation and selection of solutions may be needed. The diligence required by an investigation using a tool like Gilbert's (1996) behavior engineering model (p. 87) may help reveal flaws in the original investigation or changes that have taken place since that investigation. Of course, using good analysis tools in the first place may reduce the need to re-investigate performance.

- Is the organization capable of making these changes? Even if there is a determination that the changes will have a positive impact, the practitioner must consider the organization's capability to make them work. Environmental support for change, consequences for good and poor performance, tacit opinions on change, and motivation to change could be strong enough to influence the capability the organization has to institute further change.

- "Is it worth pursuing?" This may be the most difficult question to answer. In Mager and Pipe's model (1997), this question plays a critical role in determining whether or not to continue pursuing solutions for changing performance (p. 9). In deciding whether or not to institute further changes within an HPT project, the HPT practitioner will consider the resources used for the initial interventions, the extended costs for additional interventions, and the possibility that further change may be an inhibitor to improved performance, rather than enhancing it. Further change may also produce no results.

INFUSING CHANGE: CRITICAL SUCCESS FACTORS

The solution providers play key roles in the implementation of changes meant to improve HPT projects. In many organizations, teams of specialists are assembled to work on the initial solutions. Ergonomists, organizational effectiveness experts, management, training experts, to mention a few, gather to work on problems or opportunities, each playing a unique role on the team. The hope is that, within the solution set, experts will have attended to that part of the solution they are most capable of recommending. There may be an additional hope that all the solutions work in concert with one another and one solution does not offset the success of another. Also tied into that hope is that the organization provides support for each and all of the solutions.

Accounting for the interactions of solutions is as critical when the solutions are changed and interventions are adjusted as it was the first time they were created. There is a delicate balance among the solutions in HPT-based interventions. Factors such as support, timing, practitioner skill, external influences, and worker characteristics must still be aligned after making changes to interventions. Any loss of balance among these factors can cause the revised and existing interventions to fail.

IMPLEMENTING CHANGE—VALUE, SEQUENCE, AND TIMING

Our company is now at the point at which everything has been done correctly. The company did a robust needs assessment, proposed solid solutions, and designed and implemented them appropriately. Even the evaluation was good. Evaluation results showed that more changes were necessary. Next, the HPT practitioner questioned the value of those changes, asking whether the changes should be implemented and, if so, in what order and when.

Here is the story thus far. First solution set and evaluation: The human resources department trained a new process, added a shift, and implemented new work stations to drive more efficient productivity. Evaluation of the interventions concluded that the added shift decreased morale, the new work stations had no impact, the training didn't work, and overall individual productivity declined. Evaluation also showed that there was a genuine improvement in satisfaction with worldwide accounting coverage because of the third shift. The company had also promoted staff to be supervisors on the third shift, resulting in an increased cost for salaries.

Proposed second solution set: Based on the above evaluation data and subsequent investigation and analysis, HRD determined that:

- If the training had to change, they also had to retrain employees who had taken the original training as well as train those employees who still had to take the training.

- Next, HRD concluded that the way they introduced the third shift was flawed but that eliminating the third shift was also a problem. While it might appear obvious that cancelling the third shift would be the appropriate first step, HRD did not want to do it—and with good reasons: they needed third-shift coverage for worldwide operations, and they did not want to demote employees who had been promoted to supervision to cover the third shift, exacerbating the already low morale. They proposed to provide incentives for the third shift, including a shift premium and flex-time.

- Since the change in work stations had no immediate impact, HRD decided to do nothing about them, but reserved the right to revisit this change at a later date. They felt they could re-evaluate the impact of work stations for additional improvements once other changes had worked.

HRD deliberated. Should they commit to all the changes or only to some of the changes? Should they introduce the new interventions all at one time or stage the implementation? What, they also wondered, would be the correct sequence for introducing these changes? They looked for answers.

They first considered the value of each change to the organization. With the exception of the work stations, each proposed change was perceived critical and of high value. If both the training and the shift issues were resolved, they still believed that productivity would increase and that cost would go down. Because the money had been spent on the work stations without a positive result, subsequent changes would only increase the money spent on that intervention without the promise (initially) of significant gain. Therefore, they chose to concentrate on the training and straighten out the shift issue based on the potential value for doing each.

Next, they looked at whether or not they should do all the changes at one time or introduce them separately. They recommended a staged implementation of three interventions (training, a shift premium, and flex-time) after they weighed several factors for each of the proposed changes. Table 15.2 shows how they determined both the staging and the sequence.

Table 15.2 identifies the measures they used to determine sequence and timing for the changes they wanted to make to interventions. (Note that the criteria organizations use can and will change for each instance of multiple changes to interventions.) HRD validated this information with stakeholders and management so that the values entered represented the organization's best thinking.

THE DECISION

Because of the negative impact to the bottom line and potential lack of support, they chose to delay the shift premium intervention until a case could be made that would be strong enough to justify the increased cost and until they could gain management support. HRD did, however, reserve the right to revisit shift premiums if subsequent evaluations showed the need.

HRD wanted to measure the impact of the other two interventions to see whether the third would be necessary. Because the shift premium would increase cost and the initial goal was to decrease cost, they reasoned that they would support this effort only if the other two changes failed to produce results.

Changes to the training had to be done immediately. Some employees had been poorly trained on a new process and others had not received the training. HRD decided to rewrite the existing training and, using single-point lessons, re-educate those who had already taken the training. They did this to reduce the cost for retraining and had an additional, unplanned benefit—the single-point lessons became job aids after their initial use.

INTERRELATIONSHIPS BETWEEN CHANGED SOLUTIONS ON CLIENTS

Delaying the implementation of one change and implementing others indicates that there could be both conflicting and enabling impacts on the people affected by the changes as well. Managing such interventions requires controls and balance, and it takes more than just prioritizing and sequencing solutions to be successful. The HPT organization will have to determine the impact of multiple solutions on its clients and the organization and not just on the receivers of the interventions.

Gilley and Maycunich (2000) identify four classifications of clients that the HPT organization may have: "decision-makers" (senior executives and management with overall responsibility for the organization's success), "stakeholders" (those with risk in the implementation of solutions), "influencers" (have no direct

Table 15.2 Impact Assessment of Potential Interventions

Criteria	Intervention 1: Revised Training	Intervention 2: Add Shift Incentives	Intervention 3: Allow Flex Time
Resources			
Impact on existing resources (budget, time, headcount)	• Slight budget increase due to cost for duplication of effort. • Increase in time to redo work and take training. • No increase in headcount	• Budget increase. • Slight increase in time to process payroll • No increase in headcount	• No impact
Timing			
Time needed to institute the change	• Short-term	• Long-term due to budget approval, developing a business case, and finding a champion	• Short-term impact
Predicted Impact on Performers			
Predicted increase/ decrease in performance	• Gradual performance increase	• Immediate performance increase	• Immediate performance increase
Predicted increase/ decrease in morale	• Should increase morale	• Should increase morale	• Should increase morale
Predicted Impact on Organization			
Support for change to existing interventions	• High management support	• Low management support	• Moderate management support
Amount/ significance of risk	• Moderate to low	• High	• Low
Impact/ contribution to business goals	• Positive impact and contribution to goals if productivity increases	• Not able to determine: Initial negative impact financially, could result in high positive impact	• No impact to cost, positive impact to goals if productivity increases

impact, but can contribute knowledge and influence on decisions), and "scouts" (sponsors, subject-matter experts, with the ability to predict outcomes and supply information) (pp. 258–259). Each influences organizational change uniquely and may suffer for or benefit from these changes just as uniquely. In the previous example, support for a shift premium could be positive for the manager who is responsible for the work, negative for the manager who is responsible for budget, tentative for the stakeholders, and highly positive for sponsors and influencers who want success for the overall goals. Each has a reason to want a given outcome, but their reasons, outcomes, and measurements of success are all different.

How, then, can the HPT practitioner select and implement new changes to previously agreed-on solutions and satisfy management, influencers, stakeholders, and sponsors? The answer may rest in the compromise of high-level, uniformly adopted goals that everyone can agree to and in tradeoffs that drive consensus. High-level goals may actually enable compromise. If, for example, the HR organization sees a critical need in implementing the shift premium, they need to forge a connection between that action and the goals of the overall organization—their definition of success. A valid argument in a business case may be that the increase in salary cost could be offset by an increase in productivity, resulting in the need to use fewer employees for the same amount of work. This is a decision that may work with management and influencers, but not work with stakeholders and sponsors who may be responsible for implementing staff reductions. If, on the other hand, an increase in salary cost is offset by attrition over time or an increase in business that requires more staff, everyone is happy. Needless to say, potential for both attrition and new business will play an important role in the willingness of everyone to compromise.

BEWARE OF LURKING MONSTERS

Just like a red shirt in a load of white laundry, revising interventions may cause problems that spread beyond those originally identified. If the objective was to get a load of clothes clean, that red shirt will pose a new problem not intended by the original solution—washing the clothes. Interrelationships between solutions pose the same possibility that one intervention may cause new problems or prevent an additional intervention from working. Using the HR example, implementation of a shift premium for the third shift may offset gains that training caused because workers on the other two shifts make less money and could balk at producing the same amount of work as the premium shift workers. This is not a time to abandon caution and "give it a try," but a time to thoroughly test potential impact before doing damage.

Still another common factor with interrelated solutions is that interventions may not completely solve problems on their own, but together may reduce a problem to a manageable state. This optimal outcome is difficult to justify; there is always a drive toward perfect solutions, but justification often comes in measuring improvement against acceptable levels of performance. A classic example is the requirement for a six-sigma change. Why not seven, or eight? It is because six produces the lowest satisfactory failure levels of 99.999 percent perfection, but certainly not flawless levels (Van Tiem, Dessinger, & Moseley, 2006, p. 694).

Finally, the HPT practitioner needs to stop the cycle of evaluation and implementation of improvements when there is no business reason for change—either little to gain from further change or the cost of change is higher than the anticipated return. This also applies to a judgment call that the practitioner makes when resources are limited—to quit working on one set of solutions because others have become more critical. Sometimes, the need for that solution set has just gone away and it is time to move on.

FEEDBACK FOR THE FUTURE

Evaluation can be a dead end to an otherwise robust performance improvement project unless effort is spent to absorb the results, to make improvements based on the knowledge gained, and, finally, to capture and use lessons learned. Brinkerhoff (2006) points out that a valuable result of evaluation is that it "improves future HPT efforts by helping stakeholders investigate past efforts and decide what has worked and what has not, guiding them to allocate resources and organizational energy to subsequent efforts that have the greatest promise for paying off" (p. 289). In proposing continuous evaluation, continuous improvement should be an end-result, but not the only result. Knowledge gained by evaluating the processes and tools used to achieve performance improvement deserve the same importance as the improvements themselves. Therefore, feeding back process lessons learned should be a goal of every human performance technology project. Typical questions to answer would be: "What went right?" "What went wrong?" and "What should we do differently?"

CONCLUSION

Evaluation of HPT solutions cannot be a one-time effort. Continuous evaluation provides organizations with data from a variety of sources and at a frequency that allows for quick response and adjustment to interventions. The within and between effects that are measured for multiple solutions can help the HPT practitioner fine-tune interventions, even at a moment's notice, to help the organization maintain course. With business environments making it harder for organizations to survive, even a few days of going in the wrong direction can have dire consequences. Waiting to evaluate no longer makes sense and can waste limited resources. Waiting to correct a flawed course of action can be lethal. The simple conclusion is that HPT practitioners should and must evaluate every impact on interventions and choose changes carefully. The very life of the organization may depend on that behavior.

References

Anderson, M. C. (2003). *Bottom-line organizational development: Implementing and evaluating strategic change for lasting value.* Amsterdam: Elsevier Butterworth-Heinemann.

Brinkerhoff, R. O. (2006). Using evalution to measure and improve the effectiveness of human performance technology initiatives. In H. S. Stolovitch & E. J. Keeps (Eds.), *Handbook of human performance technology* (3rd ed.) (pp. 287–311). San Francisco: Pfeiffer.

Gilbert, T. F. (1996). *Human competence: Engineering worthy performance* (tribute ed.). Silver Spring, MD: The International Society for Performance Improvement.

Gilley, J. W., & Maycunich, A. (2000). *Organizational learning, performance, and change.* Cambridge, MA: Perseus.

Kirkpatrick, D. L., & Kirkpatrick, J. D. (2006). *Evaluating training programs: The four levels* (3rd ed.). San Francisco: Berrett-Koehler.

Mager, R. F., & Pipe, P. (1997). *Analyzing performance problems or you really oughta wanna* (3rd ed.). Atlanta, GA: CEP Press.

Phillips, J. J. (1996). *Accountability in human resource management.* Houston: Gulf.

Shrock, S. A., & Geis, G. L. (1999). Evaluation. In H. S. Stolovitch & E. J. Keeps (Eds.), *Handbook of human performance technology* (2nd ed.) (pp. 185–209). San Francisco: Pfeiffer.

Van Tiem, D. M., Moseley, J. L., & Dessinger, J. C. (2004). *Fundamentals of performance technology* (2nd ed.). Silver Spring, MD: International Society for Performance Improvement.

Van Tiem, D. M., Dessinger, J. C., & Moseley, J. L. (2006). Six sigma: Increasing human performance technology value and results. In H. S. Stolovitch & E. J. Keeps (Eds.), *Handbook of human performance technology* (3rd ed.) (pp. 287–311). San Francisco: Pfeiffer.

FRONTIERS IN MEASUREMENT AND EVALUATION

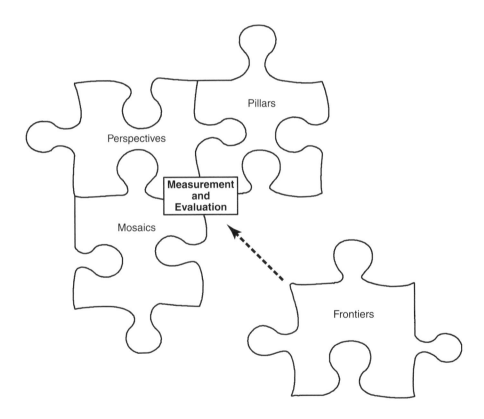

Inspired by their ideas and motivated by their hopes and dreams to change the direction of their future, the pioneers of long ago made pathways toward new frontiers as they faced challenges and dangers unlike anything they had ever known or imagined. Their determination was based in the belief that the power

273

to change was in their own hands. That precept is still very true today, since we have the knowledge, tools, and power to create our own futures. Part Four, "Frontiers in Measurement and Evaluation," looks at new beginnings, new horizons, and new arenas on the proverbial "yellow brick road" to measurement and evaluation. The authors address ideas that involve taking thoughtful and reflective risks based on current theories and practices, providing educated guesses, looking at trends, and forecasting visions and directions.

Chapter Sixteen: Understanding Context: Evaluation and Measurement in Not-for-Profit Sectors. According to Brandenburg, the emphasis in evaluation in non-profit sectors in recent years has shifted to outcome measurement, impact evaluation, and sustainability from administrative and process evaluation. The formulations of evaluation plans rely heavily on stakeholder analysis and the development of logic models. The former is needed to structure the often politically charged evaluation context; the latter is required to connect program design to intended results.

Chapter Seventeen: Using New Technology to Create a User-Friendly Evaluation Process. Rothwell and Whiteford discuss the impact that emerging technologies will continue to have on evaluation practice. They examine some of the new technology-based tools that expand the scope of evaluation in terms of the number and geographic distribution of participants; types of data that can be collected; size and relational capabilities of storage and retrieval systems; types of analysis conducted; and type of reports generated. They offer the promise of exciting new ways to "do" evaluation.

Chapter Eighteen: New Kids on the Block: Evaluation in Practice. Smith's chapter discusses the best way to tell the workplace story using five measurement and evaluation plans. She describes and discusses them and talks about their implications for the workplace. She provides a workplace alignment guide to assist practitioners with their measurement and evaluation plan.

Chapter Nineteen: Expanding Scope of Evaluation in Today's Organization. For Russ-Eft, evaluation use is expanding and evaluations are being used to aid decision making around priorities, resources, and quality, as well as to support shared learning. Future challenges revolve around global competency and ethical standards, the use of meta evaluation to inform practice, and increased professionalism and accountability within the evaluation community.

Chapter Twenty: The Changing Role of Evaluators and Evaluation. Chevalier makes the case for evaluation as a profession. He highlights major journals, associations, standards, competencies, and ethics of evaluation. He addresses various types of professional certifications for the busy practitioner and ends with some thoughts on the changing role of evaluation practice.

CHAPTER SIXTEEN

Understanding Context

Evaluation and Measurement in
Not-for-Profit Sectors

Dale C. Brandenburg

M any individuals associated with community agencies, health care, public workforce development, and similar not-for-profit organizations view program evaluation akin to a visit to the dentist's office. It's painful, but at some point it cannot be avoided. A major reason for this perspective is that evaluation is seen as taking money away from program activities that perform good for others, that is, intruding on valuable resources that are intended for delivering the "real" services of the organization (Kopczynski & Pritchard, 2004). A major reason for this logic is that since there are limited funds available to serve the public good, why must a portion of program delivery be allocated to something other than serving people in need? This is not an unreasonable point and one that program managers in not-for-profits face on a continuing basis.

The focus of evaluation in not-for-profit organization has shifted in recent years from administrative data to outcome measurement, impact evaluation, and sustainability (Aspen Institute, 2000), thus a shift from short-term to long-term effects of interventions. Evaluators in the not-for-profit sector view their world as the combination of technical knowledge, communication skills, and political savvy that can make or break the utility and value of the program under consideration. Evaluation in not-for-profit settings tends to value the importance of teamwork, collaboration, and generally working together. This chapter is meant to provide a glimpse at a minor portion of the evaluation efforts that take place in the not-for-profit sector. It excludes, for example, the efforts in public education, but does provide some context for workforce development efforts.

CONTRAST OF CONTEXTS

Evaluation in not-for-profit settings tends to have different criteria for the judgment of its worth than is typically found in corporate and similar settings. Such criteria are likely to include the following:

- How useful is the evaluation?
- Is the evaluation feasible and practical?
- Does the evaluation hold high ethical principles?
- Does the evaluation measure the right things, and is it accurate?

Using criteria such as the above seems a far cry from concepts of return on investment that are of vital importance in the profit sector. Even the cause of transfer of training can sometimes be of secondary importance to assuring that the program is described accurately. Another difference is the pressure of time. Programs offered by not-for-profit organizations, such as an alcohol recovery program, take a long time to see the effects and, by the time results are viewable, the organization has moved on to the next program. Instead we often see that evaluation is relegated to measuring the countable, the numbers of people who have completed the program, rather than the life-changing impact that decreased alcohol abuse has on participants. While the latter is certainly important, the typical community-based organization (CBO) is limited in its resources to perform the long-term follow-through needed to answer the ultimate utility question. Thus, the choice of what is measured tends to be the result of negotiation with stakeholders. The broad goals of evaluation tend to be grouped among the following:

- Understanding and sharing what works with other organizations and communities;
- Building sustainability of programs and ensuring funding;
- Strengthening the accountability of the programs with various public constituencies;
- Influencing the decisions of relevant policy makers and program funders;
- Building community capacity so that future engagements have greater community participation; and
- Understanding where the program is going so that it results in reflecting on progress that can improve future programs.

These goals reflect some of the typical objectives for applying evaluation in not-for-profit settings. The goals embody specific activities that can be designed to collect evidence on a program's effectiveness, be accountable to stakeholders, identify projects for improvement, clarify program plans, and improve communication among all groups of stakeholders. The types of programs or actions that are designed to improve outcomes for particular individuals, groups, or communities considered in this chapter include the following:

- Direct service interventions: improve the nutrition of pre-school children;
- Research endeavors: determine whether race disparities in emergency room care can be reduced;
- Advocacy efforts: campaign to influence legislation on proper use of infant car seats; and
- Workforce training programs: job training program to reduce unemployment among economically disadvantaged urban residents.

The results of evaluation in not-for-profit settings are typically designed to provide information for future decision making. Most efforts can be grouped into three categories: process evaluation, short-term evaluation, or long-term (outcome) evaluation. In fact, it is rare to see a program evaluation effort that does not include some process evaluation. Process evaluation is considered important because it typically yields an external view of how the program was conducted; in other words, it provides a detailed description of the objectives, activities, resources used, management of the program, and involvement of stakeholders. It would be difficult to judge any outcomes of a program without understanding the components of the program in detail. That is why process evaluation is important. Short-term evaluation deals with the accomplishment of program objectives or the intermediate links between the program activities and the long-term outcomes. Outcome evaluation is associated with the long-term effects such as health status or system changes that are often beyond the range of a typical evaluation effort.

STAKEHOLDER ANALYSIS

One of the key tools used to structure the evaluation process in not-for-profit settings is the stakeholder analysis. It is a key initial stage to develop the primary issues and evaluation questions from which other stages of the evaluation process can be built. The stakeholder analysis is designed to identify the needs and values of the separate stakeholders and combine the results so that an adequate plan can be developed. It is rare to find an evaluation effort in not-for-profit situations for which there are at least three stakeholder groups with a major interest in the effort. The stakeholder analysis is a means to organize the political process and create an evaluation plan, as well as satisfy the desires of the different perspectives and needs for information. A first step in the process is to identify all groups or individuals with a stake in the process, followed by a second dividing the groups into primary and secondary members. *Primary members* are those stakeholders who are likely to be direct *users* of the evaluation results; whereas *secondary stakeholders* may have an interest in the findings, but the results of the evaluation are not likely to impact them directly.

For example, in the evaluation of a workforce development project for urban adults, primary stakeholders would include the sponsoring agency or funder, the manager of program delivery, program developers, instructors, a third-party program organizer, and partner organizations that might include community-based organizations, a local business association, and a representative from the city government. Secondary stakeholders might include parents or relatives of program participants, local welfare officials, advocacy groups, and the participants themselves. A list of stakeholders can be determined by answering the following questions:

- Who pays for program staff time?
- Who selects the participants?
- Who champions the desired change?
- Who is responsible for after-program behavior/performance?
- Who determines success?
- Who provides advice and counsel on program conditions?
- Who provides critical guidance?
- Who provides critical facts?
- Who provides the necessary assistance?

Note that these questions do not identify any of the purposes of the evaluation, only a means to distinguish who should be involved in evaluation planning. The amount of stakeholder involvement in the evaluation can be limited or it can be substantial enough so that they assist in the design of the overall process, including the development of data collection protocols. The involvement of stakeholders should also lead to increasing the value and usefulness of the evaluation (Greene, 1988) as well increasing the use of the findings. Such a process increases the ownership in the report and possibly leads to a common vision of collective goals (Kopczynski & Pritchard, 2004).

The second step of performing a stakeholder analysis involves the identification of the requirements, or primary evaluation purposes, and aligning those against the list of primary stakeholders. The matrix shown in Table 16.1 is an example of this analysis for a publicly funded workforce development program for inner city adults.

The "requirements" or purposes of the evaluation can be developed in a number of ways, but the major sources of the list usually come from the published description of the program, supplemented by interviews with the stakeholders. It would be ideal if the matrix could be completed in a group setting, but it is more likely that the evaluator develops the chart independently and then shares the

Table 16.1 Stakeholder Requirements Matrix for a Public Workforce Program

	Requirements				
Stakeholders	*List of Program Activities*	*Business Acceptance*	*Identification of Strengths and Weaknesses*	*Sustainability of the Program*	*Cultural Bias Issues*
Program Sponsor	X	X		X	X
Program Manager	X	X	X	X	
Developers	X		X		X
Partner 1–CBO		X		X	X
Partner 2–Business Assoc.		X		X	
Instructors	X		X		

results in a program advisory meeting. The "X" in a given box represents where a requirement matches the possible use of that information by the selected stakeholder. One can note, for example, that program Strengths and Weaknesses are needed for staff internal to the development and execution of the program but not of particular interest to those outside that environment. Another outcome of this process is at least a general expectation of reporting relationships that would occur during the communication of the interim and final results of the evaluation.

While it might seem that the stakeholder analysis might focus on the program itself, there are other outputs that could be entered into the analysis. Results of evaluation data are often used to tell compelling stories that can increase the visibility and marketing of the organization and increase accountability with board members and community, as well as attract additional sources of revenue. These findings were supported by a national survey of local United Way organizations as reported by Kopczynski & Pritchard (2004).

EVALUATION PURPOSES

While the stakeholder analysis establishes the initial phase of understanding evaluation purposes, further definition is supplied by a list of evaluation issues.

These issues are typically generated during the stakeholder analysis after further understanding of the program description. Evaluation issues can range from general questions about program impact to detailed questions on the selection of service providers. A sample (Gorman, 2001) set of questions or primary issues from a low-income workforce development project that leverages resources from a local housing authority are listed below:

- Describe the major partners leading, managing, and staffing each major activity area.

- Describe the major program areas and the target population service goals by area. What are the major strategies to be employed to reach these service goals?

- To what extent does the program assist in decreasing or alleviating educational barriers to sustained employment? What were the major instructional and training strategies employed to attain the stated goals and objectives?

- To what extent does the program assist in decreasing or alleviating personal and social barriers to employment: poor work histories, cultural barriers, substance abuse and developmental disabilities, and limitations of transportation and adequate childcare?

- What were the participant impacts: wages, self-efficacy, and employability?

- Was there differential effectiveness of the program relative to categories of the target population: public housing residents, non-custodial parents, learning-disabled individuals, persons with limited English proficiency, and other economically disadvantaged groups?

- Was there differential effectiveness relative to the categories of high-demand sectors targeted by the program: building/construction trades, health care, and hospitality?

- What evidence indicates that the program management and its partners can actively disseminate/replicate this program in other regions via its current programs?

- What are some key success stories that serve to illustrate overall program value to participants and community?

- How cost-effective was the project in general terms? By program area? How did costs or efficiency of service change over the course of the project?

- What were the major lessons learned in the project? How do these relate to self-sufficiency for the target population? Community economic development? Leadership effectiveness?

These results were obtained from a stakeholder analysis and are not yet grouped into evaluation components. Combining these results with the stakeholder analysis assists in defining the overall evaluation plan. It provides the framework for developing the data requirements as well as the type of measurement needed for instrumentation.

LOGIC MODELS

The final phase for planning the evaluation is the development of a logic model, a description or map of how the major components of an evaluation are aligned; that is, the connection between how the program is designed and its intended results. Logic models can be used in any phase of the program development cycle (McLaughlin & Jordan, 2004) from initial design to examining long-term impact. It is a means to make the underlying theory behind the intervention more explicit and to discover its underlying assumptions. Even the development of a model, that is, mapping out all of its components, can be instructive for program staff and other stakeholders. A logic model is particularly useful for evaluators both as an advance organizer as well as a planning tool for assessment development (McLaughlin & Jordan, 2004). In many situations, such as community or public health, the specification of a logic model is a proposal requirement. Whether or not an evaluator builds on an existing logic model or develops a preliminary version for the evaluation plan, the map created is a visualization of how the human and financial investments are intended to satisfy program goals and lead to program improvements. Logic models contain the theoretical and practical program concepts in a sequence from input of resources to the ultimate impact.

Most logic models have a standard nomenclature (see the Kellogg Foundation guidelines [W.K. Kellogg Foundation, 2007] and McLaughlin & Jordan) that contain the following elements:

- *Resources:* program inputs like needs assessment data and capabilities (financial, human, organizational partnerships, and community relationships) that can be allocated to the project.
- *Activities:* the tasks or actions the program implements with its resources to include events, uses of tools, processes, or technology to perform actions to bring about intended changes or results.
- *Outputs:* the direct products of program activities or services delivered by the program, even reports of findings that may be useful to other researchers.
- *Outcomes:* both short-term (one to three years) and longer-term (four to six years) specific changes in the targeted individuals or organizations

associated with behavior, functioning, knowledge, skills, or status within the community. Short-term outcomes are those that are assumed to be "caused" by the outputs; long-term outcomes are benefits derived from intermediate outcomes.

• *Impact:* the ultimate consequences or results of change that are both intended and unintended for the individuals, organizations, or communities that are part of the system, generally occurring after program conclusion.

Whatever the process, such as a focus group, used to create a logic model, another useful outcome is a listing of key contextual factors not under the control of the program that might have both positive and negative influences on the program. These context factors can be divided into two components—antecedent conditions and mediating variables (McLaughlin & Jordan, 2004). Geography, economic conditions, and characteristics of the target group to be served are examples of the former; whereas staff turnover, new government incentives, and layoffs for a local major employer are examples of the latter.

The example shown in Figure 16.1 is a portion of a logic model from public health and concerns a neighborhood violence prevention program (Freddolino, 2005). The needs were derived from data that showed that poverty and violence were significant threats to the health of residents in Central County. The general goals of the program were to increase the capacity of local neighborhood groups to plan and implement local prevention programs and work to establish links between existing programs and agencies. Many logic models are likely more complex than the example shown in that specific actions are linked to given outputs and outcomes in order to differentiate the various conceptual links in a program.

Logic models can be constructed in various ways to illustrate various perspectives of a program. Figure 16.1 represents an *activities*-based approach that concentrates on the implementation of the program, and it is most useful for program management and monitoring. A second approach based on *outcomes* seeks to connect the resources to the desired results and is specifically geared to subdivide the short-term, long-term, and ultimate impact of the program. Such models are most useful for designing evaluation and reporting strategies. The logic model developed for a program should suggest the type of measurement required in order to prove or improve the model specified. Since the model is related to performance objectives, it can also lead to assist in judging the merit or worth of the outcomes observed.

A third type, the *theory* approach emphasizes the theoretical constructs behind the idea for the program. Such models concentrate on solution strategies and prior empirical evidence that connect the selected strategies to potential activities and assumptions. These are most useful for program planning and

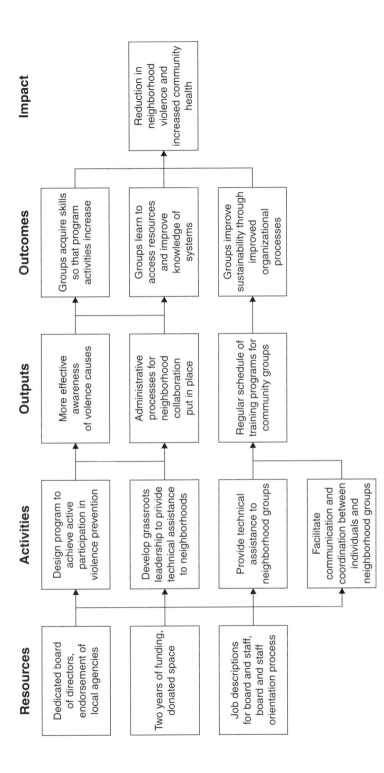

Figure 16.1 Sample Logic Model from Public Health Program.

design. Regardless of the type of model selected, each is useful for the evaluator to provide more comprehensive descriptive information that can lead to effective evaluation design and planning.

METHODOLOGIES

CDC Framework

One of the popular, if not often mandated, approaches to evaluation in the public health field is the six-step framework advocated by the Centers for Disease Control and Prevention (1999). The six steps in sequence are (1) engage stakeholders, (2) describe the program, (3) focus the evaluation design, (4) gather credible evidence, (5) justify conclusions, and (6) ensure the use and share lessons learned. To these steps, the CDC applies the following standards (as originally published by the Joint Committee on Standards for Educational Programs: *utility, feasibility, propriety*, and *accuracy*. The standard of utility can be characterized as face validity and applies to assuring that stakeholders obtain the information that is needed. The evaluation should be conducted in a manner in which the data collection makes sense, is credible, and the reports are prepared to foster use. Feasibility applies to the realism and diplomatic nature to the way evaluation is handled. Keeping in mind the politics of the situation, the evaluation should take into account potential disruptions and pay attention to keeping costs prudent. Propriety refers to the ethics and legality of the evaluation process keeping in mind the needs of the program participants and that their rights are protected. Accuracy is associated with ensuring that the evaluation is honest and technically adequate. This means that information must be included to describe the context of the program, that all instrumentation is reliable and valid, and that conclusions are based on empirical evidence. An example (Reischl, 2001) of an evaluation design following this framework is displayed in Table 16.2.

Workforce Development Framework

The CDC framework stands in stark contrast to evaluation frameworks typically used in public workforce development programs, where the evaluation plan is more subject to negotiation and the bias of the sponsoring program officer as well as available funding. The past ten years of workforce development projects have seen a large increase in consortia projects, that is, involving multiple partner organizations operating either on a regional basis or even broader, in which case one organization acts as a systems integrator. The growth of collaborative projects is in response to decreased public funding for large-scale projects operated by a single grantee or vendor to serve a narrow need. Such collaborative projects increase the evaluation complexity of the politics, management responsibility, and

Table 16.2 Evaluation Work Plan Using CDC Framework

Summer Youth Initiative Evaluation Plan

Overview: C. S. Mott Foundation has provided an annual gift to the Flint area community-based organizations (CBOs) to provide job training, recreation, and learning activities designed to develop academic skills. Each year various CBOs compete for these funds.

Step 1: Engaging Stakeholders	Stakeholders include the board of C. S. Mott, boards of local CBOs, parents and youth served, project staff.
Step 2: Describing the Program	A process evaluation (site visits and observations) will be conducted to include data on needs, stage of development, activities, resources, expectation, context, and program performance ratings.
Step 3: Focusing the Design	Three valuation designs: process, implementation, and a modest impact design. Resources include senior staff and graduate students and funds for postage, travel, data collection materials, participant incentives. CBO records needed. The impact design is pre-test/post-test using a customized tool.
Step 4: Gathering Credible Evidence	Data collection will follow standard procedures for assuring confidentiality of participants and data collected. The site visit will involve direct observations and interviews with project staff. Records will be copied from originals. Data from the impact survey require the honesty of participants.
Step 5: Justifying Conclusions	Analysis will be shared with stakeholders to promote interpretation. Standards include: needs addressed: meet goals; change in attitudes: benefits to economically disadvantaged. Recommendations will follow.
Step 6: Ensuring Use and Sharing Lessons Learned	Stakeholder counsel on use will be sought. Evaluation report will be written clearly with an executive summary, data analyses and interpretations, strengths and weaknesses of methods and recommendations. PowerPoint presentation of findings will be delivered to stimulate discussion of implications.

project organization; thus it encompasses significant stakeholder risks to implementing an effective evaluation plan. This often results in a tradeoff between the rigor of evaluation data and the need to satisfy multiple stakeholders operating in different contexts.

Collaborative projects can also suffer from lack of comparability in implementation due to inconsistent allocation or availability of resources across partner organizations. This lack of comparability in program resources often thwarts attempts at gathering data to compare results across sites and leads to misinterpretation of findings or no consistent findings. An example evaluation plan (Gorman & Brandenburg, 2002) from a multiple-site consortia project managed by a systems integrator and funded by the U.S. Department of Labor is provided in Table 16.3. In this case, the systems integrator, American Community Partnerships, is an affiliated organization associated with a large U.S. labor union whose goals, in part, are to promote high-wage jobs in union roles for economically disadvantaged urban residents. This particular program operated in some of the very poorest neighborhoods in the respective cities involved.

One can note that in complex arrangements represented in Exhibit 16.1, that the management of internal and external partner organizations is crucial to obtaining the needed services for the target population as well as attempting to meet the long-range goal of program sustainability. Initial sponsor-allocated funds cover the start-up of the partnership, but the leveraging of existing funds and other resources are required for the overall effort to be successful. Other evaluation can be considerably more complex when funded by two or more federal agencies. The report provided by Hamilton and others (2001) is such an example and provides a description of an evaluation funded over five years by the U.S. Departments of Labor and Education.

Foundation Guidelines

Numerous resources are available on outcome measurements that are designed to assist not-for-profit organizations. A current major source of information can be found through the website of the Utica (New York) Public Library, associated with the Foundation Center, a foundation collaborative. The site is annotated and contains links to major foundations, professional associations, government sponsors, technology uses, data sources, statistical information, best practices, benchmarking, and assessment tools.

Another set of evaluation models can be derived from an examination of community change efforts. Two organizations that have funded a considerable number of these actions include the W. K. Kellogg Foundation and the Annie E. Casey Foundation. Both organizations offer assistance in designing evaluation efforts. These foundations, among others, want their grantees to be successful in their efforts, so they have developed evaluation guidelines for potential grantees to build in evaluation efforts at the time of proposal writing. More extensive guidelines exist for larger-scale efforts. Especially instructive in

Table 16.3 Working Together: A Public Workforce Development Project

Objectives	Provide an external review of working together to (1) plan and manage an evaluation under guidance of program manager; (2) collect data on the effectiveness of the training and program implementation; (3) document the process of organizational partner relationships; and (4) develop recommendations for the collaborative arrangements.
Stakeholder Consensus	Build confirmation and consensus on set of evaluation questions that assure all stakeholder needs.

Evaluation Questions

Program Description	How has the training program been conducted at each site? Establish "what is" description of program with organizational relationships.
Participant Learning Outcomes	How were pre-post differences of participant training measured at each location? Examine short- and long-term learning and behavior changes. Document use of varied strategies and technology on observed outcomes?
Career and Employment Outcomes	Were observed outcomes consistent with overall program objectives? Compare enrollment numbers to "graduation" rates? What happened after graduation? Document short and long-term employment outcomes. Develop success stories to illustrate overall program value.
Internal Stakeholder Collaboration	Who were the major partners managing and staffing each collaborative? What were the elements of a successful collaborative across sites? Which programs and components appeared sustainable?
External Stakeholder Collaboration	How were partnerships established and maintained? Identify roles of various external stakeholders—unions, employers, banks, local housing authority, community-based organizations, government agencies, vendors, educators? Does the program leverage resources and avoid duplication of effort?

this regard is Kellogg's perspective on evaluating social change in that they have constructed a framework especially for external evaluators. Based on the dynamics of social change and the context of the program, they detail four types of evaluation designs: exploratory, predictive, self-organizing, and initiative renewal. Given the complexity of the type of program under review, evaluators are charged to pay attention primarily to the major aspects of the system change and disregard those features that are of minor consequence.

The Casey Foundation's (1997) approach is similar with regard to preparing evaluation guidelines for grantees, but they devote considerable advice on stakeholder analysis in the context of their major goal to serve children and families. They emphasize the utility of evaluation to understand the complex variables existing in distressed neighborhoods, where most projects are located. Using rigorous evaluation methods must be balanced with the need to document compelling stories on the resultant impact of funding. Data collected by evaluators for Casey projects consist of primarily three types: survey data (group, phone, personal, and electronic), administrative (agency collected data needed for operations), and qualitative (case studies, interviews, and observations). While some rigorous standards can be developed for preparing these instruments, the vast majority could not be classified as experimental design, which are more likely to be found in public health efforts. Another example of a very popular guide for not-for-profits at the community level is the *Measuring Program Outcomes* guide published by the United Way of America (2004). It has sold more then 150,000 copies to date. Historically, until the early 1990's, most evaluation in not-for-profits was focused on inputs and immediate outputs. The United Way guide had a strong influence on shifting that focus to outcomes (Kopczynski & Pritchard, 2004), thus concentrating on impact or the true benefits of an intervention.

The use of guidelines and standards, while commonplace in many not-for-profit projects, especially larger-scale efforts, has spawned a considerable third-party industry of businesses that specialize in this evaluation context. While many such organizations exist inside the Washington, D.C., beltway, others are local or regional in scope and can offer valuable services to clients. The question as whether to employ an external evaluator or train an internal person can be answered by these firms. Evaluators can serve many roles as facilitators, technical directors of evaluation, trainers, or some combination (Kopczynski & Pritchard, 2004). One organization that serves exclusively workforce development programs in the Midwest, Corporation for Skilled Workforce, has developed a methodology for training in-house evaluators to meet most Department of Labor standards. Given the importance of outcome evaluation and measurement for even smaller projects, another organization, Authenticity Consulting, has developed a guide (McNamara, 2007) for the typical small project funded by United Way. One of the important elements of this work is a guide to developing a basic logic model for a proposed intervention that can assist potential funding agencies and program staff in understanding the major issues to be considered. These organizations can be quite effective because they understand the local and regional context.

DATA COLLECTION AND MEASUREMENT

As can be concluded from some of the previous discussion, data collection and measurement for evaluation in not-for-profit settings can range from the deceptively simple to the complex. Most data collection schemes tend to be customized to the environment of the program being evaluated. There are a number of reasons for this. The measurement of a program is most often linked to stakeholder considerations and the needs of the sponsoring organization, as opposed to creating an elegant experimental design. The use of both quantitative and qualitative data is applied to answer the evaluation questions posed at the outset of the investigation.

Second, there is a strong bias for producing data that are useful for all stakeholders, and many users, such as directors of community-based organizations are not used to interpreting sophisticated statistical analyses. Data on effectiveness of programs often can be derived from solid descriptions of program activities and survey data. This is not to say that measurement is based on the lowest common denominator of sophistication, but the end-result is to use the findings in a way that can improve program activities. The availability of resources within not-for-profits generally implies that program staff collects data for monitoring purposes, that is, what is countable from an administrative perspective (Kopczynski & Pritchard, 2004). Other not-for-profit organizational shortcomings may enter into the development of a plan for a comprehensives data collection scheme, namely ''the lack of appreciation of data, lack of training, poorly developed information systems, and high turnover rates'' (Kopczynski & Pritchard, 2004, p. 652), besides the issue of limited budgets.

A third reason to customize data collection is that they may be limited by budget considerations. Elegant and rigorous designs cost more to implement and can have an indirect effect on program activities if certain target participants cannot participate in the primary intervention. This is not to say that rigorous designs are not applied in not-for-profit settings, especially in the public health domain. One such effort (Huffman & others, 2002) funded by the Packard Foundation presents a wealth of information on outcome measurement, valid evaluation constructs, and a set of principles to apply in such settings. Subjects of workforce development programs, for example, are often difficult to recruit, so allocating a portion of participants to a control setting is not cost-effective in many cases. Even more challenging would be follow-up data collection efforts on a homeless population (Kopczynski & Pritchard, 2004).

It is probably instructive at this point to introduce an example of the type and range of data needed to satisfy requirements in a large-scale workforce development effort. Using the same program (Gorman & Brandenburg, 2002) from the example in Table 16.3, Exhibit 16.1 represents a listing of the data elements selected to provide a comprehensive evaluation.

Exhibit 16.1 Data Collection for Working Together

A. Establish baseline measure of environment:
- Number of jobs offered to housing residents
- Number of housing residents enrolled in apprentice programs
- Infrastructure status
  - Partnership engaged in recruiting minorities and housing residents
  - Outreach and recruitment programs of local government and workforce boards
  - Outreach and recruitment programs by employers
  - Internal and external collaboration/partnerships status
  - Service provider status: capabilities; training of staff
  - Curriculum materials
  - Implementation process model: written and formal agreements established

B. Establish program objectives:
- Objectives and goals across programs
- Specific goals and objectives for particular sites
- Implementation model and components

C. Training program:
- Measures of change: attitude, behavior, learning, career aspirations and expectations
- Learning pre-and post measures: appropriate, quality, measures
- Exit testing: apprentice entrance exam; results
- What are the variations in training delivery strategy? Comparisons on effectiveness and efficiency (gains) by skill or content area
- What are the baselines measures for literacy? Standardized exams versus in-house exams

D. Post training and job results:
- Components of tracking system:
  - Number graduated
  - Number in apprenticeships
  - Number in technical training—related or not
  - Number in jobs
  - Number promoted

- Qualitative changes:
  - Changes in lifestyle
  - Changes to family and children
  - Personal financial status—before and after
E. Infrastructure development:
  - Stakeholder identification
  - Roles of partnership organizations
  - Elements of successful collaboration
  - Program leadership and management
  - Development and implementation—recruitment, retention, selection of providers
  - Strategies of organizational effectiveness
  - Effectiveness and efficiency for use of resources
  - Adequacy of sustainability plans

REPORTING RESULTS

If evaluation reports are to be useful for all stakeholders, it is important to consider the communication of evaluation results early in the design of the evaluation process. Such considerations are needed because the demand for clear and credible information from not-for-profits is high (Kopczynski & Pritchard, 2004). In general, it is prudent to negotiate what results are to be presented to whom at the time the stakeholder analysis is conducted. Final reports of evaluation are typically reported in two stages: (1) a formal written report that contains all details of the design, implementation, data collection, data analysis, findings, and conclusion with possible recommendations and (2) a second summary version, such as a PowerPoint presentation that lists the highlights of the investigation. Other reports, such as interim findings or data from a single site in a multiple-site investigation, results of a set of interviews or a survey, or case descriptions, may also be added, depending on funding and stakeholder needs.

Regardless of the type of report, there is still a need to organize reports so that stakeholders may be guided to make appropriate decisions and plan future actions based on the findings. An evaluation that contains as many data elements as depicted in Exhibit 16.1 would need to be organized efficiently if stakeholders were to be able to comprehend and sift through the volume of data likely to be generated. Smock & Brandenburg (1982) suggest a tool to aid in the process of organizing data and presenting findings as portrayed in Table 16.4.

Table 16.4 Classes of Information

Class	Inference Required	Type of Judgment	Range of Setting	Amount of Information	Focus of Outcome/Comparative Reference
I. Global	High	General Summary	Virtually All	Limited to Few	General Success or Failure; Useful for Management Decision Making; Comparison Across Settings
II. General Concept	Moderate	General Strengths and Weaknesses	Most with Common Elements	As many as Legitimate Elements	General Feedback to Target Stakeholders; Useful for Local Management and Design Decisions
III. Specific	Low	Specific (Limited)	Unique to Setting	Potentially Infinite	Specific Feedback to Target Stakeholders; Useful for Improvements and Design Decisions Only; Comparison to Other Settings Possibly Misleading

While the classification shown may be an oversimplification of available data, it is nonetheless quite useful in presenting data to unsophisticated users. The concept underlying its structure is that the entirety of information may be ranked hierarchically from its continuous mode into three levels. These three levels represent an artificial trichotomy from very general (overall success) to success or failure of specific program components to very specific findings that have meaning to possibly a single stakeholder. Level I information is the most general, must be inferred from a variety of findings (rolled up across data elements), permits a general summary of findings, can be applied to most settings in which the question asked is limited to a few statements, and is useful for general management "go or no go" decisions, the kind of final judgment that a sponsoring program officer would be interested in. This type of data would be the primary target to use in a summary presentation of the findings.

Level II information represents data useful for identifying the strengths and weaknesses of a program by its representative components, for example: the materials worked well, instructional delivery could be improved, stakeholders were satisfied, recruitment should be strengthened, or case work referrals worked well. Comparisons across sites can be made only in cases in which program elements are identical or very similar and this comparison information, when legitimate, could be included in the Level I report. The Level II information is most useful for local program staff to identify areas in which program development and delivery could be improved. It provides a starting point to delve into specifics. Both Level I and Level II information tend to be reliable due to the fact that judgments made are cross-referenced and double-checked during the data collection and analysis, whereas Level III information is more site-specific and detailed.

Level III information is the most detailed, such as open-ended comments on surveys or specific references to incidents made during interviews, and while such data tend to be rich in detail, they are also less reliable in that general judgments about success or failure of a program component cannot be made. On the other hand, they can provide very useful information for improving specific aspects of a program as well as offer explanations as to why Level II information yielded results in a particular direction.

CONCLUSIONS

If one wishes to compare how evaluation work is done in not-for-profit settings to how it is done in corporate training or organizational development efforts, there are at least three points of distinction. First, not-for-profit evaluation planning tends to be more complex in that it requires a formal, comprehensive stakeholder analysis. The Aspen Institute (2000) study pointed out stakeholder analysis as the initial best practice in not-for-profit program evaluation. The complexity is driven more from the political side because there are likely to be more stakeholders, with considerable variance in levels of sophistication regarding evaluation methods, not all of whom share the desire to even conduct the evaluation. Specific attempts must be made to, first, identify all relevant stakeholders, and then perform a process of consensus-building to assure that all legitimate evaluation questions have been posed. What happens during this initial stage has considerable influence on the remainder of the evaluation process.

Second, evaluation methodologies employed tend to be dictated by the sponsoring organizations, which can be quite varied in their standards. With minor requirements, an evaluation conducted under a U.S. Department of Labor or Housing and Urban Development are quite flexible, whereas projects under the Centers for Disease Control and Prevention, Health and Human Services or a major grant from a private foundation are more prescriptive. In fact, some foundations require a form of "certification" for many of their external evaluators. Most evaluation efforts are likely to assign to an external evaluator due to the fact that most not-for-profit organizations do not have the requisite capabilities to fulfill that role. This fact adds to project complexity, but especially adds to the politics in dealing with the recipient organization.

Third, evaluation efforts in not-for-profits can be as rigorous as those in the private sector: employing sophisticated experimental designs, requiring validated data collection tools, and using complex analysis of qualitative data, but there is an underlying requirement that the program must be described adequately. This requirement that evaluation must address the description of the target activities leads to the use of logic models not often found in private or corporate evaluation efforts. This author believes that a similar process might be useful in those settings.

References

Annie E. Casey Foundation. (1997). *Evaluating comprehensive community change.* Baltimore, MD: Author.

Aspen Institute. (2000, February). Current evaluation practice in the nonprofit sector. *Snapshots, Research Highlights for the Nonprofit Sector Research Fund, 9.*

Centers for Disease Control and Prevention. (1999). *Framework for program evaluation in public health* (MMWR 48, No. RR–11). Atlanta, GA: Author.

Corporation for a Skilled Workforce. (2008, January 23). Private interview with Jeannine LaPrad, president.

Freddolino, P. (2005). *Conducting useful program evaluations.* Ann Arbor, MI: Michigan Public Health Training Center, School of Public Health, University of Michigan.

Gorman, E. (2001). *Results of stakeholder analysis for JOLI evaluation design.* Washington, DC: American Community Partnerships. [Internal document obtained from author August 12, 2002.]

Gorman, E., & Brandenburg, D. C. (2002). *Evaluation plan for working together for jobs program.* Washington, DC: American Community Partnerships.

Greene, J. (1988). Stakeholder participation and utilization in program evaluation. *Evaluation Review*, *12*(2), 91–116.

Hamilton, G., Freedman, S., Gennetian, L., Michalopoulos, C., Walter, J., Adams-Ciardullo, D., & Gassman-Pines, A. (2001). *How effective are different welfare-to-work approaches? Five-year adult and child impacts for eleven programs.* Washington, DC: Manpower Demonstration Research Corporation.

Huffman, L., Koopman, C., Blasey, C., Botcheva, L., Hill, K. E., Marks, A. S. K., Mcnee, I., Nichols, M., & Dyer-Friedman, J. (2002). A program evaluation strategy in a community-based behavioral health and education services agency for children and families. *The Journal of Applied Behavioral Science*, *38*(2), 191–215.

Utica Public Library. (2007, October). *Internet resources of nonprofits.* Foundation Center Cooperating Collection. www.uticapubliclibrary.org/not-for-profit/outcomes.html.

Joint Committee on Standards for Educational Programs. (1994). *The program evaluation standards* (2nd ed.). Thousand Oaks, CA, Sage.

Kopczynski, M., & Pritchard, K. (2004). The use of evaluation by nonprofit organizations. In J. S. Wholey, H. P. Hatry, & K. E. Newcomer (Eds.), *Handbook of practical program evaluation* (2nd ed.). San Francisco: Jossey-Bass.

McLaughlin, J., & Jordan, G. (2004). Using logic models. In J. S. Wholey, H. P. Hatry, & K. E. Newcomer (Eds.), *Handbook of practical program evaluation* (2nd ed.). San Francisco: Jossey-Bass.

McNamara, C. (2007). *Basic guide to outcomes-based evaluation for nonprofit organizations with very limited resources.* www.liveunited.org/.

Reischl, T. (2005). *Conducting useful program evaluations.* Ann Arbor, MI: Michigan Public Health Training Center, School of Public Health, University of Michigan.

Smock, R., & Brandenburg, D. C. (1982). *Levels of information: A tool to assist in assessment development and reporting evaluation data.* Champaign, IL: Measurement & Research Division, University of Illinois.

United Way of America. (2004). *Measuring program outcomes: A practical approach.* Washington, DC: Author.

W. K. Kellogg Foundation (2007, September). *Designing initiative evaluation: A systems oriented framework for evaluating social change efforts.* Battle Creek, MI: Author.

CHAPTER SEVENTEEN

Using New Technology to Create a User-Friendly Evaluation Process

William J. Rothwell
Anita Pane Whiteford

Much interest has been focused on emerging technologies in instructional design and delivery (see, for instance, Rothwell, Butler, Maldonado, Hunt, Peters, Li, & Stern, 2004). However, less attention has focused on applying new technology to evaluating instructional or other performance improvement interventions (see Rothwell, 2005; Rothwell, Hohne, & King, 2007). After all, emerging technologies do have the potential to expand the scope of evaluation in terms of number and geographic distribution of participants; types of data that can be collected; size and relational capabilities of storage and retrieval systems; types of analysis conducted; and type of reports generated. Emerging technologies also offer the promise of exciting new ways to select or design data collection tools; collect and analyze data; store and retrieve data and results; and report evaluation results.

This chapter examines some of the new technology-based evaluation tools. The chapter will answer the following questions: (1) What technology-based evaluation tools are available to human performance technology (HPT) practitioners? (2) How can HPT practitioners use these tools to evaluate performance interventions? (3) Are HPT practitioners conducting evaluations of performance interventions? Why or why not? (4) Why use technology-based tools? (5) What does the future hold for HPT practitioners who use technology-based tools to evaluate performance interventions? In addition, this chapter will discuss ethical issues that could be posed by new technology that could take HPT practitioners into uncharted territory.

WHAT TECHNOLOGY-BASED EVALUATION TOOLS ARE AVAILABLE TO HPT PRACTITIONERS?

Technology-based evaluation tools can be understood to mean any electronically enabled applications that have experienced accelerating growth the last few years in assisting HPT practitioners and evaluators with ability to perform work faster, better, and with increased skills. With new technology-based applications appearing almost daily, it remains difficult to catalog all the new technologies. Therefore, this section will discuss only some technology-based tools that are expanding the scope of evaluation, collecting evaluation data, storing and retrieving evaluation data, analyzing evaluation data, and reporting evaluation results.

General Characteristics: Multi-Tasking and Engagement

All evaluation tools that are available to HPT practitioners expand the scope of evaluation in some way. Most tools have the ability to allow users to multi-task: collect, store, retrieve, analyze, and report data. Engagement theory is perhaps the most well-applied theory to explain the reasons for the successes for technology-based applications for HPT practitioners. "Engagement theory is best applied because the theory is based on three primary means to accomplish engagement: an emphasis on collaborative effort, project-based assignments, and non-academic focus" (Kearsley & Shneiderman, 1999, p. 5). "Engagement theory is intended to be a conceptual framework for technology-based learning and teaching because technology can facilitate engagement in different ways that are difficult to achieve without technology-based applications" (Kearsley & Shneiderman, 1999, p. 1). The theory is based on the foundation of *engaged learning*, defined by Kearsley and Shneiderman (1999) as "participant activities that involve active cognitive processes such as creating, problem-solving, reasoning, making decisions, and evaluating" (p. 1). HPT practitioners can use engagement theory to aid in selecting the appropriate tools for evaluating HPT applications. Practitioners can use the theory to formulate such critical thought-provoking questions as (1) For what target audience is engagement theory most and least effective? (2) What skills, required of participants to be effectively evaluated, are essential to collaborative activities? (3) How should individual differences be evaluated in collaborative work? and (4) What tools would be most appropriate to evaluate collaborative software tools that might be used during the intervention (Kearsley & Shneiderman, 1999)?

As mentioned previously, most technology-based evaluation tools are multi-tasked whereby the tools can collectively gather data, store and retrieve data, analyze data, and report data. All features, as well as some prime examples of technology-based tools, will be discussed in the following sections about stand-alone evaluation tools, built-in evaluation features, tools to evaluate one-way communication interventions, and tools to evaluate two-way communication interventions.

Stand-Alone Evaluation Tools

Some technology-based evaluation tools can be used on their own or can be blended with performance interventions such as, for example, Questionmark (see www.questionmark.com) and One-Touch system (see www.one.touch .com).

Questionmark. Perception Assessment Management System enables educators and trainers to author, schedule, deliver, and report on surveys, quizzes, tests, and exams. Questionmark offers evaluators the ability to author questions and assessments easily; bank questions by learning objective; deliver to browser, PDA, CD-ROM, or paper; provide instant feedback to enhance learning; provide a secure delivery platform for high-stakes exams; give administrators on-demand results, reports, and item analysis; and randomize the presentation of questions and choices (see www.questionmark.com/us/perception/index .aspx).

Idaho Power is a case study in using Questionmark. The company provides electricity to Idaho and to sections of Oregon and Nevada. It employs eighteen hundred line service workers and field engineers. Idaho Power sponsors a rigorous apprenticeship program of four and half years' duration and administers an average of three to four hundred exams per week as well as a final examination at the program's end. Idaho Power began to use Questionmark to maintain all exams in one database and to have the ability to work continuously on new exams or improve existing ones.

One-Touch. One-Touch System is the leading provider of interactive distance communication and learning solutions for corporate, educational institutions, and governmental offices. One-Touch integrates video, voice, and data over any broadband network with measurable and certifiable results, extending the reach of communication and learning sessions to geographically dispersed participants.

J.C. Penney became a customer of One-Touch System in 1996 after closing its management training facility in Texas. J.C. Penney decided to use distance learning to train 149,000 store associates so as to ensure consistency in its training. Store associates see the facilitators' video live on a classroom television and interact by using the One Touch interactive touch pad. Facilitators can pose questions and post quizzes, providing an important means to measure and establish accountability among associates for their learning. All participant data are gathered in a central database for further analysis, including attendance training records, the number of times an associate calls in, and question and quiz performance. J.C. Penney saved $58,000 in delivering one training class and reduced travel costs for training by $12 million.

Built-In Evaluation Features

Sometimes "evaluation" features are built into a technology-based performance intervention. A good example is a learning management system (LMS). An LMS is a set of software tools designed to manage user learning interventions. LMS has become a popular method of technology-based application in both the corporate and academic worlds. An LMS allows an organization to manage users, roles, courses, instructors, and facilities; post course calendars; post messages to learners; offer assessment and testing, including administering participant pre-tests and post-tests; display scores and transcripts; grade course-work; and host web-based or blended learning (see http://en.wikipedia.org/wiki/learning_management_system).

Ilias is an example of an LMS that has a built-in evaluator tool (see www.ilias.de/docu/ilias.php?ref_id = 392&frame = maincontent&obj_id = 11674&cmd = layout&cmdClas). Ilias is a powerful web-based learning management system that supports tools for collaboration, communication, evaluation, and assessment. The evaluation and assessment component of Ilias permits evaluators to create assessments based on multiple choice, single choice, allocation questions, cloze questions (free text, select box) arrangement duties, hot spots (search images to click on), and unsettled questions.

TOOLS PRACTITIONERS USE TO EVALUATE ONE-WAY COMMUNICATION INTERVENTIONS

Webcasts, podcasts, and web-based surveys rely primarily on one-way communication. A presenter broadcasts a message, or a series of messages, that can only be received by participants over the web, iPod, or other channels. Participants cannot respond in real time, so they may properly be termed as forms of one-way communication.

Podcasts and Webcasts

"A *podcast* is a digital audio program, a multimedia computer file that can be downloaded to a computer, an iPod, or another device, and then played or replayed on demand" (Islam, 2007, p. 5). A *webcast* is used on the Internet to broadcast live or delayed audio and/or video transmissions, like traditional television and radio broadcasts (see www.webopedia,com/term/w/webcast.html). Unlike webcasts, podcasts are always available, portable, user-friendly, immediately useable, and inexpensive (Islam, 2007). Podcasts and webcasts can be used in the evaluation phase of performance improvement interventions. The intervention is recorded and that allows multiple reviews to measure the effectiveness of the intervention and assess its outcomes (Islam, 2007). Facilitators could also evaluate their training skills after a training session so as to identify possible improvements for future training sessions.

Web-Based Surveys

Web-based surveys are assessment tools designed by evaluators and posted on the Internet for participants to evaluate the technology-based application used to deliver the learning intervention. Web-based surveys collect data through self-administered electronic sets of questions on the web (Archer, 2003). Software tools for web-based surveys include, among others, Survey Monkey (see www.surveymonkey.com) and Zoomerang (see www.zoomerang.com).

According to Granello and Wheaton (2004) and Archer (2003), web-based surveys can be administered easily by following several important steps:

1. Determine the target population to be assessed and the purpose of the survey;

2. Design the layout of the survey and format questions, remembering to keep the survey short and simple or else risk skewed answers;

3. Provide a welcome screen that is user friendly from the start that explains the easiness of responding to questions with instructions;

4. Post questions that have a consistent format and flow;

5. Test the system before launching it to make certain the glitches are worked out;

6. Pilot test the survey with a small group similar to the targeted audience; and

7. Strategically plan the survey distribution with only a few email reminders.

TOOLS PRACTITIONERS USE TO EVALUATE TWO-WAY COMMUNICATION INTERVENTIONS

Many new technologies facilitate the interaction of people in real time. These technologies are called *social networks*. Examples include group decision support systems, webinars, web conferences, virtual classrooms, instant messages, chat rooms, blogs, Facebook, YouTube, Twitter, wikipedias (wikis), second-life virtual reality applications—and many others.

Social network websites are legion and their range encompasses every imaginable topic. Examples include Facebook, MySpace, Windows Live Spaces, LinkedIn, and Broadcaster.com. HPT practitioners may pose questions and then receive real-time—or near-real-time—responses. The greatest promise for real-time data collection and analysis probably exists with group decision support systems in which live participants interact in real time—or virtual participants interact concurrently—to reach decisions. Participants can reach some level of agreement collaboratively on:

1. What performance problems are important;

2. How important they are;

3. What causes them;

4. What solutions should be applied to solving those problems by addressing root causes;

5. How those solutions can be implemented, and

6. How results may be evaluated.

As a result, those affected by the problems can have a stake in diagnosing the problem, solving it, and establishing and tracking relevant metrics (Rothwell, 2005).

HPT practitioners can pose questions, generate responses from many people, and then facilitate group activities as members analyze their own results. Data collected from these activities are useful for evaluating the process and the results of the group decision support system intervention itself. HPT practitioners using social networks can get many different views to evaluate interventions. They can, for instance, benchmark how other HPT practitioners have done evaluations for similar interventions and share knowledge on the latest evaluation tools and techniques.

ARE HPT PRACTITIONERS USING TECHNOLOGY-BASED EVALUATION TOOLS?

The most common method of evaluation used by HPT practitioners is a Level 1 on Donald Kirkpatrick's four-level evaluation model. Level 1 is the reaction level, and it focuses on how much people liked the intervention. Participant evaluations—also called "smile sheets"—remain the most popular way to evaluate training, and most smile sheets are administered using paper-and-pencil forms. Some large training companies have advanced as far as using scannable sheets to collect participant reactions. Some are even using web-assisted survey tools.

Web-Assisted Survey Tools

Several organizations have gone the next step to use *Survey Monkey* and similar web-assisted survey software packages to administer participant evaluations. These organizations also post results of participant evaluations online for participants and managers to review.

For instance, the leaders of one company experiencing high turnover asked human resources to explore the root cause of the turnover. The human resources manager, using *Survey Monkey*, surveyed middle managers and production supervisors. The software made it easy to collect and analyze the data. The human resources manager then fed the results of the survey back to company leaders. Online survey-based methods are particularly popular to use with distance education methods, since online data collection just seems appropriate to use with online training delivery.

Another organization has experimented with real-time data collection using wireless personal digital assistants (PDAs). At the end of a training program, participants are polled in real time to determine their perceptions of the training. Their reactions are compiled in front of them and projected on a screen. They are then asked by the facilitator to offer immediate ideas about how to improve the training for subsequent delivery. This approach, of course, is really an application of a group decision support system.

Beyond Level 1

Why do most HPT practitioners typically evaluate only participant reactions and learning? What about evaluating HPT performance interventions for transfer of skill and impact on the organization? Few HPT practitioners conduct transfer of learning studies and impact studies. They typically give several reasons. Some are that such evaluation studies are more time-consuming; evaluators lack resources and sometimes an understanding of how to conduct sophisticated evaluation studies using robust research designs; and organizational leaders do not ask for evaluation studies.

But it is critically important that HPT practitioners conduct evaluation studies at all levels of Kirkpatrick's pyramid—including transfer and impact studies—to build support from organizational leaders (Kirkpatrick & Kirkpatrick, 2006; Phillips & Phillips, 2005).Technology-based evaluation tools can help HPT practitioners achieve this goal.

WHY USE TECHNOLOGY-BASED TOOLS IN EVALUATION?

There are many advantages and disadvantages to HPT practitioners using technology-based tools for evaluation. This section will examine those advantages and disadvantages.

Advantages to Using Technology-Based Tools in Evaluation

The advantages of using technology-based tools in evaluation include decreased cost, immediacy, and ease of use for the respondee and the evaluator:

Cost. New technology offers the promise of reducing the cost of collecting and analyzing data. Instead of paying for postage on mail questionnaires, participants can use survey software at a per-use cost. And it is less expensive for an organization to email surveys to hundreds of people than to mail a hard copy of a survey.

Immediacy. In most cases, the greatest appeal of new technology when applied to evaluating performance interventions is its immediacy—that is, how quickly it can be collected and used. Gone are the days when lengthy analysis could be painstakingly applied in step-by-step, linear project approaches and then followed up by deliberate action. Time has become the only strategic resource. Fast approaches to addressing performance problems have grown more appealing to time-pressured, stressed-out managers and workers alike. Many of these approaches call for concurrent project management approaches that combine steps or carry them out at the same time.

Ease of Use. From the participants' point of view, it is easier to complete web-based surveys. The respondent does not have to hassle mailing back a survey form. From the evaluator's standpoint, some survey software permits back-end statistical analysis so that an entire data set can be recomputed every time one user completes a survey. That can also reduce both the time and cost to collect and analyze survey data.

Disadvantages to Using Technology-Based Tools in Evaluation

Of course, new technology is no panacea. It does introduce new challenges. According to Lefever, Dal, and Matthiasdottir (2007), the disadvantages of using online surveys including the following:

1. Target population being surveyed may lack computer skills, not accept using a computer, or may not have easy access to a computer;

2. Technological problems could occur with the equipment or the Internet service;

3. Emails sent to participants asking for their voluntary participation to complete the survey may be routed to the junk mail box, instead of the inbox, and participants may delete the email from researchers without opening it;

4. Challenges may occur when attempting to get a representative sample of the target population for the study by identifying email addresses; and

5. It may be difficult to verify the identity of participants completing the survey.

Verifying Participants. When using technology-based data collection tools, evaluators often face problems in determining whether the right people are actually responding (Do we really know who logged in?), whether those completing online forms actually completed instruction or participated in a performance intervention, and whether data collected are kept secure and confidential.

Security. Security is a major concern when using the Internet for data collection. Virtual private networks (VPN) are a common, popular vehicle used by researchers to ensure the security of respondents completing data collection instruments, although VPNs are by no means foolproof or hacker proof. According to Wikipedia, *virtual private networks* (VPNs) are computer networks in which some links between nodes are carried by open connections or virtual circuits in some larger network (for example, the Internet) instead of by physical wires. The link-layer protocols of the virtual network are said to be "tunneled" through the larger network. One common application is to secure communications through the public Internet, but a VPN need not have explicit security features, such as authentication or content encryption. VPNs, for example, can be used to separate the traffic of different user communities over an underlying, secure network (see http://en.wikipedia.org/wiki/virtual_private_network).

Overcoming the Disadvantages

With these new problems come new opportunities. Here are some suggestions:

Security. In addition to using a VPN, HPT practitioners may select programming language based on security needs. Use JavaScript to validate responses given by participants in online surveys. JavaScript is a programming language that alerts respondents participating in online studies if the fields were completed incorrectly or if fields were left blank during submission (White, Carey, & Dailey, 2000). Respondents receive error messages to fix the issue(s) in the survey before the final survey submission can be made. Perl is another programming language that can avoid both the cost and the potential for error incurred by the tedious data processing. Perl automatically deletes field names and other extraneous characters; transforms the various data fields into a single subject record; aggregates the subject records into single files maintained on the server; and performs any required algorithmic data re-coding before the researcher sees it (White, Carey, & Dailey, 2000).

Identifying Participants. One way to make sure that the intended participants are responding is to ask the participants to provide information that only would be able to identify—such as a password, an encrypted code, or an email address).

WHAT DOES THE FUTURE HOLD IN STORE?

The future holds exciting possibilities for applying emerging technology to evaluating performance interventions. Here are a few examples for the immediate future and beyond.

Time Travel with Kirkpatrick . . .

It may be necessary to rethink Kirkpatrick's well-known four levels of evaluation to include a consideration of *time*. The three time points are before the intervention, during the intervention, and after the intervention. (See Figure 17.1.)

Kirkpatrick's four levels are, of course, quite well known, although often criticized (see Holton, 1996). Level 1 focuses on *reactions*, addressing how

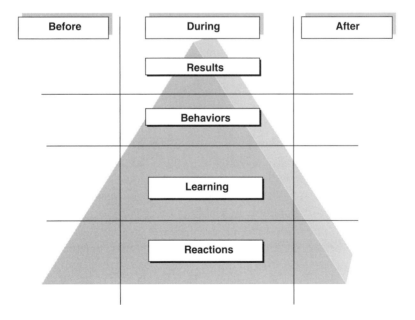

Figure 17.1 Kirkpatrick's Four Levels Reinvented to Show Different Time Periods.

Copyright © 2008 by William J. Rothwell, Ph.D., SPHR

much people liked the training or other performance interventions in which they participated. Level 2 focuses on *learning*, addressing how much people learned from training or from other performance interventions in which they participated. Level 3 focuses on *behavior*, addressing how much people changed their on-the-job behavior based on the performance intervention. Level 4 focuses on *results*, addressing how much the organization gained in productivity improvement as a result of the performance intervention. But each level may also be examined at three points in time—before, during, and after the performance intervention.

Adding the time element transforms the "hierarchy" into a "grid." Each cell of the grid suggests a range of different approaches and focal points of concern. For instance, reaction viewed *before* the performance intervention focuses on what expectations the participants targeted for change have about the intervention; reaction viewed *during* the performance intervention focuses on monitoring changing attitudes about the intervention while the intervention is implemented; and reaction viewed *after* the performance intervention measures how much people liked the change effort upon completion. Each cell of the grid may prompt HPT practitioners to think of several ways by which to measure at each point in time. New, emerging technology may support evaluation in each cell of the grid. Possible ideas about doing that are summarized in Table 17.1.

Of course, creative HPT practitioners may come up with additional ideas about ways to apply new technology in conducting evaluation. Use the worksheet in Exhibit 17.1 to stimulate thinking about other ways to evaluate performance interventions on different levels of the hierarchy and at different points in time.

Getting Help from Avatars

Futurists already predict a time when *avatars*, representations of people often used in second-life applications, will be guided by artificial intelligence and not just by people (see Hill, 2008). That will mean that second-life avatars may be able to interact with people in simulated ways, giving them opportunities to rehearse actions in real life that might not otherwise be possible due to safety or other concerns. If that happens, then it may be possible to simulate efforts to collect, analyze, and evaluate data about instruction—or other performance interventions—before the change effort is implemented. It would go the step beyond mere guesswork forecasting to actual, robust, and simulated pilot-testing of interventions assisted by new technology.

Getting on the Grid

Futurists predict that the Internet and the web will be transformed into the grid in which people, objects, and data can be linked together as "nodes." That will

Table 17.1 Possible Ways That Emerging Technologies May Be Used to Evaluate Performance Technology Interventions

Results

Before	Poll workers and managers online before a performance technology intervention to assess what level of measurable change is expected and desired as a direct consequence of the intervention.
During	Poll workers and managers online during a performance technology intervention to assess what level of measurable change is being achieved as a direct consequence of the intervention.
After	Poll workers and managers online after a performance technology intervention is fully implemented to assess what level of measurable change was achieved as a direct consequence of the intervention.

Behavior

Before	Hold a web conference before a performance technology intervention to shape expectations about what behavioral change is desired, why it is necessary, and how results will eventually be measured.
During	Follow up with people as they do their work in real time to see what behavioral changes are occurring on the job. Use video to observe behavior and count the frequency with which desired behavior is demonstrated.
After	Conduct web conferences with the peers, subordinates, and immediate supervisors of participants in training or in other performance technology interventions to gather their real-time opinions on how behavior has changed for those participating in the intervention.

Learning

Before	Conduct a pre-test online.
During	Conduct a concurrent test online while the performance technology intervention is under way.
After	Conduct a post-test online. Conduct a post-session post-mortem using virtual classroom or web conference capability to encourage interactive information sharing.

Reaction

Before	Survey participants in the performance technology interventions about their expectations and what results they expect to see from the change effect. Conduct a web conference before a performance technology intervention is implemented to collect perceptions and gauge expectations.

(*Continued*)

Table 17.1 (*Continued*)

During	Conduct focus groups in real time to capture perceptions about "how things are going." Use wireless technology to periodically poll participants on how they think things are going.
After	Follow up with a pod-cast about what happened in the performance technology intervention and then invite people to contribute success stories or other information about impact.

Exhibit 17.1 A Worksheet to Explore Possible Ways That Emerging Technologies May Be Used to Evaluate Performance Technology Interventions

Directions: Use this worksheet to structure your thinking. Think of each type of evaluation in the left column below. Then note ways that each of Kirkpatrick's four levels can be evaluated, using different emerging technology, in the right column. Be prepared to share what you wrote with others.

Results

    Before _____

    During _____

    After _____

Behavior

    Before _____

    During _____

    After _____

Learning

    Before _____

    During _____

    After _____

Reaction

    Before _____

    During _____

    After _____

speed up efforts to achieve results by seamlessly integrating interactions between humans and technology. It will mean that *assistive technology*, now associated with technology that helps the disabled to perform like the able-bodied, may become associated with the means to integrate technology seamlessly with human efforts to perform work (Foroohar, 2002).

Already *Accenture* is working to create items of clothing that will prompt users to match colors properly (Foroohar, 2002). Chips are being embedded into humans to enhance the central nervous system; and chips may eventually be used to speed up the quality and operations of the human brain ("Professor to wire computer chip into his nervous system," 2000). As artificial intelligence advances to the point that computers approximate the human capacity to "think creatively," then humans can only stay ahead by enhancing their own thinking and creative talents through real-time computer-aided technology. That will open up vistas in which evaluation can be conducted in real time, perhaps through the mind-boggling idea of computer-assisted wireless telepathy.

Using Technology to Improve Performance with Everyday Objects

Futurists already believe that technology will become embedded into everyday objects to enhance human performance, for example, eyeglasses that permit users to see while also permitting them to access real-time Internet and video (see "Newer design of close-up computer monitors increases ease of use," 2002). This could permit real-time, task-specific coaching on how to perform work. It could also give HPT practitioners the ability to analyze data even as they collect it, thereby slashing the time it takes to make data usable.

Another example: cell phones that do everything from access the Internet to permit instant messaging. Those cell phones are already with us, but their applications in collecting, analyzing, and evaluating real-time performance information is only now being considered. Cell-phone-based training and wristwatch-based training, perhaps in three dimensions, may be the next wave after podcasting, and that opens up the potential to give learners real-time performance assistance and give HPT practitioners the capability to do real-time data collection, analysis, and evaluation.

What Ethical and Confidentiality Issues Arise When Using New Technology to Evaluate Performance Interventions?

With new forms of technology arise new challenges in ethics and confidentiality. For example, there are issues with almost every method of online intervention technology—especially blogs, wikipedias, Facebook, YouTube, Twitter, seminars, and web conferences. Blogs, wikipedias, Facebook, YouTube, and Twitter are technological avenues (social networks) where it is easy to be unethical and violate copyright because the individuals posting information need not identify themselves and are not held accountable or mandated to publish the source. Just Google "media and confidentiality" to find instances in which clients have been specifically discussed by healthcare professionals.

Blogs. Some organizations are beginning to encourage employee groups to create blogs. Yet, blogs can also prompt many ethical, confidentiality, and copyright dilemmas. Blogs are a highly popular method to communicate by media. There are a multitude of blogs that are not controlled and that permit individuals to display text, images, audio files, and video available on the Internet without permission from the original creator or copyright holder (Kuhn, 2007). Currently, no code of ethics exists for bloggers, and so blogging on the web can be as lawless as the Old West. However, if a code of ethics were to be established, accountability and anonymity should be two key critical components. Bloggers should be accountable for the information that they post to give proper credit when due and should preserve anonymity when posting information (Kuhn, 2007). Evaluation of blogging as a performance intervention would require the evaluator to identify and evaluate the ethical issues as well as the performance results of the blogging intervention.

Digital Media. The U. S. government has considered issues of ethics and digital media. This has prompted the government to legislate a few federal acts in the hopes of upholding ethical standards. A few of these acts are as follows:

- *Audio Home Recording Act of 1992 (Pub.L.No-102-563):* Exempts from copyright infringement the making of copies for personal use of music files in digital form, provided that those copies are made with approved equipment.
- *No Electronic Theft Act of 1997 (Pub. L. No. 105-147):* Establishes penalties for unauthorized sharing and redistribution of copyrighted material over the Internet.
- *Digital Millennium Copyright Act of 1998 (Pub. L. No. 105-304):* Creates several protection and enforcement mechanisms for copyrighted works in digital form.

Copyright. HPT practitioners should be aware of resources available from the U.S. Copyright Office (see www.copyright.gov). This link provides information about copyright issues. It also explains how to copyright a work or record a document and reviews applicable copyright laws and policies. If there is uncertainty or questions of issues with copyright, HPT practitioners should refer to this site for additional information. They may also consult The Congress of the United States Congressional Budget Office (2004).

The federal laws listed in this chapter are based on copyright issues to protect individuals' work that is displayed on the Internet. It is very important that HPT practitioners follow the federal laws when conducting technology-based evaluations. A significant case would be if a practitioner is using an evaluation assessment tool that he or she found online and the practitioner feels that, since the assessment tool was found online, there is no need to obtain copyright permission for subsequent use. This is a common misconception. Whether evaluation material is obtained online or off-line, proper permission must be obtained from the copyright holder.

Use of Information. One dilemma for HPT practitioners is how to use information on ethics and confidentiality when selecting the appropriate evaluation tool for their needs. Practitioners must know how utilizing the information obtained from the data collection methods may impact the participants in regard to ethics and confidentiality. For example, as with any data collection method to be selected for a study, HPT practitioners have to first gauge the conditions under which the data will be collected, the population to be sampled, and then the most appropriate method that will yield the most desirable results—while also protecting confidentiality and well-being of human subjects. Internal Review Boards (IRBs) are helpful to HPT practitioners in the sense that IRBs can help practitioners remain ethical and preserve confidentiality as they collect data. The IRBs will also educate practitioners on legal issues that can arise during data collection. Many federal government guidelines exist to protect human subjects when data are collected.

SUMMARY

This chapter listed some examples of technology-based evaluation tools that could be used to evaluate performance interventions. Each new technology holds the promise of providing new, exciting ways to select or create data collection tools and to collect, store, retrieve, analyze, and communicate data in faster, more effective ways. Each new technology may also challenge HPT practitioners to come up with new ways to think about evaluating performance interventions. Indeed, it may be necessary to reinvent Kirkpatrick's famous hierarchy into a grid that addresses times before, during, and after performance interventions.

The future is likely to offer even more opportunities to apply technology to how HPT practitioners evaluate. Just a few exciting possibilities include avatars that "think"; the emergence of the grid to replace the web and the Internet; and human-machine interactions that are seamlessly integrated in real time.

It is critically important to obey the appropriate copyright laws when using evaluation tools owned by others. Following the copyright laws means obtaining permission from copyright holders to use their work in your evaluation studies. Equally important, it is the duty of HPT practitioners to abide by all ethical standards and confidentiality laws of the U.S. government.

References

Archer, T. M. (2003, August). Web-based surveys. Retrieved July 7, 2008, from www.joe .org/joe/2003august/tt6.shtml.

Foroohar, R. (2002). Life in the grid. Retrieved July 7, 2008, from www.newsweek.com/ id/65626.

Granello, D. H., & Wheaton, J. E. (2004). Online data collection: Strategies for research. *Journal of Counseling and Development*, *82*(4), 387–393.

Hill, M. (2008). Researchers teach "second life" avatar to think. Retrieved July 7, 2008, from http://apnews.myway.com/article/20080518/D90O7EDG0.html.

Holton, E. F. III (1996). The flawed four-level evaluation model. *Human Resource Development Quarterly*, *7*(1), 5–21.

Ilias information center. (2008). Retrieved July 12, 2008, from www.ilias.de/docu/ilias .php?ref_id = 392&frame = maincontent&obj_id = 11674&cmd = layout&cmdClas.

Islam, K. A. (2007). *Podcasting 101: For training and development*. San Francisco: Pfeiffer.

Kearsley, G., & Shneiderman, B. (1999, April). Engagement theory: *A framework for technology-based teaching and learning*. Retrieved July 7, 2008, from http://home .sprynet.com/gkearsley/engage.htm.

Kirkpatrick, D. L., & Kirkpatrick, J. D. (3rd ed.) (2006). *Evaluating training programs: The four levels*. San Francisco: Berrett-Koehler.

Kuhn, M. (2007). Interactivity and prioritizing the human: A code of blogging ethics. *Journal of Mass Media Ethics*, *22*(1), 18–36.

Lefever, S., Dal, M., & Matthiasdottir, A. (2007). Online data collection in academic research: Advantages and limitations. *British Journal of Educational Technology*, *38*(4), 574–582.

Learning Circuits. (2008). Lexicon update. *Training & Development*, *62*(10), 18–20.

Learning management system. Retrieved July 7, 2008, from http://en.wikipedia.org/ wiki/learning_management_system.

Newer design of close-up computer monitors increases ease of use. (2002). Retrieved July 12, 2008, from www.sciencedaily.com/releases/2002/08/020830071407.htm.

One-touch systems. (2008). Retrieved July 12, 2008, from www.one.touch.com.

Phillips, P. P., & Phillips, J. J. (2005). *Return on investment basics*. Alexandria, VA: ASTD.

Professor to wire computer chip into his nervous system. (2000). Retrieved July 12, 2008, from http://archives.cnn.com/2000/TECH/computing/12/07/robot.man/

Questionmark. (2008). Retrieved July 12, 2008, from www.questionmark.com/us/ perception/index.apx.

Rothwell, W. (2005). *Beyond training and development: The groundbreaking classic* (2nd ed.). New York: AMACOM.

Rothwell, W., Butler, M., Maldonado, C., Hunt, D., Peters, K., Li, J., & Stern, J. (2006). *Handbook of training technology: An introductory guide to facilitating learning with technology—from planning through evaluation*. San Francisco: Pfeiffer.

Rothwell, W., Hohne, C., & King, S. (2007). *Human performance improvement: Building practitioner performance* (2nd ed.). Boston: Butterworth-Heinemann.

The Congress of the United States Congressional Budget Office (2004, August). *Copyright issues in digital media*. Retrieved May 22, 2008, from www.cbo.gov/ftpdocs/57xx/doc5738/08_09_copyright.pdf.

U.S. Copyright Office. (2008). Retrieved July 12, 2008, from www.copyright.gov.

Virtual private network. Retrieved May 25, 2008, from http://en.wikipedia.org/wiki/Virtual_private_network.

Webcast. Retrieved July 7, 2008, from www.webopedia.com/term/w/webcast.html.

White, J. A., Carey, L. M., & Dailey, K. A. (2000, April). *Improving web-based survey research data collection*. Paper presented at the Annual Meeting of the American Educational Research Association. Retrieved May 25, 2008, from www.coedu.usf.edu/jwhite/survey1/SURV-E-2.pdf.

Additional Resources

Galagan, P. (2008). Second that. *Training + Development*, *62*(2), 34–37.

Gronstedt, A. (2007a). Basics of podcasting. *Info-line*, No. 250705.

Gronsted, A. (2007b). The changing face of workplace learning. *Training + Development*, *61*(1), 20–24.

Karrer, T. (2007). Learning and networking with a blog. *Training + Development*, *61*(9), 20–22.

Laff, M. (2007). The world according to WIKI. *Training + Development*, *61*(5), 28–31.

Rothwell, W., & Sullivan, R. (Eds.). (2005). *Practicing organization development: A guide for consultants* (2nd ed.) San Francisco: Pfeiffer.

Virtual education. Retrieved May 25, 2008, from http://en.wikipedia.org/wiki/Virtual_classroom.

CHAPTER EIGHTEEN

New Kids on the Block

Evaluation in Practice

Debra M. Smith

Workplaces have a story to tell. They begin their story by defining and communicating what they do, what they aspire to become, and what they believe in. These messages are their mission or what they do, the vision or what they aspire to become, and the values or what they believe in. This framework sets the stage for what happens in the middle of the workplace story. In traditional stories, the middle is the best part, it is where the characters spring to life and the action occurs. The workplace story is no different; employees become engaged and actions are initiated when the workplace shares what it is going to do to attain the vision through its goals, defines what success looks like in its strategy, and identifies the activities required to accomplish the goals with specific objectives. This stage setting enables the workplace performers, but the actual performance, or middle of the story, determines how the story will end.

Workplaces expect their stories to end with the achievement of their visions. To be certain that the goals, strategy, and objectives move the workplace toward the realization of that vision, quantifiable success factors called "performance indicators" are used to measure progress. Performance indicators are a numerical expression: a simple, relevant value in the language of the workplace that represents the success factor. They are defined by the strategy. Performance indicator numbers are snapshots in time; they provide perspective by freezing the action so the workplace can see where it is in relationship to where it wants to be. Performance indicators are evaluated to determine if the workplace performance meets the objectives. Evaluation reveals the results of the workplace activities. It shows what works and what does not work. It is through the evaluation process that meaning is assigned to the performance indicator numbers.

Table 18.1 shows a workplace storyboard, an overall sequential plan. This workplace storyboard is read from the top down. Notice how the output of each aspect is the input to the next aspect. The aspects of mission, vision, and values set the stage for the beginning of the workplace story. The goals, strategy, and objectives drive performance in the action-oriented story middle. Performance indicators and evaluation deliver results and identify next steps at the story conclusion.

In workplace stories, evaluation data are used to set the stage for the next workplace story. This continuous improvement feedback enables the workplace to adjust its mission, vision, and values to set the stage for the next story or business year. The time frame for a workplace storyboard is typically one year. If the workplace storyboard is being used as an overall strategic plan, the duration is three to five years.

MEASUREMENT AND EVALUATION PROCESS

Measurement and evaluation enable the workplace to see clearly where it is in relationship to where it aspires to be. These measurements and how the results are interpreted are predicated on the workplace strategy. The measurement and evaluation process consists of six steps: (1) describe the purpose, (2) build the plan, (3) collect data, (4) analyze the data, (5) make recommendations, and (6) take action, which are displayed in Figure 18.1 and briefly described thereafter.

1. *Describe the purpose:* Explain why data are needed. The purpose should be traceable to the strategy.

2. *Build the plan:* Define what data will be collected, its location, the time and frequency of collection, and who is responsible for collecting the data. Use this information to create a data collection table.

3. *Collect data:* Populate the data collection table.

4. *Analyze the data:* Group the data into related performance indicator categories, synthesize the data by putting together related elements, then summarize the data and present it in a form stakeholders can understand.

5. *Make recommendations:* Use the data summary to highlight areas that require attention.

6. *Take action:* Make process changes based on the recommendations.

Measurement and evaluation plans provide workplace snapshots. Selecting a measurement and evaluation plan for a strong workplace fit is about deciding

Table 18.1 Workplace Storyboard

		Defining Question	Definition	How Does It Work?
Setting the stage	Mission	What does the workplace do?	Statement describing the business and purpose of the workplace.	The workplace is defined by the products and services provided.
	Vision	What does the workplace aspire to be in the future?	Describes the future state of the workplace.	The vision is defined by the goals. The vision is realized when the goals are achieved.
	Values	What does the workplace believe in?	Guiding principles that define what is important to the workplace.	Serve as a platform for the achievement of the goals.
Performance	Goals	What is the workplace going to do to attain the vision?	Statements about what must be done to achieve the vision.	Goals translate the vision into categories of activity.
	Strategy	What does success look like?	An action plan to attain the goals; it describes success factors.	Making choices about how best to accomplish the goals.
	Objectives	What are the activities required to accomplish the goals?	Steps required to reach the goal.	Provide direction and drive processes; their sum should equal the goal.
Results	Performance Indicators	What is going to be measured?	Quantifiable signs of the success factors.	Ask the right questions to measure the performance story.
	Evaluation	Does the workplace meet the goals?	Assessing effectiveness.	Data are studied to determine if the performance meets the objectives.

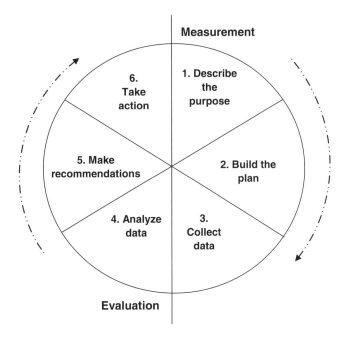

Figure 18.1 Measurement and Evaluation Process.

which snapshot best captures the workplace landscape. There are five measurement and evaluation plans commonly used in business today: Balanced Scorecard, Strategy Maps, Appreciative Inquiry, Total Quality Management, and Six Sigma. Each plan can be customized to align with an organization's workplace storyboard to tell its story. This chapter describes these plans and explains how they work. A Workplace Alignment Guide is provided to match specific workplace attributes to one of the five measurement and evaluation plans.

BALANCED SCORECARD

One approach to translating workplace strategy into a management system is the balanced scorecard (BSC). It was developed by Robert S. Kaplan and David P. Norton in 1992 in response to changes in business perspective brought about by the shift from the industrial age to the information age. Characterized by service organizations, knowledge workers, global markets, and technological change, the information age moved business from a non-competitive environment in which, if a product is produced, the consumer will buy it, to a highly competitive environment in which continuous improvement is expected.

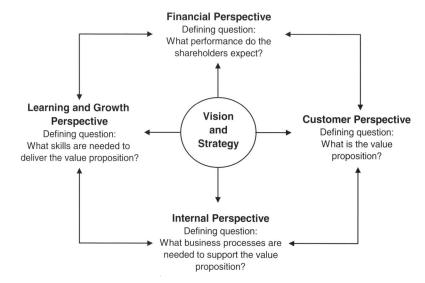

Identify objectives and performance indicators for each perspective

Figure 18.2 Using the Balanced Scorecard to Translate Strategy into Operational Terms.

Source: Adapted from Kaplan and Norton, 1996, p. 9.

In the industrial age, the workplace story was told through financial measures. To build the competitive capabilities to survive in the information age, Kaplan and Norton (1996) recognized that the workplace must identify drivers of future performance. To accomplish this, the balanced scorecard aligns workplace performance activities—goals, strategy, and objectives—with the vision. The balanced scorecard combines industrial age historical financial measures and information age non-financial performance drivers to create a "balanced" look at the workplace.

The balanced scorecard framework views the workplace from four perspectives: financial, customer, internal business process, and learning and growth. Figure 18.2 shows how the framework is used to operationalize workplace strategy. Objectives and performance indicators should be developed and data collected and analyzed for each of the four perspectives.

Financial Perspective

The balanced scorecard tells the workplace story by setting the financial objectives that are derived from the strategy and linking those objectives to internal and external processes and people to deliver performance. Indicators such as cash flow, return on investment (ROI), earned value added (EVA), net operating income, and profit margin are selected based on the workplace strategy and evaluated to determine whether the strategy or action plan is contributing to bottom-line workplace improvement.

Customer Perspective

This perspective identifies the workplace market segments, their customers, and the value proposition. The value proposition defines what the customer perceives as valuable. This value assessment leads to their decision to purchase products or services in preference to competitors' products or services. The value proposition defines, communicates, and delivers value to the customer. Value-centric performance indicators are quality, cost, time, performance, and service.

Internal Business Process Perspective

The value proposition and its performance indicators are used to build the internal business processes deemed necessary to deliver performance that meets or exceeds customer expectations. The processes must be both efficient, that is, they must deliver the product or service without waste in a short amount of time, and be effective, since processes must consistently meet their performance targets.

Internal business processes are arranged in four process groups based on their functional similarity: *operations management* is comprised of the internal processes used to create products and provide service; *customer management* contains processes used to select and retain existing customers and processes used to acquire new customers; *innovation* includes market research, design, development and marketing processes; and *regulatory and social processes* are the environmental, health and safety processes leading to the betterment of both internal and external stakeholders (Kaplan & Norton, 2004, p. 11).

Learning and Growth Perspective

This perspective examines how the workplace resources of human capital or people, knowledge capital or information, and organization capital or culture are working to build the skills necessary to deliver value creating internal processes that enable the value proposition. The learning and growth perspective is the foundation for the Balanced Scorecard framework; it provides the "infrastructure to enable ambitious objectives in the other three perspectives to be achieved" (Kaplan & Norton, 1996, p. 126).

Using Balanced Scorecard for Evaluation

The performance indicators chosen for each perspective originate from the strategy defined as part of the workplace storyboard. One of the defining features of the balanced scorecard is the cause-and-effect relationship that links the perspectives together to build the desired performance. The arrows in Figure 18.3 highlight these relationships. For example, ROI is an indicator of quality;

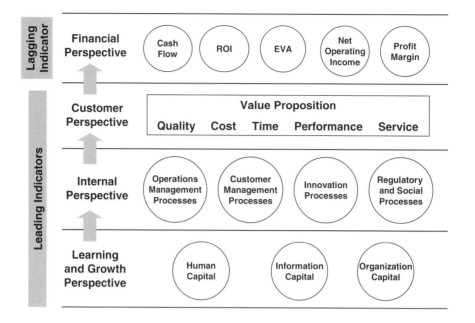

Figure 18.3 Balanced Scorecard Perspectives and Relationships.

Source: Adapted from Kaplan and Norton, 2004, p. 11.

quality is achieved through robust operating processes, and these operating processes are built by people using information and organizational capital. Each aspect selected for measurement is connected to a related indicator.

Typically, the balanced scorecard is populated quarterly. The aspect of balance is achieved by evaluating the lagging indicators: financial performance, how the workplace performed in the last quarter against the leading indicators of customer, internal business process, and learning and growth performance in the current quarter. By comparing the leading and lagging indicators it is easy to see where workplace performance has improved or deteriorated. The balanced scorecard is considered to be a micro performance management tool.

STRATEGY MAPS

Operationalizing strategy is not an easy task. Kaplan and Norton (2004) discovered that using the balanced scorecard approach to determine "what" a workplace should measure was only one part of converting strategy into action. Workplaces must also be able to describe "how" the workplace will create value and meet its goals. Building "how" actually precedes developing the measures; it is a macro view of workplace strategy. Strategy maps address building "how" by adding detail to each of the balanced scorecard perspectives and graphically showing their relationships.

Strategy map construction involves asking "What is needed?" and linking each need to one of the perspectives so the need can be met. This need question is used as part of a workplace conversation about what to measure to meet the need. For example, from the financial perspective, if the workplace profit margin is declining, ask: "What is needed to improve profitability?" Look at the customer perspective. Discuss what could be done to increase profitability in terms of quality, cost, time, performance, and service. Start with quality. Identify an internal business process that could be studied or changed to positively influence quality, ask: "What should be measured?" Identify the specific performance indicator that will show whether or not specific workplace actions are making a difference. Consider the learning and growth perspective. Ask: "If the workplace changes an operating process, will it require changes in human, information, or organization capital?" Since the customer, internal, and learning and growth perspectives are leading indicators, actions implemented here will drive the desired performance. This performance is measured by the lagging or financial perspective indicators. This is how value is built into the workplace.

Strategy maps are built from the top down but read from the bottom up. A strategy map showing how a workplace creates value is shown in Figure 18.4. Notice that the financial or lagging indicator contains two separate paths. One path describes how productivity could be improved. A second path shows how the workplace intends to create growth. The customer perspective is the key driver for building both the productivity and growth strategies depicted in the financial perspective. The customer value proposition is the strategy driver in this perspective. The customer perspective also measures lagging indicators of customer success. The delivery of the value proposition is enabled by the internal processes. These are leading indicators of improvements in the customer and financial perspectives. Objectives for the internal processes are linked to intangible assets: the people, information, and culture in the learning and growth perspective that are required to support them. Learning and growth measures are "lead indicators for internal process, customer, and financial performance" (Kaplan & Norton, 2004, p. 7). A well-built strategy map is a powerful tool that can be used to tell the workplace story in a compelling way. It enables stakeholders to visually follow the paths that lead to the realization of the workplace vision.

Using Strategy Maps for Evaluation

Each of the four perspectives is one attribute of the overall strategy. For each perspective, objectives are developed and performance indicators are established. Each measurable is associated with a performance target so that the gap between the actual and target performance can be evaluated. Strategy maps

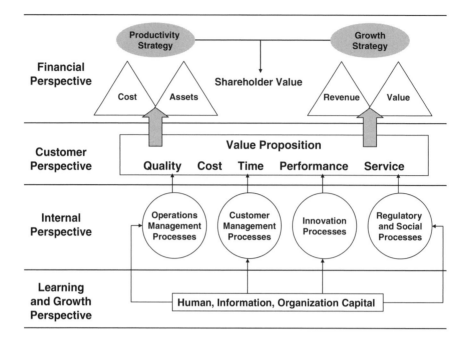

Figure 18.4 Strategy Map Showing How the Workplace Creates Value.

Source: Adapted from Kaplan and Norton, 2004, p. 11.

present a picture of how the four perspectives linked in cause-and-effect relationships are working together to deliver the strategy. The aspects of objectives, performance indicators, and evaluation from the workplace storyboard are the drivers behind each relationship drawn on the strategy map. By showing how changes in one performance area will influence another, strategy maps provide a robust framework for evaluation data analysis and recommendations.

APPRECIATIVE INQUIRY

Appreciative inquiry (AI) is an approach to finding out what is working right in the workplace. It is a systematic search for uncovering the best in people, processes, and the environment. Appreciative inquiry was developed in the mid-1980s by David Cooperrider, then a doctoral student at Case Western University. Cooperrider's research into physician leadership led him to direct his attention toward stories of success rather than failures or workplace problems. Discovering what gives life to the workplace became the focus of his research. He discovered that productivity and morale increased when questions were directed at workplace successes.

Appreciative Inquiry Defined

Appreciative inquiry is both a philosophy, a study of the fundamental nature of reality, and a process, a series of actions or steps. The process begins with a question. Inquiry is the act of asking for information. The way questions are asked is guided by the word "appreciative." To appreciate something means that its value or worth is recognized, its situational context is understood, and an importance can be assigned to it. The appreciative inquiry process "inquires into, identifies, and further develops the best of "what is" in organizations in order to create a better future" (Preskill & Catsambas, 2006, p. 1).

How Appreciative Inquiry Works

Appreciative inquiry uses five principles: *constructionist, simultaneity, poetic, anticipatory*, and *positive*, to describe the way the world works.

Constructionist Principle. Social knowledge and the future or destiny of the workplace are intertwined. To be effective in our workplace role, we must become proficient in assessing, understanding and "reading" the workplace like a fortune teller reads a palm. Workplaces are "living, human constructions" (Cooperrider & Whitney, 2000, p. 17). According to constructivist theory, knowledge is not inherent in a single person, but "constructed" as people use language to assign meaning and describe their experiences. This means that, since reality is built or constructed through social interaction, there should be consensus by the group about what constitutes reality. These meaningful conversations describe the past (what was) and the future (what could be). This reality is based on what is true, good, and possible in the workplace.

Simultaneity Principle. Inquiry and change occur simultaneously. Inquiry itself is intervention because change begins at the moment a question is asked. Asking questions and engaging associates in conversation affects how they think and act. Questions set the stage for what is found. These findings become workplace stories that enable the future to be conceived, discussed, and constructed.

Poetic Principle. Workplace stories are continually being rewritten by the associates who are living in them and by those outside the workplace who interact with the workplace. There is an endless stream of past, present, and future to learn from, inspire, or interpret in the same way that good poetry is open to endless interpretation. Any topic related to workplace life in any workplace can be studied. Appreciative inquiry provides an opportunity to consider the workplace vision and goals from a fresh perspective.

Anticipatory Principle. Creating and talking about a clear picture of the workplace's future state guides current workplace behavior toward that future state. Inquiries geared toward this anticipatory reality enable very powerful positive images of the future to foster positive actions toward that future. Applying the anticipatory principle energizes the workplace.

Positive Principle. Positive questions enable the change effort to be more enduring and successful. A positive approach leads to stories that are like snapshots of workplace life when its associates are engaged in their best performance.

In *The Thin Book of Appreciative Inquiry*, Hammond (1998, pp. 20–21) suggests that as practitioners put these principles to work, they are guided by eight assumptions or truths:

1. "In every society, organization or group, something works.
2. What we focus on becomes our reality.
3. Reality is created in the moment, and there are multiple realities.
4. The act of asking questions of an organization or group influences the group in some way.
5. People have more confidence and comfort to journey to the future (the unknown) when they carry forward parts of the past (the known).
6. If we carry parts of the past forward, they should be what is best about the past.
7. It is important to value differences.
8. The language we use creates our reality."

These principles and assumptions form the framework for the appreciative inquiry process. To practically apply the principles, Cooperrider developed the 4D process. This process model breaks the appreciative inquiry process into four distinct but related phases: *discovery, dream, design*, and *destiny*. The output from each phase is the input to the next phase. This is depicted in Figure 18.5 and briefly described.

- *Discover:* This phase involves starting a positive dialogue with associates focusing on stories of their positive experiences in the workplace. For example, associates describe a good day at work, discuss what is important about their work and their workplace, and describe what could be changed to positively improve the culture. These stories are shared and common factors are identified.

- *Dream:* Information from the discovery phase is fed into the dream phase. Associates "play" with the dialogue data from the discovery phase until they can envision what would work well in the future.

- *Design:* In this phase associate dreams are used to spark proposals on new processes and systems that support positive change. The output of the design phase is a clear, well-defined vision rooted in past successes.

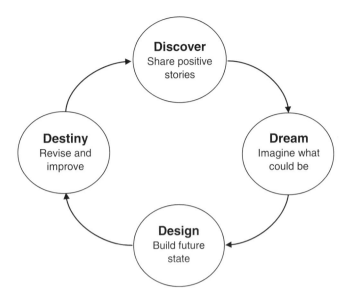

Figure 18.5 Appreciative Inquiry 4D Process.

Source: Adapted from Cooperrider and Whitney, 2005, p. 16.

- *Destiny:* The vision from the design phase is implemented in the destiny phase. This phase is iterative; as associates carry out the design, new associate conversations may trigger another round of appreciative inquiries. Workplace acceptance of the new vision is obtained through the collaborative format inherent in the 4D process.

Using Appreciative Inquiry for Evaluation

Although the focus of appreciative inquiry is workplace development and change, Preskill and Catsambas (2006) found a substantial amount of similarity between appreciative inquiry and evaluation. For example, both appreciative inquiry and evaluation use interviews and storytelling as data collection methods; both processes are iterative and integrated in the workplace; and both use a whole-systems approach that considers workplace relationships and information resource flows.

Appreciative inquiry is a participatory and collaborative approach to evaluation. Appreciative inquiry can be used to create an evaluation plan by using the discover and dream phases to collect information. These activities engage the stakeholders, communicate the purpose, and provide input to the design phase. Appreciative inquiry can also be used to conduct interviews and surveys. This entails engaging associates in the discover and dream phases and refocusing evaluation questions into a positive, appreciative form.

Discover, dream, and design can also be used to create a workplace evaluation system. Information gathering would be centered on exceptional workplace performance.

TOTAL QUALITY MANAGEMENT

Total quality management (TQM) is a holistic approach to workplace management. It can be described by breaking each word into its respective definition and then assembling each attribute into a working definition. This graphic definition is displayed in Figure 18.6 and briefly described thereafter.

- *"Total":* refers to the engagement of the whole workplace, all workplace stakeholders, associates, suppliers, and customers. Empowering associates is an integral part of the workplace storyboard; associates who are engaged in the workplace strategy seek out best practices and new ideas to meet the objectives and are able to use the performance indicators to assess effectiveness through the evaluation process.

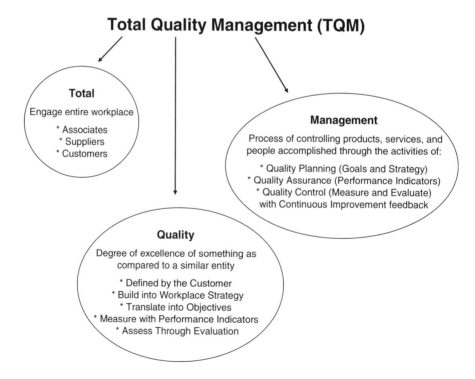

Figure 18.6 Total Quality Management Definition.

- *"Quality":* is the degree of excellence found in comparing one thing to something similar. It is defined by the customer, built into the workplace strategy, translated into objectives, measured with specific performance indicators, and assessed through evaluation.

- *"Management":* is the process of controlling products, services, and people. It is comprised of quality planning, assurance, and control activities.

Putting these three attributes together, total quality management can be defined as the engagement of all workplace stakeholders to define, build, measure, and assess quality by controlling products, services, and people through planning, assurance, control, and continuous improvement feedback activities.

Quality Planning, Assurance, and Control

The management process addresses the work associates will engage in to achieve customer quality. This work begins with quality planning. Armed with the customer quality definition, a cross-functional team of empowered associates uses the workplace goals and strategy to identify specific standards, for example, quality, time, cost, performance, and service, and determines how best to meet them. A good quality plan includes internal and external customers, designs the process to meet customer requirements, engages suppliers early, is responsive to customer changes, and will prove that the process is working. Processes designed during the quality planning phase are not perfect; they will produce waste in the form of scrap, rework, and errors. The quality control process sets controls to minimize this waste. The output of quality planning is an action plan that will be used to achieve the goals.

Quality assurance describes the work done by associates to ensure that the processes specified in the quality plan are producing products and services at the required quality level. A good quality assurance system identifies objectives and performance indicators, is prevention oriented, and includes a plan to collect and maintain performance data. Quality audits are conducted at regular intervals to ensure that processes are working as they are supposed to work. Information obtained from the quality audit is used to reduce waste and eliminate non-value-added activities.

Quality control is concerned with process activities that create specific quality characteristics. A characteristic is a distinguishing feature, dimension, or process property that can be used to collect data. Characteristics are sensitive to variation. Quality control monitors processes and uses statistical process control to reduce variability and increase process efficiency. It certifies that the workplace quality objectives are met. A good quality control system selects the characteristics to control, establishes standards for corrective action, specifies

Figure 18.7 Plan-Do-Check-Act Cycle of Continuous Improvement.

Source: Adapted from Brocka and Brocka, 1992, p. 202.

measurement methods, and documents work processes using a graphic representation or flowchart of the process steps. Associates compare process performance results to the quality standard and take action to bring nonconforming processes back to the standard.

Continuous Improvement

Continuous improvement is an integral part of both quality assurance and quality control activities. Continuous improvement is defined as "small improvements done continuously" (Brocka & Brocka, 1992, p. 32). This systematic approach engages workplace associates in making small changes over time using quality audit and control data to make processes work better. The Plan-Do-Check-Act (PDCA) cycle or Deming Wheel (Brocka & Brocka, 1992, p. 106) provides a framework for continuous improvement. Figure 18.7 shows how each of the four phases in the cycle is related to both the workplace storyboard and total quality management.

How Total Quality Management Works

Total quality management works by engaging every associate and valuing their contributions by reaching out to the customer to see, learn, and comprehend quality through their eyes and by using a continuous improvement feedback process to meet or exceed those customer expectations.

Figure 18.8 is a diagram showing the total quality management methodology. Each process step is accompanied by a number. The following is a ''by the numbers walk'' through the process:

1. Workplace leadership sets the stage by establishing the initial building blocks of the workplace storyboard: mission, vision, and values.
2. Workplace associates are engaged. Similarly, customers are engaged and asked to define their quality expectations. This associate and customer engagement occurs concurrently.
3. Customer quality expectations are translated by associates into the goals and strategy.
4. Objectives are developed based on the goals and strategy.
5. Quality planning designs the product, services, and people processes used to meet customer expectations. These processes and their outputs must align to the objectives.
6. Quality assurance builds the plans to collect and maintain process data.
7. Quality control identifies quality characteristics and measurement methods.
8. Performance indicators are used to measure performance based on the quality control criteria. Data is collected using the method defined during quality assurance.
9. Data obtained through the measurement process are evaluated.
10. Continuous improvement: Evaluation results are routed back to the quality planning step so that the quality plan can be updated. This feedback loop enables changes to be made to bring the process closer to meeting customer expectations.

Using Total Quality Management and Continuous Improvement for Evaluation

Total quality management and continuous improvement are very powerful measurement and evaluation strategies. Successful use is predicated on alignment, linkage, and replication (Godfrey, 1999, pp. 14.8–14.11). Alignment refers to the incorporation of customer expectations into the workplace storyboard. This means that customer expectations are translated into goals, and that an action plan or strategy that provides direction or objectives on how best to accomplish those goals is implemented. The objectives are used to determine what needs to be measured to show that processes are performing correctly. These performance indicators are studied during the evaluation process to determine whether the performance meets the objectives. Linkage is the clear connection of each attribute: goals, strategy, objectives, performance indicators,

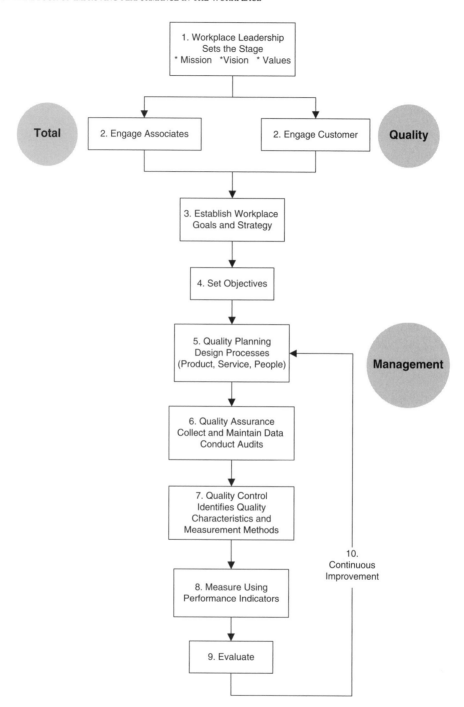

Figure 18.8 How Total Quality Management Works.

and evaluation to the next level attribute. Replication refers to the ability of robust processes to be repeated. Evaluation determines replication by measuring consistent performance over time.

SIX SIGMA

Six sigma is both a philosophy and a business management methodology. As a philosophy it provides a framework for achieving breakthrough achievements in quality and customer satisfaction by reducing fluctuation in process performance or variation. The six sigma methodology originated at Motorola in the early 1980s in response to an executive comment that product quality was poor. Their search for a quality improvement process led to the discovery that producing products right the first time lowered production costs.

The term "six sigma" refers to the goal of the methodology, that is, the production of nearly perfect products and services. Sigma is the eighteenth letter of the Greek alphabet; in mathematical statistics it is used to represent standard deviation. Standard deviation is used to measure process capability. Process capability is a qualitative description of how a process is performing. Table 18.2 shows sigma levels and the corresponding defects per million opportunities (DPMO) associated with each level. As the sigma increases, the number of DPMO decreases. When a process is performing at a six sigma level it means the percentage of perfect product or service produced is 99.99966 percent. This is considered to be Best-in-Class.

Table 18.2 Sigma Levels for Product/Service Quality

Sigma	Yield % of Perfect Product/Service	DPMO*	Revenue Cost	Standard	Industry View
1	31%	690,000	—	—	—
2	69.2%	308,000	30–40%	—	—
3	93.3%	66,800	20–30%	Historical	Average
4	99.4%	6,210	15–20%	Current	—
5	99.97%	230	10–15%	Intermediate	World Class
6	**99.99966%**	**3.4**	**Less than 10%**	**Long-term**	**Best-in-Class**

*Defects Per Million Opportunities

Counted defects divided by the number of opportunities multiplied by one million
Source: Adapted from Kumar, 2006, p. 11.

Notice that as products and services are produced or provided at levels approaching the defect-free six sigma level, the revenue cost is decreasing. High-quality products and services actually cost less. Defect management, waste reduction efforts, and problem solving cost more than designing processes whereby products and services are produced or provided defect- and error-free. It costs less to do things right the first time.

Historically, products and services have been produced at 3.8 sigma or 99 percent good. The quality difference between products and services produced/provided at this level compared to those same products and services produced or provided at six sigma or 99.99966 percent are significant. Table 18.3 shows some practical examples highlighting these differences.

Table 18.3 Practical Meaning of Six Sigma

99% Good: 3.8 Sigma	99.99966% Good: 6 Sigma
20,000 pieces of mail lost per hour	7 pieces of mail lost per hour
15 minutes of unsafe drinking water daily	1 minute of unsafe drinking water every 7 months
5,000 incorrect surgical procedures per week	1.7 incorrect surgical procedures per week
200,000 wrong drug prescriptions per year	68 wrong drug prescriptions per year
7 hours without electricity every month	1 hour without electricity every 34 years

Source: Adapted from Visteon Corporation, 2003, slide 23.

How Six Sigma Works

Six sigma methodology is based on the premise that "companies don't know what they don't know" (Harry & Schroeder, 2000, p.71). This means that unless a process is described numerically it cannot be understood by the workplace. This understanding is critical to controlling the process. Processes should be measured with performance indicators that are aligned to the workplace strategy. This is the only way to improve quality and increase customer satisfaction. Metrics provide a common language that can be used to communicate objectively, collect facts, establish a baseline, make comparisons, and enable cost-benefit analysis.

Six sigma is a systematic approach to reducing variation that uses statistical tools to measure process capability and analyze the results to both control and improve processes. The methodology enables the achievement of excellence by consistently creating conditions under which problems simply cease to exist.

The six sigma methodology can be used for both technical or manufacturing and non-technical applications such as service or transactional. It can be used at the business, operational, and process levels. Key concepts identified by Kumar (2006, p. 9) include:

- *Critical to quality (CTQ):* Measurable characteristics linked to customer expectations;
- *Process capability:* What the process can deliver;
- *Defects, errors, mistakes:* An output that does not meet a defined specification;
- *Variation:* Fluctuation of process performance; and
- *Stable operation:* Consistent performance over time in alignment with customer expectations.

Six sigma uses two different application methods for implementation. DMAIC (pronounced duh-may-ik), an acronym for "define, measure, analyze, improve, and control" is used to improve an existing product or process by finding and fixing defects. Design for six sigma (DFSS) offers several variations of DMAIC that are used to design new products or processes and prevent defects. One DFSS method is DMADV (pronounced duh-may-dove), an acronym for "define, measure, analyze, design, and validate." The DMAIC method is used to find and fix defects on existing projects, and the DMADV design for six sigma prevents defects. Five-step methods are shown and described in Figure 18.9.

Successful six sigma deployment is a cultural change that requires:

- Agreement by top management to drive the six sigma approach;
- Development of competency by top leadership in statistical data analysis;
- Engagement of associates on six sigma projects; and
- Dedicated teams responsible for using methods and tools to reduce variation.

The six sigma framework can be used to build the workplace storyboard; it can be deployed as an operational process improvement initiative or as a measurement and evaluation tool. Six sigma works by embedding the methodology in the workplace storyboard. Implementation occurs in the performance and result phases after the mission, vision, and values are in place. Goal setting and strategy development include customer expectation input. The performance indicators must be linked to the goals.

Using Six Sigma for Evaluation

Evaluation using the six sigma methodology involves assessing process capability using the sigma levels. Performance indicator measurements of capability are compared with the workplace targets established by customer expectations.

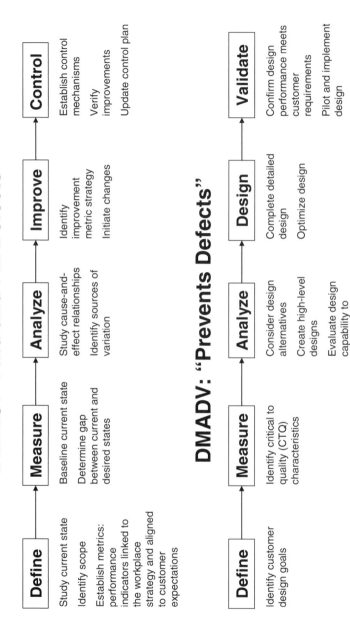

DMAIC: "Find and Fix Defects"

Define	Measure	Analyze	Improve	Control

Define
Study current state

Identify scope

Establish metrics: performance indicators linked to the workplace strategy and aligned to customer expectations

Measure
Baseline current state

Determine gap between current and desired states

Analyze
Study cause-and-effect relationships

Identify sources of variation

Improve
Identify improvement metric strategy

Initiate changes

Control
Establish control mechanisms

Verify improvements

Update control plan

DMADV: "Prevents Defects"

Define	Measure	Analyze	Design	Validate

Define
Identify customer design goals

Measure
Identify critical to quality (CTQ) characteristics

Analyze
Consider design alternatives

Create high-level designs

Evaluate design capability to determine best design

Design
Complete detailed design

Optimize design

Validate
Confirm design performance meets customer requirements

Pilot and implement design

Figure 18.9 Six Sigma Methodology.

This is the measurement step in the DMAIC process. If there is a gap between the current and desired state, cause-and-effect relationships are studied, and sources of variation are identified in the DMAIC analyze step.

HOW TO MATCH THE WORKPLACE TO A MEASUREMENT AND EVALUATION PLAN

All five of the profiled measurement and evaluation plans: balanced scorecard (BSC), strategy maps (SM), appreciative inquiry (AI), total quality management (TQM), and six sigma (SS) have one common attribute: they all obtain their measurement and evaluation information from the workplace storyboard. Successful use of any measurement and evaluation plan is predicated on a well-built, workplace storyboard showing the logical connection of its aspects. When this aspect relationship is simple and clear, it enables translation into any measurement and evaluation plan.

Matching the workplace to a measurement and evaluation plan is a three-step process consisting of studying or analyzing what is going to be built, selecting a framework or methodology for the construction and aligning it to the workplace, and then modifying attributes to adapt the plan to the workplace landscape. Here is a summarization of the analyze, align, and adapt process:

1. *Analyze:* Use the workplace storyboard to study the detailed structure of the workplace. Consider the workplace nature. Is it technical or manufacturing oriented or does it have a non-technical service or transactional orientation?

2. *Align:* Identify criteria that are important to the workplace. For example, approach, simplicity, linkage, performance, and results. Table 18.4 is a workplace alignment guide that includes these criteria, their associated defining statements, and the five profiled measurement and evaluation plans to assist in determining which plan would be a good workplace fit.

3. *Adapt:* Customize the plan selected to be a "best fit" for the workplace by adding other required elements or subtracting extraneous elements. All of the measurement and evaluation plans profiled are customizable. Guided by the workplace storyboard, associates can select and implement only those pieces of the chosen methodology or philosophy that complement the workplace.

Future Measurement and Evaluation Plans

The future of measurement and evaluation plans is not about new philosophies or methodologies; it's about learning how to build a robust workplace storyboard, aligning it to a measurement and evaluation plan, and customizing the plan.

Table 18.4 Workplace Alignment Guide

Criteria	BSC	SM	AI	TQM	SS
Approach					
Workplace storyboard required	X	X	X	X	X
Philosophy defined			X	X	X
Methodology provided	X	X	X	X	X
Technical framework		X		X	X
Service or transactional framework	X	X	X	X	
Use as a tool	X	X	X	X	X
Problem-solving approach		X		X	X
Proactive (preventive) approach			X	X	X
Simplicity					
Easy to adapt	X	X	X	X	X
Graphic elements displayed	X	X			
Shows "how"		X		X	
Linkage					
Customer focus	X	X	X	X	X
Baselines available	X			X	X
Cause and effect relationships shown	X	X	X	X	X
Performance					
Planning included	X	X	X	X	X
Control available				X	X
Continuous improvement used			X	X	X
Results					
Quantitative metrics used				X	X
Qualitative metrics used	X		X		

Criteria	BSC	SM	AI	TQM	SS
Results can be replicated			X	X	X
Implementation					
Management agreement needed?	X	X	X	X	X
Dedicated teams used			X	X	X
Training needed			X	X	X

SUMMARY

Evaluation tools are as diverse as the workplaces that use them. This chapter described five measurement and evaluation plans and explained how they could be used to enable workplace measurement and evaluation. All of the plans require management agreement, customer engagement, and a workplace storyboard to capture the plan.

How each measurement and evaluation plan tells the workplace story is decided by the workplace associates who translate customer expectations into measurable activities. The workplace snapshots provided by measurement and evaluation plans must align with the strategy. They should be easy to understand and should be used to drive workplace decisions. It is through the successful implementation of robust measurement and evaluation plans that workplaces will continuously improve.

References

Brocka, B., & Brocka, M. (1992). *Quality management: Implementing the best ideas of the masters*. New York: Irwin/McGraw-Hill.

Cooperrider, D., & Whitney, D. (2005). *Appreciative inquiry: A positive revolution in change*. San Francisco: Berrett-Koehler.

Cooperrider, D., & Whitney, D. (2000). A positive revolution in change: Appreciative inquiry. In D. Cooperrider, P. Sorensen, D. Whitney, & T. Yaeger (Eds.), *Appreciative inquiry: Rethinking human organization toward a positive change theory*. Champaign, IL: Stipes Publishing.

Godfrey, A. B. (1999). Total quality management. In J. M. Juran & A. B. Godfrey, (Eds.), *Juran's quality handbook*. New York: McGraw-Hill.

Hammond, S. A. (1998). *The thin book of appreciative inquiry*. Bend, OR: Thin Book Publishing.

Harry, M., & Schroeder, R. (2000). *Six sigma: The breakthrough management strategy revolutionizing the world's top corporations*. New York: Doubleday.

Kaplan, R. S., & Norton, D. P. (2004). *Strategy maps: Converting intangible assets into tangible outcomes*. Boston: Harvard Business School Press.

Kaplan, R. S., & Norton, D. P. (1996). *Balanced scorecard*. Boston: Harvard Business School Press.

Kumar, D. (2006). *Six sigma best practices: A guide to business process excellence for diverse industries*. Fort Lauderdale, FL: J. Ross Publishing.

Preskill, H., & Catsambas, T. (2006). *Reframing evaluation through appreciative inquiry*. Thousand Oaks, CA: Sage.

Visteon Corporation. (2003). *Six sigma and continuous improvement methodologies*. (GB Module #3). Van Buren Township, MI: Visteon Corporation.

CHAPTER NINETEEN

Expanding Scope of Evaluation in Today's Organizations*

Darlene Russ-Eft

Human resource development (HRD) professionals and organizational managers and executives are increasingly recognizing the importance of measurement and evaluations of organizational programs and processes. A study by the Conference Board (Gates, 2005) found that executives plan to make increasing use of human capital metrics. The reason for this is the role that such measurement and evaluation play in helping the organization achieve its strategic goals. As confirmation, LaBonte and Necessary (2007) emphasized the use of measurement for decision making. In other cases, line managers, including those in HR, HRD, and human performance technology (HPT), recognize the importance of measuring the effects and impacts of their interventions. Such information can also be used to determine what changes, if any, are needed in the interventions in order to meet their objectives. All of these trends point toward the importance of evaluation and also the expanding approaches and scope of evaluation.

The purpose of this chapter is to examine the expanding scope of evaluation in organizations. The discussion begins with a brief examination of the expansion in the contexts in which evaluations are occurring. The discussion then turns to a presentation of two major types of approaches to evaluation: *outcome-based* approaches and *process or systems* approaches. This discussion highlights

---

* Note: An earlier version of this paper was presented in May 2008 at the Ninth Annual HRD Research and Practice Across Europe conference held in Lille, France.

the expansion that has taken place in recent years in terms of evaluation approaches. The final section of the chapter describes the expansion of evaluation in terms of uses of evaluation.

EXPANDING CONTEXTS FOR EVALUATION

Some might argue that evaluations took place in the early Chinese dynasties (Guba & Lincoln, 1981; Mathison, 1994; Worthen, Sanders, & Fitzpatrick, 1997) or by the early Greek scholars (Stufflebeam & Shinkfield, 1985; Worthen, Sanders, & Fitzpatrick, 1997). Moving to more modern times, however, the first assessment of student achievement took place in 1845 when Horace Mann used a written essay exam to supplement the oral exam in the Boston Public Schools (Madaus & O'Dwyer, 1999). The first formal educational program evaluation was undertaken by Joseph Rice and published in *The Forum* in 1897 in an article titled "The Futility of the Spelling Grind," in which he showed no relationship between time spent on spelling and spelling competency (Colwell, 1998; Stufflebeam, Madaus, & Kellaghn, 2000). Within management, Frederick W. Taylor (1911) undertook time-and-motion studies in order to identify ways to improve employees' skills. During World War I, mental tests were used to classify inductees based on skills, and military leaders requested that the American Psychological Association develop a group intelligence test (Guba & Lincoln, 1989). Thus, evaluation began with a rich array of organizational contexts. [For those interested in more of the history of evaluation, good background is provided in the citations above as well as in Russ-Eft and Preskill (2001) and Hogan (2007).]

Today much evaluation work is conducted on federal and state government programs. Some examples include evaluation of the U.S. Head Start program (for example, Karoly, Kilburn, & Cannon, 2006), of changes in K-12 education (for example, Yin & Davis, 2006), and of the federally funded Adult Education Program (for example, Russ-Eft, 1986). Evaluations also include a focus on public health campaigns (Scherer, 2004) and of community partnerships focused on social and economic development and increased crime and violence prevention (Rog & others, 2004). In addition, training and development efforts are evaluated in private, for-profit organizations (Russ-Eft, Krishnamurthi, & Ravishankar, 1994), in non-governmental organizations, private voluntary organizations, faith-based organizations, and community-based organizations (for example, LeMay & Ellis, 2007), in university settings (for example, Collins & Hopson, 2007), and in foundations (for example, Chelimsky, 2001).

Over the years evaluation activities and evaluation associations have developed in countries throughout the world. In 1998, the presidents of several national evaluation associations debated the pros and cons of entering into a partnership. The associations represented on the panel and in position papers came from Australasia, Canada, Germany, Italy, Kenya, Malaysia, the United Kingdom, and the United States. A second panel session was held the following year. Support was received from the W.K. Kellogg Foundation to establish this international partnership, called the International Organization for Cooperation in Evaluation (www.internationalevaluation.com/). As of January 17, 2008, there were over sixty national organizations affiliated with the International Association for Cooperation in Evaluation (IOCE) and representing all continents.

EXPANDING APPROACHES FOR EVALUATION

As evaluation expands into different contexts, the approaches to evaluation also expand. This section reviews some of the approaches that have been suggested by various researchers, evaluators, and practitioners. The discussion separates these approaches into two major types: outcomes-based approaches and process or systems approaches.

Outcomes-Based Approaches

Much of the work on evaluation within organizational settings began with Donald Kirkpatrick. He focused on whether programs are achieving their objectives or what might be called an "outcomes-based" approach. He created a taxonomy, variously called the "four-step approach to evaluation," "the four levels of evaluation," or the "four-level model." We will begin with a presentation of Kirkpatrick's four levels and will describe some other outcomes-based approaches, many of them representing a variation of the Kirkpatrick approach.

Kirkpatrick's Four-Level Evaluation Model. Kirkpatrick (1959a, b; 1960a, b; 1994) described the outcomes of training as *reactions, learning, behavior*, and *results*. Training evaluations, then, should measure each of these outcomes. A Level 1 evaluation gathers reactions to the training, which are typically called "smile sheets"; a Level 2 evaluation measures trainees' learning, typically with some sort of test; a Level 3 evaluation measures the behavior of trainees (typically on the job or through observation); and a Level 4 evaluation examines the business results for training. A more detailed discussion of Kirkpatrick's levels appears in Chapter Nine of this volume of the handbook.

Although Kirkpatrick's approach has been discussed widely, organizations have not tended to implement all four levels of evaluation. Typically, training evaluation gather data only at the reaction and learning levels. For example, Taylor, Russ-Eft, and Chan (2005) undertook a meta-analysis of studies, both published and unpublished, that evaluated the effectiveness of behavior-modeling training. Of these studies, fifty-two measured attitudes, fourteen measured declarative knowledge, thirty-two measured procedural knowledge, sixty-six measured job behavior, and none measured business results. Certainly reaction and learning measures may be easier and less expensive to obtain. But at the same time, improvements in the effectiveness, efficiency, and profitability of the organization provide the best business case for a learning/training investment.

Training Effectiveness Evaluation (TEE) System. Similar to the Kirkpatrick approach, the training effectiveness evaluation system or TEE (Swanson & Sleezer, 1987) suggested evaluating programs at the satisfaction, learning, and performance levels. Specifically, they recommended developing tools to measure participants' and supervisors' satisfaction; trainees' knowledge and skills; and financial performance. Scores from each of the tools are then assessed before and after an intervention.

Hamblin's Five-Level Model. Hamblin (1974) proposed a five-level model. Similar to Kirkpatrick's approach, evaluations should measure reactions, learning, job behavior, and organizational impact (non-economic outcomes of training). In addition, there should be a Level 5 that examines "ultimate value variables" or "human good" (economic outcomes).

Kaufman, Keller, Watkins Five-Level Model. Kaufman and Keller (1994) and Kaufman, Keller, and Watkins (1995) proposed a model that expanded on the ideas of both Kirkpatrick and Hamblin. They suggested the four previously mentioned. In addition, they recognized the societal impact of training and other HRD interventions. This model, then, includes *societal outcomes* as a fifth level, recognizing that organizations can affect suppliers, clients, and the larger society.

Swanson and Holton's Results Model. Swanson and Holton (1999, p. 8) claimed that "assessment and evaluation are different. Assessment of results is a core organizational process. Evaluation is optional." This text described approaches to assessing results rather than "evaluating." Organizational performance results can be assessed (or evaluated) by examining systems outcomes and financial outcomes. Learning results can be assessed (or evaluated) by measuring knowledge and expertise outcomes. Finally, reaction results can be assessed (or evaluated) through participant and stakeholder measures. It is important to note that they described some specific approaches such as the critical outcome technique, auditing program practices and effectiveness, and certification of core expertise.

Return on Investment. Literature describing the evaluation of business results, financial results, and return on investment (ROI) has become increasingly popular. Jack and Patti Phillips (2005) and Patti and Jack Phillips (2006) have written extensively about ROI and consider this to equate to Kirkpatrick's Level 5 evaluation. "Impact measures are converted to monetary values and compared with the fully loaded program costs" (Phillips & Phillips, 2006, p. 3). Evaluation at this level is typically represented by the benefit-cost ratio (BCR) or by ROI. The following provide the basic formula:

$$BCR = Program\ Benefits/Program\ Costs$$

$$ROI = [Program\ Benefits/Program\ Costs] \times 100$$

Well-designed and well-documented ROI evaluation efforts are hard to find, as suggested by the Taylor, Russ-Eft, and Chan (2005) work. Although organizations and executives claim to be interested in ROI, Russ-Eft and Preskill (2005) suggest that more often evaluation stakeholders have other key questions that are of greater importance.

Process and Systems Approaches

Rather than simply focusing on the outcomes of a program, various other approaches focus on processes, either within programs or within the evaluation. Wang and Spitzer (2005) suggested that some of these approaches tend to have a practice base but are also research and theory driven.

Brinkerhoff's Stage Model. Brinkerhoff (1988, 1989) suggested a cyclical approach, in which every phase of a program can be evaluated. The stages include (a) the needs analysis, (b) the program design, (c) the training program's operation or implementation, (d) later stages in terms of outcomes that are similar to the Kirkpatrick approach. Nevertheless, this stage model provides a type of formative evaluation in that the evaluation findings can be used to aid in decision making and improvement throughout the planning, design, and implementation of the program. This stage model is very similar to the training efficiency and effectiveness Model (TEEM) developed by Lincoln and Dunet (1995).

Input, Process, Output Model. Bushnell (1990) described the "input, process, output model" as IBM's corporate education strategy for the year 2000. This model, similar to Brinkerhoff's stage model, views the evaluation as a cyclical process. Furthermore, such a model appears related to the CIPP model (or context, input, process, and product evaluation) suggested by Stufflebeam (1983, 2000). The input, process, output model begins by examining the *input* factors, such as trainee qualifications, program design, instructor quality and qualifications, materials quality, facilities, and equipment. The *process* factors include such variables as the planning, developing, and delivery of the training. Only after the input and process factors have been examined can the outputs and outcomes be evaluated. *Outputs* are the short-term results, such as trainee reactions, knowledge and skill gains, and job performance improvement. *Outcomes*, or long-term results, include what might be considered business results, such as profits, customer satisfaction, and productivity.

Systemic Model of Factors Predicting Employee Training Outcomes. Richey (1992) developed a model that focuses on factors affecting training outcomes, particularly the trainee characteristics and perceptions of the organization. Thus, it posits that the trainee attitudes are affected by such background characteristics as age, education, previous training, ability to learn, and motivation. The working conditions and the management approach also affect trainee attitudes. Although instructional design and delivery may have some effect on training outcomes, these trainee attitudes have a direct effect on knowledge and behavior resulting from training.

Brinkerhoff's Impact Map. Brinkerhoff and Gill (1994) suggested that too often the wrong people get sent to the training or that the right people attend, but that other factors prevent use of the training. These factors include poor program design, inadequate instructors, the lack of supervisory or peer support, a fear of failure, or a system that punishes the new behaviors. In such cases, the intervention can have little or no impact. The suggestion, then, is for the evaluator to create a "map" showing the entire process from an input phase to the desired outcomes. This "impact map" can help to identify both the process and the factors that can affect the outcomes. This impact map notion is similar to the idea of evaluability assessment introduced by Joseph Wholey (1975, 1976, 1979).

Brinkerhoff's Success Case Method. Recently, Brinkerhoff (2003, 2006) introduced "the success case method." This method enables the evaluator to examine the ways in which the training is or is not aligned with the business strategy. It begins by recognizing that "programs are almost never completely successful such that 100 percent of the participants use learning on the job in a way that drives business results. Similarly, almost no program is ever a 100 percent failure such that no trainee ever uses anything for any worthwhile outcome" (Brinkerhoff, 2005, p. 92). The method focuses on examining the successful and the unsuccessful cases. These findings document the individual and business effects and can identify the factors that support or hinder those effects. (A more detailed analysis of the success case method is discussed in Chapter Five of this handbook.)

Holton's HRD Evaluation Research and Measurement Model. Holton (1996) argued that the Kirkpatrick model is not a model or a theory but rather a taxonomy. He then proposed that the three outcomes of training (learning, individual performance, and organizational results) are influenced by primary and secondary factors. More recently, Holton (2005) has elaborated on the original model. While the outcomes remain as learning, individual performance, and organizational performance, the various factors influencing these involve ability, environment, motivation, and secondary influences on each of these outcomes.

Preskill and Russ-Eft Systems Model. Preskill and Russ-Eft (2003, 2005) and Russ-Eft and Preskill (2001, 2005) recommended that evaluations within organizations use a systems model. Such a model recognizes not only the various factors affecting the individuals and the program or process but also the factors that influence the evaluation itself. Figure 19.1 provides a depiction of this systems model.

This framework recognizes that a number of variables can affect design, conduct, and findings of an evaluation—all of which may influence how the findings may be used or not used. At the heart of the evaluation is the evaluation process. This process includes *focusing* the evaluation, *designing* the evaluation and instrument and *collecting* the data, *analyzing* the data, and *communicating and reporting* on the process and the findings. All of the evaluation depends on *managing* the process and the resources. Russ-Eft and Preskill (2001) provide details on the various steps in the evaluation process.) The systems model recognizes that the evaluator's choices in the various steps within the evaluation process are influenced by the *evaluator's characteristics* (for example, level and type of evaluation expertise, credibility with the program staff), the stakeholders' reasons for conducting the evaluation (that is, their *intended use* of the findings), and the *political context* for the program and the evaluation.

The model moves beyond factors and variables directly involved with the evaluation and suggests that the organization's infrastructure is also important (Preskill & Russ-Eft, 2003; Preskill & Torres, 1999; Russ-Eft & Preskill, 2005). Certainly, the *organization's mission, vision, and strategic goals* can and should influence and even direct the focus and resources of the evaluation; furthermore, the evaluation can and should provide needed information to help shape that mission, vision, and strategy. *Leadership* can provide support for the evaluation or can undermine the entire effort; and the evaluation process can yield important insights to the leadership. An organization's *culture* can lead to active participation and interest in the evaluation, and the evaluation can also help to shape and influence that culture. An effective *communication* system facilitates disseminating evaluation information and findings, contributing to increased use of those findings for decision making and action (Torres, Preskill, & Piontek, 2005). The organization's *systems and structures*, such as a rewards and recognition system that supports the evaluation, can contribute to

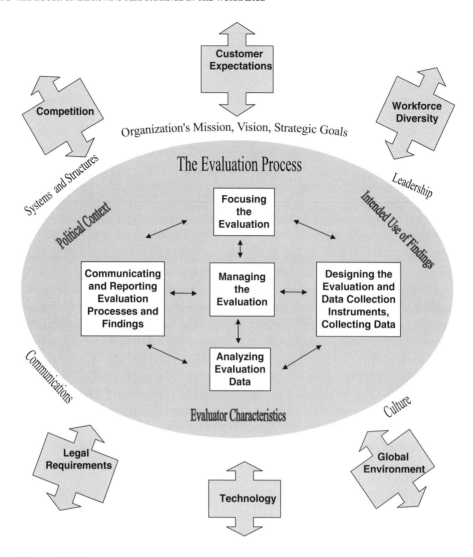

Figure 19.1 A Systems Model of Evaluation.

© H. Preskill & D. Russ-Eft (2004). An earlier version of this figure can be found in H. Preskill & D. Russ-Eft (2003). A framework for reframing HRD evaluation practice and research. In A. Gilley, J. Callahan, & L. Bierema (Eds.), *Critical issues in HRD: A new agenda for the twenty-first century*. Cambridge, MA: Perseus. Reprinted with permission.

participation in the evaluation; furthermore, the evaluation may yield information to make needed changes to the systems and structures.

Finally, the systems approach recognizes the importance of the external environment for the organization and for the evaluation. Some of the elements of this environment include the organization's competition, increasing customer expectations, needs for diversity in the workforce, legal requirements, changes in technology, and the demands of the global environment. These external elements can, in turn, influence stakeholder's information needs, which can affect the focus and conduct of the evaluation.

Conclusions

A variety of approaches to evaluate HRD and other organizational interventions exist for use within many different organizational settings; these include small, medium, and large companies; local, state, and national government agencies; and local, regional, national, and international non-governmental organizations. As more and more of these organizations undertake evaluation efforts, the various approaches to evaluation continue to evolve.

EXPANDING USES OF EVALUATION

Evaluation involves the determining of the merit, worth, or value of a program, process, or product (Scriven, 1991). Furthermore, such determinations are made in order to inform decision making. Thus, organizations and the people within these organizations undertake evaluations on a daily basis. Decisions are made as to whether to undertake certain projects, make specific purchases, and engage in various activities. As a result, more and more organizations and communities are using formal evaluation processes to aid and inform decision making. Such decisions tend to revolve around prioritizing resources, improving quality, and increasing organizational knowledge and learning.

Within any organization, decisions need to be made concerning what programs, services, and products are most critical (for example, Gibson, Martin, & Singer, 2004; Hong & Jun, 2006). Since resources are not infinite, priorities must be set. Evaluation findings can be used to highlight the potential and actual benefits and effects of a program, service, or product. Rather than simply relying on intuition or "gut feeling," evaluation can help determine what directions should be taken, what is worthwhile, what should be continued, and, perhaps, what should be discontinued. Such an evaluation use can be considered a summative evaluation (Scriven, 1991, 1996). Such summative evaluation can include activities that focus on monitoring and auditing (Rossi, Freeman, & Lipsey, 1999) or on outcomes and impacts, as described in the previous section.

Evaluation can help to improve the quality of programs and processes or what has been called formative evaluation (Scriven, 1991, 1996). As suggested in some of the systems approaches above, an examination of the factors and the systems surrounding the HRD intervention, as well as a review of the intervention itself, can provide needed information for program improvement. An examination of the program documents, implementation, and processes can lead to suggestions for improvement that can come from participants in the program, as well as those outside of the program or even the organization. Certainly, formative evaluation can be considered part of the development process.

Both summative and formative evaluations comprise what might be considered "instrumental use" of evaluation, or the direct application of the evaluation findings. Patton (1997), however, suggests other uses of evaluation. Indeed, Russ-Eft, Atwood, and Egherman (2002) demonstrated process use, even while there was limited instrumental use of evaluation findings, because of organizational changes. In this case, consultants within the organization were able to use the experience and understandings emanating from the evaluation to examine their own processes and workflows, separate from the outcomes of the evaluation.

Other uses of evaluation findings include conceptual use and shared learning. Certainly, the involvement of stakeholders in determining the focus of the evaluation can aid in greater understanding of the program or intervention and the organizational processes that can support or hinder its effectiveness (Russ-Eft & Preskill, 2005). Indeed, an increasing use of evaluative inquiry (Parson, 2001; Preskill & Torres, 1999) and appreciative inquiry (Preskill & Coghlan, 2003) enables all stakeholders to learn from and use the evaluation process and the findings.

FUTURE DIRECTIONS AND CHALLENGES

There are areas that show the continued expansion of evaluation research and practice. Each area represents both opportunities and challenges. These three areas involve the continued international growth in evaluation, the increasing interest in meta-evaluation, and the increasing calls for professionalism and accountability of evaluators and the evaluation community.

As discussed above, evaluation activity and evaluation associations exist throughout the world. The development of the IOCE is helping to ensure that support for evaluation and evaluators will continue and will increase. Indeed, this organization holds several specific goals: (a) build evaluation leadership and evaluation capacity in developing countries, (b) help practitioners take a more worldly approach to the issues, problems, and questions that they investigate, and (c) foster global collaboration, information sharing, and theory building. Such globalization does not, however, come without some challenges. First, if evaluators are to practice globally, they must possess some competence to interact with the various constituencies. Second, the ethical standards used in one national or organizational setting may not be able to be translated or adapted to another national or organizational setting. Both of these challenges then relate to the interest in meta-evaluation and the calls for certification.

Meta-evaluation refers to evaluation that looks inward on its own practice, or what might be considered an evaluation of an evaluation (Scriven, 1991; Russ-Eft & Preskill, 2001). Such a meta-evaluation can be undertaken by the evaluator or evaluation team as a kind of reflection process. It may be undertaken by the program staff or stakeholders as a means of providing a critique of the evaluation. Or it may be undertaken by a peer evaluator or group of peer evaluators. Through such meta-evaluation, both the evaluators and the stakeholders can learn more about the evaluation processes. In addition, such meta-evaluation can bring greater clarity and greater credibility to the original evaluation findings. Russ-Eft and Preskill (2008) provide an example of a meta-evaluation of a beta-test process within a private organization. Even though meta-evaluations can yield important learnings and findings, the challenge for evaluators is to identify ways to build such meta-evaluations into an already expensive (potentially in the minds of the client) process.

A final area of expanding scope for evaluation involves the increasing calls for professionalism and accountability within the evaluation community. Such interest stems partly from the growth of the evaluation throughout the world and partly from evaluators' recognition of their own need for increased learning and development. Thus, sets of standards and guidelines have been developed by various national evaluation associations. In addition, recent studies have been undertaken to identify evaluator competencies (King, Stevahn, Ghere, & Minnema, 2001; Russ-Eft, Bober, de la Teja, Foxon, & Koszalka, 2008; Stevahn, King, Ghere, & Minnema, 2005). The challenge will be to determine the most effective methods for incorporating such standards and competencies into the future education, training, and development of evaluators and those who plan to undertake evaluations.

References

Brinkerhoff, R. O. (1988). An integrated evaluation model for HRD. *Training and Development Journal, 42*(2), 66–68.

Brinkerhoff, R. O. (1989). *Achieving results from training.* San Francisco: Jossey-Bass.

Brinkerhoff, R. O. (2003). *The success case method: Find out quickly what's working and what's not.* San Francisco: Berrett-Koehler.

Brinkerhoff, R. O. (2005). The success case method: A strategic evaluation approach to increasing the value and effect of training. In G. G. Wang & D. R. Spitzer (Eds.), *Advances in HRD measurement and evaluation: Theory and practice. Thousand Oaks, CA: Sage.*

Brinkerhoff, R. O. (2006). *Telling training's story: Evaluation made simple, credible, and effective.* San Francisco: Berrett-Koehler.

Brinkerhoff, R. O., & Gill, S. J. (1994). *The learning alliance: Systems thinking in human resource development.* San Francisco: Jossey-Bass.

Bushnell, D. S. (1990). Input, process, output: A model for evaluating training. *Training and Development Journal, 42*(3), 41–43.

Chelimsky, E. (2001). What evaluation could do to support foundations: A framework with nine component parts. *American Journal of Evaluation, 22*, 13–28.

Collins, P. M., & Hopson, R. K. (2007). Building leadership development, social justice, and social change in evaluation through a pipeline program. In K. M. Hannum, J. W. Martineau, & C. Reinelt (Eds.), *Handbook of leadership development evaluation.* San Francisco: Jossey-Bass.

Colwell, R. (1998). A long trail a winding: Issues, interests, and priorities in arts education. *Arts Education Policy Review, 99*(5), 21–30.

Gates, S. (2005) *Measuring more than efficiency.* (Report No. R-1356-04-RR). New York: Conference Board.

Gibson, J., Martin, D., & Singer, P. (2004). Setting priorities in health care organizations: Criteria, processes and parameters of success. *Biomedical Central Health Services Research, 4.*

Guba, E. G., & Lincoln, Y. S. (1981). *Effective evaluations.* San Francisco: Jossey-Bass.

Guba, E. G., & Lincoln, Y. S. (1989). *Fourth generation evaluation.* San Francisco: Jossey-Bass.

Hamblin, A. C. (1974). *Evaluation and control of training.* London: McGraw-Hill.

Hogan, R. L. (2007). The historical development of program evaluation: Exploring the past and present. *Online Journal of Workforce Education and Development, 2*(4). Retrieved April 1, 2008, from http://wed.siu.edu/Journal/VolIInum4/Article_4.pdf.

Holton, E. F., III. (1996). The flawed four-level evaluation model. *Human Resource Development Quarterly, 7*(1), 5–21.

Holton, E. F., III. (2005). Holton's evaluation model: New evidence and construct elaboration. In G. G. Wang & D. R. Spitzer (Eds.), *Advances in HRD measurement and evaluation: Theory and practice.* Thousand Oaks, CA: Sage.

Hong, S.-J., & Jun, I.-S. (2006). An evaluation of the service quality priorities of air cargo service providers and customers. *Review of Intermodal Transportation Research, 1*, 55–68.

Karoly, L, Kilburn, R., & Cannon, J. (2006). *Early childhood interventions: Proven results, future promise.* Washington, DC: Rand.

Kaufman, R. A., & Keller, J. M. (1994). Levels of evaluation: Beyond Kirkpatrick. *Human Resource Development Quarterly, 5*(4), 371–380.

Kaufman, R. A., Keller, J. M., & Watkins, R. (1995). What works and what doesn't: Evaluation beyond Kirkpatrick. *Performance and Instruction, 35*(2), 8–12.

King, J., Stevahn, L., Ghere, G., & Minnema, J. (2001). Toward a taxonomy of essential evaluator competencies. *American Journal of Evaluation, 22*, 229–247.

Kirkpatrick, D. L. (1959a, November). Techniques for evaluating programs. *Journal of the American Society of Training Directors (Training and Development Journal)*, *13*(11), 3–9.

Kirkpatrick, D. L. (1959b, December). Techniques for evaluating programs—Part 2: Learning. *Journal of the American Society of Training Directors (Training and Development Journal)*, *13*(12), 21–26.

Kirkpatrick, D. L. (1960a, January). Techniques for evaluating programs—Part 3: Behavior. *Journal of the American Society of Training Directors (Training and Development Journal)*, *14*(1), 13–18.

Kirkpatrick, D. L. (1960b, January). Techniques for evaluating programs—Part 4: Results. *Journal of the American Society of Training Directors (Training and Development Journal)*, *14*(1), 28–32.

Kirkpatrick, D. L. (1994). *Evaluating training programs: The four levels*. San Francisco: Berrett-Koehler.

LaBonte, T., & Necessary, M. (2007, August). Stand firm in quest for true data. *T&D*, *61*, 50–53.

LeMay, N. V., & Ellis, A. (2007). Evaluating leadership development and organizational performance. In K. M. Hannum, J. W. Martineau, & C. Reinelt (Eds.), *Handbook of leadership development evaluation*. San Francisco: Jossey-Bass.

Lincoln, R. E., & Dunet, D. O. (1995). Training efficiency and effectiveness model (TEEM). *Performance and Instruction*, *34*(3), 40–47.

Madaus, G. F., & O'Dwyer, L. M. (1999, May). A short history of performance assessment: Lessons learned. *Phi Delta Kappan*, pp. 688–695.

Mathison, S. (1994). Evaluation. In A. C. Purves (Ed.), *Encyclopedia of English studies language arts*. Champaign, IL: NCTE and Scholastic.

Parson, B. A. (2001). *Evaluative inquiry: Using evaluation to promote student success*. Thousand Oaks, CA: Corwin.

Patton, M. Q. (1997). *Utilization-focused evaluation: A new century text* (3rd ed.). Thousand Oaks, CA: Sage.

Phillips, J. J., & Phillips, P. P. (2005). *ROI at work*. Alexandria, VA: American Society for Training and Development.

Phillips, P. P., & Phillips, J. J. (2006). *Return on investment (ROI) basics*. Alexandria, VA: American Society for Training and Development.

Preskill, H., & Coghlan, A. (2003). Using appreciative inquiry in evaluation. *New Directions in Program Evaluation* (No. 100). San Francisco: Jossey-Bass.

Preskill, H., & Russ-Eft, D. (2003). A framework for reframing HRD evaluation practice and research (pp. 199–257). In A. M. Gilley, L. Bierema, & J. Callahan (Eds.), *Critical issues in HRD*. Cambridge, MA: Perseus.

Preskill, H., & Russ-Eft, D. (2005). *Building evaluation capacity: 72 activities for teaching and training*. Thousand Oaks, CA: Sage.

Preskill, H., & Torres, R. T. (1999). *Evaluative inquiry for learning in organizations.* Thousand Oaks, CA: Sage.

Richey, R. C. (1992). *Designing instruction for the adult learner.* London: Kogan Page.

Rog, D. J., Boback, N., Barton-Villagrana, H., Marrone-Bennett, P., Cardwell, J., Hawdon, J., Diazs, J., Jenkins, P. I., Kridler, J., & Reischl, T. (2004). Sustaining collaboratives: A cross-site analysis of the National Funding Collaborative on Violence Prevention. *Evaluation and Program Planning, 27*(3), 249–261.

Rossi, P. H., Freeman, H. E., & Lipsey, M. W. (1999). *Evaluation: A systematic approach* (6th ed.). Thousand Oaks, CA: Sage.

Russ-Eft, D. (1986). Evaluability assessment of the Adult Education Program (AEP). *Evaluation and Program Planning, 9*, 39–47.

Russ-Eft, D., Atwood, R., & Egherman, T. (2002). Use and non-use of evaluation results: A case study of environmental influences in the private sector. *American Journal of Evaluation, 23*, 19–31.

Russ-Eft, D., Bober, M. J., de la Taja, I., Foxon, M. J., & Koszalka, T. A. (2008). *Evaluator competencies: Standards for the practice of evaluation in organizations.* San Francisco: Jossey-Bass.

Russ-Eft, D., Krishnamurthi, S., & Ravishankar, L. (1994). Getting results with inter-personal training. In J. J. Phillips (Ed.), *In action: Measuring return on investment* (1st ed.) (pp. 199–212). Alexandria, VA: American Society for Training and Development.

Russ-Eft, D., & Preskill, H. (2001). *Evaluation in organizations: A systematic approach to enhancing learning, performance, and change.* Cambridge, MA: Perseus.

Russ-Eft, D., & Preskill, H. (2005). In search of the holy grail: ROI evaluation in HRD. In G. G. Wang & D. R. Spitzer (Eds.), *Advances in HRD measurement and evaluation: Theory and practice. Thousand Oaks, CA: Sage.*

Russ-Eft, D., & Preskill, H. (2008). Improving the quality of evaluation participation: A meta-evaluation. *Human Resource Development International, 11*, 35–50.

Scherer, J. A. (2004, February). *A guide to collecting data on performance indicators for the Centers for Disease Control and Prevention's Prevention Research Center.* Bethesda, MD: COSMOS.

Scriven, M. (1991). *Evaluation thesaurus* (4th ed.). Thousand Oaks, CA: Sage.

Scriven, M. (1996). Types of evaluation and types of evaluator. *Evaluation Practice, 17*(2), 151–161.

Stevahn, L., King, J. A., Ghere, G., & Minnema, J. (2005). Establishing essential competencies for evaluators. *American Journal of Evaluation, 26*(1), 43–59.

Stufflebeam, D. L. (1983). The CIPP model for program evaluation. In G. F. Madaus, M. Scriven, & D. L. Stufflebeam (Eds.), *Evaluation models* (pp. 117–141). Boston: Kluwer-Nijhoff.

Stufflebeam, D. L. (2000). The CIPP model for evaluation. In D. L. Stufflebeam, G. F. Madaus, & T. Kellaghan (Eds.), *Evaluation models* (2nd ed.). Boston: Kluwer Academic.

Stufflebeam, D. L., Madaus, G. F., & Kellaghn, T. (2000). *Evaluation models: Viewpoints on educational and human services evaluation* (2nd ed.). Boston: Kluwer Academic.

Stufflebeam, D. L., & Shinkfield, A. J. (1985). *Systematic evaluation.* Boston: Kluwer-Nijhoff.

Swanson, R. A., & Holton, E. F., III (1999). *Results: How to assess performance, learning, and perceptions in organizations.* San Francisco: Berrett-Koehler.

Swanson, R. A., & Sleezer, C. M. (1987). Training effectiveness evaluation. *Journal of European Industrial Training, 11*(4), 7–16.

Taylor, F. W. (1911). *The principles of scientific management.* New York: Harper.

Taylor, P., Russ-Eft, D., & Chan, D. (2005). The effectiveness of behavior modeling training across settings and features of study design. *Journal of Applied Psychology, 90,* 692–709.

Torres, R. T., Preskill, H., & Piontek, M. E. (2005). *Evaluation strategies for communicating and reporting: Enhancing learning in organizations* (2nd ed.). Thousand Oaks, CA: Sage.

Wang, G. G., & Spitzer, D. R. (Eds.) (2005). *Advances in HRD Measurement and Evaluation: Theory and Practice. Thousand Oaks, CA: Sage.*

Wholey, J. S. (1975). Evaluation: When is it really needed? *Evaluation Magazine, 2*(2).

Wholey, J. S. (1976). *A methodology for planning and conducting project impact evaluation in UNESCO fields.* Washington, DC: Urban Institute.

Wholey, J. S. (1979). *Evaluation: Promise and performance.* Washington, DC: Urban Institute.

Worthen, B. R., Sanders, J. R., & Fitzpatrick, J. L. (1997). *Program evaluation* (2nd ed.). New York: Longman.

Yin, R. K., & Davis, D. (2006). State-level education reform: Putting all the pieces together. In K. Wong & S. Rutledge (Eds.), *District-wide efforts to improve students' achievement.* Greenwich, CT: Information Age.

CHAPTER TWENTY

The Changing Role of Evaluators and Evaluation

Roger Chevalier

I s evaluation a true profession, a field of study and activity, or a subset of other professions? For every individual who practices evaluation as a full-time role, there are thousands who use evaluation to support broader professions. And while there are advantages for an individual to work full-time as an evaluator, there are other advantages of having evaluation embedded in other professions.

Evaluation is used to measures such things as the effectiveness of public and organizational programs, the quality of goods and services, the impact of training, the performance of personnel and equipment, and the potential value of proposed actions. "Evaluation should be seen as a process of knowledge production, which rests on the use of empirical inquiry" (Owen, 2006). In other words, evaluation is making a value judgment of the merit or worth of an object based upon a set of standards or criteria. With such a wide range of uses, it's not surprising that a number of professions have established standards and guidelines to encourage its correct use.

WHAT IS A PROFESSION?

One of the earliest and most accepted definitions of a profession comes from the highly respected educator, Jim Finn, as he reviewed the audiovisual field to see whether it was a true profession. According to Finn (1953), "A profession has, at least, these characteristics: (a) an intellectual technique, (b) an application of that technique to the practical affairs of man, (c) a period of long training necessary before entering into the profession, (d) an association of the members of the profession into a closely knit group with a high quality of communication between members, (e) a series of standards and a statement of ethics which is enforced, and (f) an organized body of intellectual theory constantly expanding by research."

In 1967 the Department of Labor co-sponsored a meeting with Cornell University and the American Society for Personnel Administration (ASPA) (the forerunner of the Society for Human Resources Management (SHRM). According to Fred Wilkins (2008), who worked for ASPA at the time of the meeting, five distinct characteristics of a profession were developed:

1. A profession is defined by the existence of a national organization that can speak as a unified voice for its members and foster development of the field.

2. A profession has a code of ethics that identifies standards of behavior relating to fairness, justice, truthfulness, and social responsibility.

3. A profession is also marked by the existence of applied research related to the field.

4. A profession has a defined body of knowledge.

5. A profession has a credentialing organization that sets standards in the field.

These characteristics are also referenced in Raymond Weinberg's book, *Certification Guide* (2002). It is interesting to note that the Department of Labor does not identify evaluation as a profession in the list of professional and related occupations in the *Occupational Outlook Handbook* (Wilkins, 2008); nor does the Department of Labor currently have a definition or list of characteristics of a profession on their website.

The Society for Human Resource Management's Human Resource Certification Institute defines a profession (Cherrington & Leonard, 1993) as having the following characteristics:

1. A profession must be full-time.

2. Schools and curricula must be aimed specifically at teaching the basic ideas of the profession, and there must be a defined common body of knowledge.

3. A profession must have a national professional association.

4. A profession must have a certification program.

5. A profession must have a code of ethics.

The most notable additions by SHRM are the additions that a profession must be "full-time" and that there must be a "certification program."

THE CASE FOR EVALUATION AS A PROFESSION

Evaluation is an intellectual technique that is applied to the practical affairs of man. In order to be viewed as a profession, it requires significant education and training; an association of the members of the profession into a closely knit group with high-quality communications between members; an organized body of intellectual theory that is constantly expanding by research; evidence of practical application; plus a set of standards and a statement of ethics.

Education and Training

Education and training in evaluation may be formal or informal. Formal programs can help prepare individuals for doing systematic evaluation. In addition to lectures, textbooks, and articles that deal with the subject, evaluation techniques can be learned with simulations and research projects as well as during internships as part of the formal education process. Informal programs may include attending professional meetings or conferences; participating in mentoring and coaching programs; reading professional books and journals, and other professional-development-type activities.

Formal Programs. It is interesting to note that nearly all of the formal education resources identified on the American Evaluation Association (AEA) website available for evaluators to learn their craft are parts of broader fields of study (AEA University Programs, n.d.). Some university graduate programs or certificate programs deal directly with evaluation, but most were imbedded in graduate programs for psychology, education, educational psychology, professional and public sociology, public administration and policy, education and educational research, and organizational development. It should be noted that there are also many undergraduate and graduate courses in evaluation in instructional technology and performance technology programs.

Informal Programs. In addition to formal education programs, practitioners can develop evaluation knowledge and skills by participating in coaching, mentoring, or other on-the-job programs, or by attending professional conferences and training programs hosted by professional organizations such as AEA, the Project Managers Institute (PMI), SHRM, ISPI, ASTD, and so forth, as well as by commercial vendors.

Books. Amazon.com lists over 127,000 entries when evaluation is searched in their non-fiction book section. That number drops quickly to about seven hundred books that address research methodologies for the social sciences. Four examples of excellent evaluation books follow.

Evaluation Theory, Models, and Applications is a comprehensive resource for students of evaluation to learn its history, theory and standards, models and approaches, procedures, and inclusion of personnel and program evaluation (Stufflebeam & Shinkfield, 2007).

The book that I have found most valuable as I worked to assess the impact of training and performance improvement interventions is Donald Kirkpatrick's *Evaluating Training Programs: The Four Levels*, first published in 1994 and now in its third edition (1998). Kirkpatrick first published his ideas regarding four levels of evaluation in 1959 in a series of four articles called "Techniques for Evaluating Training Programs" in *Training and Development*. His four-level model focused on student reaction (what they thought about what they learned), learning (increase in knowledge and skills), behavior (changed behavior when returned to the workplace), and results (impact on desired business outcomes (Chevalier, 2004).

Another book that has gained a lot of attention in recent years is *Return on Investment in Training and Performance Improvement Programs* by Jack Phillips (1997). Later described by Phillips as Level 5, many view return on investment as a subset of Kirkpatrick's Level 4. That being said, many organizations have embraced the idea of comparing the cost of an intervention with its impact on organizational performance. The question that applies here is: "Was the gain worth the pain?"

A less traditional approach to evaluation is offered by Rob Brinkerhoff in his book, *The Success Case Method* (2003), in which he focuses on factual and verifiable accounts that demonstrate how and how valuably a person used some new method, tool, or capability.

Professional Journals. Practitioners can also read professional journals such as:

- *American Journal of Evaluation (AJE):* Formerly known as *Evaluation Practice*, AJE "publishes original papers about the methods, theory, practice, and findings of evaluation. The general goal of *AJE* is to present the best work in and about evaluation, in order to improve the knowledge base and practice of its readers" (www.eval.org/Publications/AJE.asp).

- *Educational Evaluation and Policy Analysis (EEPA):* EEPA "publishes scholarly manuscripts of theoretical, methodological, or policy interest to those engaged in educational policy analysis, evaluation, and decision making" (*Educational Evaluation and Policy Analysis*, n.d.).

- *Educational Researcher(ER):* ER "contains scholarly articles that come from a wide range of disciplines and are of general significance to the education research community" (*Educational Researcher*, n.d.).

- *Evaluation and Program Planning (EPP)":* EPP publishes "articles from the private and public sectors in a wide range of areas: organizational development and behavior, training, planning, human resource development, health and mental, social services, mental retardation, corrections, substance abuse, and education" (*Evaluation and Program Planning*, n.d.).

- *Evaluation Review (ER):* ER contains "the latest quantitative and qualitative methodological developments, as well as related applied research issues" in such fields as "education, public health, criminal justice, child development, mental health, social work, public administration, and environmental studies" (*Evaluation Review*, n.d.).

- *New Directions for Evaluation (NDE):* NDE is "a quarterly sourcebook . . . an official publication of the American Evaluation Association. It is a peer-reviewed journal that publishes empirical, methodological, and theoretical works on all aspects of evaluation" (*New Directions for Evaluation*, n.d.).

- *Performance Improvement Quarterly (PIQ):* PIQ "is a peer-reviewed journal created to stimulate professional discussion in the field and to advance the discipline of HPT through publishing scholarly works. Its emphasis is on human performance technologies such as front-end analysis or evaluation" (*Performance Improvement Quarterly*, n.d.).

- There are also many other evaluation journals published by the various evaluation professional groups around the world.

Professional Evaluation Associations

The American Evaluation Association (AEA) is the largest evaluation association in the world with 5,500 national and international members and an annual conference attended by 2,500 participants. AEA's mission (AEA About Us, n.d.) is to:

- Improve evaluation practices and methods,

- Increase evaluation use,

- Promote evaluation as a profession, and

- Support the contribution of evaluation to the generation of theory and knowledge about effective human action.

There are many countries around the world that sponsor and support professional evaluation associations. These include:

- *Africa:* African Evaluation Association, Nigerian Network of Monitoring and Evaluation, Ghana Evaluators Association, South African Evaluation Network, and Uganda Evaluation Association

- *Asia:* Japan Evaluation Society, Malaysian Evaluation Society, and Sri Lanka Evaluation

- *Australia:* Australasian Evaluation Society
- *Canada:* Canadian Evaluation Society and Quebec Society for Program Evaluation
- *Europe:* Danish Evaluation Society, Dutch Evaluation Society, European Evaluation Society, Finnish Evaluation Society, French Evaluation Society, German Evaluation Society, International Program Evaluation Network (Russia), Italian Evaluation Society, Spanish Public Policy Evaluation Society, Swedish Evaluation Society, Swiss Evaluation Society, United Kingdom Evaluation Society
- *Latin America:* Latin American and Caribbean Programme for Strengthening the Regional Capacity and Evaluation of Rural Poverty Alleviation Projects, and Red de Evaluacion de American Latina y el Caribe
- *Middle East:* Israeli Association for Program Evaluation

Defined Common Body of Knowledge

In researching for this chapter, I was unable to identify a common body of evaluation knowledge. Evaluation is such a broad field that overlaps with many other professions that it would be difficult to identify a clear body of knowledge that all practitioners should have. Perhaps the best collection of evaluation resources is published on the American Evaluation Association website in their Resource Category.

Practical Application

Mentors and coaches can help accelerate this hands-on learning process. Publishing evaluation results and receiving feedback can also help to further refine these skills. However, to truly develop and refine their skills, evaluators must practice their craft in the real world by measuring results on a full-time or part-time basis.

For example, many AEA members work full-time in the field of evaluation, although their job titles may vary from evaluator to project analyst, program evaluator, market researcher, educational analyst, auditor, and so forth. Other members work in fields in which evaluation is only part-time for their roles.

Full-Time Evaluators. Evaluators who work full-time at their craft have the advantage of greater focus and experience in the evaluation process. The disadvantage is that they typically are not involved in a project until after it has been completed. At that point they have to reconstruct what has happened, identify what measures are appropriate, and determine whether performance was actually improved. In many cases, evaluation is limited, as the performance shortfall was not adequately defined in measurable terms at the beginning of the

performance improvement process so it is more difficult to measure improvement when the project is complete.

The role of full-time evaluators is to "look backwards," since they typically
start their work after a project has been implemented. They then try to
measure the impact of the initiative by reconstructing what has happened.
Part-time evaluators, who begin the measurement process at the beginning to
determine the present and desired levels of performance, look forward with
their evaluations. The starting point for them is not the end of a project but the
beginning (Chevalier, 2003). The gap analysis process is depicted in Figure 20.1.

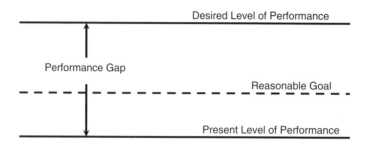

Figure 20.1 Performance Gap Analysis.

By clearly describing the present and desired levels of performance and
setting a reasonable goal in measurable terms, the part-time evaluators are
better able to track changes in performance as a result of the interventions made.
This is far superior to beginning the evaluation process after the intervention has
been made because it may be difficult if not impossible to reconstruct a baseline
with which to measure the effects of the changes made.

Part-Time Evaluators. Evaluation is more commonly seen as part of project
management, quality assurance, performance improvement, and instructional
design. Here are some examples:

- Project managers are the largest identifiable group that uses evaluation as
  part of their field. Project managers need to measure the impact of their
  interventions as part of the monitoring and controlling process to ensure
  that they have met the requirements of a particular project.

- Human resource managers must continuously monitor the effectiveness of
  their programs in terms of impact on individual and organizational
  performance. Evaluation provides feedback on the state of the human
  assets that make up the organization.

- Instructional designers use a systematic approach to developing training.
  Practitioners must be able to perform a needs assessment to determine the

knowledge and skills required to do a specific job; design, develop, and deliver the training and evaluate the results.

• Performance technologists also use a systematic approach to improving workplace performance. The process used includes identification of a performance gap as the difference between the present and desired levels of performance, determination of the underlying causes for the gap, design, development and implementation of solutions, and evaluation of the results.

• Evaluation is an integral part of the quality assurance professional's role. Quality assurance is done to ensure that an organization's products and services meet customer expectations. Evaluation allows organizations to systematically assess the degree to which their products and services meet the standards they have set. This systematic assessment of quality is a necessary step for continuous improvement of those products and services.

Evaluation practitioners who do evaluation as part of a greater performance improvement process have the advantage of being involved in the project from its beginning.

Ideally, part-time evaluators have determined present and desired levels of performance and set a reasonable goal or milestone with which to measure progress in terms of quality, quantity, time, and cost at the most basic level; for sales, service, customer service, customer retention, and customer referrals at an intermediary level; or for profitability and market share at the business outcome level. For these part-time evaluators, the evaluation process begins as the performance shortfall is defined.

Another important aspect of gap analysis is found in establishing trends in performance before the intervention is made. Too often evaluation begins by determining the present level of performance as a single point in time. The impact of the intervention is then determined by the change from that point after the intervention as shown in Figure 20.2. The results could be misleading if the performance trend before the intervention is not known.

But how does the evaluation of the result of the intervention change when we know the trends in performance that existed before the intervention? Was performance declining, steady, or already improving? Did the intervention positively increase the trend that was already there? By starting the evaluation process at the beginning of the project, part-time evaluators can determine existing trends that will serve to demonstrate how much performance has actually improved as a result of the intervention. This trend analysis is depicted in Figure 20.3.

Depending on the trend before the intervention, the various outcomes have different values. If there was a downward trend before the intervention, an upward performance is desirable, but leveling the performance downturn may also show a measure of success. If there was steady performance before the intervention, then only upward performance would indicate that the intervention was successful. If there was an upward trend before the intervention, continued upward performance may not necessarily be an indication that the intervention added value, because performance was headed that way anyway.

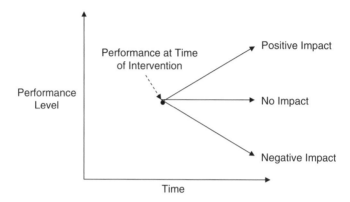

Figure 20.2 Performance Improvement Measured from a Single Point.

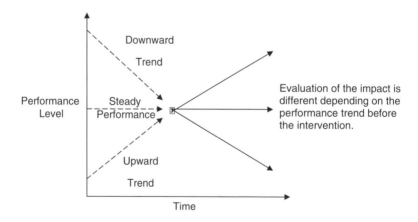

Figure 20.3 Performance Improvement Measured from Performance Trends.

Standards, Competencies, and Ethics

National and international evaluation associations have developed standards for conducting evaluation. Indeed, evaluation standards suffer from too many sources; sources that cannot be used to hold evaluation practitioners accountable for their professional ethical practices. "There is evidence to suggest that these voluntary standards have not yet met their full potential" (Russon, 2005).

AEA's Guiding Principles. In AEA's *Guiding Principles for Evaluators* (2004), the following five principles are established to guide their members:

1. *Systematic Inquiry:* Evaluators conduct systematic, data-based inquiries about whatever is being evaluated.

2. *Competence:* Evaluators provide competent performance to stakeholders.

3. *Integrity/Honesty:* Evaluators ensure the honesty and integrity of the entire evaluation process.

4. *Respect for People:* Evaluators respect the security, dignity, and self-worth of the respondents, program participants, clients, and other stakeholders with whom they interact.

5. *Responsibilities for General and Public Welfare:* Evaluators articulate and take into account the diversity of interests and values that may be related to the general and public welfare.

The Joint Committee's Program Evaluation Standards. Located in the Evaluation Center of Western Michigan University, The Joint Committee's stated role is to guide and improve the quality of program, personnel, and student evaluations (The Joint Committee, 1994). The program evaluation standards are clustered under four headings:

1. Utility with standards for evaluator credibility, attention to stakeholders, clear purposes, explicit values, selection of relevant information, meaningful processes and products, responsive communication and reporting, and concern for consequences and responsiveness.

2. Feasibility with standards for practical procedures, political viability, resources use, and project management;

3. Proprietary with standards for responsiveness and inclusiveness, formal and informal agreements, human rights and respect, balance, transparency and disclosure, conflicts of interest, and fiscal responsibility;

4. Accuracy with standards for trustworthy conclusions and decisions, explicit evaluation reasoning, valid constructs, reliable information, sound qualitative and quantitative methods, sound designs and analyses, trustworthy evaluation and context portrayals, and valid communication and reporting; and

Government Auditing Standards. In 2003, the United States Government Accountability Office released the *Government Auditing Standards*. They are often used in conjunction with the AEA *Guiding Principles for Evaluators* and The Joint Committee *Program Evaluation Standards*. Their chief purpose is "to help ensure that program evaluations and audits provide an independent assessment of the performance and management of programs against objective criteria or best practices'' (Stufflebeam & Shinkfield, 2007, p. 99). The four general standards applicable to program evaluations and evaluators are *independence, professional judgment, competence*, and *quality control and assurance* (Stufflebeam & Shinkfield, 2007).

IBSTPI Competencies. The International Board of Standards for Training, Performance, and Instruction (IBSTPI) has identified fourteen evaluator competencies clustered in four general domains that are ''required by internal staff or external consultants conducting evaluations in organizational settings, such as for-profit and not-for-profit organizations, military, and government agencies evaluating their own internal programs'' (IBSTPI, 2006).

Competency is defined as the knowledge, skill, or characteristic required to effectively perform a role in an organization (Lucia & Lepsinger, 1999). Competency has also been defined as the knowledge, attitudes, or skills that define the core abilities required for successful performance in a given job (Parry, 1998). The IBSTPI competencies for evaluators include:

1. Professional Foundations:
   - Communicate effectively in written, oral, and visual form.
   - Establish and maintain professional credibility.
   - Demonstrate effective interpersonal skills.
   - Observe ethical and legal standards.
   - Demonstrate awareness of the politics of evaluation.
2. Planning and Designing the Evaluation:
   - Develop an effective evaluation plan.
   - Develop a management plan for the evaluation.
   - Devise data collection strategies to support the evaluation questions and design.
   - Pilot test the data collection instruments and procedures.
3. Implementing the Evaluation Plan:
   - Collect data.
   - Analyze and interpret data.
   - Disseminate and follow up the findings and recommendations.
4. Managing the Evaluation:
   - Monitor the management plan.
   - Work effectively with personnel and stakeholders.

The development of these evaluator competencies is yet another step in making evaluation a true profession.

These competencies "represent more than the knowledge, skills, and attitudes expected of professionals in various settings. They also provide operational definitions that can be used by organizations to define job requirements and position descriptions, establish performance indicators, and improve professional development programs" (Klein & Richey, 2005).

Ethics

AEA, The Joint Committee, and IBSTPI do include ethical considerations in their standards and competencies. Ethical standards were adopted by the American Educational Research Association (AERA) in June 1992 and revised in 1996 and 2000 as "an educational document to stimulate collegial debate and to evoke voluntary compliance by moral persuasion" (About AERA, n.d.). However, a lack of ethical accountability can be seen when professional associations guide members involved in evaluation without a means to monitor or investigate infractions.

THE ISSUE OF CERTIFICATION

Certification of evaluators is the next step in moving the field of evaluation toward becoming a profession. By certifying evaluators, professional and ethical standards could be enforced by the certifying body if a certified evaluator was found to be incompetent or unethical in conducting evaluations.

Certification for Full-Time Evaluators

The greatest problem in defining evaluation as a profession is that there is no certification process or credential for full-time evaluators to demonstrate that they have acquired the necessary body of knowledge and are performing to a given set of standards. Without a certification that would be at risk for professional or ethical shortfalls, full-time evaluators cannot be held accountable for their performance by the evaluation associations to which they belong.

Certification for Part-Time Evaluators

When the evaluation role is only a part-time function, evaluation standards for performance and accountability for adherence through certification are available for individuals working in these professions. Here are some examples:

Project Management. Founded in 1969, the Project Manager's Institute (PMI) is the leading membership association for project managers with more than 260,000 members in more than 171 countries (PMI, n.d.b). According to Joseph Patterson, PMI's Public Relations Manager, PMI has certified 267,000 project managers worldwide as Project Management Professionals (Patterson, 2008).

To be eligible for the PMP credential, applicants must have a bachelor's degree with three years of experience and 4,500 hours spent leading and directing project tasks or 7,500 hours spent leading and directing project tasks without a bachelor's degree. Applicants for the credential must agree to adhere to a code of ethics and professional conduct and pass a two-hundred-multiple-choice-question examination that includes forty-two questions (21 percent) related to evaluation under the heading of monitoring and controlling (PMI, n.d.a).

Human Resource Management. Human resource management includes such organizational functions as recruitment, selection, training, performance management, and compensation. Founded in 1948, the Society for Human Resource Management (SHRM) is the world's largest professional association devoted to human resource management. SHRM represents more than 225,000 individual members in over 125 countries, and has a network of more than 575 affiliated chapters in the United States and abroad (About SHRM, n.d.).

Human Resource Certification Institute (HRCI) began certifying HR professionals in 1976. Since then, the HRCI has certified over ninety thousand HR professionals in three certification areas: Professional in Human Resources (PHR), Senior Professional in Human Resources (SPHR), and Global Professional in Human Resources (GPHR) (HRCI Overview, n.d.).

For the PHR and SPHR certifications, six functional areas are described: strategic management, workplace planning and employment, human resource development, total rewards, employee and labor relations, and risk management. Of the seventy-four responsibilities listed for these functional areas, twenty include evaluation (PHR/SPHR Test Specifications, n.d.).

The HRCI certification requirements include work experience, adherence to standards of honor and integrity, and two hundred multiple-choice test questions for the PHR and SPHR certifications and a 150-question multiple-choice test for the GPHR certification. Certifications may be denied or revoked for falsification of work experience or other information on the exam application, misrepresentation of work experience or other information, violation of testing procedures, failure to pass the certification exam, or failure to meet recertification requirements (PHR SPHR GPHR Certification Handbook, 2008).

Quality Assurance. Formed in 1946 and with more than 100,000 individual and organizational members in over one hundred countries, the American Society for Quality (ASQ) is the leading professional association that advances learning, quality improvement, and knowledge exchange to improve business results. ASQ has certified over 120,000 individuals in fourteen different certification programs for various aspects of quality in such industries as education, government, healthcare, manufacturing and service (ASQ: Who we are, n.d.).

Each certification candidate is required to pass a multiple-choice examination that measures comprehension of the related body of knowledge. The Certified Manager of Quality program also has two essay questions. All exams have questions on evaluation of quality improvement initiatives, but to varying degrees based on the program. ASQ also has a code of ethics (ASQ: Code of Ethics, n.d.) to guide its members in their actions as they work to improve quality in the organizations they serve. ASQ uses its Ethics Committee to review complaints regarding performance and ethics of their certified people.

Performance Technology. Founded in 1962 as the National Society for Programmed Instruction (NSPI), the International Society for Performance Improvement (ISPI) represents about ten thousand performance improvement professionals in forty countries and offers the Certified Performance Technologist (CPT) designation (About ISPI, n.d.). Applicants must demonstrate proficiency in ten standards of performance technology and adhere to a code of ethics. Certification is performance-based, with applicants having to document three examples of meeting each of the ten standards using from three to seven projects. The descriptions of these projects must be attested to by clients and/or supervisors to ensure the accuracy of the submissions (CPT Apply, n.d.).

Human performance technology (HPT) has been described as the systematic and systemic identification and removal of barriers to individual and organizational performance (Chevalier, 2004). The ten standards of performance technology are based on four principles and six steps that make up a systematic process for performance improvement (Standards of Performance Technology, n.d.). These standards are summarized below:

1. Focus on results and help clients focus on results.
2. Look at situations systemically, taking into consideration the larger context including competing pressures, resource constraints, and anticipated change.
3. Add value in how you do the work and through the work itself.
4. Utilize partnerships or collaborate with clients and other experts as required.
5. Be systematic in all aspects of the process, including the assessment of the need or opportunity.
6. Be systematic in all aspects of the process, including the analysis of the work and workplace to identify the cause or factors that limit performance.
7. Be systematic in all aspects of the process, including the design of the solution or specification of the requirements of the solution.

8. Be systematic in all aspects of the process, including the development of all or some of the solution and its elements.

9. Be systematic in all aspects of the process, including the implementation of the solution.

10. Be systematic in all aspects of the process, including the evaluation of the process and the results.

Approximately 1,040 CPTs have been designated since the program began in April 2002, with all successful applicants demonstrating proficiency in evaluation (Standard 10). Consequences for violations of the Standards for professional performance and the Code of Ethics include penalties that include letter of reprimand, suspension of the credential, and denial of re-certification (*CPT Policy & Procedures Manual*, 2007).

Instructional Design. Founded in 1944, ASTD represents about seventy thousand members from more than one hundred countries and connects locally in almost 140 U.S. chapters and twenty-five global networks (ASTD: About Us, n. d.). ASTD is the world's largest association dedicated to workplace learning and performance professionals. In July 2006, ASTD began offering certification to instructional designers with the Certified Professional in Learning and Performance (CPLP) credential.

The certification process involves a 150-question, multiple-choice test and submission of a work product in one of six areas: designing learning, delivering training, improving human performance, measuring and evaluating, facilitating organizational change, and managing the learning function. Eighteen (12 percent) of the 150 questions are on measuring and evaluating (Candidate Bulletin, 2007). Applicants must also agree to adhere to a code of ethics for workplace learning and performance professionals. According to Jennifer Naughton, ASTD Certification Institute's director of credentialing, 543 training professionals have been certified (Naughton, 2008).

ASTD has procedures in place to remove the credential where there is evidence and a documentable case of falsifying information/misrepresentation, dishonesty, and cheating. They have a variety of sanctions including de-certification, denial of results, denial of certification, and possible legal action, determined on a case-by-case basis.

THE CHANGING ROLE OF EVALUATION

With a much greater management emphasis on achieving bottom-line results, the role of evaluation has become more important. Results-based M (measurement) and E (evaluation) has become a global phenomenon as national and international stakeholders in the development process have sought increased accountability, transparency, and results from governments and organizations'' (Kusek & Rist, 2004).

Evaluation is done to measure the impact of the performance improvement initiative on desired business outcomes such as improved productivity and quality, reduced time and cost, greater customer satisfaction, retention, and referrals, and more sales, profitability, and market share. Line managers and supervisors are responsible for improving performance and need to be able to measure progress. The managers need good information with which to make decisions, and much of this knowledge comes from evaluation of existing performance.

This is particularly apparent in management decisions about training departments. If results are not measured in terms of improving a desired business outcome, the training department is seen as being a cost center, part of the overhead of doing business. When organizational value is not measured, the training department is more likely to suffer budget and personnel cuts during a business downturn, since measurable impact on organizational performance cannot be demonstrated. Outsourcing is a common way of attempting to reduce costs by designing and delivering training more efficiently, sometimes without concern for effectiveness.

The role of evaluation has also become more important for all who practice it as part of another role because they too need to demonstrate value to the organizations they serve. The questions to be answered by evaluation include, ''Was individual performance improved?'' and ''Did that change in individual and group performance improve bottom-line results?''

But evaluation is underutilized, as can be seen in the research on training. Instructional designers follow a systematic approach that includes assessment, design, development, implementation, and evaluation. Unfortunately, most evaluation done in the training industry has been limited to Level 1 (reaction) and Level 2 (learning), since these can be measured in the classroom. Far fewer attempts have been made to measure Level 3 (change in behavior) and Level 4 (impact on a desired business outcome).

Annual studies done by the ASTD have revealed consistent results from surveys of benchmarked organizations with the last results published in their 2004 *State of the Industry Report* for 213 organizations (ASTD, 2004). The percentages that follow reveal the number of benchmarked organizations that use each level of evaluation.

Level 1: Participant Reaction 74 percent

Level 2: Knowledge and Skills 31 percent

Level 3: Behavior Change 14 percent

Level 4: Business Outcome 8 percent

An earlier ASTD study published in their 1996 *State of the Industry Report* (ASTD, 1996) measured the percentage of courses that the benchmarked organizations conducted on the various levels of evaluation. For the years 1994 to 1996, the benchmarked organizations indicated that between 92 and 95 percent of their courses received Level 1 evaluations, 30 to 34 percent received Level 2 evaluations, 11 to 14 percent received Level 3 evaluations, and between 2 and 3 percent received Level 4 evaluations.

Evaluation should now be considered a part of the intervention itself, as the act of measurement encourages individuals to improve their performance (Chevalier, 2004). The Hawthorne studies revealed that groups that believe they are being observed will outperform their unobserved counterparts. It follows that, measurement, which is a form of observation, can therefore help to improve performance. It is also a way of demonstrating value.

Evaluation continues to develop as a field of study, with many professional associations contributing to the field with guidelines, standards, and competencies. "The 1990s saw the evaluation profession evolve even further. Increased emphasis on government program accountability and organization's efforts to be lean, efficient, global, and more competitive have led to more urgent calls for evaluation" (Russ-Eft & Preskill, 2001). The next step appears to be that of certification that would set and enforce professional and ethical standards for full-time practitioners.

CONCLUSIONS

Although there are many who measure the impact of programs and other interventions on a full-time basis, evaluation is not yet a true profession. Rather than lacking one set of standards to guide practitioners, there are too many sources and descriptions of evaluation standards.

Further, there is no certification of evaluators and therefore no consequences for violating standards for professional and ethical activity. "One reason to do that [certify practitioners] is to ensure some quality control for people who purport to be professionals in a field that does not require state licensure" (Rothwell & Wang, 2008).

"Evaluators are perhaps better described as a 'near-group' than as a profession. The field is marked by diversity in disciplinary training, type of schooling, perspectives on appropriate methods, and an absence of strong communication among its practitioners" (Rossi, Freeman, & Lipsey, 1999). This is reinforced by the number of professions that include evaluation as part of the body of knowledge for their certification processes.

While the importance of evaluation continues to grow as organizations become more results oriented, so does the need for greater professionalism among its practitioners. Certification of distinct groups, such as program evaluators, may be the next step in moving evaluation from a field of study to a profession.

Similarly, the role of evaluation is evolving. While measuring impact is important, evaluation is best defined as gathering information with which to make decisions. "Ultimately, the potential of evaluation is more likely to be realized if informing rather than influencing policies and programs is the criterion for success" (Henry, 2000).

References

2008 PHR SPHR GPHR certification handbook. Retrieved April 18, 2008, from http://www.hrci.org/certification/2008hb.

ASTD. (1996). *State of the industry report*. Alexandria, VA: Author.

ASTD. (2004). *State of the industry report*. Alexandria, VA: Author.

About AERA. Retrieved April 18, 2008, from www.aera.net/AboutAERA/Default.aspx?menu_id=90&id=222

About ISPI. Retrieved April 18, 2008, from www.ispi.org/info/about.htm.

About SHRM. Retrieved April 18, 2008, from www.shrm.org/about/

AEA. About us. Retrieved April 18, 2008, from www.eval.org/aboutus/organization/aboutus.asp.

AEA. Professional groups. Retrieved April 18, 2008, from www.eval.org/Resources/ProfessionalGroups.asp//www.certifiedpt.org/index.cfm?section=standards.

AEA. University programs. Retrieved April 18, 2008, from www.eval.org/Training/university_programs.asp.

AEA. Resources. Retrieved August 18, 2008, from www.eval.org/resources.asp

American Evaluation Association. (2004, July). Guiding principles for evaluators. Retrieved April 18, 2008, from www.eval.org/GPTraining/GP%20Training%20Final/gp.principles.pdf.

American Educational Research Association (AERA). Retrieved April 19, 2008, from www.aera.net.

American Evaluation Association (AEA). Retrieved April 19, 2008, from www.eval.org.

American Journal of Education. www.eval.org/Publications/AJE.asp.

American Society for Training and Development (ASTD). www.astd.org.

ASQ. Code of ethics. Retrieved April 30, 2008, from www.asq.org/about-asq/who-we-are/ethics.html.

ASQ. Who we are. Retrieved April 18, 2008, from www.asq.org/about-asq/who-we-are/index.html.

ASTD. About us. Retrieved April 19, 2008, from www.astd.org/ASTD/aboutus/ about_inside.htm.

ASTD. Candidate bulletin—revised November 2007. Retrieved April 19, 2008, from www.astd.org/NR/rdonlyres/7B0E3A00-9C07-400D-9BE1-1649BB8B9BD4/0/ CPLP_Candidate_Bulletin_FINAL012308.pdf.

Brinkerhoff, R. O. (2003). *The success case method.* San Francisco: Berrett-Koehler.

Bureau of Labor Statistics, U.S. Department of Labor (2008–2009). *Occupational outlook handbook.* Retrieved April 18, 2008, from www.bls.gov/oco/oco1002.htm

Cherrington, D. J., & Leonard, B. (1993, November). HR pioneers' long road to certification. *HR Magazine, 38*(11), 63–75.

Chevalier, R. (2003, May/June). Updating the behavioral engineering model. *Performance Improvement, 42*(4), 8–13.

Chevalier, R. (2004, April). Evaluation: The link between learning and performance. *Performance Improvement, 43*(4), 40–44.

Chevalier, R. (2004). Foreword. In R. Chevalier (Ed.), *Human performance technology revisited* (pp. i–iv). Silver Spring, MD: International Society for Performance Improvement.

CPT Apply. Retrieved May 1, 2008, from www.certifiedpt.org/index.cfm?section = apply.

CPT Policy & Procedures Manual (Vol. 2). (2007, October). Silver Spring, MD: International Society for Performance Improvement.

Educational evaluation and policy analysis. Retrieved April 19, 2008, from www .sagepub.com/journalsProdDesc.nav?prodId = Journal201852.

Educational researcher. Retrieved April 19, 2008, from www.sagepub.com/journals ProdDesc.nav?prodId = Journal201856.

Evaluation and program planning. Retrieved April 19, 2008, from www.elsevier.com/ wps/find/journaldescription.cws_home/593/description#description.

Evaluation review. Retrieved April 19, 2008, from www.sagepub.com/journalsProdDesc .nav?prodId = Journal200935.

Finn, J. (1953). Professionalizing the audio-visual field. In D. P. Ely & T. Plomp (Eds.), *Classic writings on instructional technology* (Vol. 1, pp. 231–241). Englewood, CO: Libraries Unlimited.

Henry, G. T. (2000). In V. J. Caracelli & H. Preskill (Eds.), *The expanding scope of evaluation use* (No. 88, pp. 85–98). San Francisco: Jossey-Bass.

HRCI Overview. Retrieved April 18, 2008, from www.hrci.org/certification/ov/

IBSTPI. (2006). *Evaluator competencies.* Retrieved April 18, 2008, from www.ibstpi.org/ Competencies/evaluatorcompetencies.htm.

International Society for Performance Improvement (ISPI). www.ispi.org.

Kirkpatrick, D. L. (1998). *Evaluating training programs: The four levels* (2nd ed.). San Francisco: Berrett-Koehler.

Klein, J. D., & Richey, R. C. (2005, November/December). The case for international standards. *Performance Improvement*, 44(10), 9–14.

Kusek, J. Z., & Rist, R. C. (2004). *Ten steps to a results-based monitoring and evaluation system*. Washington, DC: The World Bank.

Lucia, A. D., & Lepsinger, R. (1999). *The art and science of competency models: Pinpointing critical success factors in organizations*. San Francisco: Pfeiffer.

Naughton e-mail, February 13, 2008.

New directions for evaluation. Retrieved April 19, 2008, from www.eval.org/Publications/NDE.asp.

Owen, J. M. (2006). *Program evaluation: Forms and approaches* (3rd ed.). New York: The Guilford Press.

Parry, S. B. (1998, June). Just what is a competency? (And why should you care?). *Training*, 35(6), 58–64.

Patterson, J. (2008). e-mail, March 10, 2008.

Performance Improvement Quarterly. www.ispi.org/publications/piq.htm.

Phillips, J. J. (1997). *Return on investment in training and performance improvement programs*. Houston, TX: Gulf.

PHR SPHR GPHR. (2008). *Certification handbook*. Retrieved April 18, 2008, from www.hrci.org/HRCI_Files/_Items/HRCI-MR-TAB2-1329/Docs/2008%20Cert%20Handbook.pdf.

PHR/SPHR Test Specifications. Retrieved April 18, 2008, from http://www.hrci.org/Certification/2008HB/APX-A/

PMI Career Development. (n.d.). Retrieved May 1, 2008, from www.pmi.org/CareerDevelopment/Pages/Obtaining-Credential.aspx.

PMI Who we are. Retrieved April 18, 2008, from www.pmi.org/WhoWeAre/Pages/Default.aspx.

Program Evaluation Standards. Retrieved April 18, 2008, from www.wmich.edu/evalctr/jc/ProgramEvaluationStandardStatementsOct2007(3).pdf.

Project Managers Institute (PMI). www.pmi.org.

Society for Human Resources Management (SHRM). www.shrm.org

Rossi, P. H., Freeman, H. E., & Lipsey, M. W. (1999). *Evaluation: A systematic approach* (6th ed.). Thousand Oaks, CA: Sage.

Rothwell, W. J., & Wang, G. G. (2008, June). Training soapbox: Accreditation advantages. *Training*, 45(5), 14–15.

Russ-Eft, D., & Preskill, H. (2001). *Evaluation in organizations: A systematic approach to enhancing learning, performance, and change*. New York: Basic Books.

Russon, C. (2005). Cross-cutting issues in international standards development. In C. Russon & G. Russon (Eds.), *International perspectives on evaluation standards* (pp. 89–93). San Francisco: Jossey-Bass.

Standards of performance technology. Retrieved April 18, 2008, from www.certifiedpt .org/index.cfm?section = standards.

Stufflebeam.D. L., & Shinkfield, A. J. (2007). *Evaluation theory, models, and applications.* San Francisco: Jossey-Bass.

The Joint Committee on Standards for Educational Evaluation (1994). *The program evaluation standards: How to assess evaluations of educational programs* (2nd ed.). Thousand Oaks, CA: Sage.

Weinberg, R. B. (2002). *Certification guide* (7th ed.) (pp. 15–16). Alexandria, VA: Human Resources Certification Institute.

Wilkins, F. (2008, February 28). Personal conversation.

ABOUT THE EDITORS

James L. Moseley, Ed.D., LPC, CHES, CPT, is an associate professor at Wayne State University's College of Education Instructional Technology Program. He is a licensed professional counselor, a certified health education specialist, and a certified performance technologist. He teaches and advises doctoral students in program evaluation, performance improvement and consulting, and adult learning. He is the recipient of many honors and awards and has published and presented in our discipline. He is co-author, with Darlene M. Van Tiem and Joan C. Dessinger, of *Fundamentals of Performance Technology: A Guide to Improving People, Process, and Performance* (1st & 2nd editions) and *Performance Improvement Interventions: Enhancing People, Processes, and Organizations Through Performance Technology* and co-author with Joan C. Dessinger of *Confirmative Evaluation: Practical Strategies for Valuing Continuous Improvement* and *Training Older Workers and Learners: Maximizing the Performance of an Aging Workforce*. Moseley is a member of ISPI and ASTD and is frequently invited to present at local, regional, national, and international conferences.

Joan C. Dessinger, Ed.D., CPT, is an author, consultant, editor, and educator. She is the founder of and senior consultant with *The Lake Group,* a performance improvement consulting group, and an adjunct faculty member in Wayne State University's Instructional Technology Program. She is co-author with Darlene M. Van Tiem and James L. Moseley of *Fundamentals of Performance Technology* (1st & 2nd editions) and *Performance Improvement Interventions* and co-author with James L. Moseley of *Confirmative Evaluation: Practical Strategies for Valuing Continuous Improvement* and *Training Older Workers and Learners: Maximizing the Performance of an Aging Workforce*. She has also contributed articles and chapters to professional books and other publications on such topics as adult learning, distance learning, older worker-learners (OWLS), performance support tools (PST), program and product evaluation, and storytelling. As a performance improvement consultant, Dessinger has worked with national and international companies from a variety of industries, including automotive, insurance, pharmaceutical, retail, and manufacturing. She is a member of ISPI and ASTD and is frequently invited to present at local, regional, national, and international conferences.

ABOUT THE CONTRIBUTORS

*A*nne M. Apking, M.A. CPT, a learning and performance improvement consultant since 1983, has worked successfully with a wide array of industries and clients, designing and implementing solutions that create business impact. Within the expansive field of "human performance technology," Apking specializes in curriculum design, development, and measurement, as well as the creation of learning strategies and learning business plans. For much of her professional career (1988 to 2004), she fulfilled the role of leader and principal consultant at Triad Performance Technologies, Inc., a well-respected and award-winning learning and performance improvement consulting company. Also during this time, Anne co-authored an award-winning book with Dr. Robert Brinkerhoff, *High-Impact Learning: Strategies for Leveraging Business Results from Training* (2001). Since 2004, Apking has worked independently as a performance improvement consultant with clients such as ArvinMeritor, Ceridian, Farmers and Foremost Insurance, Merillat Industries, and Steelcase Inc. She holds B.A. and M.A. degrees from Western Michigan University in organizational psychology and is a Certified Performance Technologist (CPT). She is very active in the International Society for Performance Improvement (ISPI). Apking can be reached at anne@anneapking.com.

Eileen R. Banchoff, Ph.D., CPT, is the president of Banchoff Associates, Inc., a business partner to automotive, financial, and health care institutions in southeast Michigan, specializing in eliminating human performance problems that have been clearly mapped to core business needs. Banchoff earned her doctor of philosophy degree from Wayne State University in the field of instructional technology and did her doctoral research on the use of formal instructional design models and project success. While continuing to do extensive research on the instructional design process, her firm also helps clients develop their own internal ISD and performance improvement processes/models. As adjunct faculty, Banchoff has taught performance consulting and technology courses for Wayne State University and ASTD's Analyzing Human Performance course for the University of Michigan-Dearborn. She is an active member in the International Society of Performance Improvement locally, having served as local chapter president and board member for over fifteen years, and nationally, having served as track chair and reviewer for six international conferences, chair of the 2008-2009 Nominations Committee, and chair of the Awards of Excellence Task Force, rewriting the submission guidelines. She earned Certified Performance Consultant status in 2003 and recertified in 2006. She can be contacted at www.banchoff.com.

Carl Binder, Ph.D., CPT, has been helping organizations accelerate performance and improve results for over thirty years, after beginning his career as a graduate fellow at Harvard University with B.F. Skinner and associate director of a human behavior research laboratory. He has authored dozens of articles and chapters in human learning and performance, training and development, sales and marketing, customer service, performance measurement, and educational policy and has worked with scores of public organizations and companies in a dozen industries in the United States and abroad. Founder of three consulting firms, workshop leader, and lecturer, Binder has twice been invited as an ISPI Master's Series Speaker and received the Fred S. Keller Award from the American Psychological Association for contributions to education and training. He is known for developing plain-English, easy-to-apply methodologies based on principles from the science of behavior. A long-time contributor to ISPI conferences and publications, Binder is known for his FluencyBuilding™ instructional methodology, The Six Boxes® Approach to performance improvement, and for practical performance measurement methods based on the work of Ogden R. Lindsley. You can contact him by email at carl@binder-riha.com, download many of his publications at www.Binder-Riha.com/publications.htm, and learn more about the Six Boxes® Approach at www.SixBoxes.com.

Lori G. Bosteder, Ed.M., is a graduate of the Adult Education and Higher Education Leadership Program at Oregon State University. She also holds a B.A. in business management. Her focus of interest is organizational training, communication design, and social/emotional learning. She has been a marketer, graphic designer, and educator over the last thirty years. She was a managing partner in a design firm for ten of those years. Bosteder works closely with a home builder in Eugene, Oregon. She has been their marketing consultant/designer for twenty years and is currently assisting in an organizational change process. She has also worked with a wide variety of clients such as Egghead Software, Dynamix's (video games), public utilities, numerous small businesses from restaurants to paint stores, and several non-profits. She is principal in EQsmarts, a training and coaching company focused on emotional intelligence and stress management skills for educational professionals, organizations, and individuals. Bosteder co-conducted a research study at the Oregon women's penitentiary with an OSU colleague. They created an in-depth training program in emotional intelligence (EQ) skills for women inmates in a vocational program. The Institute of HeartMath skill set was the key methodology and the program created a remarkable new emotional resiliency and stability in these women. Bosteder is a certified trainer in TalentSmart's *Discovering EQ*, a licensed institute of HeartMath Resilient Educator® Instructor and a Licensed HeartMath® 1:1 Provider. She is adjunct faculty at Oregon State University and at Linn-Benton Community College and can be reached at bostedel@onid.orst.edu.

Dale C. Brandenburg, Ph.D., CPT, is a Senior Fellow of the Institute for Learning and Performance Improvement at Wayne State University in Detroit, Michigan, and senior partner in Rothwell & Associates, a human resources consulting firm. He specializes in needs assessment, evaluation, training strategy, and the impacts of technology deployment on workforce issues. Previously he worked for a private research and development firm and at the University of Illinois. His primary publications in research journals, books, and book chapters involve training evaluations and the implication of workplace performance models. He received his B.S. degree in mathematics education and his M.A. degree in behavioral psychology, both from Michigan State University, and his Ph.D. degree in educational measurement and statistics from the University of Iowa. He is a Certified Performance Technologist. He can be reached at d.brandenburg@wayne.edu.

Dr. Roger Chevalier, Ph.D., CPT, has over forty years of experience in management and performance improvement. He is an independent consultant who specializes in embedding training into comprehensive performance improvement solutions. He is the author of *A Manager's Guide to Improving Workplace Performance*, which received a 2008 Award of Excellence from the International Society for Performance Improvement. Chevalier has personally trained more than thirty thousand managers, supervisors, and salespeople in performance improvement, leadership, coaching, change management, and sales programs. His past clients include a wide range of businesses, government agencies, and non-profits. His work experience includes having been the ISPI director of information and certification, vice president of Century 21 Real Estate's Performance Division, and director of training for the U.S. Coast Guard's West Coast Training Center. Chevalier earned a doctorate in applied behavioral science as well as two master of science degrees in organizational behavior and personnel management. He can be reached at Roger@aboutiwp. com or through his website, www.aboutiwp.com.

Joan C. Dessinger, Ed.D, CPT, is an author, consultant, editor, and educator. She is the founder of and senior consultant with The Lake Group, a performance improvement consulting group, and an adjunct faculty member in Wayne State University's Instructional Technology Program. She is co-author with Darlene VanTiem and James Moseley of *Fundamentals of Performance Technology* (1st and 2nd eds.) and *Performance Improvement Interventions* and co-author with James Moseley of *Confirmative Evaluation* and *Training Older Workers and Learners*. She has also contributed articles and chapters to professional publications on such topics as adult learning, distance learning, older worker-learners (OWLS), performance support tools (PST), program and product evaluation, and storytelling. She and James Moseley are the editors of the ISPI/Wiley *Handbook of Improving Performance in the Workplace: Volume Three: Measurement and Evaluation*. As a performance improvement consultant, Dessinger has worked with national and international companies from a variety of industries, including automotive, insurance, pharmaceutical, retail, and manufacturing. She is a member of ISPI and ASTD and is frequently invited to present at local, regional, national, and international conferences. You may contact Dessinger via email at jdessinger@aol.com.

Carol K. Diroff, Ph.D., holds a doctorate from Wayne State University in instructional technology. She studied human performance technology under Dr. James Moseley. She has twenty-six years of management experience working for a variety of companies. Diroff joined the field of instructional design in 1990 and has been fortunate to practice her trade at a major automotive manufacturer, where she has been employed for fifteen years. Currently, she manages a staff of instructional designers and developers specializing in technical training and performance support. Diroff is also a six-year member of the adjunct instructional technology faculty at Wayne State University and has taught needs assessment, introduction to instructional systems design, and advanced instructional design theory and research. She has been a guest speaker for local Human Performance Technology organizations and recently spoke at ISPI-Michigan on the topic of continuous evaluation for multiple interventions. She can be reached at cdiroff@comcast.net.

Ingrid J. Guerra-López, Ph.D., is an associate professor and director of the Institute for Learning and Performance Improvement at Wayne State University and an associate research professor at the Sonora Institute of Technology in Mexico. Guerra-López is also principal and chief innovation officer of Intelligence Gathering Systems, a consultancy organization focused on designing and implementing automated performance tracking and management systems that improve performance by providing just-in-time data and intelligence to improve management decision making. Guerra-López's research, teaching, and consulting focus on managing and improving performance through its measurement and evaluation. Specifically, she is engaged in improving management decision making through the design, development, and use of performance measurement and management systems. She is the author of five evaluation and assessment books, various book chapters related to performance improvement, and over two dozen articles in performance, management, and human resource journals. Her research is currently focused on performance measurement systems and their impact on decision making and organizational effectiveness. She can be contacted by email at: iguerra@wayne.edu.

Judith A. Hale, Ph.D., CPT, is the author of *Performance-Based Evaluation: Tools and Techniques for Measuring the Impact of Training* (2002), the *Performance Consultant's Fieldbook: Tools and Techniques for Improving Organizations and People* (2nd ed.) (2007), *Outsourcing Training and Development* (2006), *Performance-Based Management: What Every Manager Should Do to Get Results* (2003), and *Performance-Based Certification: How to Design a Valid, Defensible, Cost-Effective Program* (2000). She is a contributing author to the *Handbook of Performance Technology* (3rd ed.) (2006). She has dedicated her professional career to helping management develop effective and practical ways to improve individual and organizational performance. She is known for making sense out of confusion and helping others stay focused on what matters. She is able to explain complex ideas so people understand their relevance and how to apply them. Hale was awarded a B.A. from Ohio State University, an M.A. from Miami University, and a Ph.D. from Purdue University. She can be reached at Haleassoci@aol.com.

Nancy B. Hastings, Ph.D., is an assistant professor of instructional and performance technology at the University of West Florida. She teaches online classes in instructional technology, technology planning and change, project management, and distance learning at the master's, specialist, and doctoral level. She is also the internship coordinator for the Master's of Education in Instructional and Performance Technology program. Hastings received her Ph.D. from Wayne State University, Detroit, Michigan. Prior to joining the faculty of the University of West Florida, Hastings was employed as a lecturer and research associate in the instructional technology program at Wayne State, where she was responsible for the development and implementation of the program's fully online instructional technology program. Hastings also has extensive practical experience, having worked in corporate training and performance improvement for over fifteen years, in both manufacturing and service related settings. She can be reached by email at nhastings@uwf.edu.

Peter R. Hybert, M.S. Ed., CPT, has been in the training and performance improvement field since 1984 and has worked as a consultant since 1989. He spent five years as a training designer at MCC Powers (now Siemens), then nine years at SWI before becoming one of the founding partners of CADDI, a firm dedicated to developing and marketing a rapid instructional design methodology. Four years later, he founded his own company, PRH Consulting Inc., which focuses on consulting projects—using a comprehensive set of tools, skills, and experience to work with clients to leverage know-how for performance. His clients include several Fortune 500 firms, as well as small and mid-sized organizations. He has analyzed, designed, and developed training and performance systems and programs for almost every type of business function and process. He is the author of more than twenty articles and has presented at international conferences and local chapters of ISPI and ASTD. He has also served as the chairperson for ISPI's Awards of Excellence Committee, ISPI's Nominations Committee, and as Chicago ISPI chapter president. He completed his master's degree at Northern Illinois University. Hybert is a Certified Performance Technologist (CPT). He can be reached at Pete@prhconsulting.com.

Tim Mooney, M.A., is a vice president with the Advantage Performance Group (APG), a wholly owned subsidiary of BTS Group AB. A seasoned international performance consulting expert who specializes in assessment, measurement, organizational change, and sales effectiveness, Mooney has delivered projects in Great Britain, France, Germany, South Africa, and North America. In his role as the practice leader for *The Advantage Way^{SM}*, he is responsible for developing the practice capabilities, growing the business, and working closely with APG and BTS clients to ensure measurable results on all projects. With more than twenty-five years of corporate sales management and consulting experience, Mooney is a frequent speaker and writer on the topic of achieving measurable business impact from training. His recent book, *Courageous Training*, describes how iconoclastic L&D leaders are consistently producing business results for their organizations. Prior to joining APG in 2000, he served in a senior management capacity for DDI, where his roles included vice president of sales and marketing for assessment and regional vice president. Mooney earned a B.A. degree in psychology from Butler University in

Indianapolis and an M.A. degree in industrial/organizational psychology from the University of Akron. He can be contacted at tmooney@ameritech.net.

James L. Moseley, Ed.D, LPC, CHES, CPT, is an associate professor at Wayne State University's College of Education Instructional Technology Program. He is a licensed professional counselor, a certified health education specialist, and a certified performance technologist. He teaches and advises doctoral students in program evaluation, performance improvement and consulting, and adult learning. He is the recipient of many honors and awards and he has published and presented in our discipline. Moseley is currently co-editor with Joan Dessinger of the ISPI/Wiley *Handbook of Improving Performance in the Workplace: Volume Three: Measurement and Evaluation*. He is also co-author with Darlene VanTiem and Joan Dessinger of *Fundamentals of Performance Technology: A Guide to Improving People, Process, and Performance* (1st and 2nd eds.) and *Performance Improvement Interventions: Enhancing People, Processes, and Organizations Through Performance Technology* and co-author with Joan C. Dessinger of *Confirmative Evaluation: Practical Strategies for Valuing Continuous Improvement* and *Training Older Workers and Learners: Maximizing the Performance of an Aging Workforce*. Moseley is a member of ISPI and ASTD and is frequently invited to present at local, regional, national, and international conferences. You may contact him via email at jmosele@comcast.net.

Richard B. Pearlstein, Ph.D., has devoted more than thirty-five years to designing, implementing, and evaluating performance improvement systems in major corporations and federal agencies. He takes a practical approach to evaluation—seeing its organizational role as a research-based means of providing key information to decision-makers. Pearlstein has senior-level experience in conducting evaluations. For a key member of the U.S. intelligence community, he recently led a team that gathered and analyzed quantitative and qualitative data. Senior management used the resulting recommendations to improve a major development program. For the American Red Cross, he designed human performance measurement systems for biomedical services functions and conducted evaluations to improve outcomes of nationwide training curricula. For a major telecommunications company, he designed and managed research projects that enabled it to meet the terms of a federal consent decree by finding ways to help more women move into technical management. Pearlstein presents frequently for national and international human performance improvement organizations and has written numerous journal articles. He was vice president for research and development for the International Society for Performance Improvement for two terms and was selected twice as a National Benchmark Expert in Training Evaluation by the

American Society of Training and Development. He can be reached at rpearl stein@csm.com.

Jack J. Phillips, Ph.D., a world-renowned expert on measurement and evaluation, is chairman of the ROI Institute. Through the Institute, Phillips provides consulting services for Fortune 500 companies and major global organizations. The author or editor of more than fifty books, he has conducted workshops and presented at conferences in forty-four countries. His most recent books include *ROI for Technology Projects: Measuring and Delivering Value* (2008); *Return on Investment in Meetings and Events: Tools and Techniques to Measure the Success of all Types of Meetings and Events* (2008); *Show Me the Money: How to Determine ROI in People, Projects, and Programs* (2007); *The Value of Learning* (2007); and *How to Build a Successful Consulting Practice* (2006). His expertise in measurement and evaluation is based on extensive research and more than twenty-seven years of corporate experience in five industries (aerospace, textiles, metals, construction materials, and banking). Phillips has served as training and development manager at two Fortune 500 firms, senior HR officer at two firms, president of a regional federal savings bank, and a professor of management at a major state university. Phillips can be reached at jack@roiinstitute.net.

Patti P. Phillips, Ph.D., president and CEO, ROI Institute, Inc., is a renowned expert in measurement and evaluation; she helps organizations around the world implement the ROI Methodology. Since 1997, following a thirteen-year career in the electric utility industry, Phillips has embraced the ROI Methodology by committing herself to ongoing research and practice. To this end, she has implemented ROI in private-sector and public-sector organizations. Phillips teaches others to implement the ROI Methodology through the ROI certification process, as a facilitator for ASTD's ROI and Measuring and Evaluating Learning Workshops, and as adjunct professor for graduate-level evaluation courses. She serves on numerous doctoral dissertation committees, assisting students as they develop their own research on measurement, evaluation, and ROI. She contributes to a variety of journals and has authored a number of books on the subject of accountability and ROI, including *ROI in Action* (2008); *Show Me the Money: How to Determine ROI in People, Projects, and Programs* (2007); *The Value of Learning* (2007); *Return on Investment Basics* (2005); *Proving the Value of HR: How and Why to Measure ROI* (2005); *Retaining Your Best Employees* (2002), and *The Human Resources Scorecard: Measuring Return on Investment* (2001). Phillips can be reached at patti@roiinstitute.net.

William J. Rothwell, Ph.D., SPHR, is professor of workforce education and development on the University Park campus of The Pennsylvania State

University. Prior to entering academe in 1993, he was a training professional in a large insurance company and, before that, a state government agency. He has consulted with over forty multinational companies and has authored, co-authored, edited, or co-edited over three hundred books, book chapters, and articles. He can be reached by email at wjr9@psu.edu.

Darlene Russ-Eft, Ph.D., is professor and chair of the Department of Adult Education and Higher Education Leadership in the College of Education at Oregon State University, where she teaches master's and doctoral courses in research, program evaluation, and learning theory. Her most recent books are *Evaluator Competencies: Standards for the Practice of Evaluation in Organizations: A Practical Guide to Needs Assessment; Building Evaluation Capacity: 72 Activities for Teaching and Training; and Evaluation in Organizations: A Systematic Approach to Enhancing Learning, Performance, and Change.* Russ-Eft is president-elect for the Academy of Human Resource Development (www.ahrd.org) and is a current director of the International Board of Standards for Training, Performance, and Instruction (www.ibstpi.org). She is immediate past editor of the research journal, *Human Resource Development Quarterly.* She received the 1996 Editor of the Year Award from Times Mirror, the Outstanding Scholar Award from AHRD, and the Outstanding Research Article Award from ASTD. Prior to joining Oregon State University in 2002, she was director of research at AchieveGlobal and division director of Research for Zenger-Miller. Her B.A. in psychology is from the College of Wooster; her M.A. and Ph.D. in psychology are from the University of Michigan. She can be reached at zmresearch@aol.com.

Catherine M. Sleezer, Ph.D., is the training manager at Centrilift, a division of Baker Hughes. Prior to accepting a position in the private sector, she was a university faculty member and taught human resource development and needs assessment courses at the master's and doctoral levels. She also consulted with many organizations in the private, public, and government sectors to address their learning and performance needs. Sleezer has a record of research publications and presentations. She is a former board member of the Academy of Human Resource Development and a former member of the ASTD Research Committee. Her books include *Human Resources Development Review: Research and Implications; Human Resource Development and Information Technology: Making Global Connections*; and *A Practical Guide to Needs Assessment* (2nd ed.). She can be reached by email at catherine.sleezer@centrilift.com.

Debra M. Smith, M.B.A., PMP, is the former global strategic applications training leader at Visteon Corporation, where she developed training solutions leveraging application experts to provide rapid, focused face-to-face and online training. She teaches project management and mentors corporate trainers. Smith is a member of the Project Management Institute (PMI) and has achieved Project Management Professional (PMP) certification. She is a member of the Association for Educational Communications and Technology (AECT) and the International Society for Performance Improvement (ISPI). Smith earned associate's and bachelor's degrees from Ferris State University and an MBA from Madonna University. She is presently a doctoral candidate in instructional technology with a human performance emphasis at Wayne State University, Detroit, Michigan. She can be reached at dmsmith398@comcast.net.

David L. Solomon, Ph.D., received his doctorate in instructional technology from Wayne State University. He is vice president, innovation and strategic planning, at Big Communications (Ferndale, MI), the leading healthcare communications agency focused on driving brand growth through innovative and strategic multi-channel solutions. Solomon has traveled the globe designing product launch events and supporting world-famous brands with performance improvement initiatives that integrate people, processes, and technology. During his tenure at BBDO, Solomon was responsible for the international training team, where he designed, developed, and implemented Chrysler International's retail training strategies, which included a competency-based sales certification program that fulfilled all compliance requirements for the Block Exemption Regulation (BER) in the European Union. During this time, Solomon was the architect of the DaimlerChrysler Academy Measurement Task Force, which was honored with the American Society for Training and Development Excellence in Practice Award for 2005. Currently, he is leading the design effort at Big Communications with emphasis on measuring the impact of communications, training, and performance improvement interventions. In addition, he is responsible for managing Big's innovation process, a process committed to transforming breakthrough ideas into refined products and services for Big clients. He can be reached at dsolomon@bigcommunications.com.

Dean R. Spitzer, Ph.D., is president of Dean R. Spitzer & Associates and is widely recognized as one of the world's leading experts on performance measurement and management. For many years previously, he was a senior researcher, consultant, and quality expert with IBM Corporation. He has over thirty years of experience in helping individuals and organizations achieve superior performance.

Prior to joining IBM, he led his own consulting firm. In that capacity, Dr. Spitzer directed over one hundred successful performance improvement projects. Prior to leading his consulting firm, Dr. Spitzer was a manager and internal consultant with several Fortune 100 companies and government agencies and served as a professor at five universities. He has been a keynote speaker, lecturer, and consultant on five continents.

Dr. Spitzer is the author of eight books and over 150 articles on various areas of human performance improvement, organizational development, and performance management. His latest book is the much acclaimed *Transforming Performance Measurement: Rethinking the Way We Measure and Drive Organizational Success*.

Dr. Spitzer earned his Ph.D. degree with honors from the University of Southern California and his M.A. from Northwestern University. He also pursued both undergraduate and graduate studies at the London School of Economics. He can be contacted at www.deanspitzer.com or deanrspitzer@gmail.com.

William J. Tarnacki II, M.Ed., MBA, MHCS, is director of human resources and organizational development at ProQuest Company, based in Ann Arbor, Michigan, a subsidiary of Cambridge Information Group, based in Bethesda, Maryland. Prior to joining ProQuest, Tarnacki had six years of successful human resources leadership experiences as a division human resources manager and a plant human resources leader at Eaton Corporation and General Electric Corporation, respectively. Tarnacki also spent over five years serving in specialist roles for Ford Motor Company and Ford Motor Credit Company as an instructional designer, performance consultant, and human resources associate in labor relations. Before going into the HR field, he spent time as a shop supervisor and quality coordinator for a small manufacturing company and as a consultant for a boutique consulting firm in Michigan. He has an extensive background in business, human resources strategy, organizational development, manufacturing operations, lean manufacturing principles, and training and development. Tarnacki holds a bachelor's degree in psychology, a master's degree in instructional technology from Wayne State University, and an MBA from the University of Michigan. He is also trained as a Six Sigma Greenbelt and earned his certification as a Master Human Capital Strategist (MHCS) in 2008. He can be reached at Bill.tarnacki@proquest.com.

Anita Pane Whiteford, Ph.D., PHR, is a graduate of the Workforce Education and Development Program at the University Park campus of the Pennsylvania State University. Currently, Whiteford works in the workplace learning and performance profession as a training professional. She holds graduate degrees in human resource administration and social work. Whiteford holds her professional human resources certificate from the Society for Human Resource Management. Her research interests focus on evaluation, transfer of learning, and ROI. She can be reached by email at apw129@psu.edu or anita.whiteford@gmail.com.

NAME INDEX

SUBJECT INDEX

Page references followed by *fig* indicate an illustrated diagram; followed by *t* indicate a table; followed by *e* indicate an exhibit.

Pfeiffer Publications Guide

This guide is designed to familiarize you with the various types of Pfeiffer publications. The formats section describes the various types of products that we publish; the methodologies section describes the many different ways that content might be provided within a product. We also provide a list of the topic areas in which we publish.

FORMATS

In addition to its extensive book-publishing program, Pfeiffer offers content in an array of formats, from fieldbooks for the practitioner to complete, ready-to-use training packages that support group learning.

FIELDBOOK Designed to provide information and guidance to practitioners in the midst of action. Most fieldbooks are companions to another, sometimes earlier, work, from which its ideas are derived; the fieldbook makes practical what was theoretical in the original text. Fieldbooks can certainly be read from cover to cover. More likely, though, you'll find yourself bouncing around following a particular theme, or dipping in as the mood, and the situation, dictate.

HANDBOOK A contributed volume of work on a single topic, comprising an eclectic mix of ideas, case studies, and best practices sourced by practitioners and experts in the field.

An editor or team of editors usually is appointed to seek out contributors and to evaluate content for relevance to the topic. Think of a handbook not as a ready-to-eat meal, but as a cookbook of ingredients that enables you to create the most fitting experience for the occasion.

RESOURCE Materials designed to support group learning. They come in many forms: a complete, ready-to-use exercise (such as a game); a comprehensive resource on one topic (such as conflict management) containing a variety of methods and approaches; or a collection of like-minded activities (such as icebreakers) on multiple subjects and situations.

TRAINING PACKAGE An entire, ready-to-use learning program that focuses on a particular topic or skill. All packages comprise a guide for the facilitator/trainer and a workbook for the participants. Some packages are supported with additional media—such as video—or learning aids, instruments, or other devices to help participants understand concepts or practice and develop skills.

- *Facilitator/trainer's guide* Contains an introduction to the program, advice on how to organize and facilitate the learning event, and step-by-step instructor notes. The guide also contains copies of presentation materials—handouts, presentations, and overhead designs, for example—used in the program.

- *Participant's workbook* Contains exercises and reading materials that support the learning goal and serves as a valuable reference and support guide for participants in the weeks and months that follow the learning event. Typically, each participant will require his or her own workbook.

ELECTRONIC CD-ROMs and web-based products transform static Pfeiffer content into dynamic, interactive experiences. Designed to take advantage of the searchability, automation, and ease-of-use that technology provides, our e-products bring convenience and immediate accessibility to your workspace.

METHODOLOGIES

CASE STUDY A presentation, in narrative form, of an actual event that has occurred inside an organization. Case studies are not prescriptive, nor are they used to prove a point; they are designed to develop critical analysis and decision-making skills. A case study has a specific time frame, specifies a sequence of events, is narrative in structure, and contains a plot structure—an issue (what should be/have been done?). Use case studies when the goal is to enable participants to apply previously learned theories to the circumstances in the case, decide what is pertinent, identify the real issues, decide what should have been done, and develop a plan of action.

ENERGIZER A short activity that develops readiness for the next session or learning event. Energizers are most commonly used after a break or lunch to stimulate or refocus the group. Many involve some form of physical activity, so they are a useful way to counter post-lunch lethargy. Other uses include transitioning from one topic to another, where "mental" distancing is important.

EXPERIENTIAL LEARNING ACTIVITY (ELA) A facilitator-led intervention that moves participants through the learning cycle from experience to application (also known as a Structured Experience). ELAs are carefully thought-out designs in which there is a definite learning purpose and intended outcome. Each step—everything that participants do during the activity—facilitates the accomplishment of the stated goal. Each ELA includes complete instructions for facilitating the intervention and a clear statement of goals, suggested group size and timing, materials required, an explanation of the process, and, where appropriate, possible variations to the activity. (For more detail on Experiential Learning Activities, see the Introduction to the *Reference Guide to Handbooks and Annuals*, 1999 edition, Pfeiffer, San Francisco.)

GAME A group activity that has the purpose of fostering team spirit and togetherness in addition to the achievement of a pre-stated goal. Usually contrived—undertaking a desert expedition, for example—this type of learning method offers an engaging means for participants to demonstrate and practice business and interpersonal skills. Games are effective for team building and personal development mainly because the goal is subordinate to the process—the means through which participants reach decisions, collaborate, communicate, and generate trust and understanding. Games often engage teams in "friendly" competition.

ICEBREAKER A (usually) short activity designed to help participants overcome initial anxiety in a training session and/or to acquaint the participants with one another. An icebreaker can be a fun activity or can be tied to specific topics or training goals. While a useful tool in itself, the icebreaker comes into its own in situations where tension or resistance exists within a group.

INSTRUMENT A device used to assess, appraise, evaluate, describe, classify, and summarize various aspects of human behavior. The term used to describe an instrument depends primarily on its format and purpose. These terms include survey, questionnaire, inventory, diagnostic, survey, and poll. Some uses of instruments include providing instrumental feedback to group members, studying here-and-now processes or functioning within a group, manipulating group composition, and evaluating outcomes of training and other interventions.

Instruments are popular in the training and HR field because, in general, more growth can occur if an individual is provided with a method for focusing specifically on his or her own behavior. Instruments also are used to obtain information that will serve as a basis for change and to assist in workforce planning efforts.

Paper-and-pencil tests still dominate the instrument landscape with a typical package comprising a facilitator's guide, which offers advice on administering the instrument and interpreting the collected data, and an initial set of instruments. Additional instruments are available separately. Pfeiffer, though, is investing heavily in e-instruments. Electronic instrumentation provides effortless distribution and, for larger groups particularly, offers advantages over paper-and-pencil tests in the time it takes to analyze data and provide feedback.

LECTURETTE A short talk that provides an explanation of a principle, model, or process that is pertinent to the participants' current learning needs. A lecturette is intended to establish a common language bond between the trainer and the participants by providing a mutual frame of reference. Use a lecturette as an introduction to a group activity or event, as an interjection during an event, or as a handout.

MODEL A graphic depiction of a system or process and the relationship among its elements. Models provide a frame of reference and something more tangible, and more easily remembered, than a verbal explanation. They also give participants something to "go on," enabling them to track their own progress as they experience the dynamics, processes, and relationships being depicted in the model.

ROLE PLAY A technique in which people assume a role in a situation/scenario: a customer service rep in an angry-customer exchange, for example. The way in which the role is approached is then discussed and feedback is offered. The role play is often repeated using a different approach and/or incorporating changes made based on feedback received. In other words, role playing is a spontaneous interaction involving realistic behavior under artificial (and safe) conditions.

SIMULATION A methodology for understanding the interrelationships among components of a system or process. Simulations differ from games in that they test or use a model that depicts or mirrors some aspect of reality in form, if not necessarily in content. Learning occurs by studying the effects of change on one or more factors of the model. Simulations are commonly used to test hypotheses about what happens in a system—often referred to as "what if?" analysis—or to examine best-case/worst-case scenarios.

THEORY A presentation of an idea from a conjectural perspective. Theories are useful because they encourage us to examine behavior and phenomena through a different lens.

TOPICS

The twin goals of providing effective and practical solutions for workforce training and organization development and meeting the educational needs of training and human resource professionals shape Pfeiffer's publishing program. Core topics include the following:

    Leadership & Management

    Communication & Presentation

    Coaching & Mentoring

    Training & Development

    E-Learning

    Teams & Collaboration

    OD & Strategic Planning

    Human Resources

    Consulting

What will you find on pfeiffer.com?

- The best in workplace performance solutions for training and HR professionals

- Downloadable training tools, exercises, and content

- Web-exclusive offers

- Training tips, articles, and news

- Seamless on-line ordering

- Author guidelines, information on becoming a Pfeiffer Partner, and much more

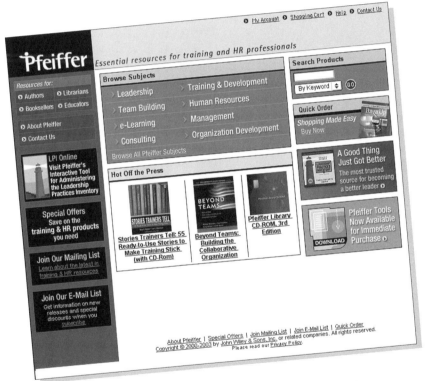

Discover more at www.pfeiffer.com